AA Essential

explorer
SPAIN

AA Publishing

Essential

Written by Adam Hopkins and Gabrielle Macphedran
Additional writing and research by Tony Evans
Series Adviser: Ingrid Morgan
Series Editor: Nia Williams
Copy Editor: Audrey Horne
Designer: Geoff Hayes

Revised second edition 1995
First published 1993

Edited, designed, produced and distributed by AA Publishing, Norfolk House, Priestley Road, Basingstoke, Hampshire RG24 9NY.

A catalogue record for this book is available from the British Library.

ISBN 0 7495 0567 2
This book was produced using QuarkXpress ™ , Aldus Freehand ™ and Microsoft Word ™ on Apple Macintosh ™ computers.

Colour origination by Fotographics Ltd
Printed and bound in Italy by LEGO SpA, Vicenza

Published by AA Publishing (a trading name of Automobile Association Developments Limited, whose registered office is Norfolk House, Priestley Road, Basingstoke, Hampshire, RG24 9NY. Registered number 1878835).

Montserrat Monastery in Catalonia, much visited by pilgrims and tourists

Adam Hopkins, a regular contributor to the *Daily Telegraph, The European* and other newspapers, has written books about Spain and Crete. He and journalist and broadcaster Gabrielle Macphedran are also joint authors of several AA Essential Guides.

The village of Potes Frama in North Spain's Picos de Europa

About this book

This book is divided into three principal sections.

The first part of the book discusses aspects of life today and in the past. Places to visit are then covered, along with Focus on... and Close-up features, which highlight areas and subjects in more detail. Drives and walks are also suggested in this section of the book. Finally, day-to-day practical information for the visitor is given in the Travel Facts section, which is followed by a selective Hotels and Restaurants listing.

Some of the places described in this book have been given a special rating:

▶▶▶ Do not miss

▶▶▷ Highly recommended

▶▷▷ See if you can

General Contents

Spain through voices past and present 8-9

Spain is...
- A Land of Many Selves 12-13
- Landscape and Cityscape 14-15
- People and Institutions 16-17
- Pleasures and Diversions 18-19
- Food and Drink 20-1
- Diverse Nations 22-3
- The Future 24-5

Spain was...
- Another Country 26-7
- Inhabitants and Invaders 28
- Roman 29
- The Moors 30-1
- Reconquest 32-3
- The Catholic Kings 34-5
- The Habsburgs 36-7
- The Golden Age 38-9
- The Bourbons 40-1
- At War 42-3
- In Turmoil 44
- The Republic 45
- Civil War 46-7
- Franco and Beyond 48-9

Madrid 50-71
Galicia 72-82
The North Coast 83-97
Aragon and Navarre 98-113
Barcelona 114-27
Catalonia 128-49
Castilla, León and La Rioja 150-79
Extremadura 180-9
Castilla-La Mancha and the Madrid region 190-207
Levante 208-23
Andalucía 224-54

Travel Facts 255-73
Hotels and Restaurants 274-84

Index 285-88

Maps

Spain 10-11
Spain in 1604 26
Madrid 50-1
Madrid: Old Town 53
Madrid: Palacio Real 57
Madrid: Parque del Retiro 64
Galicia 72
Santiago de Compostela 79
Cantabrian Coast 84-5
Aragon and Navarre 98
Barcelona 114
Barcelona: Barri Gòtic 116
Barcelona: Ramblas 119
Barcelona: Eixample 120
Catalonia 128
Tarragona 146
Castilla, León and La Rioja 150-1
Avila 154
León 162
Segovia 175
Extremadura 180
Guadalupe Monastery 184
Castilla-La Mancha 190-1
El Escorial 200
Toledo 204
Levante 208
Valencia 222
Andalucía 224-5
Córdoba 232
Granada 242
Granada: the Alhambra 243
Seville 248
Alpujarras 252

Features

Focus on...Santiago de Compostela 78–9
Focus on...Prehistoric Cave Paintings 88–9
Close-up...Picos de Europa 92–3
Focus on...Spanish Flora and Fauna 104–5
Focus on...The Pyrenees 108–9
Close-up...Empúries 133

Close-up...The Catalan Pyrenees 139
Focus on...Religious Processions 140–1
Focus on...Creative Catalonia 144
Close-up...Gaudí and Co 145
Focus on...The Pilgrims' Way 168–9
Close-up...Cáceres 183
Focus on...Conquistadores 188–9
Focus on...Quixote Country 198
Close-up...El Escorial 200
Focus on...Albufera 211
Close-up...Elche 216
Focus on...Maestrazgo 218–9
Close-up...Baeza 228
Focus on...Coto Doñana 229
Focus on...Bullfighting 240–1

Walks

Madrid: Old Town 53
Madrid: Palacio Real 57
Madrid: Parque del Retiro 64
Reserva Nacional Dos Ancares/Vigo 81
Taramundi 87
San Sebastián 95
Ordesa National Park/ Señorio de Bertiz 111
Barcelona: The Ramblas 118
Barcelona: Eixample 120
Costa Brava Patrol Path 137
The Gredos Mountains 161
Laguna Negra 177
Parque Nacional de las Tablas de Daimiel/ Ciudad Encantada 195
Gardens of Valencia 212
El Torcal de Antequera 231

Drives

The Miño to Cabo de Fisterra 82
Alto Campoo 96
Aragon: Mountains and plain 103
Behind the Costa Brava 132
Historic Castile 159
Along the Tiétar Valley/ Scenic Extremadura 186
Sigüenza circular route 203
To the heart of the Levante 221
Alpujarras 252
White Towns 253

Spain

through voices past and present

'Their bodies inured to abstinence and toil, their minds composed against death, all practise a stern and constant moderation. They prefer war to ease and should they lack foes without, seek them within.'
– Roman traveller, 1st century BC, on the Asturians

'Seek not for Paradise! It is here – it is here – it is here!'
– Arab poet, on Granada

'Wherever we are we weep for Spain, for we were born there and it is our native land.'
– Morisco on expulsion of the Moriscos after 1609

'The Spaniards are good Christians, but immoral.'
– Venetian diplomat, 16th century

'Never in seven hundred years of continuous war, nor in a hundred years of continuous peace, has Spain been as ruined and poor as it is now.'
– A contemporary observer, 1600

'Since God created the world there has been no empire in it as extensive as that of Spain, for from its rising to its setting the sun never ceases to shine for one instant on its lands.'
– Francisco Ugate de Hermosa, 1655

'Spain is essentially the nation of gentlemen, which for three centuries has lived by doing nothing at the expense of the Indies and America. In Spain they used to await the galleons as, in France, they vote the budget.'
– Victor Hugo

'Let others repine at the lack of turnpike-roads and sumptuous hotels and all the elaborate comforts of a country cultivated into tameness and the commonplace, but give me the rude mountain scramble, the roving, haphazard wayfaring, the frank, hospitable though half wild manners that give such a true game flavour to romantic Spain.'
– Washington Irving

Frog fountain in Tarifa, the Andalucian coastal town where the invading Moors landed in 711

'The Spanish struggle is the fight of reaction against the people, against freedom. My whole life as an artist has been nothing more than a continuous struggle against reaction and the death of art... In the panel on which I am working and which I shall call *Guernica*... I clearly express my abhorrence of the military caste which has sunk Spain in an ocean of pain and death.'
– Pablo Picasso, May 1937

'In Spain the dead are more alive than the dead of any other country in the world.'
– Federico Garcia Lorca

'A cloud of dust, left in the air when a great people went galloping down the highroad of history.'
– José Ortega y Gasset

'If the people of Spain have one common trait it is pride, and if they have another, it is common sense, and if they have a third, it is impracticality... This common sense that they possess is as hard and dry as the plains and mesas of Castilla and it diminishes in hardness and dryness as it goes away from Castilla. At its best it is combined with a complete impracticality. In the south it becomes picturesque; along the littoral it becomes mannerless and Mediterranean; in the north, Navarra and Aragon, there is such tradition of bravery that it becomes romantic; and along the Atlantic coast, as in all countries bounded by a cold sea, life is so practical that there is no time for common sense.'

– Ernest Hemingway, in *Death in the Afternoon*

'Absurdity is the nerve and mainstay of Spain.'

– Angel Ganivet, historian

'Even Spanishness itself, *casticismo,* the quality that binds the nation and makes its flavour instantly recognisable – even this is tempered by the provinces, and has its lights, shades and distortions. The archetypal Castilian has to him something of the gaunt meditative quality that El Greco gave to his saints, or Velázquez to his Habsburgs; his eyes are deep-set, his expression is concentrated, and whether he is jogging to a shack on a big mule, or stepping into a night club out of an Alfa-Romeo, he looks as though he is pursued by some mighty preoccupation. This grave model is coarsened by the Catalans, dullened by the Galicians, solidified by the Basques, and parodied by the flamboyant Andalusians.'

– Jan Morris, in *Spain*

Mountains near Requena in the Levante region

A Coruña-
La Coruña
Ferrol
Avilés
Gijón
Santander
Oviedo
Asturias
Cantabria
Santiago de
Compostela
Lugo
Cordillera Cantábrica
Galicia
León
Pontevedra
Ponferrada
Montes de León
Ourense-
Orense
Vigo
Miño
Burgos
Esla
Palencia
Aranda
de Duero
Valladolid
Zamora
Castilla y León
Segovia
Salamanca
Sistema Central
Avila
Sierra de Guada-r
MADRID
Sierra de Gredos
Plasencia
Talavera de
la Reina
Aranjuez
PORTUGAL
Tajo
Toledo
Extremadura
Cáceres
Montes de Toledo
Castilla
Ciudad
Real
Mérida
Badajoz
Guadiana
Valdepeñas
Puertollano
Sierra Morena
Aracena
Córdoba
Guadalquivir
Jaén
Andalucía
Sevilla
Huelva
Granada
Antequera
Mulhacen
3478m
Golfo de
Cádiz
Costa de la Luz
Jerez de
la Frontera
Ronda
Sistemas
Málaga
Costa del Sol
Cádiz
Marbella
SPAIN
Gibraltar (U.K.)
Algeciras
0
50
100
150
200 km
0
50
100 miles
Estrecho de Gibraltar
MOROCCO

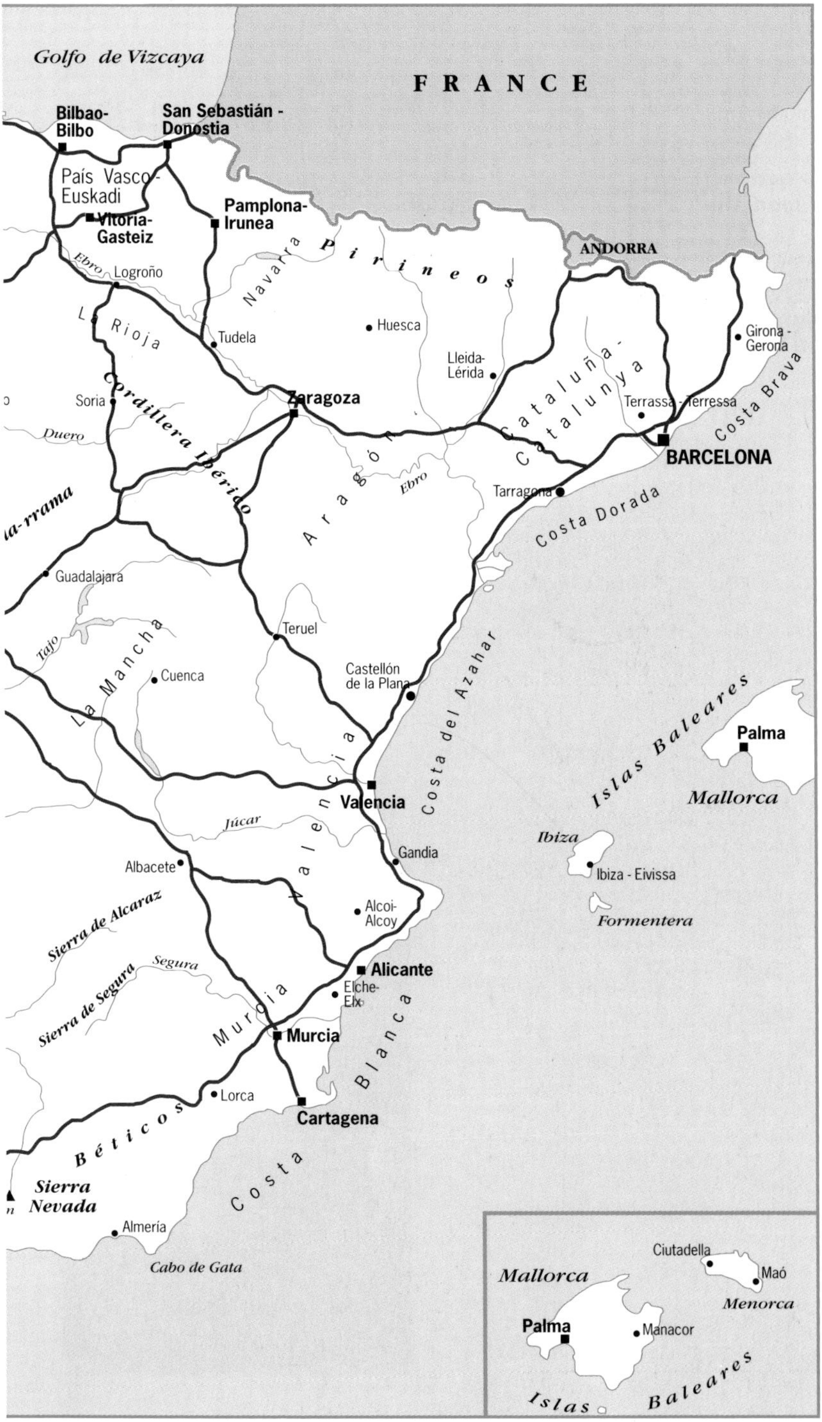
Golfo de Vizcaya
FRANCE
Bilbao-Bilbo
San Sebastián - Donostia
País Vasco-Euskadi
Vitoria-Gasteiz
Pamplona-Irunea
Navarra
Pirineos
ANDORRA
Logroño
La Rioja
Tudela
Huesca
Lleida-Lérida
Cataluña-Catalunya
Girona-Gerona
Costa Brava
Terrassa - Terressa
BARCELONA
Zaragoza
Soria
Duero
Cordillera Ibérico
Aragón
Ebro
Tarragona
Costa Dorada
Guadalajara
Teruel
Tajo
La Mancha
Cuenca
Castellón de la Plana
Costa del Azahar
Islas Baleares
Palma
Mallorca
Valencia
Júcar
Gandia
Ibiza
Ibiza - Eivissa
Formentera
Albacete
Alcoi-Alcoy
Sierra de Alcaraz
Segura
Sierra de Segura
Alicante
Elche-Elx
Murcia
Costa Blanca
Lorca
Cartagena
Béticos
Sierra Nevada
Costa
Almería
Cabo de Gata
Ciutadella
Maó
Menorca
Manacor
Islas Baleares

11

A Land of Many Selves

■ The Land beyond the Pyrenees, exotic, strange, romantic; a part of Europe, member of the European Community; land of the guitar and the carnation; land of steel foundries and tough fishermen; land of extravagant Easter processions, where hooded penitents go barefoot and beat their backs with chains; land of artistic invention; land above all of a new democracy. The point about Spain is that all these images and many others have more than a grain of truth to them. This is a country of many selves. .....■

From the visitor's point of view, the first attraction may well be the climate and the sea, in which case Spain's Mediterranean coast will be the target. This is where the post-war package-tour boom began in the late '50s and '60s, with heavy overbuilding and a start to the Concrete Costas, so much discussed and criticised – and, yes, they do look horrible in many places. But lately, after a scare at the prospect of losing visitors, the Costas have tidied themselves up considerably, with better facilities, clean beaches and safe drinking water. Visiting them can be a crowded, cheerful, good-fun kind of experience, not by any means 'real Spain', but something, nevertheless, that many will still find unbeatable for a holiday. And some places on the Costas, as visitors and readers of this book will soon discover, do remain remarkably attractive.

The real thing Behind, in the mountains that line the coast, 'real Spain' breaks out almost instantly. It is the cities, villages and landscapes of the interior – and of the North Atlantic coast – which make up the vast bulk of this book, reflecting the astonishing depth of interest and historical richness of Spain-behind-the-Costas. Often one will see sights and encounter attitudes that seem to belong to a distant past. Often it is modernity that will most impress. Spaniards tend to prefer the latter version, in case a recitation of their age-old differences should sound like backwardness. But the differences between Spain and other countries, long symbolised by the barrier of the Pyrenees, are real, may well be permanent, and are often thrilling.

<< *España es muy de moda.*
Spain is very fashionable. **>>**

Flamenco, one of the many and varied faces of Spain

Favoured nation In Europe and North America, and in Japan, where flamenco classes are all the rage, Spain is the place of the moment. This general enthusiasm was endorsed in 1992 when both the Barcelona Olympics and the Seville Expo were thumping successes, marking not only the quincentenary of Columbus's first voyage but also a high point for modern Spain. Having 'been away' under the Franco dictatorship right up to 1975, Spain had entered the concert of nations at a bound. Meanwhile a new federal system of 'autonomous regions' has replaced the old central structure, allowing Spain's constituent parts to reveal, as never before, the astonishing differences between them. Those who have been familiar only with tourist Spain are left gasping at the richness of the wider country as it unfolds before their eyes.

Spanish animation Always a large part of the experience, this is perhaps most obvious in the smartness and high-style fashion and the glitzy, all-night hullabaloo of nightclubbers and disco-dancers in Madrid and Barcelona. But that is only a beginning. The arts are burgeoning. New books are being published at a great rate. You cannot miss the snappy design of posters and other graphic art, or the confident liveliness of street life. Spain, with all the immensity of its up-and-down history behind it, is once again on the move. It is as exhilarating for its present as it is remarkable for its age-old survivals.

The other Spain Naturally there is also a down-side, of which the Spanish themselves are very conscious. Having been highly centralised for centuries, the country still stumbles under the weight of an ancient bureaucracy, well capable of causing frustration and delays. Crime, though it has not reached the level of northern Europe, is on the increase. Corruption in public administration and politics is allegedly rife. Unemployment and the Basque terrorist movement ETA cast their shadow (see pages 23 and 24). Except for crime, which is a worry in all countries, these problems affect Spaniards rather more than visitors; what seems to count most is the exuberance, even the brilliance, of modern Spain.

The Mezquita mosque in Córdoba, a magnificent reminder of Spain's Moorish past.

■ Spain is a big country, and most of its people are gathered in the cities. This means that much of the interior is empty. The landscape is often hard and challenging, green enough in spring but sun-hammered by summer. Yet there are zones of fertility and pleasing ease. Valencia, on the Mediterranean, luxuriates in fruit and vegetables; gardens and fruit trees line the valleys of the southern rivers, the Guadiana and the Guadalquivir. And, along the north Atlantic coast, the countryside is intensely, lushly green. .....■

Cuenca in its arid surroundings – archetypal Spanish landscape

Mountains and plains The central fact is that the gaunter inland parts are high, and Spain is more mountainous than any European country except Switzerland. Madrid is one of the highest capitals of the continent. The land climbs quickly up from the narrow strip of the north coast (except for Galicia, a plateau in the northwest corner). Once across the northern mountains, or Cordillera Cantabrica, the open plains begin. This high level country is known as the *meseta*. Rivers criss-cross it, running considerable distances. The Ebro, starting towards the northwest, flows right across the country to the Mediterranean east, providing fertile ground along its length – including the vineyard country of the Rioja. Next river down is the Duero (Douro in Portuguese and, often, English), accompanied by vines and wheat. Now, working southward to the River Tagus, the country, still *meseta*, grows rougher and more rugged, broken by a series of inland mountain ranges, the sierras of Cuenca, Guadarrama, magnificent Gredos and other, lesser outcrops. Last of all, dividing the southern region of Andalucía from the sea, comes the Sierra Morena. Of all this countryside, only 10 per cent is truly fertile. Some 40 per cent is 'moderately arable'. Another 40 per cent can be used for agriculture only with difficulty. And 10 per cent is absolutely useless.

Towns and cities Within this challenging terrain, the Spaniards and the Moors – an Arab and Berber people who held much of the peninsula for centuries (see pages 30–1) – have managed to construct an extraordinary range of villages, towns and cities.

Start in the warm south with Andalucía, and the romantic images are true – the cobbled streets with whitewashed houses, black grilles over windows and a tumble of geraniums. Castles abound, legacy of centuries of contention. Of the cities the great stars are Córdoba, Seville and Granada.

Move on to the central *meseta*, where the climate is punishingly hot in summer, cold in winter, and the villages are low and often poor, many built of claybricks – adobe – and clustered round a dominant, stone-built church. The cities here are sturdily heroic, each with a historic centre or *casco viejo*. Often the major buildings are heraldically emblazoned; often there will be a Gothic cathedral. Around the *casco viejo*, 20th-century apartment blocks rise in often depressing array.

The most beautiful cities of the centre are Toledo, Avila, Segovia, Salamanca and Cuenca, with Burgos a little further north. Two of Spain's three biggest cities also fall into this zone: Valencia, down on the coast, is largely modern, though with a rich scattering of architectural and artistic treasures. Madrid, 17th-century or later, with a huge 20th-century extension, is hardly a connoisseur's capital to look at. But it is one of the most exciting places in Europe, with a large concentration of art.

Barcelona falls into the northern band but is a Mediterranean city, most confident and lively of any in Spain, enriched by the extraordinary phenomenon of Modernist architecture, with the genius Gaudí as chief exponent. Of north coast cities, San Sebastián is most memorable at one end, and at the other Santiago de Compostela, goal of pilgrims. And to all this, of course, must naturally be added those tourist honey-pots, the Costas.

The limestone massif of northern Spain's dramatic Picos de Europa

People and Institutions

■ What do the Spaniards look like and how do they behave? Traditional answers have been sexist. Writers through the ages, being mostly male, have been unstinting in their praise of Spanish women. What one can say for sure is that the physical presence of the Spanish people is highly arresting, less because of their generally dark complexions and hair than on account of their style. Men in cities often go suited, women wear clothes that look extremely smart on them but might be considered overdressing elsewhere. .....■

The young assert themselves through informality, picking up Europe's latest fashions and, in the big cities, even anticipating them. Spain may seem to be characterised by a young woman in jeans strolling arm-in-arm down a village street with her black-clad grandmother.
Vigour of speech and gesture is an abiding characteristic of the Spaniards. In Aragon and Navarre people speak so forcefully that they may sound quite angry during an exchange of pleasantries. The traditional notion that Spain is the slothful country of *mañana* or 'tomorrow' may be true enough of the bureaucracy, but most Spaniards work hard and often briskly.

Work and play Spanish hours may be a puzzle at first. The day often starts early, with offices (not shops) opening at 08.00hrs and carrying straight on till 14.00 or 15.00hrs, at which point the working day is over. Some enterprises (including all shops) have an afternoon session, starting about 17.00hrs. In either case, where possible, Spaniards take a long, late lunch hour. Lunchtime television news, for instance, is at 15.00hrs. This system is breaking down somewhat in Madrid and

Wedding in the park

Barcelona, thanks to the impact of international business and the EU, but it will be many decades before it perishes utterly. In the evening, people have a coffee or a drink in a bar or café and eat a light dinner at any time from 21.00 till 23.00hrs. Children accompany their parents.

Family bonds In all of this, even in industrial cities, the family is the key, with mutual bonds extremely strong, mutual support freely given and the mother at the centre in a style one might describe as Mediterranean-matriarchal, within a rather 'macho' society. The family is celebrated over long Sunday lunches, usually in restaurants. Most Spaniards live in apartments, often crowded and a little dingy – though new prosperity is changing this.

Though churches remain crowded, the Catholic Church itself is no longer overwhelmingly important. The number of atheists and agnostics is increasing steadily, especially in the north. Many hundreds of priests have left the church over the marriage issue and basic questions of reform versus conservatism.

<< Even in these increasingly secular days, boys are still mostly named for saints (it used to be compulsory). Girls are often named after the character in which the Virgin is venerated locally, be it the Virgin of the Immaculate Conception or Virgin of the Rocks. The very common 'Inma' is thus an abbreviation of 'Inmaculada'. **>>**

The monarchy The importance of the monarchy remains to some degree an open question. Brought to the throne after the death of Franco (see page 49), King Juan Carlos has not only defended democracy, but behaved with a prudent modesty and lack of ostentation which contrasts with the behaviour of the political classes. Neither he nor his queen, Sofia of Greece, have much truck with the old aristocracy. They keep no court, have no courtiers and have brought up a civically-minded group of children. Nevertheless, the monarchy itself appears to lack strong roots, thanks to its history during the 19th and early 20th centuries. The role of police and army has also changed. Where once the army dominated much of civilian life, now soldiers are largely invisible and fears of army intervention virtually nil, short of any attempt to dismember the state in response to Basque or Catalan separatism. The police, once feared, have re-emerged, in general, as public servants – symbolised by the fact that the Civil Guard or Guardia Civil, a paramilitary brigade, now frequently abandon their famous patent-leather tricorn hats in favour of workaday forage caps.

Spaniards know how to relax during the heat of the day

■ **Television-watching is the great pastime, in Spain as elsewhere, with blaring TV sets a fixture in cheap restaurants, and game-shows plentiful. Television also shows a lot of football and it is this, these days, which is probably the number one public passion. Real Madrid and Barça (Barcelona) dominate a league whose smallest quivers send shockwaves through the nation. Sporting papers are eagerly read; players live in a cauldron of emotion; and supporters work themselves into a frenzy of enthusiasm. .....**■

Children take over the arena after a wood-chopping contest in San Sebastián, one of the highly individual pastimes enjoyed by the Basques

Cycling is another major Spanish sport and even in the hottest weather motorists may encounter posses of brightly and tightly clad persons, heads down over handlebars, whizzing through remote and hostile territory.

Mountaineering and mountain walking are also popular, especially in the north and most of all in the Basque Country. Foreigners are the main walkers in southern sierras, mainly in the Alpujarras south of Granada and the lovely, if steep countryside around the White Towns in the provinces of Málaga and Cádiz.

Horse-riding and the management of horses is another Spanish passion, particularly in Andalucía, and visitors tap into this as well, with increasing numbers of trekking holidays now on offer, often in wildly magnificent scenery.

Bullfighting is discussed on pages 240–1. Though assaulted from abroad on grounds of cruelty, it remains almost as important as soccer, with indications that young people are starting to attend in greater numbers. Spaniards will tell you that it is not a sport but an ancient ritual, with a strong aesthetic content, and that it raises issues of life and death for man as well as bull. At all events, like it or loathe it, it is there in Spanish society – not reported on newspaper sports pages, but reviewed on the arts pages along with literature and music.

Silver screen The cinema remains exceptionally well attended, with foreign films – largely American – dubbed into Spanish. For the original language, you will need to look to specialist cinema houses. Quite a few Spanish films are made and a number of Spanish directors, like Carlos Saura, and Pedro Almodóvar, in lighter style, have gained international reputations. With Luis Buñuel among their forebears, there is certainly inspiration available.

A musical nation In music as well as dance, intensely local styles survive. The mountainous north, for example, is strongly attached to bagpipes, not to mention harps in Celtic Galicia. In Aragon they dance – and sing – the *jota*, with wonderfully rhythmic movement. In Catalonia, by contrast, the key dance is the *sardana*, very much a community affair, with ceremonious dancing in a ring, hands joined. People drop in and out; all ages circle round together in a relaxed sharing of experience. Flamenco, though it stands at the centre of the national stage, is also originally a local form – the music of the Andalucian south and especially of the gypsies. Its hypnotic singing style and dramatic dancing expresses a highly individual, sexually charged ethos, compulsively romantic and easy to subvert into the unchallenging form freqently offered to tourists. The names of the rhythms are often based on places: Malagueñas from Málaga, for instance; Sevillanas from Seville, of course; and Trianeras from that once-gypsy quarter of Seville, Triana, across the river from the city centre.

Festivals and dress Another aspect of Spanish life centres on processions and dressing up. Religious processions, full of intense passion, dripping with the sense of guilt and atonement – as well as a lot of fun, when nobody is looking – are described on pages 140–1. They are conducted in an extraordinary garb of robes and pointed hoods borrowed from the Inquisition.

Less solemn ceremonies and feast days feature a gallimaufry of giants, men on stilts invisible inside vast costumes, and roly-poly figures dressed as human heads, making their way through the cheerful throng. The battles of the Moors and Christians are evoked in annual re-enactments. The best is at Alcoy, near Valencia, where the Moors give as good as they get and one dreads to think how much the costumes have cost. New festivals are springing up elsewhere. Cartagena now lays on a lively Romans-and-Carthaginians contest, with local matrons toga-swathed, the chemist and grocer bearing a dashing line in swords and shields.

It is no surprise that every village in Spain has its own feast day, or even week of festival. Joining in can be one of the great pleasures.

Festivals mean frills and finery

■ **International food, based mainly on French cuisine, is available à la carte in Spain's better hotels; in the cheaper, package holiday hotels an attempt is made to serve narrower national interests, be it German sausages or British-style meat and veg. Fish and chips are commonplace along the Costas. Visitors should also know, however, that Spanish food, accompanied by Spanish wines, is regionally based and almost always much better than the 'international'. .....■**

Essentially, the country has four broad culinary divisions. There is a band along the northern coast where seafood and bean-dishes dominate; Catalonia, on the eastern seaboard, is full of rich and subtle mixtures; the interior (mainly Old Castile north of Madrid and New Castile to the south) goes in for meat, part grilled, part roasted in wood-fired ovens; Andalucía, finally, is the place for salad, fish and fruit. There are local drinks like sherry in the south or cider in the north. Many areas produce good cheese, once again highly distinctive in character. Excellent mineral waters abound, from Vichy Catalan in the Costa Brava, to Lanjarón from the springs of the Alpujarra mountains south of Granada. Madrid has a great range of regional and foreign restaurants – and some very good dishes of its own.

Pavement café in Valencia

Sweetmeats and snacks Desserts are less distinguished, except where they have Arab origins. But bar-snacks are a vital part of Spanish eating. Known as *pinchos* when they consist of a mere morsel alongside a drink, *tapas* when they are a little more substantial – the most common and most delicious form of bar-snack – and *raciónes* or rations when they amount to something the size of a restaurant dish, they come in huge varieties, ranging from mussels in vinaigrette, through Russian salad and kidneys in sherry to the wilder shores of fried pig's ear or snails and garlic.

The north San Sebastián in the Basque Country has arguably the best food in Spain. *Merluza en salsa verde* – hake in a green parsley sauce – is the dish most praised. Asturias, in the middle of the coast, specialises in cider and *fabada*, a bean-and-sausage stew served as a first course. Galicia offers a feast of shellfish – spider crab, oysters, scallops (*vieiras*). Humbler dishes are also excellent – *caldo gallego*, a soup/stew with greens and meat, and *lacón con grelos*, pork hock with turnip tops. Wines are drunk young, often from little white china cups on pedestals.

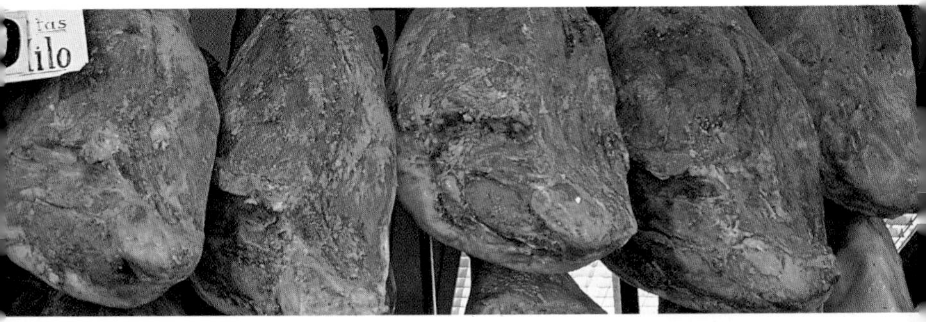

Catalonia and Valencia Catalonia yields such surprises as goose with pears and chicken with peach, or the *mar i muntanya* dishes, literally 'sea and mountain', mixing meat with fish and shellfish. Game is also good. The Raimat wine region produces Spain's best (still) white wines. *Cava*, a sparkling white made by the *méthode champenoise*, comes from the Penedès district. Valencia, of course, is the home of paella, a dish of rice, chicken, shellfish and mutton, made to order in great iron pans.

Castile and the centre *Cochinillo* and *cordero asado*, respectively roast suckling pig and lamb, crisp outside and tender within, leave space for little else. Vegetables are scarce, except in La Mancha, south of Madrid, where *pisto manchego* is close to ratatouille. La Rioja, in the northeast, produces Spain's best known red wines. The best of all, however, come from the Riba del Duero in the northwest, with a vast and less spectacular production from the area round Valdepeñas in La Mancha. Madrid's most famous dish is *caldo Madrileño*, a broth with chick peas, then ham and chicken, served in its successive stages.

Andalucía and the south To get the classic salad of lettuce, tomato, onions and olives, ask for *ensalada verde. Ensalada mixta* comes with tuna and other extras. Fried fish, light and varied, is called *fritura mixta*, or, in the case of tiny fish, *pescaíta frita.* Asparagus and artichokes are wonderful. Many Andalucians drink sherry as a regular tipple.

You can eat well and relatively cheaply at the counter in a tapas bar. The days of free tapas with drinks are, however, virtually a thing of the past

The landscapes Spaniards inhabit and the food they eat are certainly pointers to Spain's diversity. Language is a deeper indication. There are four separate languages and numerous dialects. The language we call Spanish and which is spoken by hundreds of millions in Latin America, as well as in the Iberian peninsula, is really 'Castilian' and known as such by Spaniards. This is the language of Old Castile, a Romance or Latin-derived tongue also containing thousands of Arabic words. .....

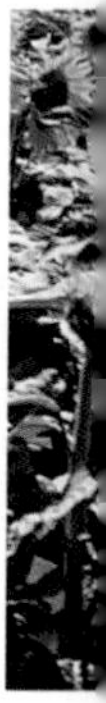

Two of Spain's other languages are also Latin-derived. Catalan is spoken – and written – not just in Catalonia but also in slightly differing forms which locals claim as distinct languages, right down the Valencian seaboard and as far as the Balearic islands. Galicia has preserved a distinct Romance tongue akin to Portuguese, now, after some falling off, once again surprisingly widely spoken in this northwesterly region.

Ancient tongue The fourth language, completely separate, is Basque, which has no firm connection with any other language (though it does have some affinities with Georgian in the old Soviet Union). It is believed to be extremely ancient, certainly from before the times of literacy, though, like Castilian or any language, it contains many later borrowings and adaptations. The fact that the Basque word for 'knife' derives from the word for 'stone' is taken as an indication that it may really be that linguistic rarity – a language with elements surviving from the Neolithic period.

Conflict There is some mutual hostility between the languages. Road signs and place names are now almost all in the local languages, but, where they are not, campaigning enthusiasts still paint out the Castilian names. Nor do committed Basques or Catalans particularly enjoy speaking Castilian. The history of each of these peoples is touched upon in the next chapter. Some of the differences in character are sketched in opposite, at risk of outrageous generalisations.

A flamenco show in Seville

Castilians and Aragonese Outside the villages of Castile, Old and New, it is hard to spot a genuinely Castilian personality. Movement of population has made the people 'Spanish' in a general sense. Country people, however, are marked by a certain pride and reserve. The people of Aragon, the other great historic area which teamed up with Castile, are trenchant and direct. Those who live in the enclosed valleys of the high Pyrenees are inward-looking, not always a barrel of fun.

Basques The Basque Country, for all its differences and present sense of grievance, shared the destiny of central Spain for centuries, incidentally producing a disproportionate number of mathematicians and bankers. Today the Basque country is industrial as well as rural. The Basques are lively, hospitable and sports-minded, and also great gamblers. Their passionate insistence on their own identity has thrown up ETA, the separatist terrorist movement which has caused so great a headache to the rest of Spain (though disavowed by many Basques it still receives some popular support). It is possible, just possible, however, that ETA will soon disintegrate (see page 24). Meanwhile, the group has posed no threat to tourists in the Basque country, and elsewhere only the episodic threat with which all Spaniards live constantly.

Catalans The Catalans are European-minded, with strong French connections across the Pyrenees. Their area has the heavy tourism of the Costa Brava and still some textile industry, with a good deal of electronics and light-engineering. But there is also a deep rurality which is most attractive to encounter. The Catalans are both level-headed and great producers of surprises, in art as in food. Their nationalist impulses will be satisfied by something well short of independent statehood.

Galicians (Gallegos) Nothing is more wistful than Galician poetry, full of loss and homesickness. Many Gallegos emigrate. Those who stay are a little canny, but endlessly loyal and hospitable when friendship is established. They are often conservative in temperament. 'None of this nonsense about independence', they say.

Village line-up in the rugged Picos de Europa region

■ Spain was a military dictatorship till 1975. By the '80s it was changing, at giddying pace and with no intermediate stages, into a post-industrial democracy, while also retaining a great many features which were seemingly changeless and immemorial. It had entered NATO, it had wholeheartedly embraced the European Community – and this despite severe competition in agriculture from more 'efficient', more highly mechanised neighbours. Since then, most Spanish cities have prospered (incidentally putting up prices for tourists). Meanwhile, many rural areas have been driven even further below the poverty line. What comes next? .....■

The problems Spain's first, worst problem is unemployment, relating to recession, agricultural prices, technological change and the restructuring of industry. There seems no easy end to it. The second is Basque terrorism at the hands of ETA, that group whose name stands for 'Basque Land and Liberty'. After increasingly random acts of violence, ETA's top military commanders were detained in the early 90s, leading to hopes of greater tranquillity. But the call for a separate state will not simply go away, even though other Basque groups have grown far more cooperative with the centre. Another all-Spanish problem is immigration from North Africa. This has not yet led to a right-wing backlash as in France, but that possibility is certainly a worry at the political level. In summing up, one might say that Spain has so far managed to sustain itself and succeed despite these problems but few of them are likely to go away.

Rural Andalucía, a harsh land from which to scrape a living

Environment The environment is another area of concern and has a direct bearing on visitors. Here, too, one must start with the positive, for Spain has more wild and untamed space, more mountain and forest than anywhere else in Europe. Flora and fauna are splendid, ranging from high Pyrenean to lowland Mediterranean species, and with such fine 'extras' as the Ebro delta and especially the wetlands of the Coto Doñana at the mouth of the Guadalquivir. Against this, it must be said that environmental consciousness has been particularly slow to develop in Spain. Individuals dump litter indiscriminately, especially plastic. Agriculturalists show little awareness of the consequences of over-using pesticides and fertilisers.

Industry, particularly the old Franco period plant, causes serious pollution as well as being often an eyesore. Solutions are often being attempted to all these problems, though industry is particularly intractable. The tourist trade wishes to smarten up its image and has made considerable improvements along the coast. But the Spaniards feel that some of the criticism they have received has been unfair, and the point has been made that if it is the foreigners who want the wild spaces inviolate, then perhaps it is foreigners who should pay, if necessary through international agencies.

The future of tourism Package tours and large resorts were and remain the staples of Spain's coastal tourism. Independent travel has always existed side by side with the tours, though on a far smaller scale. Recently, however, more and more people have become aware of the beauties and pleasures of inland Spain and, as a result, more beds and eating places are now called for. Whether they will be created in a way that is sympathetic to the environment and adds to the pleasures of travelling, is a key question for the future. If the government and planning authorities have learned the lessons of the Costas, then there are grounds for hope.

Way back in the '20s, Spain invented a unique feature (later copied by Portugal). This was to turn some of its ancient buildings, of which there are so many that any use for them is an act of rescue rather than appropriation, into a chain of state-run hotels. These are the paradors, in Spanish *paradores*. The chain has been enlarged by the construction of well-designed modern paradors in key spots where touring hotels are – or were – in short supply.

With this as a model at the top end of the market, perhaps something equally imaginative can be achieved for budget travellers.

Time will tell.

The upmarket face of tourism – parador at Jaén in Andalucía

SPAIN WAS *Another Country*

■ Somehow, from a history dogged by misfortune, Spain has delivered itself into a vibrant present, enthusiastically received by its European partners and moving fast to close the economic gap between itself and northern Europe. How has the trick been managed, one may well ask, considering the dark days of the 20th-century Civil War and the long period of military dictatorship that followed? .....■

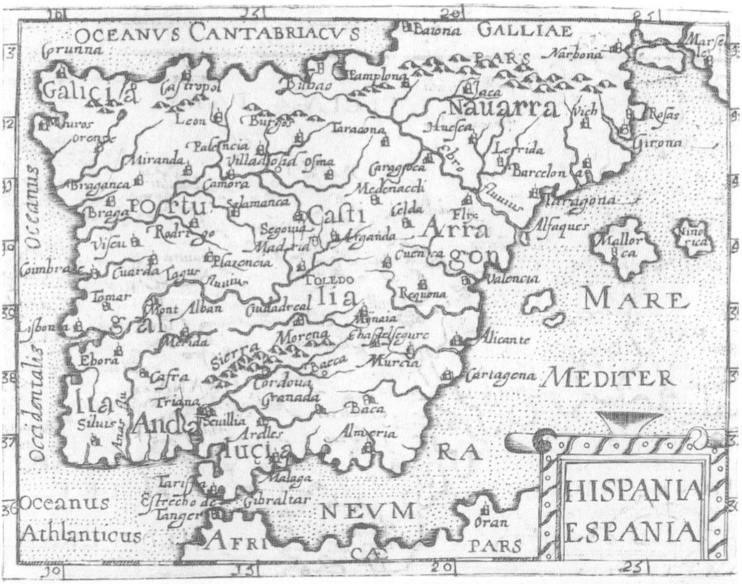

Moorish castle, relic of a significant period in Spain's past

Behind the phenomenon of the present, there looms another, longer history, encountered all over Spain where castles, cathedrals, churches, arcaded squares and streets still stand, a glorious architectural accumulation. Much of this inheritance also bears witness to decay, for collapse has been as strong a theme in Spain as growth and empire. The magnificent and sometimes jagged edges of Spanish art and sculpture form an electric part of the inheritance, sufficient reason in itself to visit Spain.

The Spanish story Spain's long prehistory was a tale of cave-dwelling hunter-gatherers, farmers and traders from far-off places. The Romans ruled for four centuries, then the Visigoths, and then, through most of the peninsula, the Moors. The Christians slowly pushed them back again. By the 16th century Spain was the centre of an empire stretching over much of Europe and Latin America. In the 17th century, with the nation nearly bankrupt, Spain was producing her greatest works of art and literature in a profuse Golden Age. The empire was lost during the 19th century. From 1936 to 1939, after a brief Republic, Spain tore itself to pieces in a Civil War won by the right-wing Nationalists under General Franco. He died in 1975, to be succeeded by democracy and King Juan Carlos. The pages that follow look at the story in greater detail and outline the course of art and architecture.

Inhabitants and Invaders

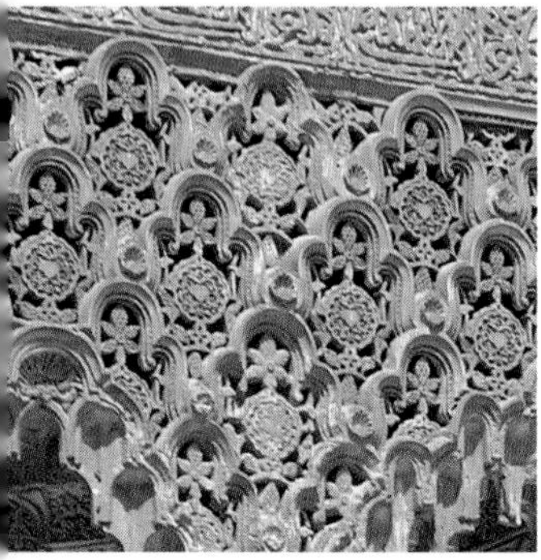

■ The first inhabitants of the peninsula included the palaeolithic cave-dwellers of northern Spain, responsible, among many other works, for the extraordinary and naturalistically painted bison of Altamira (around 13000BC). There are other interesting but less spectacular palaeolithic caves and rock shelters in eastern and southern Spain. The neolithic period has left behind quite a wide range of dolmens, including huge burial chambers, with beautifully cut stone, at Antequera in the south, dating from about 2500BC. .....■

In the second millennium BC, probably from points east, there arrived the tribal peoples known to the Greeks, after the River Ebro, as the Iberians. They were joined by a wave of Celts, creating a warlike people now called the Celtiberians. They left behind them, especially round Avila in the centre, scores of sculpted bulls or boars, mysterious, sad-looking creatures. The round foundations of Celtic homes, and some that survive as inhabited structures, may still be encountered in Galicia. The most advanced populations were in the east, close to the Mediterranean. This area produced the stone-carved female bust, probably 5th century BC, known as *La Dama de Elche*.

Tales of the past Somewhere along the southern Atlantic coast, according to the ancients, lay the kingdom of Tartessos, famed for the wealth of its mines. Hercules killed its king in performing one of his twelve labours. He also set the rock of Gibraltar on one side of the exit of the Mediterranean and Ceuta on the other. Though the site has not been found, it is clear that the kingdom of Tartessos really existed in some form.

Newcomers The Phoenicians began to arrive as traders at about 1000BC. In due course, as Tyre collapsed, they shifted to Carthage, in Tunisia, and were known henceforth as Carthaginians. They founded a city on the site of modern Cádiz and traded with the Iberian settlements along the Spanish coast. They were joined in due course by ancient Greek traders, moving into such sites as Empúries in modern Catalonia and Denia, on the Costa Blanca.

The dolmen of Menga at Antequera in Andalucía dates back 4,500 years

■ **After losing the first Punic War, the Carthaginians fell back on the Spanish coast, founding the city of New Carthage, modern Cartagena. In 219BC their leader, Hannibal, attacked Sagunto further up the coast, starting the Second Punic War. He won – but only after the mass suicide of the inhabitants – and moved north against the Greek settlements. But the Greeks allied themselves with the Romans, who subdued Spain with great difficulty, themselves provoking a mass suicide in Numantia in 133BC. The conquest ended in 19BC. .....■**

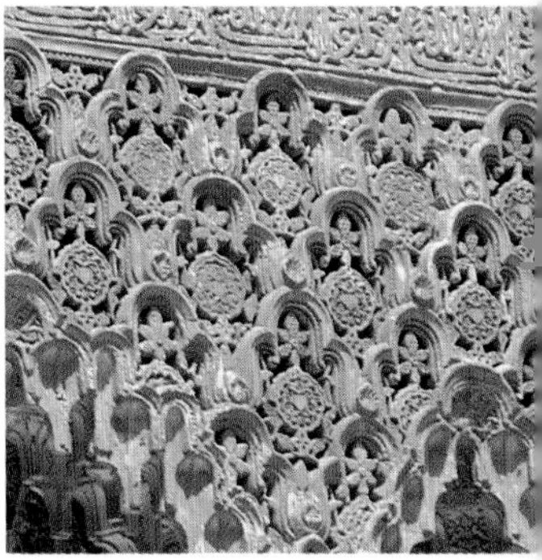

Itálica: the Roman amphitheatre...

The country they took over was on the backward side, raising cattle and sheep rather than crops. It also had a powerful military aristocracy. The Romans contributed social order and a uniform system of justice, widespread irrigation and, extremely important, roads. They divided the peninsula into three provinces: Lusitania, approximately Galicia and modern Portugal; Baetica, more or less modern Andalucía; and Tarraconensis, with Tarragona as capital and controlling much of the rest of Spain. They met constant resistance along the Cantabrian coast; the Basques proved totally resistant to Roman culture.

Traces of an empire Numerous Roman ruins remain, and some still functional pieces of architecture. The soaring aqueduct of Segovia was used until modern times; the bridge over the Tagus at Alcántara is 80m high; Tarragona has a massive quantity of Roman remnants; and there are substantial remains at Itálica, near Seville. The greatest concentration of all is at Mérida in Extremadura, the former Augustus Emerita. A Roman palace has recently been unearthed at Córdoba, though it may disappear again under a new railway station.
Roman Spain produced grain, wine and olive oil for export to Rome. Spanish-born emperors included Trajan, Hadrian and Marcus Aurelius. Of writers, Lucan, Martial and the two Senecas were all born in Spain.

...and remains of the city

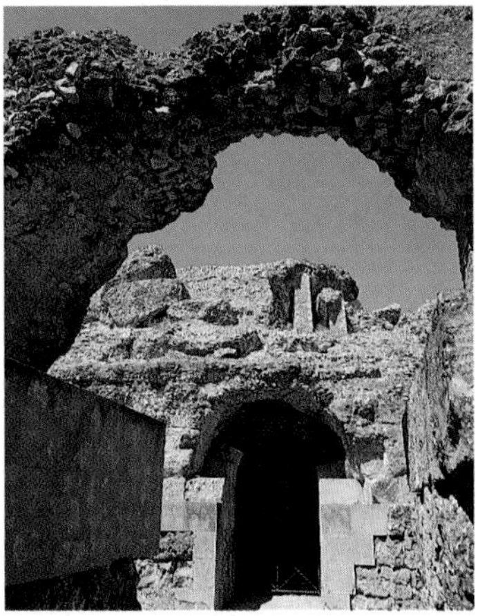

The Moors

■ The Visigoths followed the Romans, and ruled for three centuries. They built small churches with horseshoe arches; their carved stonework can be seen at the National Archaeological Museum in Madrid. Their country was known as Vandalusia. In AD711 and AD712, came Berber troops from the Atlas Mountains in North Africa under Arab leadership. These people, united only in Islam, are called the Moors. They captured the Visigothic capital, Toledo, and within four years had taken most of the rest of Spain. .....■

Moorish castle, Vélez Málaga

Córdoba on the Guadalquivir became the Moors' capital and prospered to an extraordinary degree. In 785, the territory of the Moors declared itself an emirate, under Abd al-Rahman I, the last surviving member of the Umayyad dynasty, who had escaped from a coup in Baghdad. Abd al-Rahman founded a great mosque in Córdoba, the Mezquita, using ancient capitals and columns and constructing over them a double tier of horseshoe arches, brilliant in red and white segments. The city was by now the largest in Europe, specialising in silks, leather and luxury goods. The Moors had brought with them rice, citrus fruit, cotton, saffron, artichokes – a huge collection of useful plants. They developed the Roman irrigation system into a complex network still intensely admired. They loved poetry above all other arts.

Building power Maintaining central control was always a problem. Abd al-Rahman III (912–61) smashed several separatist movements and proclaimed al-Andalus an independent caliphate in 785. He enlarged the Mezquita as place of worship for a swelling population, and for himself, 8km from Córdoba, he built the splendid palace of Medina Azahara.

This was the zenith, a period of *convivencia* or mutual toleration in which the three civilisations of Islam, Christianity and the Jews all lived together fairly peaceably. Córdoba had great libraries and nurtured philosophers, doctors and mathematicians. Soon, however, power passed to a military dictator, al-Mansur, in Spanish Almanzor, who launched devastating raids against the Christian north and built the last extension of the Mezquita, giving it a capacity of 25,000 worshippers.

Decline and fall Following Almanzor, at the start of the 11th century, the caliphate collapsed in sudden chaos, from which there emerged some 30

petty kingdoms, called the *taifas*. Seville and Zaragoza were the greatest. Soon, however, the Christians were pressing hard, and the *taifas* summoned help from the fundamentalist north African Almoravids who simply took over tottering al-Andalus. Another fundamentalist group from Africa, the Almohads, followed. In Seville, their Spanish capital, they built a great tower for the mosque, the Giralda. Seville's famous Golden Tower or Torre del Oro is also their work.

Even the Almohads, however, could not hold off the Christians. Seville was lost in 1248 and then only the kingdom of Granada survived. It endured in artistic brilliance, creating the Alhambra palace and other splendours, till finally defeated in 1492. Granada's capture brought to an end one of the most brilliant civilisations ever seen in Europe.

Moorish architecture Moorish building depended on delicacy, elaboration and brilliant colour, with horseshoe arches, patios, paired windows divided by a single slender column (*ajimez/ajimeces*) and hanging ceilings of extraordinary complexity that look like wasps' or swallows' nests (*muqarnas*). Decoration was in abstract plaster patterning, again amazingly complex, and often used Koranic script. Wall tiles, or *azulejos*, again elaborate and multi-coloured, were another major feature. They remain so in Spain today. The *alcazaba* was the principal Moorish fortress; the *alcázar* was a fortified palace.

Both terms were adopted by the Spaniards.

The Torre del Oro, Seville

■ Some time in the 720s, starting at Covadonga in Asturias, the small, surviving pockets of Christians began to expand their territory. In the 8th and 9th centuries, the Asturians built themselves tiny but accomplished churches and palaces in Oviedo and round about, and then expanded south to León, only to be overwhelmed by Almanzor in 996. In Santiago, further west, a tomb claimed as that of the Apostle James was discovered in the early 9th century. Almanzor devastated Santiago, too, sparing the tomb but stealing the cathedral bells. .....■

Alfonso VI of Castile, conqueror of Moorish Toledo

Expansion Undaunted, the Christians once again began their expansion, now extending south and east into an area they filled with castles and called Castilla. In the mid-10th century, it proclaimed its own independence and from that point on dominated both its Christian neighbours and the advance into central Spain. To the south of Castile and León lay a wild frontier area, only lightly inhabited but always dangerous. To cope with this, the Castilians developed an extraordinary mixture of spirituality and military might, two qualities which infused future Spain.

Meanwhile, over in the east, Barcelona and the Catalan region had been won from the Moors by the Carolingian kings of France, giving the area a quite different beginning. Barcelona became an independent country in 878 under Wilfred the Hairy. Aragon and Navarre had also become tiny independent kingdoms, joining in the general southern movement.

The difficulty facing the Christian expansion was lack of people to resettle conquered areas. When Alfonso VI of Castile recaptured Toledo in 1085 he was taking on an awesome responsibility. Moorish villagers and townspeople often remained as labourers, while the Christians, often unable to press on further, instead exacted tribute from the weakened *taifa* kingdoms. There was a great deal of coming and going across the lines. Christian kings often had Moorish wives and Moorish leaders Christian wives. The Christian hero El Cid (1026–99) fought for years as a mercenary for Moorish Zaragoza. The Moors supplied the Christian aristocracy with silks and luxuries. Their learning was much admired and, so far as possible, absorbed. Meanwhile the Christian kingdoms welcomed French pilgrims and settlers.

New hostility In the 12th and 13th centuries both sides hardened up, the Moors now throwing Christians out of their territories, the Christians aiming for total reconquest under the banner of St James the Moorslayer (the form into which poor St James the Apostle had been transmuted). The Christians, though more primitive, were by now the stronger, and slowly, over the centuries, accomplished their goal. The key Christian victory was at Navas de Tolosa near Jaén in 1212. Jaume I of Aragon-Catalonia pushed down the eastern seaboard in the 13th century, retaking Valencia, earlier El Cid's private fief. Fernando III of Castile, who became a saint, retook almost all of Andalucía. Now it was all over bar Granada. But this meant a wait of more than two centuries.

Art and architecture French influence soon combined with Spanish taste to usher in the Romanesque style. Its key, of course, is the use of the round arch, in which the Romans had specialised. The ground plan took on the form of the cross, with transepts and a rounded apse. Another great feature of Spanish Romanesque, which spread along the Pilgrims' Way and through the territories first reconquered, was its gloriously elaborate and usually good-humoured sculpture. There was also fine Romanesque painting, especially in Catalonia and León. Gothic architecture, based on height, with pointed arches and tall windows, came in, again from France, by the 13th century. This was the style of Spain's great cathedrals and was used in the later territories of the Reconquest.

Two other important styles originated in the south. In the early centuries, Christians moving north out of al-Andalus brought Moorish building habits, returning the horseshoe arch borrowed long before from the Visigoths. These were the Mozarabs, their style Mozarabic. As the Reconquest progressed, many Moorish craftsmen continued to work in a style called Mudéjar, creating some of Spain's most characteristic buildings. Towers are patterned in raised brick and ceramics (Aragon is the best place for these, especially Teruel). Their other trademark was the *artesonado*, or coffered wooden ceiling, often star-patterned and with elaborate pendants. Mudéjar means almost as much to Spain as Romanesque or Gothic.

Mudéjar-style church in the Moorish town of Vélez Málaga, Andalucía

The Catholic Kings

■ **Aragon absorbed Catalonia and the two of them established a Mediterranean empire which included, with historic consequences, Sardinia, Sicily and Naples and even, for a century or so, Athens and much of mainland Greece. Nevertheless, the king of Aragon was in bad trouble with his nobles when his son Ferdinand, still a teenager, travelled to Valladolid in 1469 to be married secretly, in a private house, to Isabella of Castile, one of two future claimants to the Castilian throne. .....■**

This marriage of Ferdinand and Isabella, which might have amounted to nothing, proved the making of the Spain we know today. Ferdinand and his father won their civil war at home; Isabella overcame her rival, known as La Beltraneja, in another civil war, sealed by a victory at Toro in 1474. It was a ruthless progress to the throne, and though the two monarchs represented separate kingdoms – and were careful to maintain the constitutional difference – the alliance created a formidable power-block which later evolved into a single nation-state.

> **<<** *Tanto monta, monta tanto* was the motto of Ferdinand and Isabella, meaning roughly *'However high one climbs, so high climbs the other'*. Castile, however, was the dominant partner and Castilian the dominant language. **>>**

Formidable team They were an extraordinary couple. Ferdinand was a military leader and crafty diplomat, much praised by Machiavelli. The apparently simpler Isabella, rather plain in looks and deeply resentful of her husband's many amours, was an administrator of extraordinary gifts, a true 'conviction monarch' who fought fiercely for her own vision of Castile and Catholic expansion. Together they imposed civic order through a vicious local police force

Isabella of Castile. No woman had a stronger influence on Spanish history than this queen

called the Santa Hermandad or Holy Brotherhood; they tamed the hitherto warring nobles, forbidding them to build more castles. Though themselves of middle-brow tastes, at least in reading, they promoted sculpture, architecture and painting to an extraordinary degree. They governed by itineration, that is to say, continual movement about their kingdoms, rather than ruling from a fixed capital.
In their own day they were best known for the conquest of Granada, Spain's last Moorish kingdom, which

fell in 1492 after a 10-year war. Meanwhile, they had established the Spanish Inquisition. Its targets were those members of Spain's half-million strong Jewish community who were accused of making false conversions to Christianity. These *conversos* were mercilessly harried with burning, imprisonment and seizure of property.

Expulsion and expansion With the defeat of Islam, the Catholic Kings (they received this title from the Pope) now banished the Jews from Spain. At the same time, they acceded to the pleas of the Genoese navigator Christopher Columbus to carry Christianity to the Far East. Columbus was convinced that Japan lay on the far side of the Atlantic. He wanted to keep one tenth of all his discoveries and demanded the hereditary title of Lord High Admiral. A disagreeable man of extraordinary courage and tenacity, he sailed with his three tiny caravels from Palos de la Frontera near Huelva on 3 August 1492, but it was not till his third voyage that he passed right through the Caribbean islands to reach the continent of Latin America. The Catholic Kings, as it happened, never kept their side of the bargain and Columbus died surrounded by acrimony. Isabella herself died in 1504, Ferdinand in 1516.

Art and architecture The reign of Ferdinand and Isabella coincided with a new form of Gothic architecture, full of sweeping curves, with thrilling tracery and vaulting, in which style the Catholic Kings commissioned many buildings. Their shields, monograms and other emblems contributed to the effect of Isabelline Gothic as it is known. There are major royal buildings in Toledo and Granada. Finest of all in this style is the Chapel of the Constables in Burgos Cathedral. Isabella commissioned some of the most elaborate Gothic sculpture ever carved (see Burgos, Cartuja de Miraflores; page 157).
Another style, named Plateresque from silver-smithery, involved the shallow carving of façades in extraordinary, sinuous elaboration, often carrying messages connected with the Humanist movement, now arriving from Italy. Plateresque façades could be married either to Gothic or Renaissance buildings. Key examples are the University façade in Salamanca, and the Colegio de San Gregorio in Valladolid.

Ferdinand II of Aragon. His marriage to Isabella of Castile united two great kingdoms and instigated a period of conquest, discovery... and oppression

■ **The epoch of the Spanish Habsburgs was even more extraordinary than that of the Catholic Kings. For within three years of the death of Ferdinand, Spain and its territories had become the biggest, most feared force on earth. Another 100 years and all was near collapse. But as national fortunes ebbed, so Spain produced the writers and painters of its Golden Age. Their brilliance in literature, painting and sculpture remains an astonishment. .....■**

Emperor Charles V, grandson of Ferdinand and Isabella

Emperor, kings and happenings Charles I of Spain, Charles V of the Holy Roman Empire, was born with the century. He came to the Spanish throne in 1516, acquiring by inheritance not only Spain, its Italian possessions and Flanders, but the vast colonial spaces, all except Brazil, now opening out in Latin and Central America. He became Emperor in 1519, bringing in most of Germany and Eastern Europe. Nothing on this scale had ever been seen before, unless perhaps the empires of Alexander the Great and Tamburlaine. Yet when this grandson of Ferdinand and Isabella was called to the Spanish throne his language was Flemish, his experience foreign. He spent the greater part of his reign travelling and fighting in distant territories and ruled more from Brussels than from any Spanish centre. Nevertheless, he learned good Spanish, became hispanicised to a surprising degree and was in the end much loved by the Spanish people, retiring from empire in 1556 to live a monastic life at Yuste in Extremadura.

In 1521, right at the beginning, the Spanish towns had erupted against him in the revolt of the Comuneros, successfully suppressed. From that point, Charles's life as emperor was overshadowed by the Reformation and the rise of Protestantism, which to him was heresy, in Germany and the Low Countries. He extended the Inquisition to Flanders and became involved in an unwinnable war there. This sucked in resources from the rest of the empire, first Italy and then Castile, which was easier to tax than Aragon for constitutional reasons. This meant that just as Castile achieved its peak as a wool-rearing and trading kingdom, it began to be devastated economically for reasons that were non-Spanish.

Mixed legacy Charles conducted other ruinous wars, fighting the French in Italy and at one point even sacking Rome. When he retired to Yuste, passing the Spanish (but not the imperial) throne to his son Philip II, Philip was obliged almost at once to declare bankruptcy. Even so,

Spain remained the superpower of the western world, with American gold and silver bullion entering in huge quantities (though often passing straight through to foreign creditors). Philip fought the Turks in the Mediterranean, stopping their up-to-now remorseless advance in the great sea battle of Lepanto in 1571 (his half-brother, Don John of Austria, was admiral). Married briefly to Mary Tudor of England (among four wives), he fought bitterly against her Protestant successor, Queen Elizabeth, unleashing the Invincible Armada in 1588. Devastated mainly by storm, this proved a ruinous enterprise.

Philip established Madrid as Spain's first fixed capital and ruled by an infinity of written memoranda, largely from the Monastery of El Escorial in the Guadarrama mountains and for two years from Lisbon – Portugal was under Spanish rule from 1580 to 1640. Nothing was stronger than his sense of duty; his self-control was iron.

This dedication skipped a generation in the case of his son Philip III who frittered away 23 years, removing the capital to Valladolid and back again to Madrid. Spain, and especially Castile, continued helter-skelter towards financial ruin. In 1609, the Moriscos, the remaining Moorish population, were expelled under cruel circumstances, with devastating consequences to Spanish agriculture, which they had sustained with their skills and labour. Philip III's successor Philip IV, grave and sombre in his many royal portraits by Velázquez, fought more expensive wars, further impoverishing the country. A 10-year secession by Catalonia had disastrous consequences for that region. Moreover, Philip married his daughter Maria Teresa to Louis XIV of France, with fateful results. When the Spanish crown fell vacant in 1700, after a long reign under the ailing Charles II, the French were ready and waiting.

Philip II, whose reign saw much warfare and religious intolerance

The Golden Age

■ Cervantes in literature, Velázquez in painting – two names synonymous with Spain's Golden Age, an ill-defined period with its first intimations under Ferdinand and Isabella, some slight consolidation under Charles V, a deepening and intensification under Philip II and then, from the start of the 17th century, a flood of almost unbelievable achievement. .....■

We have seen the earliest traces under Ferdinand and Isabella, with Plateresque façades laid on early Renaissance buildings. The Catholic Monarchs also imported some of the finest paintings from the Low Countries, introducing a grave note of realism. In the world of ideas, the Golden Age began with the arrival of Renaissance, man-centred humanism to add a softening layer to the Castilian cocktail of mysticism and military might. The works of Erasmus, written in the Spanish Netherlands, became hugely popular, and the Spanish writer, Bartolomé de las Casas, shocked at the way millions of Indians were dying in Latin America as a result of Spanish actions, indicted his own country in a volume of protest which rings down the centuries. With the best painters in the world at his imperial command, Charles V employed the Italian Titian as his court painter, starting up a memorable tradition of royal portraiture.

Court painter Velázquez, whose own paintings scorn flattery

El Escorial Philip II made his own massive contribution when he used the architect Herrera to build the huge monastery of El Escorial in a bare unornamented style – *desornamentado* – to express the grand sobriety of the Spanish monarchy. This was the other side of the coin to the exuberantly decorative elements of Spanish style, and both were to endure as permanent currents.
Philip's court painters were now Spanish, with Sanchez Coello dominating. Outside the court, Renaissance models had now given way to the elongations and contortions of Mannerism.

<< Luis Morales, El Divino, a painter from Badajoz, was an early Mannerist. The greatest was the learned Cretan, El Greco, who settled in Toledo, failed to find work with the court, and painted an unbroken flow of searing, saintly images. Meanwhile, St Teresa of Avila and St John of the Cross were living out their spiritual ecstasies, expressing them in literature which used the erotic as a metaphor for the divine. **>>**

San Lorenzo de El Escorial, the great monastery and mausoleum built by Philip II, a gloomy memorial to the Habsburg dynasty in Spain

Miguel Cervantes Saavedra (1547–1616) is the great figure who spans the junction of the centuries. Cervantes lost the use of an arm at the Battle of Lepanto, was captured at sea and held as a slave in North Africa, and finally ransomed, to resume a literary career which left him poor and complaining. But in his great creation Don Quixote, he poked fun at the somewhat strangulated values of Spain and used the earthy squire Sancho Panza as a coarser, comic version of humanity to contrast with the lofty follies of his master.

Artistic flowering Now Spain's greatest literature came in a torrent: Lope de Vega, who wrote more than 1,800 plays, and Calderón de la Barca, the other great classic playwright; Tirso de Molina who created Don Juan; the poet Quevedo, who denounced the errors of his age and was imprisoned by the state; Gongora, who struck a note of sonorous splendour. Historically, this was now the era of the Counter-Reformation, with Catholicism actively wishing to put forward a clearer imagery. This coincided with the clarifying spirit of early baroque. In Spain it ran along with the prodigious new wealth of Seville, which enjoyed a trade monopoly with America. Not too surprisingly, Seville and Andalucía became the source of a multitude of painters and sculptors.

Velázquez (1599–1660) moved from his Sevillian beginnings as a realist, whose works were full of contrasting light and darkness, to become the greatest of Spanish court painters, with an all-seeing eye. (He came on the heels of two very fine non-Andalucian Spanish painters, Ribalta in Valencia and Ribera in Naples.)

Southern masters The greatest after Velázquez was Zurbarán, grave painter of monks and their white robes (Extremaduran-born, he worked in Seville). Juan Martinez Montañés was slightly older, a sculptor known to his own age as *el dios de madera*, the God of wood-carving. Alonso Cano, feckless and disorganised, produced painting and sculpture which combined a simple strength with delicate purity. Among the last in this great line was the good-tempered Sevillian, Bartolomé Esteban Murillo, painter of smiling street children, soft doves and scores of angels ascending in clusters. When he died in 1682, the great tradition was coming to a close.

The Bourbons

■ With the death of Charles II of Spain, last of the Habsburgs, Louis XIV of France remarked that now there were no more Pyrenees. By this he meant that France under himself and Spain under his grandson, the Bourbon Philip of Anjou, would be effectively a single realm. The prospect of French expansionism horrified much of the rest of Europe and the War of the Spanish Succession now began. By the end of it, Spain had lost Flanders, Naples and Milan, Gibraltar and Menorca. But Philip of Anjou was there as Philip V of Spain. .....■

The siege of Barcelona in the War of the Spanish Succession

It was the misfortune of Barcelona, Valencia and the Catalan-speaking east that they had backed the losing side in the war. Adopting the vigorous centralising policies of France, Philip V subjected them to fierce repression, pulling down a chunk of Barcelona to build a fortress in its midst and closing the Catalan universities. Reaction to this was the start of the long drive towards separate Catalan status. The Basques, however, had been allies to the Bourbons and remained untouched for the moment.

Towards a modern age Philip V reigned from 1700 to 1746, interrupted in 1724 when he passed the throne to his son Luis, who promptly died. His second son, Ferdinand VI, reigned from 1746 to 1759, but it was his third son, Charles III, by his later marriage to Isabella Farnese, whose reign from 1759 to 1788 proved most decisive for Spain. Charles III was the very model of a modernising monarch. Though centralist and authoritarian, he gave an enthusiastic welcome to the more practical, project-orientated side of the 18th-century Enlightenment (in Spanish, *La Ilustración*).

Communications and harbours improved considerably. Charles himself established royal ceramics and glass factories (in Madrid and La Granja) and gave a boost to the royal tapestry factory founded by his brother Ferdinand VI (in Madrid and still existing). Under his sponsorship, the flora and fauna of Spain and its empire were collected and classified and he moved his brother's botanical gardens to a site beside the Prado Museum, a building he himself initiated. It was intended as a natural history museum, not as the great picture gallery it has now become.

> **<<** So many were Charles III's improvements to the capital that he was nicknamed the Mayor of Madrid. **>>**

Charles was succeeded in 1788, just in time for the hot breath of the French Revolution to reach Spain, by simple-looking Charles IV and his dominant but frumpish wife, María Luisa, both well known to us through Goya portraits. María Luisa was enamoured of a young Extremaduran guards officer named Manuel Godoy, and Godoy was soon propelled into control of the government. This curious trio toiled and trimmed to respond to French aggression, but in the end, after a popular revolution had all but swept them away, they were neatly displaced by Napoleon, who needed the Iberian peninsula in order to pursue his sea blockade of Britain. Spain now pursued a grievous destiny without the Bourbons.

18th-century art and architecture

The Bourbons were great palace-builders and restorers. The Royal Palace in Madrid burned down in 1734 and was rebuilt in a classic palatial style to the taste, finally, of Charles III. Another major palace was at Aranjuez south of Madrid, beside the Tagus, and yet another, north of Madrid and easily the most charming, at La Granja de San Ildefonso. Baroque had given way now to rococo as is most evident at La Granja and in the palace interiors. The doorway of the palace of the Marqués de Dos Aguas in Valencia and the churches in Priego de Córdoba in Andalucía are examples of wonderfully extravagant rococo. The name of the Churriguera dynasty of architects has been fastened on the wildest instances, but that they were not always so extravagant is demonstrated by the ordered beauty of their Plaza Mayor in Salamanca. Francisco de Goya y Lucientes, non-conformist and a late developer in art, made his way slowly towards the centre from beginnings in Zaragoza as a religious painter. Summoned to Madrid, he and his brother-in-law Francisco Bayeu became extremely accomplished painters of vivid cartoons for the royal tapestry factory. He was soon painting portraits of leading Enlightenment figures, then of the aristocracy and eventually, as court painter, of the royal family. By the time of the Bourbon abdication in 1808 he had already produced the teasing, enigmatic, bitter etchings of his *Caprichos* series and was ready to move on again to document Spain's great tragedies of war.

War of the Spanish Succession: Anglo-Dutch victory at Vigo, 12 October 1702. Spanish power in Europe was much reduced as a result of this war

On 2 May 1808, the populace of Madrid rose against the occupying French, dragging Murat's Mameluke troops from their horses in the Puerta del Sol. By 3 May it was over and the firing squads were in action. Goya was later to paint the central happenings on both days. The thwarted rising signalled the start of the first modern war of independence, with Spain fighting against France in an unofficial, undercover struggle that coined the word *guerrilla* or little war, waged by *guerrilleros*. A liberal, not to say revolutionary, constitution was promulgated in unconquered Cádiz. .....

With Napoleon's eventual defeat the Bourbons regained the crown in the shape of Ferdinand VII. Ungrateful to the *guerrilleros* he began a repression which amounted to an official terror. Meanwhile, almost without realising it, Spain lost virtually all her Latin American possessions to the continent's supposed liberators.

A wry look at Isabella II, whose succession began the Carlist Wars

The Carlist Wars After a reign, in which he was at times ascendant and at times on the defensive, Ferdinand was succeeded by his daughter Isabella II, beginning with a long regency. In bitter dispute over the legality of royal inheritance through the female line, Ferdinand's brother Carlos María Isidro unleashed the so-called Carlist Wars (1833–9). Though restricted mainly to the north, and with the Carlists based in Navarre and the Basque Country, these sanguinary contests were a great setback to Spain. The Carlists remained a political force until at least the 1960s.

Isabella (1833–68) proved a frivolous monarch and Spanish politics became a to-and-fro contest between conservatives and liberals, with a sequence of military coups. The century included a military dictatorship (under Espartero, who vigorously repressed the Basques) and, from 1873–4, a short-lived First Republic.

Throughout this period, the Basque Country and Catalonia were experiencing an industrial revolution. One result was increasing wealth among the bourgeoisie, who became great cultural patrons, especially in Catalonia. Another was the rapid growth of a strong labour movement, with radicalised trades unions and a strong anarchist movement. Anarchist atrocities were met by government atrocities, which

punctuated the last years of the century. In 1898, Spain suddenly found itself pitched against the young United States in an attempt to preserve Cuba as the last of its major colonies. Cuba was lost along with the Spanish fleet, the bulk of the Spanish army and the last shred of national dignity. It was the nadir for Spain.

Art and architecture Goya's dark vision was a beam of light to prove that Spain's brilliance was not lost. He painted great wartime canvases and documented the detail in his infinitely painful, almost grotesque etchings, *The Disasters of War*. He died in exile in France, in 1828. Queen Isabella gave her name to a new 'Isabelline' style, parallel to British mid-Victorian, with heavy furniture and profuse decoration. From now on, much Spanish art was *costumbrista* – literally 'about customs' and devoted to evoking regional and folklore scenes. It paralleled a surge of romantic writing about Spain by foreigners – including Prosper Mérimée with *Carmen*. This helped to create the dagger-and-carnations image of Spain. By mid-century, Catalan language and literature were on the upturn, in what is known as the Catalan *Renaixença* or Renaissance. Its quick successor was Modernista architecture.
This brilliant style, the most exciting artistic phenomenon in 19th-century Spain and overlapping well into the 20th century, was an amalgam of northern European Arts and Crafts, art nouveau and Jugendstil, with a recovery of Moorish and, especially, Catalan motifs of earlier centuries. Its greatest figures were Gaudí, Domènech i Montaner and Puig i Cadafalch, its best known building Gaudí's extraordinary 'temple', the Sagrada Família in Barcelona.

Gaudí extravaganza in Barcelona's Parc Güell, good hunting ground for aficionados *of Modernista*

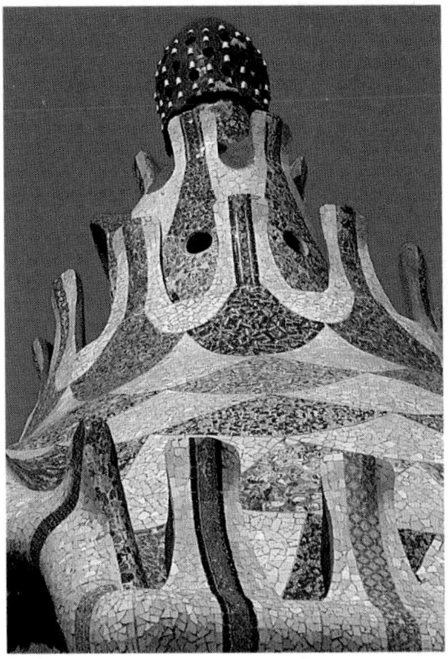

SPAIN WAS *In Turmoil*

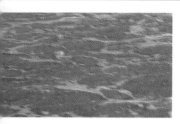

■ After the loss of Cuba, the cry was for national regeneration. It was uttered both by politicians and a new group of writers, whose work seemed to promise if not another Golden Age, at least a silver one. These were the 'Generation of '98', discussed on page 45. But serious trouble was to strike again within a decade. .....■

The flashpoint was North Africa. When Spanish interests came under threat in Morocco, the government attempted a military call-up. The Catalans refused to report for service in a national army they saw as Castilian. In Barcelona, the workers took to the streets. Churches and convents were ransacked and over 100 people died at the barricades.

Miguel Primo de Rivera, dictator from 1923 to 1930

The year was 1909 and this was the *Semana Tragica*, the Tragic Week of Barcelona. It was a grim augury for the future.

The Great War Curiously, World War I provided some relief, for though the political system came near collapse, Spain managed both to protect its own neutrality, and to export goods and particularly food to a hungry Europe. But soon Morocco, now a protectorate, brought fresh troubles. A humiliating military defeat by rebel tribesmen led to a downward spiral in Spanish political life and, in 1923, to takeover by a military dictator, Miguel Primo de Rivera. The Bourbon monarch of the day, the young Alfonso XIII, put up with it equably, even describing Primo as 'my Mussolini'. Primo's rule was, in fact, a much gentler affair, now often referred to as *la dictadura blanda*, the soft dictatorship. Meanwhile, under the surface, anti-monarchical, republican sentiment was growing, along with Catalan separatism.

Primo resigned in 1930 and in the next year republican socialists combined with Catalans to win Spain's major cities in local elections. Alfonso XIII knew his hour had come and simply left the country. Spain's Second Republic now began. Few recognised that it already contained its doom within it, in the fierce but so far submerged opposition between a long-suffering, anti-clerical left and a right wing wedded to military values and a backward-looking Catholicism. These forces were soon to polarise into a revolutionary movement on one hand, confronting a Spanish version of Fascism on the other.

The life of the Republic began quietly enough, with bourgeois-style balanced budgets and respectable intentions among the new Socialist rulers. But traditionalists were deeply offended when Catalonia was granted autonomy within Spain, and by their attempts at land reform, designed to attack shocking rural poverty. .....

Nationalists 'liberating' Toledo during the Civil War

A right-wing government was returned in 1933. In 1934, in Asturias, in northern Spain, the coal miners and their industrial allies declared a soviet. Back in Madrid, one General Francisco Franco Bahamonde was called on to suppress the rebellion, which he did, with great loss of life. Primo de Rivera's son, José Antonio – known in Spain simply by his first names – had founded a diluted Fascist party called the Falange in 1933. The hard left won national elections in February 1936 and soon Falangists were murdering government allies and government hit-squads were murdering right-wing leaders. The generals rebelled in the name of national honour and order.

Art and literature The Generation of '98 included a number of writers who achieved an international reputation, among them the Basque-born philosopher and essayist, Miguel de Unamuno (1864–1936), the intellectual and political theorist José Ortega y Gasset (1883–1955) and Salvador de Madariaga (1886–1978), who finally became a voice for Spain's intellectuals in exile. Other writers include the poet Antonio Machado (1875–1939), Juan Ramón Jiménez who won the Nobel prize for literature in 1956, and Federico García Lorca (1898–1936), who produced a stunning effect with his lyrical poetry and symbolic drama. In painting, Spain had meanwhile given the world Pablo Picasso (1881–1973), Salvador Dalí (1904–1989) and Joan Miró (1893–1983). By the mid-'30s, the work of all three had become a prophecy of war.

Generals Franco and Mola repudiated the Republic on 18 July 1936 and began a conflict that was to shatter Spain and lead to 36 years of military dictatorship. So passionately fought was the war and so burning the issues within it, that it became a representative conflict for the wider world of the 1930s, rather like Vietnam in the 1960s and '70s. It too sucked in the great powers in unequal portions; but unlike Vietnam, Spain's Civil War helped draw up the battle-lines for a World War which started immediately at its end. .....

The Generals had resolved at the outset that if they could not take over the country in what would in effect have been a protracted coup, then they would fight till they won, however long it took. This is exactly what happened. For when they rose, far from falling into their hands, the country divided itself into two zones, one Republican, one Nationalist (this was what the Generals called themselves). The Republicans held Madrid and the centre, Barcelona, Valencia and the east. Very importantly, they held the Basque iron industry and the coalfields of Asturias on the north coast. The Nationalists held the rural west and an inland band across the north. They won Seville by a brilliant ruse on the first day.
The navy split down the middle, but the Nationalists' main asset was their command of the greater part of the regular army.

General Franco, whose repressive rule spanned nearly 40 years

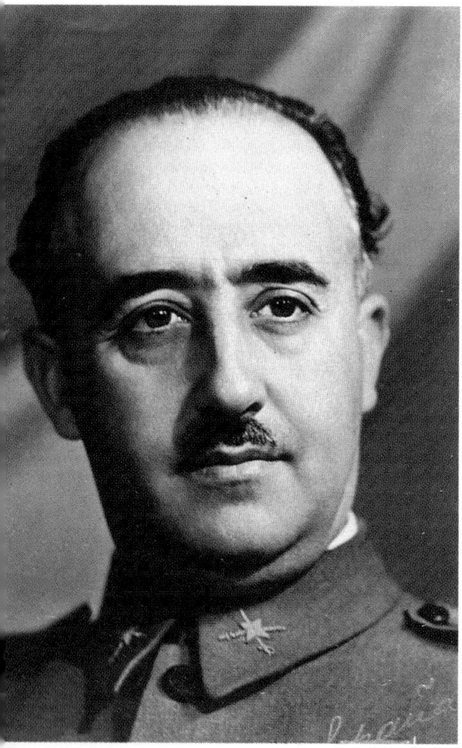

Foreign involvement Successfully transferring experienced, well-trained troops from Morocco to the south of Spain, Franco raced towards Madrid and, to the astonishment of all involved, was unable to take the city, brilliantly defended by an improvised resistance. The war now settled down for long enough for foreign countries to become involved. Nazi Germany and Mussolini's Italy sent men and war materials to Franco. The Republicans received material aid from Stalin's Russia and came increasingly, though secretly, under Russian political control. France and Britain, scared of Germany and trying to appease her, declared a policy of

non-intervention. But they allowed their citizens, along with a good many leftist Americans, to join a series of International Brigades and so to fight on the Republican side. As the battle spread round Madrid in 1936, all these various forces were involved.

Political developments Convulsive events were also occurring behind the lines. On both sides, in roughly equal proportions, slaughter was taking place. In the Republican zone, some 5,000 members of the clergy were murdered. The Nationalists more methodically eliminated the Left. Politically, Franco emerged as strongest of the Nationalist leaders and was nominated head of state. Lacking any obvious ideology, he adopted the Falangist party as his main vehicle. José Antonio had been shot by the Republicans in Alicante jail and Franco was able to dominate the party easily. Meanwhile, on the Republican side, a genuine revolution was now taking place. Barcelona became a proletarian city. In rural Aragon, anarchist collectives were formed. They cultivated their lands successfully until suppressed by their supposed allies, the communists.

Death of the Republic The course of the war now slowly flowed against the Republicans. They held Madrid but as the war moved to the north, German assistance in the air helped the Nationalists take Bilbao. Meanwhile the civilian population of the Basque town of Gernika (in Castilian, Guernica) was systematically bombed, the first time this had happened in Europe. By late 1937, the north was in Franco's hands, and the main struggle was now in the east. Some of the most fearful battles, marked by sub-zero temperatures, were fought for Teruel. By now, however, Stalin was pulling back from the war, allowing German help to Franco to become decisive.

As the war moved into its final phase and Franco remorselessly pushed eastwards, his forces were met by the Republic's last throw – a counter-attack across the Ebro, without air-cover. The long-running Battle of the Ebro became one simply of attrition and by the time it was over the Republic was lost. Franco entered Barcelona in triumph; Madrid collapsed helplessly upon itself and with its fall on 27 March 1939, the Civil War was over.

Intellectuals in exile Picasso had painted his great work *Guernica* as a protest during the war. By the end of the war, the poets Lorca and Machado were dead, one murdered, one collapsing as he reached exile. Now most of the rest of Spain's surviving artists and intellectuals were also forced into exile, leaving a country denuded of its best minds for several decades.

Franco and Beyond

■ Franco's main goals were order and the maintenance of his own authority as absolute ruler. He began his post-war career by executing more than 40,000 of his former opponents. Many others remained in prison for long periods. Meanwhile, as World War II raged all around, Spain came close to starving. But though Franco sent volunteer troops to fight on the eastern front, he resolutely refused to open Spain to his former ally, Hitler. What animated him, at the deepest level, was his own view of patriotism. .....■

Falangists on the march

After World War II, as the only surviving state that could be described, though rather inaccurately, as Fascist, Spain was profoundly isolated. Most countries withdrew their ambassadors. But soon the Americans discovered they needed Franco for their anti-Communist alliance and offered dollars in exchange for bases. From this point the tide began to turn. Spain joined the United Nations in 1953 and soon the OECD. Vitally needed foreign investment began to flow in and little by little it became possible to reconstruct Spain's devastated industrial base. Catalonia and the Basque Country acquired the lion's share, though Franco also industrialised such places as Burgos and Madrid. Above all, he was a centralist, determined not to let Spain's peripheries off their short leash. The Basque and Catalan languages were repressed, along with any political opposition anywhere. One thing Franco could not stem, however, was the rural exodus.

Rural depopulation Unable to earn a living in the countryside, millions simply decamped to the cities, settling in shanty towns which were eventually replaced by jerry-built apartment blocks. Countless thousands more migrated to northern Europe, becoming, with rural Italians, Greeks and Yugoslavs, West Germany's earliest *Gastarbeiter*. Nevertheless, it is astonishing how much of modern Spain was taking shape in the Franco period.

New Spain Where only lately Spain had been dirt-poor, the economy had come quite suddenly to life, helping create a large new middle class, a stabilising factor Spain had always lacked. This was partly because of the money sent home by migrant workers and partly foreign investment. Even more importantly, it came from tourism. Adopting what now seems a questionable course, Spain went in in a huge way for cheap mass tourism on its

King Juan Carlos, who brought in democratic rule after Franco's death

Mediterranean coast. Success was almost instant. As foreign currency poured in, so did new ideas and new ways of behaviour.

The old dictator died a lingering death in 1975. His designated successor was Prince Juan Carlos de Borbón y Borbón, grandson of Alfonso XIII and sworn to uphold the Franco state. Once crowned king, however, Juan Carlos moved swiftly, with his chosen Prime Minister Adolfo Suárez, to install democracy. By manoeuvring within the system rather than challenging it from outside, he was able to comply, in form at least, with his previous promises. This was vital if he was not to run the risk of army intervention once again. Spain now began a hectic time of transition.

All nearly came unstuck in February 1981 when Antonio Tejero, lieutenant-colonel of the paramilitary Civil Guard, entered the parliament with a troop of armed men and simply took its members captive – all this in front of television cameras.

It was the king, once more, who saved the day, ordering back to their barracks the handful of generals who stood ready to rebel. The following year it was possible for Spain, without real fear of army intervention, to elect a moderate Socialist government under the Andalucian lawyer Felipe González. The only dark shadows were growing unemployment and the Basque terrorist movement ETA.

In 1986 Spain joined the European Community, a symbolic return to a continent from which it had long been spiritually absent. In 1992, the Olympic Games were held in Barcelona and at the 'Universal Expo' in Seville Spain celebrated the double-edged quincentenary of Columbus' first voyage out over the unknown Atlantic.

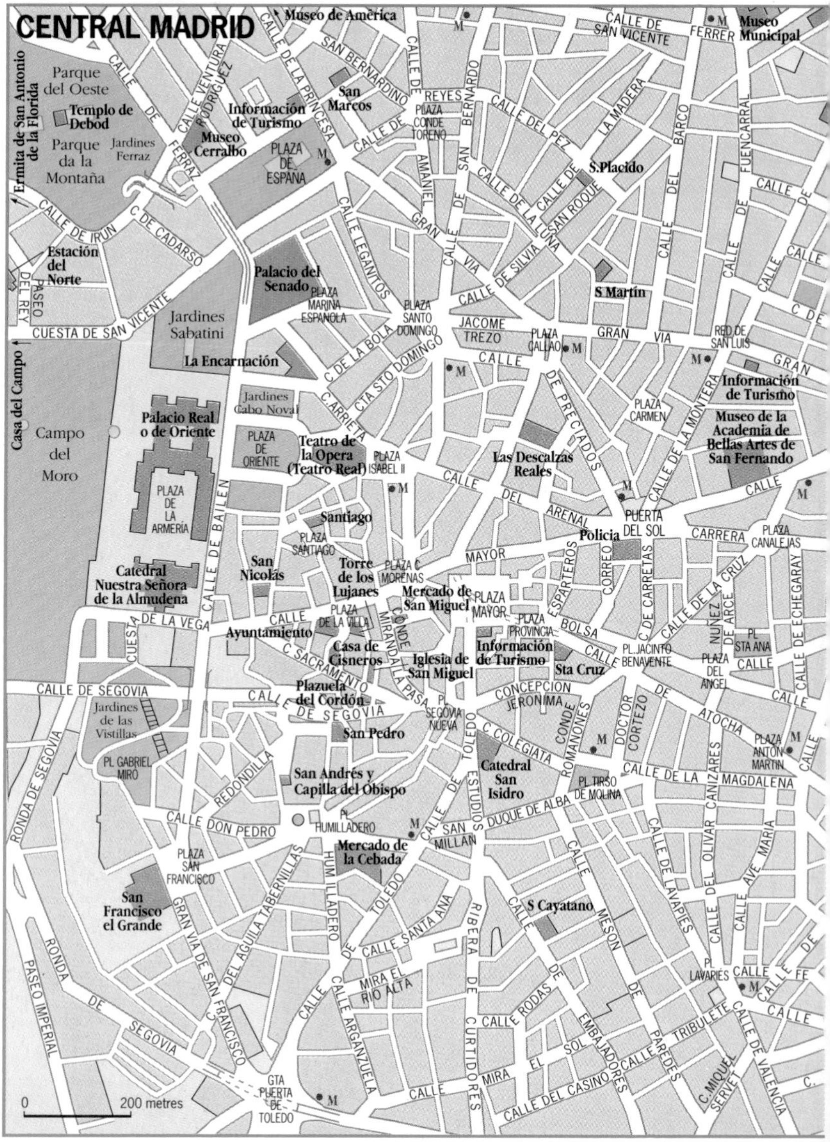
CENTRAL MADRID
Museo de América
Museo Municipal
Parque del Oeste
Templo de Debod
Parque de la Montaña
Jardines Ferraz
Ermita de San Antonio de la Florida
Información de Turismo
Museo Cerralbo
San Marcos
PLAZA DE ESPAÑA
S.Placido
Estación del Norte
Palacio del Senado
PLAZA MARINA ESPAÑOLA
S Martín
Jardines Sabatini
La Encarnación
Casa del Campo
Campo del Moro
Palacio Real o de Oriente
Jardines Cabo Noval
PLAZA DE ORIENTE
Teatro de la Opera (Teatro Real)
PLAZA ISABEL II
PLAZA DE LA ARMERÍA
Las Descalzas Reales
Información de Turismo
Museo de la Academia de Bellas Artes de San Fernando
PUERTA DEL SOL
Policia
Santiago
PLAZA SANTIAGO
Catedral Nuestra Señora de la Almudena
San Nicolás
Torre de los Lujanes
Mercado de San Miguel
PLAZA MAYOR
Ayuntamiento
PLAZA DE LA VILLA
Casa de Cisneros
Iglesia de San Miguel
Información de Turismo
Sta Cruz
PL STA ANA
PLAZA DEL ANGEL
PL.JACINTO BENAVENTE
PLAZA CANALEJAS
Plazuela del Cordón
Jardines de las Vistillas
San Pedro
PL GABRIEL MIRÓ
San Andrés y Capilla del Obispo
Catedral San Isidro
PL TIRSO DE MOLINA
PLAZA ANTÓN MARTÍN
PL HUMILLADERO
Mercado de la Cebada
PLAZA SAN FRANCISCO
San Francisco el Grande
S Cayatano
PL LAVAPIÉS
GTA PUERTA DE TOLEDO
CALLE DE SEGOVIA
CUESTA DE SAN VICENTE
CALLE DE BAILEN
GRAN VIA
CALLE MAYOR
CALLE DE TOLEDO
CALLE DE ATOCHA
CALLE DE FUENCARRAL
RONDA DE SEGOVIA
PASEO IMPERIAL
GRAN VIA DE SAN FRANCISCO
CALLE DEL ARENAL
0
200 metres

CALLE DE
SEGOVIA

MADRID

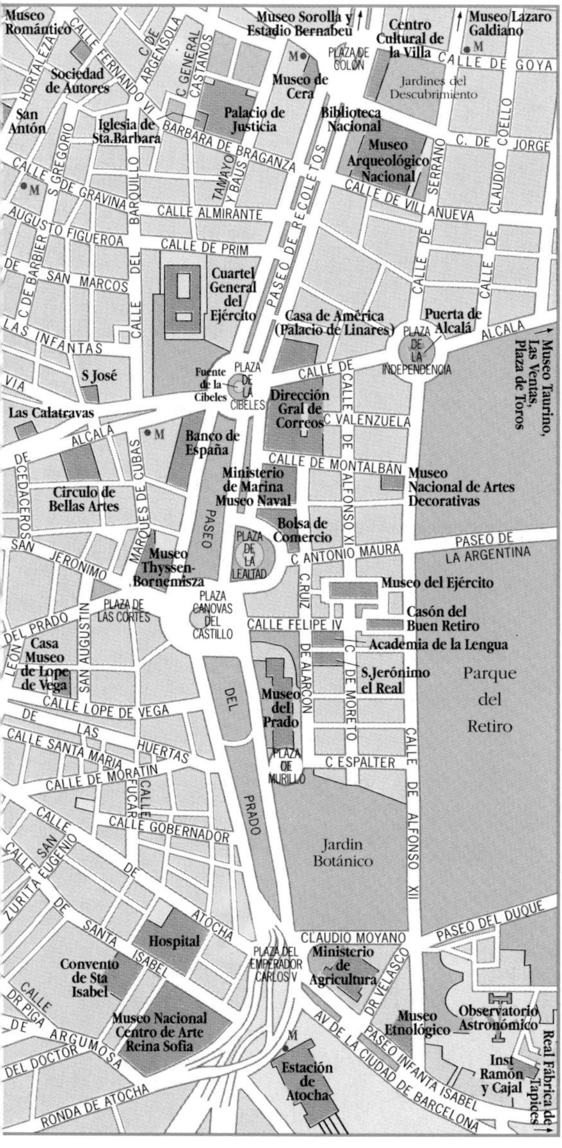
Museo Romántico
Sociedad de Autores
San Antón
Iglesia de Sta.Barbara
Palacio de Justicia
Museo Sorolla y Estadio Bernabeu
Museo de Cera
Centro Cultural de la Villa
Museo Lazaro Galdiano
PLAZA DE COLÓN
Jardines del Descubrimiento
Biblioteca Nacional
Museo Arqueológico Nacional
CALLE DE GOYA
C. DE JORGE
CALLE FERNANDO VI
C. DE ARGENSOLA
C. GENERAL CASTAÑOS
HORTALEZA
S. GREGORIO
BARBARA DE BRAGANZA
TAMAYO Y BAUS
PASEO DE RECOLETOS
CALLE DE VILLANUEVA
C. DE SERRANO
CLAUDIO COELLO
CALLE DE GRAVINA
BARQUILLO
CALLE ALMIRANTE
AUGUSTO FIGUEROA
CALLE DE PRIM
C. DE BARBIER
DE SAN MARCOS
CALLE DEL
Cuartel General del Ejército
Casa de América (Palacio de Linares)
Puerta de Alcalá
PLAZA DE LA INDEPENDENCIA
ALCALA
Museo Taurino, Las Ventas, Plaza de Toros
LAS INFANTAS
S José
Fuente de la Cibeles
PLAZA DE LA CIBELES
CALLE DE
Dirección Gral de Correos
C. VALENZUELA
Las Calatravas
ALCALA
Banco de España
CUBAS
CALLE DE MONTALBÁN
Museo Nacional de Artes Decorativas
Ministerio de Marina Museo Naval
Circulo de Bellas Artes
CEDACEROS
MARQUES DE
PASEO
Bolsa de Comercio
CALLE DE ALFONSO XI
PASEO DE LA ARGENTINA
SAN JERONIMO
Museo Thyssen-Bornemisza
PLAZA DE LA LEALTAD
C. ANTONIO MAURA
Museo del Ejército
PLAZA DE LAS CORTES
PLAZA CANOVAS DEL CASTILLO
C. RUIZ
Casón del Buen Retiro
CALLE FELIPE IV
Academia de la Lengua
DEL PRADO
Casa Museo de Lope de Vega
SAN AUGUSTIN
LEÓN
S.Jerónimo el Real
Parque del Retiro
Museo del Prado
DE ALARCÓN
C. DE MORETO
CALLE LOPE DE VEGA
DE LAS HUERTAS
CALLE SANTA MARIA
CALLE DE MORATIN
PLAZA DE MURILLO
C. ESPALTER
CALLE DE ALFONSO XII
DEL PRADO
FUCAR
CALLE GOBERNADOR
CALLE SAN EUGENIO
ZURITA
Jardin Botánico
DE ATOCHA
PASEO DEL DUQUE
DE SANTA ISABEL
Hospital
CLAUDIO MOYANO
PLAZA DEL EMPERADOR CARLOS V
Ministerio de Agricultura
Convento de Sta Isabel
DR. VELASCO
CALLE DR PIGA
Museo Etnológico
Observatorio Astronómico
Museo Nacional Centro de Arte Reina Sofia
DE ARGUMOSA
DEL DOCTOR
AV. DE LA CIUDAD DE BARCELONA
PASEO INFANTA ISABEL
Estación de Atocha
Inst Ramón y Cajal
Real Fábrica de Tapices
RONDA DE ATOCHA

Madrid has no great architectural assemblages as in Rome or Paris, and few great individual monuments other than the Prado and companion art galleries, yet it offers a captivating liveliness ... and half a dozen of Castile's most thrilling towns within day-tripping distance.

Set on a dour plain, Madrid still reflects the artificiality of choice that made it Philip II's capital in 1561. Starting life as Majerit, a tiny Moorish town around a fortress on the trickle of the Río Manzanares, it was chosen because of its central position. The court drew nobles, ecclesiastics and their retinues, as well as adventurers and a colourful low-life populace. The city's labyrinthine 17th-century quarter survives; in the 18th century the Bourbons laid out avenues and installed fountains. After rebelling against the Napoleonic occupation, Madrid grew quickly, acquiring some lovely 19th-century neighbourhoods. Trauma came in the present century when Republican Madrid was besieged by Franco. In a three-year struggle, Madrid held its own until the bitter end of the war. For almost 40 years, the city endured Franco's punitive rule. Following his death in 1975, it burst on to the modern European scene with unbridled enthusiasm.

Madrid's main square used to be the scene of bullfights, public executions and extravagant ceremonies to welcome Spanish and foreign potentates. The grandest welcome was probably that for Charles III, arriving from Italy to take up the throne in 1760. The most celebrated execution was that of Rodrigo Calderón in 1621. Though the hated servant of a corrupt minister, his bearing was so noble that his name has entered the language in the phrase 'proud as Rodrigo on the scaffold'.

Old Madrid Madrid is divided by the Castellana, a great north–south throughway. The northern end is effectively a new centre to the city. Old Madrid lies near the southern end. The Moors built their fortress here above the river, the site of the Palacio Real. Midway between this and the lower end of the throughway lies the real heart of Madrid, the Puerta del Sol and the Plaza Mayor. Buses, metro and pedestrians converge on the Puerta del Sol. The building on one side of the Plaza Puerta del

The Plaza Mayor, Madrid's central square

Sol, headquarters of the Community of Madrid, was formerly Franco's Ministry of the Interior. Opposite are streets leading to major department stores and cinemas on the Gran Vía. There is a statue of a bear guzzling the fruit of the arbutus, symbol of Madrid. The Calle Arenal leads to the Teatro de la Opera and the Palacio Real. The Calle Mayor passes the Plaza de la Villa (see page 64). Behind the Calle Mayor is the 17th-century Plaza Mayor, with restaurants and bars all around (see **Food and Drink**, page 67). Nearby are old churches and El Rastro, the Sunday flea market.

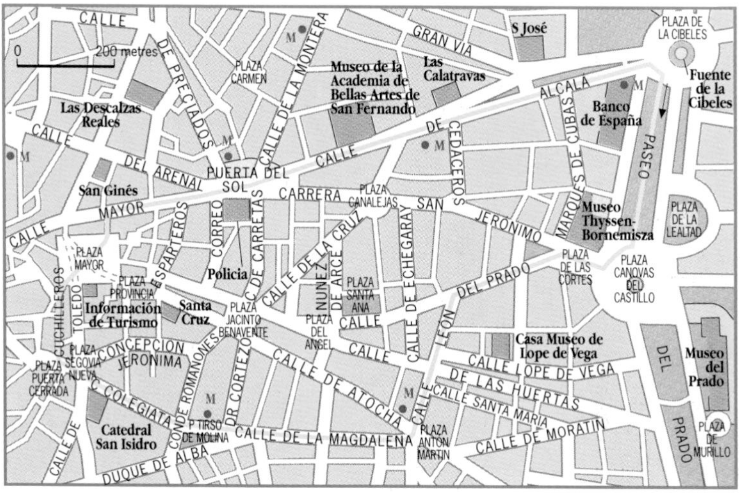

Walk Through the Old Town

From Banco de España metro station, take Paseo del Prado exit and walk south down the central reservation. Turn up right immediately after the Thyssen-Bornemisza collection into Plaza de las Cortes.
The rather small Parliament building, or Cortes, is on your right.

Angle left along Calle del Prado.
There are antique shops in this area.

Go left down Calle León to the metro at Antón Martín.
Here you enter a friendly working-class neighbourhood.

Turn right along Calle Magdalena.
The wig shop on the left stocks false beards and moustaches.

Continue to Tirso de Molina.
There are cheap restaurants and a metro station here.

Angle right by San Isidro cathedral, right up Calle Toledo, left through adjoining plazas of Segovia Nueva and Puerta Cerrada. Right up Cuchilleros (restaurants, see page 67), and so into the Plaza Mayor. Exit diagonally across and down to the Puerta del Sol. Cut diagonally across right and down Calle de Alcalá.
The Academy of San Fernando is on your left.

Continue downhill to the Banco de España metro.
Views of the Post Office and Alcalá Gate give final encouragement at the end of the walk.

Main Sights

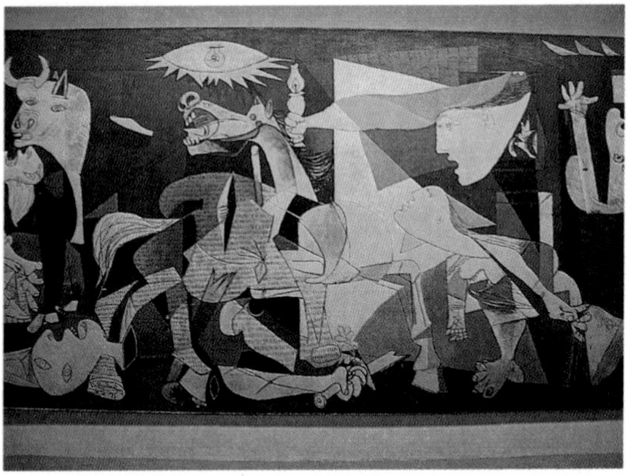

Picasso's Guernica, *inspired by the Civil War*

54

▶▷▷ Casón del Buen Retiro

A short walk uphill from the Prado, this building (part of the 17th-century Retiro royal palace) houses the Prado's 19th-century collection (Prado entry ticket valid). Notable for its *costumbrista*, or folklore elements, it documents a Spain now largely vanished, and merits a look-in.

▶▶▶ Centro de Arte Reina Sofía

Calle de Santa Isabel 52

The former hospital near Atocha station, converted some years back into a large and pleasing art venue, now holds Picasso's *Guernica*. This huge work of unrelieved angst and agony, composed in greys and black, is approached through a collection of Picasso drawings. These were formerly part of the Museo de Arte Contemporaneo, now moved as a whole into the Reina Sofía, with an illustrative array of works by Dalí, Juan Gris, Miró etc. as well as newer work by Tàpies and the sculptor Chillida.

Museo del Prado see page 55

Palacio Real see pages 56–7

▶▶▶ Palacio Villahermosa / Museo Thyssen – Bornemisza

Paseo del Prado 8

This, the greatest of 20th-century private collections, housed in the Villahermosa palace (near the Prado), ranges from 15th- and 16th-century German masters to the best of the 20th century. Start at the top; work down.

▶▶▷ Real Academia de Bellas Artes de San Fernando

Calle de Alcalá 13

This 18th-century foundation, which first excluded Goya and later welcomed him as president, has one of the country's finest collections of his works, including the gruesome *House of the Mad*. There are magnificent monks painted by Zurbarán, good Murillos, and El Greco's enchanting painting of his own family.

▶▶▶ Museo del Prado

The Prado is one of the most spectacular picture galleries in the world. The immense power of the Spanish crown meant that the monarchs, on whose collection the Prado is founded, bought in the best of paintings from their dominions and from countries closely involved with Spain, including the Low Countries of Hieronymus Bosch and Rubens, and the Italy of Titian and Tintoretto. At home both Velázquez and Goya were court painters for most of their careers. El Greco was always at odds with the court but his works were bought in after his death. Quantities of the finest religious painting, representing the whole course of Spanish art, arrived after the disestablishment of the monasteries in the 19th century. A full range of all these works, including many masterpieces of world importance, is displayed in the Prado.

It is a huge gallery and cannot comfortably be taken in on one visit. We recommend a first visit concentrating on the main Spanish masters – El Greco, Velázquez and Goya in historically correct order (all on the first floor except for part of the Goya collection which is downstairs at the southern end). A second visit could take in other Spanish masters – Zurbarán, Ribalta, Ribera, Alonso Cano, Murillo (again all on the first floor) – and Italian masters, especially Titian. The French paintings on this floor are also very fine. A third visit might concentrate on earlier works (kept downstairs), mostly from the Low Countries and mostly towards the northern end of the building. Bosch is the star here for many visitors, but the Rogier van der Weyden contribution is also magnificent. Early Spanish paintings are less impressive here but the country's individual strengths start to emerge with such Renaissance painters as Pedro Berruguete (downstairs, not far from Bosch).

For opening times, see **Travel Facts**, page 266.

The life of artist Francisco de Goya (1746–1828) was changed irretrievably by an illness which led to total deafness. It struck him when on a visit to Andalucía to stay with the Duchess of Alba, with whom he was in love. He painted her many times, but she is not 'La Maja' in his two famous paintings of that name, a woman shown both dressed and naked in the same luxuriant pose. It was after the onset of his deafness that Goya's tormented inner life began to make itself manifest in fantastical and sombre works.

One of the world's great art galleries: the Prado

Bourbon grandeur, the Palacio Real

You'd never guess it as you cross the bare plains round Madrid, but one of the reasons for having a capital city just on this site was the plentiful supply of firewood. Some inkling of how it may have once looked can be gained from the Casa del Campo, the forest and former hunting ground on the far side of the Manzanares. The views are especially beautiful from the windows of the Palacio Real.

The Arab fortress, or *alcázar*, in Madrid, was replaced by a Gothic palace, renovated and redecorated under the direction of Velázquez. This in its turn burned down, destroying many of Velázquez's own paintings.

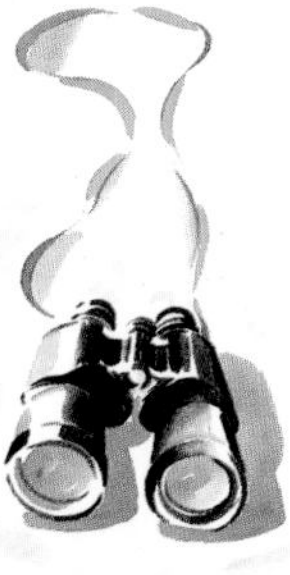

▶▶▶ **Palacio Real**

The Palacio Real (Royal Palace), stately home of the Bourbon dynasty from the 18th to the 20th centuries, is neo-classical in style, and contains 2,800 rooms. It is also known as the Palacio de Oriente, from the square located on its eastern flank.

The Bourbons preferred to live outside Madrid, but the palace which they used to act out the imperial role, was erected by Philip V from 1734, on the site of the old Arab *alcázar* in Madrid.

The new palace was built by two Italian architects, Juvara and Sachetti. They worked in a regal style, further sobered by Charles III into the battleship bulk we see today. Within, however, all is sumptuousness, for this remained the palace of the Bourbons up to the abdication of Alfonso XIII in 1931. The present king, Alfonso's grandson Juan Carlos, lives in more domestic style in the Zarzuela Palace outside Madrid. The Palacio de Oriente is still used for state functions.

Visitors enter by the impressive courtyard on the southern front and purchase their tickets on the right-hand side for a guided tour (English spoken as well as Spanish).

Highlights include: the marble double staircase at the start, with painted ceiling; Goya portraits of Queen Maria Luisa and Charles IV; the Salón de Gasparini, with oriental-style stucco ceiling; the Sala de Porcelana, its walls clad in porcelain plaques made at the royal porcelain factory of the Buen Retiro; the huge state dining room; and a sumptuous throne room with ceiling by the then aged Tiepolo.

There are several museums in the palace precincts, for which extra tickets are required. The **Biblioteca** (library) has 400,000 volumes. The **Armería Real** contains the suits of armour worn by the Spanish kings, their children and horses. The **Museo de Carruajes** (Museum of Carriages) is reached via the adjacent park, the Campo del Moro (entrance at the bottom of the hill).

Walk Circuit of the Palacio Real

From Opera metro in Plaza Isabel II, skirt round Teatro de la Opera into Plaza de Oriente. Left on Bailén, passing royal palace entrance.
Divert across the forecourt between the palace and the Almudena cathedral for views of the **Casa del Campo**.

Go first right round the cathedral on Calle Mayor.
There are excavations (left) of Moorish ruins.

If hot and tired, return along Bailén to Plaza de España (see page 63). Serious walkers only, continue steeply downhill to Paseo Virgen del Puerto beneath and right.
Here you enter (towards far end) the fine **Campo del Moro** park with carriage museum.

Go out the same way and on round the park for a steep pull up Cuesta de San Vicente, then left along Ferraz to Templo de Debod in Parque de la Montaña. Back to Ferraz, up Calle Ventura Rodriguez, then right down Martín de los Heros for Plaza de España. Start up the Gran Vía then right up Isabel la Católica.
This dingy street is redeemed by the ceramics shop **Casa Antigua de Talavera**.

Now pick your way downhill back to Opera metro.

Museums and Galleries

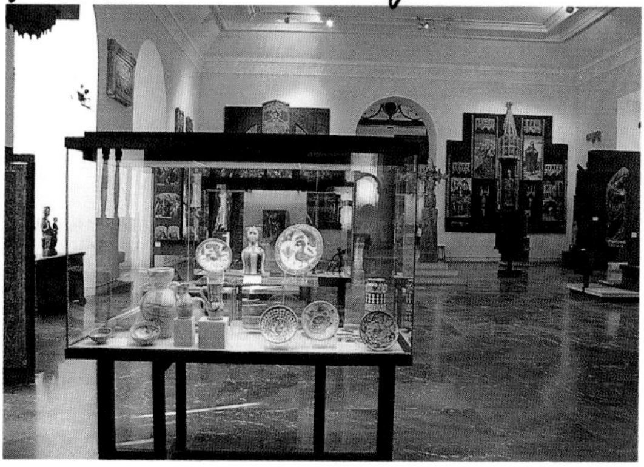

Glimpses of the past in the Museo Arqueológico

Diego Rodriguez de Silva y Velázquez (1599–1660) was more than a simple painter. Throughout his career he climbed steadily up the rungs of the court ladder, finally becoming a knight of Santiago. He is wearing the insignia in his self-portrait *Las Meninas*, his most famous painting. His jobs as courtier included long expeditions to Italy to buy paintings for the crown. He also decorated the now lost palace of the Retiro. Many of his greatest works hung in the earlier palace on the site of the Palacio Real, destroyed by fire in 1734.

▷▷▷ **Casa-Museo de Lope de Vega**
Calle de Cervantes 11
Reconstructed in period style and now converted to a study centre (open only briefly to the public), this house evokes its former inhabitant, the heroic playwright of the Golden Age and author of over 1,800 plays.

▶▶▷ **Estudio y Museo de Sorolla**
Paseo General Martínez Campos 37
The Sorolla Museum, in the artist's home-cum-studio some way north of the old centre, displays the works of the Valencia-born painter Joaquín Sorolla (1863–1923), full of the charm and radiant light of the Levante.

▷▷▷ **Museo de América**
Reyes Católicos 6
Due as ever to re-open after long closure, this museum celebrates popular art of pre-Columbian Latin America and of the Philippines.

▶▶▷ **Museo Arqueológico Nacional**
Calle de Serrano 13
Key exhibits and collections include: a replica of the Altamira caves on the Cantabrian coast (see pages 88–9); the 6,000-year-old painted and sculpted bust from Elche in the province of Murcia known most appropriately as La Dama de Elche; Roman material; Moorish exhibits and particularly fine displays of Visigothic material rarely encountered elsewhere. Galleries may be closed at short notice.
For opening times, see **Travel Facts** page 266.

▷▷▷ **Museo Cerralbo**
Calle Ventura Rodriguez 17
The private collection of the late Marqués de Cerralbo has notable art-works and floridly eclectic late 19th-century décor.

▶▶▷ **Museo del Ejército**
Calle Méndez Núñez 1
Housed in another surviving building from the Buen Retiro royal palace (see also **Casón del Buen Retiro**),

the Army Museum contains all kinds of wonders and curiosities, from the swords of El Cid and Boabdíl to a mass of regimental flags and insignia. More than a flavour here of Franco's Spain.

▶▶▶ Museo Lázaro Galdiano

Calle de Serrano 122

The Lázaro Galdiano museum, in a 19th-century palace/mansion, is named after the wealthy private collector who assembled it. It provides a rich and intriguing account of the Middle Ages in a whole variety of art forms, including enamel, ivory, gold and even that great rarity, Moorish silk. There is also a collection of paintings from Bosch to Goya.

▷▷▷ Museo Municipal

Calle de Fuencarral 78

The Municipal Museum offers a lively overview of the city's history and development, with maps and a scale model of Madrid in 1830.

The sword of Boabdíl, last king of Granada (displayed in the Museo del Ejérito), was stolen by Napoleon and returned by Hitler as a gift to Franco, after the German conquest of Paris in World War II.

▶▷▷ Museo Nacional de Artes Decorativas

Calle de Montalbán

Visit the Museo Nacional de Artes Decorativas for a display of Spanish furniture, fittings, domestic decorations and other comforts, ranging from the 15th to 19th centuries. It is all here, from Moorish-style *artesonado* ceilings to ceramics, leatherwork, clothing and kitchens. There are some charming and sumptuous whole-room reconstructions.

Decorative entrance to the Municipal Museum

Religious Buildings

While scores of major ecclesiastical monuments adorn the cities of Castile, Madrid is low on this element of the historic legacy. One or two set-pieces are excellent, however, and others, though less impressive in themselves, form a familiar part of the cityscape.

In a continent whose capitals are built on great rivers such as the Danube and the Seine, the Río Manzanares has always seemed a joke, even to Madrileños. Its feeble trickle has been proverbial for centuries.

▶▷▷ Catedral Nuestra Señora de la Almudena

Calle Mayor

A new cathedral, opposite the main entrance of the Palacio Real, this chilly white construction languished as a half-built shell for many decades, symbol of a paralysis of will. It finally opened in 1993, revealing an austere interior, its vistas blocked by heavy columns. Round behind the apse, down the Calle Mayor extension, are excavations with remains of the Moorish city.

▶▷▷ Catedral San Isidro and its neighbours

Down beneath the Plaza Mayor in the Old City, there are a number of churches to use as a focus while strolling. **San Isidro**, a twin-towered, 17th-century building, has long done temporary duty as a cathedral. **San Pedro** has a 14th-century Mudéjar tower. **San Miguel** is 18th century; the **Capilla del Obispo** has interesting tombs.

▶▷▷ Convento de la Encarnación

Plaza Encarnación

A Habsburg foundation like the Descalzas Reales (see below), this convent was founded in 1611 by Margaret of Austria. It specialises in Spanish art. Note particularly the sculptures by Gregorio Fernández (see also **Valladolid**, page 179) and work by Francisco Bayeu in the church.

Madrid's new cathedral, Catedral Nuestra Señora de la Almudena

• ***Stroll*** *Start in Plaza Mayor and exit left of the Panadería with its grand façade. Cross Calle Mayor and go down Bordadores past the church of San Ginés (shops here sell religious images) and straight on up San Martín for a visit to Convento de las Descalzas Reales. Emerging, turn right, then left to reach Calle Mayor again via Calle Fuentes. Turn right down Calle Mayor and left into Plaza de la Villa. Carry straight on down the little alleyway, Cordón, below, left, then turn 90 ° left passing the diplomats' church of San Miguel and into Plaza Puerta Cerrada. Left up Cuchilleros to the top for the lively little market of San Miguel and right into the Plaza Mayor.*

▶▶▶ Convento de las Descalzas Reales

Plaza de las Descalzas, Arenal

This convent-museum of the Barefoot Sisters, in this case royal ones (the order itself had been founded at a marginally humbler level by St Teresa), was deservedly 1987's European Museum of the Year.

Established in the 16th century by Juana de Austria, daughter of Charles V, it became a retreat for noble ladies, lavishly endowed by their families (see also Las Huelgas, **Burgos**, page 157). Along with its many chapels and grand baroque stairway (with frescos by the court painter Claudio Coello), it has a fine collection of tapestries, sculptures, art objects and paintings. There are works by Titian, Rubens and other imported artists; Spanish painters and sculptors are represented by Alonso Cano, Zurbarán, Luisa Roldán and others. Guided tours only, bossily conducted, in Spanish.

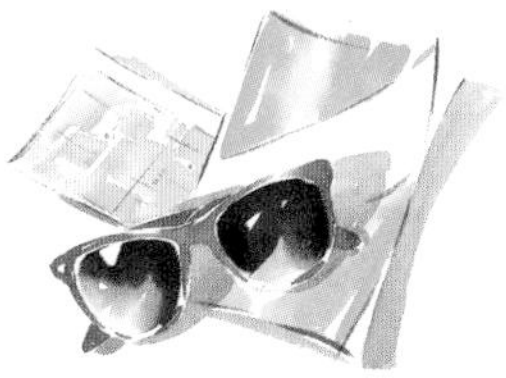

▶▶▷ **Ermita de San Antonio de la Florida (Panteón de Goya)**

Paseo de la Florida

Goya's final resting place (he died in Bordeaux in 1828) is in a little church or 'hermitage', now deconsecrated, close to the Río Manzanares. He had decorated it himself, to royal order, finishing in 1798. It is down behind the Estación del Norte, and reaching it requires a taxi or a little effort. But the fresco in the dome – the *Miracle of St Anthony*, with figures leaning over a painted railing or even sitting on it – will reward the visitor.

▷▷▷ **San Francisco el Grande**

Plaza San Francisco

On down Calle Bailén from the Royal Palace and past the new Almudena Cathedral, this large and fairly lumpy neo-classical church of the 18th century remains a considerable landmark. One chapel features a Goya scene. Tours available.

▷▷▷ **San Jerónimo el Real**

Calle de Moreto

A tall, rather gaunt building dominating the hillside above the Prado and beneath the Retiro park, San Jerónimo is all that survives of a former Hieronymite monastery. The church is famous for society weddings and royal associations. The present king, Juan Carlos, was married in Greece but crowned here at San Jerónimo.

San Jerónimo el Real, church of Spain's top people

Other Sights

▷▷▷ **Casa de Campo**

A huge green lung on the west side of Madrid, accessible by cable-car from Paseo del Pintor Rosales on the edge of Parque del Oeste, the Casa del Campo is a relatively natural tract of wooded countryside with zoo and amusement park. Once it was a royal hunting ground; seen from the windows of the Royal Palace, it continues to provide a splendid vista.

▶▶▷ **Campo del Moro**

A rather formal park, the 'Field (or Country) of the Moor' climbs steeply up from the Río Manzanares towards the Royal Palace. There is a fine vista upwards.

▷▷▷ **Ciudad Universitaria**

Madrid's main university, in the northwest of the city, was badly damaged during the Civil War. Rebuilt under Franco, it scarcely merits the visit incorporated in many city bus tours, except as the location of the Museo de América (see page 58).

▷▷▷ **Estadio Bernabeú**

Real Madrid, most glamorous of Spanish football clubs, is based at the Bernabeu stadium, quite far north along the Castellana. Great if you can get a ticket.

▶▷▷ **Jardin Botánico**

Madrid's Botanical Gardens represent one of the strongest themes of the Spanish Enlightenment in the 18th century – the commitment to the description and classification of the flora not only of Spain but of Latin America and the Philippines. Initiated by King Ferdinand VI and moved to their present site beside the Prado by Charles III, the gardens, with their methodical planting of trees, medicinal herbs, etc, make an interesting visit. The Prado building here was itself another Enlightenment phenomenon, intended originally as an observatory.

'No pasarán!'– 'They shall not pass!'...This became the war cry of Madrid throughout the Spanish Civil War, echoed all over the world by supporters of the beleaguered Republic. The point where, above all, the Nationalists 'should not pass' was in the battered University City, symbol of light and learning, under attack from the Casa de Campo and the river below.

In Madrid's 200-year-old Botanical Gardens

▶▷▷ Parque del Oeste
This green and relaxing area, set mostly on a slope above the Río Manzanares, is site of the incongruous but marvellous 4th-century BC Temple of Debod, a gift from Egypt reassembled here in recognition of Spanish engineers' work on the Aswan dam.

▶▶▷ Parque del Retiro
Madrid is fortunate to have this stylish park, originally the garden of Philip IV's now-vanished Retiro Palace, right at its heart. There are flowerbeds, a boating lake and plentiful trees to offer shade in summer. The Palacio de Cristal (Crystal Palace) and Palacio de Velázquez are both used as cultural centres. Young people whizz along on rollerskates and skateboards; old men play *petanque*; fortune-tellers, theatre groups, bands and puppeteers all perform on Sundays. See also **Walk** on page 64.

▷▷▷ Plaza Canovas del Castillo
This square, named after a turn-of-the-century prime minister, was adorned by Charles III with a fountain and statue of Neptune (the square is known to taxi-drivers and other Madrileños as 'Neptuno'). Close to the Prado, it has the Ritz Hotel on one corner and the equally famous Palace Hotel almost diagonally opposite.

▶▶▷ Plaza de la Cibeles
The fountain of the goddess Cibeles, her chariot drawn by lions, is perhaps the most familiar image of Madrid for Spaniards. It stands at the key intersection of Madrid, where the Calle de Alcalá meets the lower part of the Castellana, here called the Paseo del Prado (south of Cibeles) and the Paseo de Recoletos (north).

▷▷▷ Plaza de Colón
'Columbus Square' is a roundabout on Paseo de Recoletos. Next to it is a monument to Christopher Columbus, with rather shapeless modern sculptures round an open space. The 'gardens' abut on the National Library, with the Archaeological Museum behind. There is a theatre/arts centre below ground.

▶▷▷ Plaza de España
Across town from Plaza de la Cibeles and at the far end of the Gran Vía, the Plaza de España acts as another of the city's pivots. It contains much-loved statues of Don Quixote and Sancho Panza.

• ***Stroll*** *From the Puerta de Alcalá head northwards along Calle de Serrano, one of Madrid's prestigious shopping streets. Pass the Museo Arqueológico on your left and then the Columbus Centre heralded by huge blocks of stone etched with celebrations of Columbus' journeys. This is also Madrid's Cultural Centre. Turn left here at Calle de Goya and cross the road to the far side of Paseo de Recoletas and stroll down towards Plaza de la Cibeles, effectively doing a U-turn and passing two excellent cafés, the art nouveau Café Espejo and the old literary Café Gijón. Turn left once more at Cibeles to complete the circle.*

Neptune all aglow in the Plaza Canovas del Castillo

The Barrio de Salamanca, a smart bourgeois district north of the Parque del Retiro and centred on the Calle de Goya, was built as a real-estate speculation by the Marquis of Salamanca in the 19th century. Unbelievably, considering how central it seems today, the well-to-do of the period were reluctant to live there, so far did it seem from the Plaza Mayor.

▶▶▷ Plaza de Oriente and Teatro de la Opera

The Plaza de Oriente, across the Calle de Bailén from the Palacio Real, is a major stopping-point for tour buses. The statues of the Visigothic and Spanish kings surrounding it were originally intended for the palace skyline but rejected as being too heavy. On the far side is the **Teatro Real**, used as an opera house (due to reopen soon after some years of heavy restoration).

▶▶▷ Plaza de la Villa

This square on the historic Calle Mayor, which leads down from the Puerta del Sol towards the Almudena cathedral, contains a cluster of Madrid's finest buildings. The 17th-century but much modified ***ayuntamiento*** (town hall, open to the public Monday to Friday, 10.00–20.00hrs) on the west side is flanked by the 16th-century **Casa de Cisneros**. Opposite is the medieval **Torre de Lujanes**. Beside this is the elegant building called the **Hemeroteca**.

Walk Parque del Retiro

Start on Calle Felipe IV between the Prado and the back of the Ritz hotel, walk up to the Prado annexe immediately ahead. Cross Calle de Alfonso XII into the Retiro park.
At the end of the Paseo de la Argentina, lined with handless statues, lies the the Estanque (lake with boats for hire) and the monument to Alfonso XII.

Pass behind the monument, cross the Paseo de Venezuela to the blue-domed Palacio de Velázquez and the Palacio de Cristal.
The latter is a huge conservatory, with lake and fountains.

Continue in the same direction to the rose garden by the Glorieta (arbour) del Angel Caido on Paseo de Uruguay. Turn right at the glorieta and leave the park, cross Alfonso XII and continue down Claudio Moyano (second-hand bookstalls) to Paseo del Prado. Turn right keeping the Jardin Botánico to your right and thus back to the Prado Museum.

Monument to Alfonso XII in the Parque del Retiro, once the garden of a royal palace

The Puerta de Alcalá, a triple-arched classical gateway a little up from Plaza de la Cibeles. It was erected in honour of Charles III

Torre Picasso and Torre Europa are Madrid's two highest skyscrapers. They lie high up Castellana near the Bernabeu stadium, at the heart of Madrid's new high-rise 'downtown'. Their presence here exemplifies the city's northwards-shifting centre of gravity.

▶▶▶ **Puerta del Sol and Plaza Mayor environs**

Start in lively Puerta del Sol, then angle into the Plaza Mayor, also lively in summer, with outdoor café tables, evening performances of plays, music, etc, and strolling crowds. The 17th-century square is the work of the architect Gómez de Mora; the equestrian statue is of his sovereign Philip III. It has one particularly grand side, familiarly known as La Panadería after a bakery that once stood on the premises. The most attractive exit is in the southwest corner, down into the buttressed Calle Cuchilleros with its many restaurants. Exit by the southeast, however, and you will soon find the Foreign Office, housed in the Palacio de Santa Cruz. Cut back to Sol by side streets for a glimpse of Old Madrid.

▶▶▷ **El Rastro**

The Rastro is Madrid's flea market, liveliest on Sunday mornings. It runs downhill from the area of La Latina metro, south of Sol and the Plaza Mayor. The Plaza Cascorro, with good bars, is its heart. In Ribera de Curtidores, Sunday stalls sell Toledo tablecloths and Talavera pottery. Illegal pet vendors lurk in side streets. Regular shops sell wicker furniture, army surplus and antiques.

▶▷▷ **Real Fábrica de Tapices**

Tapestries are still woven by hand in this 19th-century descendant (now rather drab) of the 18th-century royal factory. Designs by Goya and his brother-in-law, Bayeu, are still in use.

▶▷▷ **Las Ventas (Plaza de Toros) and Museo Taurino**

Las Ventas is Madrid's enormous bullring, built in 20th-century mock-Mudéjar style, and national shrine to the art, or massacre, of the bullfight. There is a small bullfighting museum attached.

Shopping

Galería del Prado shopping centre, on Plaza de Canovas del Castillo

Traditional shops and curiosities The oldest and most picturesque of Madrid's shops naturally cluster in the oldest part of town, around the Puerta del Sol and Plaza Mayor – Calle Esparteros for cutlers, Marqués Viuda de Pontejos for haberdashers, Zaragoza and Bordadores for religious items, etc. **Ramírez**, Calle Concepción Jerónima, and **Conde Hermanos-Sobrinos de Estezo**, Otocha 53, are guitar specialists, a peculiarly Mediterranean branch of instrument making.

There are curiosities like **La Violeta** on the Canalejas roundabout selling only sweets scented or decorated with violets. **Casa Mira**, at Carrera de San Jeronimo 30, is a lovely nougat shop, while further down the road and on the Calle del Prado, there are many antique shops.

The quintessential expression of the area is the Rastro market (see page 65). The purpose-built arts and crafts market, **Puerta de Toledo**, is nearby at Calle Ronda de Toledo. Just north of Puerta del Sol, there are inner-city branches of the main department stores, **El Corte Inglés** and **Galerías Preciados**.

Ready for a break from shopping? Beware as you sit outdoors at your café table, delightful as it may be. It is said that the wind of Madrid 'can kill a man without snuffing out a candle'.

Fashion Top for fashion is the Calle Serrano and surrounding Salamanca area (mainly Calles Lagasca and Claudio Coello). One of the liveliest designers here is **Adolfo Dominguez**, Serrano 96 and Ortega y Gasset 4. At **Alfredo Villalba**, Serrano 68 and Goya 17, you'll find just a few, mildly freakish numbers on the rail – at more than high prices.

Behind the Cafe Gijon on Paseo de Recoletos an area of charming 19th-century streets has also been colonised of late by designers. Take a walk in Calle Almirante, Conde de Xiquena and Piamonte, for such beautiful boutiques as Ararat, Elisa Bracci, Tokio (gloves and boots).

Art and books For art galleries and art bookshops, consult the *Arte y Exposiciones* booklet from tourist offices. Find books at **Casa del Libros** on Gran Vía 29 and second-hand books in the stalls on Claudio Moyana.

Food and Drink

See also page 274

Madrid ranks high for the pleasures of the table, with a huge range of tapas bars, restaurants from the Spanish regions and many foreign countries, and excellent cafés for a coffee with your *coñac*.

Tapeando in Madrid The Madrileñan *tasca*, home of delicious and exceptionally varied tapas (see page 20), is one of the city's real institutions, at its best in the much-visited tourist areas close to the Plaza Mayor (down Cuchilleros and with the Plaza de Puerta Cerrada as a natural centre) and the more obviously working-class streets round about. Other good areas nearby include: Plaza Santa Ana, Calle Echegaray and the upper end of the Rastro. Be guided by eye and nose; try everything from *pimientos de Padrón* (hottish green peppers from Galicia) to *cecina*, raw, air-cured beef from León and Castile, sliced thin as Italian *prosciutto*. Tapas are available all over the rest of the city, though in less concentration, served at the counter in cafeterias and in the street-facing bars of many smaller restaurants.

Restaurants and cafés Sit-down restaurants range from popular and demotic to the very up-market indeed. There are outstanding places to eat at the top end – from the Basque **Zalacaín** to the more international **Fortuny**. Prices match those of other western European capitals. Apart from Basque cookery (expensive), traditional regional fare tends to be in the middle price-bracket. Try **Botín**, the thoroughly Castilian roast suckling-pig specialist on Cuchilleros, or **Casa Lucio** on Cava Baja. Cafés like **Café de Oriente** in Plaza Oriente or the new (though in art nouveau style) **Espejo** on Paseo de Recoletos provide informal meals as well as coffee and cakes; old-style, often turn-of-the century cafés, like the **Café Gijón** on Recoletos or the **Lyon** on Alcalá, have always been popular in Madrid. Don't ignore restaurants in department stores like **El Corte Inglés**, where the food may be surprisingly good.

<<Ah what a place Madrid is, all show! ... Façade, nothing but façade. These people have no idea of comfort in their own houses. They live in the streets and so that they can dress well and go to the theatre, some families eat nothing but potato omelettes all year round.>> Benito Pérez Galdo, *La de Bringas* (English translation by Gamel Woolsey, 1953, as *The Spendthrifts*)

Display of local sausages in a Madrid delicatessen

Nightlife and Entertainment

Disco life goes on right through until dawn

WEEKEND ITINERARY
Friday evening: Stroll to the Plaza Mayor; relax in a bar or restaurant on Calle Cuchilleros or the Plaza Puerta Cerrada.
Saturday: Visit the Prado today (you may have to queue on Sunday). Leave time for a daytime stroll through the Retiro park and a wander along up-market Serrano for window-shopping.
Sunday: Start with chocolate and *churros* before a trip to the Rastro. Have lunchtime tapas in one of the bars at the top end of the market. If you want to see a bullfight, it has to be Sunday afternoon; Las Ventas is usually booked out, so you may have to go as part of an (expensive) city tour. End the day with a simple meal at the Brasserie de Lista, Ortega y Gasset 6.

Nightlife in Madrid is fast, furious – and late. For the more staid, there are good venues for theatre, opera or film. Check the listings in *El Pais* newspaper or in the leisure magazine *Guia del Ocio*.

Theatre and cinema For Spanish-speakers, Madrid offers a rich theatrical life (watch out for the **Compañía Nacional de Teatro Clásico**). Opera and ballet will take place in the **Teatro Real**, Plaza de Oriente, when reconstruction work is complete (check listings). Cinemas abound in the Gran Vía area, mostly showing dubbed movies. A few specialist cinemas show films in the original languages (try Calle Martín de los Heros).

Flamenco Many of Spain's best flamenco artists gravitate to Madrid. They create an atmosphere in the capital's nightspots that is sometimes lacking in Andalucía. **Corral de la Morería**, Calle Morería 17, remains the best, but is expensive. The **Café de Chinitas** (Torija 7) comes cheaper and there are larger venues like **Arco de Cuchilleros** (Cuchilleros 7) catering for tours and coach parties.

The late-night thrash Nothing moves on faster than *la Movida,* the night-time perambulation of the young, with an area 'in' one month and 'out' the next. Presumably the outdoor night-spots on Castellana will go on for ever. The Malasaña district round the Plaza Dos de Mayo has been red hot, but is now much less so. Try **Archy** on Marqués de Riscal 11, and **Volereta** on Calle de Princesa 3. **Pachá**, Barceló 11 (Wednesday to Sunday only), has kept its super-trendy rating, as has **Joy Eslava**, Arenal 11, in a converted cinema.
For those who actually want to sit down with a drink, listen to music (classical) and enjoy some conversation, **La Fidula** at Calle de Huertas 57 or **Solesmes** at Calle Amnestía 5 will prove havens.

Accommodation

See also page 274

Madrid has two wonderful, old-world hotels to rival anything in London or Paris – including their high prices. One or two modern imitations are also worth considering. Then come the swisher international hotels, comfortable, clean and anonymous. The city's older hotels and pensions in the middle and down-market range are more varied, some down-at-heel, others refurbished and on the way up. Choice is made easier by the fact that each of the main groups tends to be confined to a single area. The difficulty occurs in the cheaper register because of the variation of standards.

Up-market The two flagships are the **Ritz** and **Palace**, 200m from one another across the Paseo del Prado. The Ritz was built in 1910 for the guests of King Alfonso XIII. It retains its original splendour along with the smartest of modern appurtenances. The Palace, too, has been done up but retains, despite all the shops downstairs, an air of gravity and splendour at a lesser price than the Ritz. To these should be added the modern but old-world-gracious **Villa Magna** at the nearer end of the Castellana, the new and slightly less successful imitator, **Villa Real**, close to the Palace, and the older **Arosa**, just off the near end of the Gran Vía.

The chain-style modern hotels are mostly to be found going up the Castellana. In the north, near the new 'downtown' area, the expensively anonymous and efficient **Eurobuilding** is the leading example.

Budget The older hotels cluster in the more central parts of town, lying in a rough fan shape, with its base in the Puerta del Sol, its left-hand edge by the Plaza de España and the right-hand by Atocha station. Atocha is a rough district, though the modernised **Carlton** in Delicias is perfectly acceptable. Watch your step round Calle Echegaray, where some of the cheaper hotels are to be found. There are numerous hotels along the noisy Gran Vía, but ask for an internal room on patio or stairwell.

WEEK'S ITINERARY
Sunday: Visit the Rastro flea market; take in a bullfight in the afternoon (if that is your thing) – see Weekend Itinerary, page 68 – or stroll in the old town. For dinner, fry your own steak at El Schotis, Cava Baja 11 (tel: 265 3230), quiet on Sunday.
Monday: Shopping day, as museums and public buildings are closed.
Tuesday: Make your first visit to the Prado, then take in Reina Sofia art centre for modern art.
Wednesday: Time for an excursion – take your pick of Toledo, Segovia, Avila, the Escorial.
Thursday: Morning visit to theThyssen-Bornemisza collection and/or Academy of San Fernando. An afternoon walk perhaps, and an early evening drink at the Café Gijón in Recoletos.
Friday: Time for another excursion (see Wednesday).
Saturday: Don't miss the Lázaro Galdiano museum, Madrid's most pleasing. After last-minute shopping, blow your remaining cash on dinner at atmospheric, old-fashioned 'Lhardy', San Jerónimo 8 , tel: 521 3385 – early booking essential.

Old-style hotel area – Plaza de Colón

Practical Points

Madrid's red buses are a popular way of getting about the city

EXCURSIONS
There is a tremendous range of one-day destinations around Madrid (many described in the chapter on pages 190–207). Toledo, Segovia and Avila are all quintessential Castilian cities. The monastery palace of El Escorial, like it or loathe it, is a top European sight and combines well with a visit to the disturbing Valle de los Caídos (Valley of the Fallen). The delightfully situated royal palace of Aranjuez is about an hour south of Madrid.

Getting around

Metro The Metro is both the quickest way of getting round and the easiest for those with little or no Spanish. Stations are marked with diamond-shaped signs, with red borders and with the name written in the centre. Tickets are bought in the station either from machines or manned guichets. There is one flat fare for a journey of any distance, but the ten-journey ticket is far better value. Route maps are clear (lines are numbered 1 to 10 with one short line marked 'R'). Inter-line connections are simple to make. Look at the map before a journey, remember the line number and final destination on that line, then follow the signs pointing that way. The Metro is relatively clean, and so far seems perfectly safe.

Bus Mastering the whole of the bus network is quite a business, but it is well worth the effort to identify one or two main lines – no 12, for example, runs all along the Castellana from the Santiago Bernabeu stadium to the Prado. There is also a useful circular bus route which is just as good for sightseeing as any expensive tour. Buy single tickets on the bus (valid for any distance) or a 10-ride 'bonobus' ticket, highly recommended, available from kiosks and *estancos* (the most central spots are Cibeles and Puerta del Sol). On entry to the bus, insert ticket into the machine by the door which clips the edge and so makes your ride legal. Free bus maps are available.

Taxis Taxis are metered, safe and plentiful – except when it rains or when you need one in a hurry. A green light shows when they are free. They are good value at night when streets are clear, less so during the day in busy areas of town. Madrid is often a fearful snarl-up of traffic – another good reason for using the Metro.

Trains Chamartín, way up north beyond the Plaza de Castilla, is the new mainline station for most routes. It is linked by a through line with Atocha, the old southerly station, now rebuilt, at the bottom end of the Botanical Gardens. (There is also a Metro link, no 8, Chamartín to Plaza de Castilla, then take no 1 to Atocha RENFE.) The same train may well pass through both stations. Pick it up at the point of first departure, though, at weekends and during holiday periods. 'Cercanías' refers to local and suburban trains, 'largo recorrido' to inter-city and long distance trains.

Eating hours
Madrid not only stays up later than other Spanish cities; it also takes its meals appreciably later. Add maybe half an hour to each phase of the normal Spanish day (see page 16) to stay in step. If you can adjust to this rhythm you will enjoy your stay much more than by arriving first at every restaurant.

Security
Madrid used to be one of the safest cities in Europe. This is no longer so obviously the case; and to Spaniards the change seems very shocking. To those from other countries, however, Madrid may well seem no more fear-provoking than their own capitals. Normal precautions are in order (see page 258); and while there are no out-and-out 'no-go' areas, it is wise to walk with care, especially at night, in the area south of the Plaza Mayor generally, around Atocha, the Plaza Santa Ana and Echegaray.

Tourist information
At Barajas airport, there is a desk on the departure level (tel: 205 8656). Hotel reservations are made here. In town, there are tourist offices at Torre de Madrid, Plaza de España (tel: 241 23 25); Plaza Mayor 3 (tel: 266 5477); Charmartín railway station; and at Calle Duque de Medinaceli 2, beside the Palace Hotel.

Until the early 1970s, Madrid had *serenos*. These were nightwatchmen, who carried leaded sticks which they banged on the pavement to indicate they were near and you were therefore safe. Coming home at night, people would stand by their apartment block door and clap their hands to summon the *sereno*. He would then unlock the door with a key from the mighty bundle at his waist. With the disappearance of the *serenos*, Madrileños feel less spied upon, but they badly miss their former security.

On 2 May, in the Plaza Dos de Mayo, processions mark the events portrayed in Goya's famous paintings under the title *Dos de Mayo (Second of May)*, the occasion in 1808 of a popular rising and, on the following day, executions by firing squad.
15 May, the day of San Isidro, Madrid's patron saint, is celebrated throughout the city but particularly in the Plaza Mayor, with open-air concerts. There are bullfights at Las Ventas every day for a fortnight.

Away from the bustle: a Madrid backstreet

Galician farms are characterised by the granite grain stores on legs called hórreos

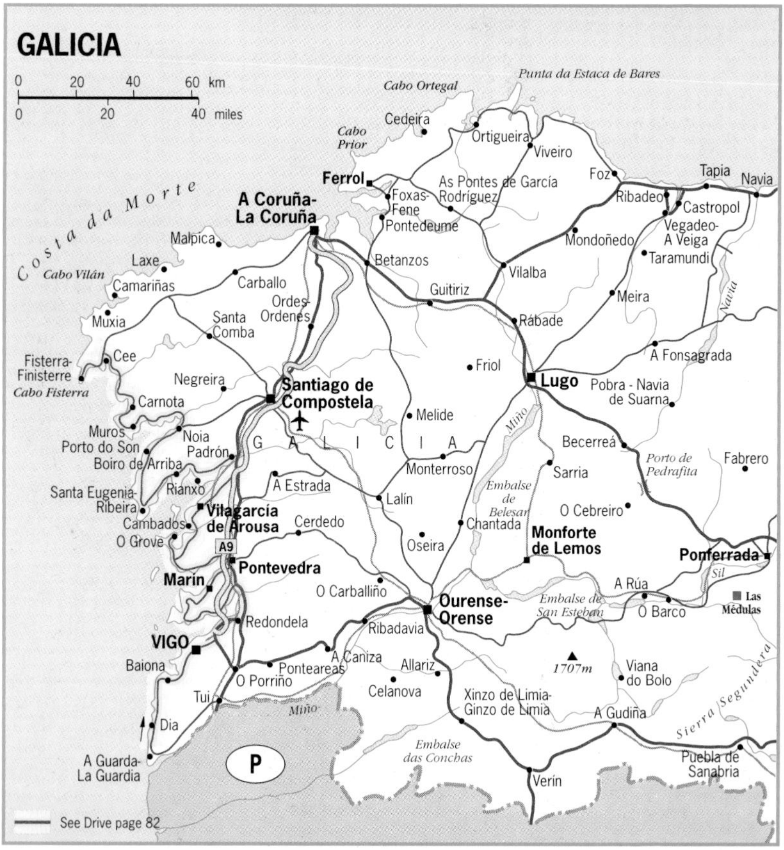

GALICIA

Green and grey are the colours of Galicia. The green stands for the meadows and eucalyptus forests of this gently rainy northwest corner of the peninsula. Grey is for the granite of great headlands which rear up skywards or tilt down gently to an Atlantic fierce in winter, often suave in summer. The landscape is melancholy, expressed in a folk music of drums, bagpipes and the harp, and in centuries of plangent poetry in the local language, Gallego, Romance dialect not far removed from Portuguese.

The coastline is exceptionally lovely, deeply indented by long inlets called *rías*. These are wild in places, in others cultivated to the water's edge. They offer many of Spain's best and least developed beaches. They are also rich in shellfish. There are good Galician (or Gallego) wines – the sharp Ribeiros and Albariños – and *caldo gallego*, soups and stews with kale or turnip greens and local ham. The elements combine to make a distinctive and surprising cuisine.

The trouble is and always has been poverty, however. Tiny, uneconomic allotments, endlessly divided by inheritance, have led to emigration on a huge scale, with Vigo and A Coruña as the ports for departing liners. So many are the emigrants that, in some parts of Argentina, the word 'Gallego' is used as a substitute for 'Spaniard'. Even today, displaced Gallegos are found all over Spain, working in the construction trade or dead-end, heavy labour. Not surprisingly, there is a drugs problem round Galicia's major ports.

Galicia above all is Celtic country. The Celts came 1,000 years BC and built their round-house settlements mostly on hilltops. Some are still in active use. The Romans built bridges and the huge city walls of Lugo. The Moors came and stayed only briefly. Soon after their departure, locals discovered a tomb that they claimed was that of St James the Apostle ('Sant Iago'), so starting off a pilgrimage that was one of the great features of the European Middle Ages and remains, with the *rías* and Galicia's unchanging country ways, among the chief reasons for visiting this most untypical and seductive region.

A wild shore under a grey sky, both typical of rainy Galicia

The harbour in A Coruña

Galicia is rich in granite-built granaries called *hórreos*. With pitched roofs and slatted sides, they resemble country chapels. Some are tiny. The biggest, at Lira near Carnota, hidden above the village and the sea, extends to a full 30m and looks like a petrified railway carriage. Galicia also has many stone crosses standing in out-of-the-way country spots.

Horses – described as wild though having human owners – range free in some parts of Galicia. You are most likely to see them along the coast south of Baiona. In spring and early summer there are festive round-ups for branding, known as *curros*.

In the gazetteer entries below, Galician place names appear in brackets after the Castilian.

▷▷▷ **Allariz**

A rustic little town rising from the River Arnoia south of Ourense, Allariz offers a delightful main square and some attractive churches.

▶▶▷ **Bayona (Baiona)**

It was to Baiona, on the southern extreme of the Ría de Vigo, that the *Pinta* first brought word of the New World in March 1493. The charming little town is still guarded by a fortified peninsula, with 16th-century walls, a modern parador within them and yachts moored beneath. The excellent beach of Praia de America is across the bay.

▶▷▷ **Betanzos**

Betanzos, at the head of the main *ría* dividing A Coruña from Ferrol, is set on a steep hill contained within a wider valley. The hilltop is crowned with an old main square, 18th-century town hall and the guild church of Santiago, an odd and pleasing complex. A little lower down is the equally irregular and pleasing 14th- to 15th-century church of Santa María del Azogue (literally 'of the market') and just opposite, the graceful, Gothic monastery church of San Francisco, a fine fusion of form and decoration. Note especially the wild boar and bear supporting the tomb of the founder, Count Fernán Pérez de Andrade.

▶▶▷ **Camariñas and Muxia**

These little fishing harbours, lively in summer, are tucked inside the mouth of the Ría de Camariñas (see **Costa de la Muerte**, page 76). On the Muxia cape is a sanctuary and two large rocks believed to have powerful healing properties. On Cabo Vilán opposite, there are, by contrast, modern electricity-generating windmills.

▷▷▷ **Cebreiro**

The pass of Pedrafita de Cebreiro is the climax of the pilgrims' climb up the final barrier that faced them, 200km from Santiago – the forested slopes of the hills of the Bierzo region. There is a sanctuary above the present road – and a radio mast.

▷▷▷ **Celanova**

This pretty little town, assembled round the Benedictine monastery of San Salvador, lies in sweeping, wooded country southwest of Ourense. The baroque monastery church contains a 10th-century Mozarabic shrine.

▶▶▷ **La Coruña (A Coruña)**

A Coruña (Corunna in English), though dismal on entry, nevertheless has much of interest within. An old town lies on an isthmus with harbour on one side and beach on the other. Beyond, on the near-island to which the isthmus leads, is La Ciudad, the City, with a Roman-founded lighthouse and ramparts that have figured large in history.

A Coruña was the final departure point of the disastrous Armada sent by Philip II of Spain against England in 1588. A year later, during an English attack, local heroine, María Pita, gave the alarm and saved the day for Spain. In the Peninsular Wars of 1808–12, a British expeditionary force was decisively defeated here by the French. It remains a garrison town. Spaniards, and especially Galicians, remember it – along with Vigo – as departure point for liners bearing emigrants to the New World.

The sights It is natural for a visitor to begin on the isthmus, where beautiful glass balconies overlook the modern fishing harbour. At the far end of the isthmus, just before it rises to La Ciudad, a left turn will take the walker into a grandiloquent if rather barren square named after María Pita. The town beach beckons over the ridge – though you may prefer to press on to the wilder beaches of the Costa de la Muerte (see page 76).
La Ciudad is the original town. On its eastern side, confined within ramparts, is the Jardín de San Carlos where Sir John Moore is buried.
Leave by the archway behind the gardens for the pretty square of Santa Barbara, backed by a monastery of the same name. Angle up through the square for the Calle Herrerías and the house of María Pita, no 28 (marked with plaques). Turn down, looping back, among fine Galician houses, granite and white, for the Romanesque church of Santa María. Beneath is the gracious Plaza del General Azcarragas and, in the far corner from this approach, the Romanesque church of Santiago, with St James himself on the main façade – at full gallop in a bowler hat. Now it is only a step down again to the Avenida Maritima on the isthmus. The lighthouse, Torre de Hercules, is a long hike or bus ride to the northern tip of the peninsula.

<< We buried him darkly at dead of night ...>>
The Burial of Sir John Moore at Corunna, written by the Reverend Charles Wolfe, mourns the loss of the general who commanded Britain's first expeditionary force to Spain's Peninsular Wars. Forced back towards Galicia, Moore died while his beaten army was embarking at Corunna. His tomb is in the garden on the San Carlos ramparts, where lines from Wolfe's poem, and others by the Galician poetess Rosalía de Castro, are inscribed on a little *mirador*.

The peace and quiet of a lonely beach on the beautiful Ría de Camariñas

Galicia's famous *rías* (sea inlets) are the region's chief delight, and are richly studded with good beaches. The Rías Altas (Upper Inlets) lie on the north coast, wild, exhilarating, sometimes rather exposed. The Rías Bajas (Lower Inlets) lie on the western coast south of Fisterra. The further south you go, the more populous they are. Though Galicia is generally rainy, the Rías are a good deal drier than inland districts. See also Drive on page 82.

Alameda: technically a poplar grove but really meaning a tree-shaded public walkway, avenue or square. Many Spanish towns are graced with one. In the best, the spreading branches of low trees are grafted together to form a single leafy canopy.

▶▶▷ Costa de la Muerte (Costa da Morte)

This is the fierce coast from A Coruña to Fisterra (Finisterre). Unfailingly, fishermen are drowned here each year, often while trying to make the difficult harbours strung along the coast. Malpica and Laxe are examples of towns which lack elegance but whose beaches are both lively and lovely in summer. The *ría* entering the coast between Camariñas and Muxia may well be reckoned the most beautiful part of the whole Spanish coast. The hinterland is deeply rural featuring a profusion of stone crosses and stone-built *hórreos* (see panel, page 74).

▷▷▷ El Ferrol (Ferrol)

Naval base and major naval dockyard to rival Cartagena (in Murcia), Ferrol was the birthplace of General Franco and once known as El Ferrol del Caudillo. The dictator holidayed nearby at Sada, making Ferrol/A Coruña the summer capital of Spain. Earlier, Ferrol had been extended under Charles III, and its central area is a grid reminiscent of 18th-century Lisbon.

▶▶▷ Lugo

A small city buried deep in the countryside of northeastern Galicia, present-day Lugo offers an agreeable animation. The Romans left a wall of slate-like slabs laid sideways. Many times restored, these are now 10m high and with 85 bastions. They still entirely ring the inner city, providing a walk of 2km plus.

A few metres downhill from the airy Praza (Plaza) Maior, the stone of the cathedral dourly confronts the stone of the bishop's palace. But the cathedral itself, a stopping-point on the Pilgrims' Way, is a real gem, tiny inside and with an air of holiness, Romanesque running into Gothic into baroque, with baroque towers and façade in rough imitation of Santiago. Inside, in the nave, note the charming, round-arched galleries for pilgrims. The Gothic church of San Pedro has given its cloister to the adjoining Museo Provincial, recently and brilliantly reorganised.

A deserted stretch of the Costa de la Muerte

Granite pillars support the plain granite buildings of Pontevedra

Galician has always been a language of literature, from the Middle Ages when it was a vehicle for courtly poetry, right up to our own day. Alfonso X, the Learned, wrote verses in Galician. But the most famous Galician writer is the poet Rosalía de Castro (1847–85) from the little town of Padrón, where her house is now a museum. Her poetry, melancholic in tone, is often compared with that of American poet Emily Dickinson. Galicia's most recent literary hero is Alvaro Cunqueiro, born in Mondoñedo. Locals are convinced that only death robbed him of the Nobel prize.

▶▶▷ **Mondoñedo**
This small but charming cathedral town has winding streets, houses of white rendering with granite trim, and glassed-in balconies. It has been a literary and religious centre for centuries. The cathedral, with baroque façade, abuts a delightful square, watched over by a seated statue of the writer Alvaro Cunqueiro.

▶▷▷ **Orense (Ourense)**
Provincial capital and home of the singer Julio Iglesias, Ourense sprawls across the Miño valley. It is approached from the north by an interesting medley of road and rail bridges, including the 13th-century 'Roman' bridge, a wonderful construction on Roman foundations. The *casco viejo*, high on the southern side, has lively bars and a succession of attractive squares tumbling down round the cathedral. The archaeological museum lies behind a handsome heraldic façade.

▶▷▷ **Osera (Oseira) Monastery**
This vast Cistercian foundation, described as the Escorial of Galicia, has a fine carved façade of 1709, three excellent cloisters, a 12th- to 13th-century church and a sacristy, with fine Gothic ribbing.

▷▷▷ **Pontedeume**
The little town pitches itself downhill through arcaded streets to the site of the famous bridge built across the River Eume by the counts of Andrade.

▶▶▷ **Pontevedra**
Old Pontevedra is a composition in granite. Centuries ago, until its river silted, it was the major port of the area. The almost circular white and granite church of the Peregrina stands above the three-sided Plaza de la Herrería. From here take Calle Odriozala down through Plaza de la Leña (beautiful home of the provincial museum), then Plaza de Mugartegui. Calle Princesa off Plaza de Teucro is full of bars. Turn left at the T-junction here (bars galore) and climb to Santa María la Mayor, with a fine baroque façade on the far side.

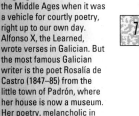

FOCUS ON *Santiago de Compostela*

■ **The great cathedral of St James in Santiago was the goal of and reward for the hardships of Europe's most celebrated pilgrimage. It stands below the crest of a hill in a city which is itself almost entirely a devotional work in stone. .....■**

Palmeros are pilgrims to Jerusalem; *Romeros* to Rome; *Pelegrinos* and *Jacobitos* to Santiago.

The strong grey granite of Galicia, glistening with mica in sunlight, smoothly shiny in the more customary rain, characterises Santiago, which was at one time the capital of the kingdom of Galicia.
From many points you can look right out of the city on to green hills beyond.

Approaching the cathedral Pilgrims came in through the Porto do Camiño (the Galician language is generally used in signs here) and up over the hilltop, passing churches and monasteries, some small and Romanesque, others huge and classically baroque. The route leads on, most impressively, down Calle Azbachería to the north transept of the cathedral.
Modern visitors still enter on foot but usually by a different route (the centre is mainly pedestrianised), taking any one of three parallel granite streets that lead from the east towards the cathedral. Rúa Nueva is highest on the gentle hillside, then comes Rúa del Villar, the traditional main street. Both of these have heavy arches and arcades, and colourful shopping. The lowest, Calle del Franco (with its side-streets) is packed with bars, restaurants and lively students, and ends with the beautiful Palacio de Fonseca, a university building with a Renaissance façade, a Mudéjar-ceilinged lecture/exhibition hall to the left and a two-storeyed cloister.
These two contrasting approaches to the cathedral, one liturgical, the other abundant with life, make a fitting preparation for a building intensely dramatic in religious terms but full, too, of a sense of welcome and good humour.

The baroque façade of the great pilgrimage cathedral of Santiago

Goal of pilgrimage The baroque façade on the Plaza de Obradoiro, with its elaborate twin towers, dominates the large square bearing the same name. Rising from the entrance to the Romanesque crypt beneath (now part of the cathedral museum) is an intertwined, double ramp stairway – gloriously baroque.

Once in through the cathedral door, however, you are back in the old cathedral of the pilgrims (mostly 12th century) and on the site of earlier buildings, destroyed by Almanzor at the end of the 10th century.

First comes the original (now cloaked) portal – the Portico de la Gloria, carved by Master Mateo from 1168. Christ sits at the centre showing his wounded hands, St James below him in intercessionary position. The central column of the Tree of Jesse beneath bears the shapes of thumbs and fingers worn by the millions of right hands of pilgrims placed there, as they bend to bump heads with the statue of Master Mateo, hoping to gain some of his wisdom. There are almost 200 figures in the full assemblage, including the 24 elders of the Apocalypse, King David (centre-left, smiling broadly), and scenes of hell (on the right-hand arch). What prevails, however, is the sense of warmth and joy.

A high gallery, typical of the great pilgrim churches, runs round the cathedral, including the transepts. Above the altar is the glisteningly ugly image of St James. His alleged remains are kept in a casket in a crypt. You may climb up behind the saint to kiss the shell on the back of his gown – the final 'amen' of the pilgrimage.

The cathedral museum, divided into several parts in different places, is an extra to the cathedral visit and of considerably less interest. The best part is the sequence of tapestry galleries.

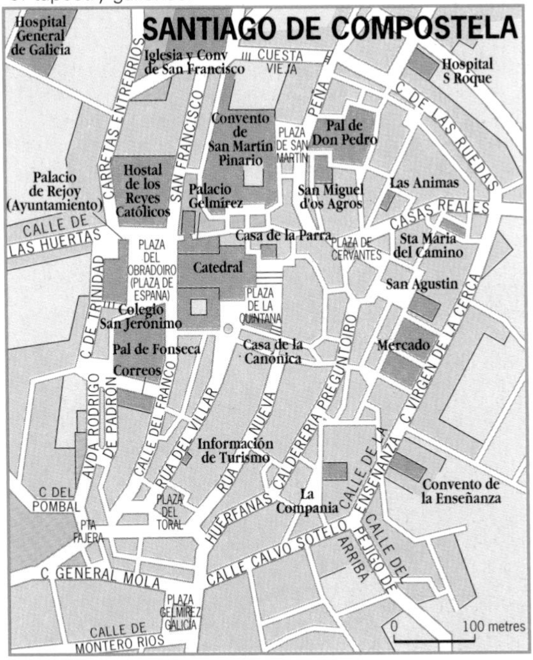

Waiting for the pilgrims... and tourists

▶▷▷ Ribadeo

Ribadeo lies on the Galician side of the mouth of the Eo estuary. The town is scruffy but agreeable. The town hall is the former mansion of Antonio Raimundo Ibañez, founder of the outstanding ceramics works near by at Sargadelos. There are good views over the *ría*.

▶▷▷ San Esteban Dam

The winding Río Sil is dammed in many spots as it makes its way to join the Miño. The biggest and best-loved dam is San Esteban, just west of Ourense. Northeast, at the centre of a circular plain, lies the excellent little town of Monforte de Lemos with castle and monastery.

▶▶▷ Túy (Tui)

The fortified cathedral at Tui, rising above the Río Miño as guardian of the Spanish border, has a stout defensible tower, pinnacles and crenellations. Inside, it is tiny, mostly Gothic with Romanesque traces and Mozarabic horseshoe arches. The old stone-built town gathered round it on the hilltop is charming, with several notable churches and a broad main street reminiscent of English or French market towns.

The most beautiful china in Spain, often in dashing shades of blue, is made at Sargadelos not far from Ribadeo, at the factory set up in the late 18th century by Antonio Raimundo Ibañez, first Marquis of Sargadelos, to provide local employment. Subject of a Goya portrait, Ibañez was killed in mob violence after the French invasion of 1808. His offence: being too keen on French ideas.

▶▷▷ Verín

This small town of decayed spas and excellent mineral waters (among them Fontenova, encountered nationwide) lies in a broad valley. Near by is Monterrey, an isolated hill topped by the most amazing castle-and-church complex in Galicia, once refuge of Pedro I, the Cruel. Castle and tower (open for climbing) provide great views, and the two-storey palace (closed) a touch of grace.

▶▷▷ Vigo

Spain's leading fishing port, this city of 260,000 dominates its *ría*, with heavy traffic and stark apartment blocks. But the old town, just above the Nautico swimming pool on the front – once a terminal for trans-Atlantic liners – offers serene old stone and wrought-iron balconies painted in silver. A neo-classical cathedral replaces the earlier version, burned down in a raid by Francis Drake. The little market of A Pedra (La Piedra in Castilian) sells tobacco and trinkets. Visitors can also buy oysters at the street stalls, then take them into the bars behind, where lemons and white wine are willingly provided. The arches of the one-time waterfront, here called Los Berbes, are full of fish restaurants and young people.

View from Tui across the Miño to Portugal

Drive/Walk Reserva Nacional Dos Ancares

This is a one-day excursion from Becerreá, on the NV1 between Lugo and Ponferrada, involving three to four hours' hard driving, and with several possibilities for walks. It takes the traveller from deeply rustic farmland right up into wild but not very high mountains and finally to Piornedo, a village much restored and popular, but in all essentials a pure, pre-Roman Celtic survival, quite thrilling in its mere existence. It consists in large part of *pallozas* (Celtic round houses).

From Becerreá, follow signs for Navia de Suarna, north on LU722. Ignore first turn at Liber (9km), but 500m further on, turn right for Os Ancares and San Román. Continue on high ridge road (but not when cloud is low).
At **Sete Caballos**, there is a possible there-and-back walk to **Quindos**.

Continue to Degrada.
From here car passengers might have a beautiful 6km walk downhill on the road, for later pick-up by their kindly driver.

Go up again to Donis and 1km further to Piornedo.
Here, after visiting the round houses, explore local paths and trackways.

Return first to Degrada then back to Liber/Puente de Gatín via Doiras, making the journey effectively a triangle.

Walk Exploring Vigo

This walk, uphill then down again, could begin or end at any one of three points depending on energy.

Fit walkers should start at the Piscina Nautico and climb up Calle Carral to the Puerta del Sol.
Note the elaborate turn-of-the-century buildings and a strange statue of a siren on a tall column.

Semi-fit people may join here in Puerta del Sol. Climb up the steps (Baixada a Principe), leaving Vigo's main shopping street, the pedestrian Calle del Principe, to the left.
At the top of the steps, the decayed red-light district lies to the right, unthreatening in daylight.

Turn left, however, up Paseo de Granada, past the town hall and cross the main road.
The least energetic should start here, at the town hall.

Take the steps up towards the cross a short way above, turn right and follow the gently climbing lane, with a park to the left.
You soon pass the round-hut foundations of a Celtic settlement.

Continue on the lane through municipal nurseries, then go up left through the park, and left again along a few metres of road to the castle entrance.
This is the great reward – a gentle garden within the ramparts and splendid views of city, *ría* and environs. (The least fit of all can drive right up to the castle.)
Castle open: 10.00hrs till dusk.

Galician shepherdess

The Rías Bajas, or Lower Inlets, of Galicia's coast

Drive From the Miño to Cabo de Fisterra

See map on page 72.

This is a drive northwards from the mouth of the Miño river on the border with Portugal, following the complicated indentations of the Rías Bajas with Cabo Fisterra (Cabo Finisterre) as its climax. Allow three to four days for a leisurely trip.

Start at the summit of Monte Tecla above La Guardia (A Garda), self-proclaimed Capital of the Lobster. The road passes through a major Romano-Celtic camp.

Follow the road north to Baiona. Left just after the bridge at Ramallosa brings you to the popular but rewarding **Praia America** and after 20km to **Vigo**.

Crossing the Ría de Vigo by motorway bridge, either cut off the next peninsula by proceeding directly overland to Pontevedra, or follow it round to complete the Ría de Vigo and continue to Ría de Pontevedra. Taking the peninsula road you will notice fleets of *bateas*, low ship-like platforms for nurturing shellfish.

After Pontevedra, head west along the northern bank of the ría *to the popular resort of El Grove (O Grove) and the island-resort of La Toja (A Toxa). Continue round the next* ría *(Arosa or Arousa).*
The whole *ría* varies between rurality and over-development. It was at **Padrón**, at the head of the estuary, that the boat from the Mediterranean, bearing the body of St James, is said to have come ashore.

Continue to Ría de Muros y Noia. This is suddenly far wilder. Bizarre headstones in the churchyard of **Noia's** Santa María a Nova record the professions of the deceased from the 9th to 19th centuries. **Muros** on the north shore has an arcaded front and tiny, steep alleyways up to fishermen's cottages.

Follow the road north from Muros. From here, views of Fisterra and the beautiful beach of Carnota emerge. At **Cabo Fisterra** itself, there is a real sense of being at the Land's End of Europe, the point beyond which – till 1492 – there was no venturing.

THE NORTH COAST

Northern Spain's encounter with the Atlantic is conducted, above all, in shades of green: meadows tilting down from the deeper green of pine forests, and the more varied green of deciduous woods.
Where land meets sea there are often rocks and cliffs – and scores of sandy beaches, ranging from super-smart town beaches to wild and little visited corners. The coastal towns themselves are hugely varied: elegant San Sebastián and smoke-belching Bilbao (both Basque cities); Santander, university city and capital of the Cantabria region; and Oviedo, capital of Asturias. You will not reach Oviedo without passing by the Picos de Europa, to many the most thrilling mountains in Spain. This coast is green, of course, because it rains here – not all the time but enough to make it totally different from Spain's Mediterranean costas.

In the gazetteer entries below, where both Castilian and Basque place names are given, the Basque appears in brackets after the Castilian.

▶▶▷ **Bilbao (Bilbo)**
Basque Bilbao, once Castile's great wool port, is now the steel and chemicals town to beat them all. Locals call it El Botxo (The Hole). Seen from the motorway, it is a concentration of apartment blocks and smoking industry. Inside is a solidly gracious 19th-century centre, badly polluted river and interesting old town. The **Museo de Bellas Artes** (Parque de Doña Casilda) is one of Spain's best regional galleries. The 1890s Teatro de Arriaga is 19th-century fake rococo; the Gothic 15th-century catedral de Santiago has a huge porch; and the San Antón was a centre of Basque resistance to Franco. The Begoña sanctuary, with good views of the city, may be reached by elevator from Calle Esperanza Ascao.

▶▷▷ **Cervatos**
Going southwest from Santander, 5km south of Reinosa, the collegiate church of Cervatos rises over a hamlet with cobbled streets. It has elaborate carvings, (some very erotic), and a set of gargoyles.

An unusual use of oxen in Bilbao

All along the north coast you see *Las Casas de los Indianos* (the Houses of the Indians). Latin American emigrants who returned home with bulging wallets were known collectively as 'Los Indianos'. Many were from Spain's north coast. They used their savings to build fine houses, most often in the towns and villages of their birth. Many of these mansions are in a serene 19th-century style, often marked with a palm tree as proof of past exoticism.

▶▶▶ Costa de Cantabria

The soft green land behind the sea is dairy country, with pine-clothed hills and mountains and a few outbreaks of fierce grey rock. The coast has good sandy beaches. Though strikingly wave-pounded in bad weather, this is the least daunting stretch of Spain's north coast.

Resorts

Castro-Urdiales is a busy little town, though its maritime promenade is calm and charming. It ends in a raised rock where a castle wraps itself round a modern lighthouse.

Pretty **Comillas** is dominated by buildings in the Barcelona Modernista style, erected in the days when King Alfonso XII came here to relax. Biggest is the hill-top seminary by Domènech i Montaner. The summer palace of the Marquis of Comillas is by Joan Martorell, and a ceramic-laden folly, El Capricho, is by Gaudí.

The little old town of **Laredo**, with cobbled streets and 13th-century church of La Asunción, has sprouted a mini-Miami, along the sandspit that points at Santoña opposite. The resort beach is excellent, the ambience lively. The old town now seems a solid mass of bars and discos.

Noja's curving golden beach, with hills behind, is a delight. The village of **Bareyo**, inland, has a restored Romanesque church.

Santoña has a narrow beach, a fort with an impressive number of gun emplacements, the revered 13th-century church of Santa María del Puerto and a large, brightly painted fishing fleet.

The pleasing estuarine settlement of **San Vicente de la Barquera** is approached from the east by a long low bridge. Its arcaded Plaza Mayor is at river level, while above, on a hill between a meeting-place of rivers, the old town is dominated by the church of Nuestra Señora de los Angeles, Gothic with Romanesque portals.

See also Santander and El Sardinero, page 96.

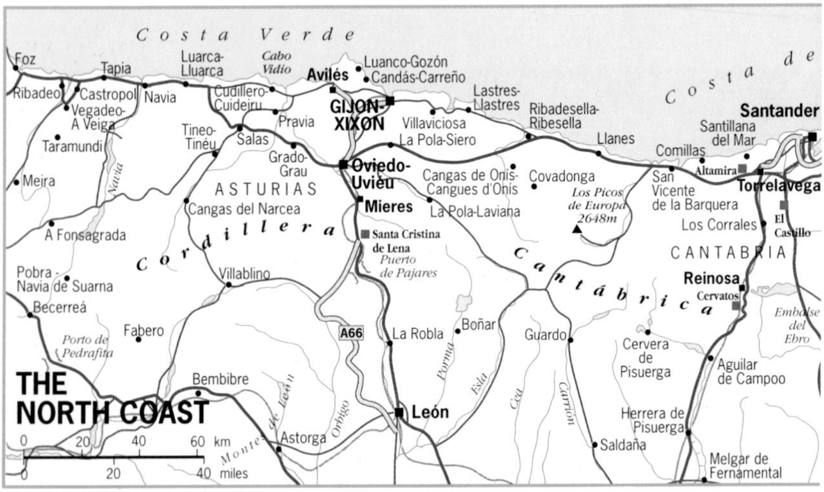

▶▶▶ Costa Vasca

The 'Basque coast' has cliffs and headlands and rivers winding down through pine-covered mountains, each with a fishing port where it meets the sea. Except for San Sebastián and Fuenterrabía (separate entries), it is used mainly by Basques.

Resorts

Bakio has a good wide beach but many apartment blocks. Before you reach it, you will pass the unfinished Lemoniz nuclear power plant, abandoned after ETA bombs (no stopping for 4km). Continuing eastwards, the coastal scenery is magnificent between Bakio and Bermeo, with access to the sanctuary-on-a-rock of San Juan des Gastelguche.

Bermeo, a major fishing port, is one of the four towns where Spanish kings swore to uphold Basque rights. The ceremony took place in Santa Eufemia above the harbour. There is a fisherman's museum in the 'Tower of Ercilla'. Basque fishing boats in primary colours, are brilliant *en masse*.

Elantxobe is thrillingly sited under the rock face of a tall cape. The upper road offers views of harbour and trawlers far below.

A huge rock called El Ratón stands off **Getaria**, joined to it by an isthmus with a fishing harbour. The steep little town sizzles with grilled fish.

Lekeitio is a river-mouth fishing port, with coloured boats, houses with glass balconies and a pinnacled and buttressed church. A pine-clad island stands in the river mouth with an excellent beach beyond. The tortuous but lovely coast between Lekeitio and Ondarroa has high capes, bracken, pine, and eucalyptus.

At **Ondarroa** the river winds round an arrow-point of land, where church and old town rise dramatically. Glass balconies and half-timbered houses abound.

The stately resort of **Zarautz**, popular with the élite of Madrid in the 19th century, has a wide beach, a pair of historic palaces and an attractive main square.

The Basques are great sportsmen and, to a lesser degree in a macho society, sportswomen. Competitive team rowing, town versus town, is very popular – straight out into the fearsome Bay of Biscay, around a buoy and home again, regardless of the weather. Other sports involve chopping logs, shifting enormous weights with teams of oxen (and human assistance) and, especially, *frontón* and *pelota* – ball games played in a walled court. In the former, the ball is struck with the bare hands, which often bleed. In *pelota*, said to be the fastest game on earth, a curved basket is used to hit the ball.

The Basque navigator Juan Sebastián Elcano of Getaria shipped with Magellan in 1521. After Magellan's death in the Philippines, Elcano took charge, becoming the first circumnavigator of the world.

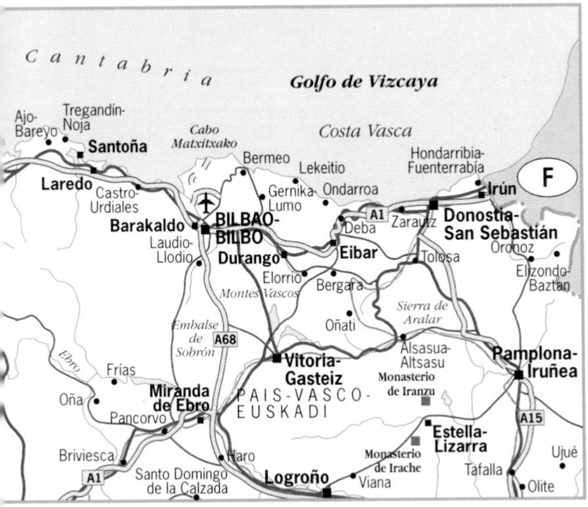

▶▶▶ Costa Verde

The 'Green Coast' is no misnomer for Atlantic Asturias, despite one or two large towns like steel-making Avilés and, especially, Gijón. East of Gijón, the Picos de Europa rise high behind a friendly coastline. Westwards the shore becomes wilder and rockier. There are great beaches all along.

While the rest of the peninsula was in Moorish hands, way back in the 8th century, the Asturians, in their distant fastness, were developing a delicate and assured pre-Romanesque style of architecture. It is seen at its best near Oviedo in the little mountainside church – once probably a palace dining-hall – of Santa María del Naranco. In Oviedo itself, the church of Santullano has very early frescos. Other delightful and strangely moving churches are to be found at Valdedíos near Villaviciosa and at Santa Cristina de Lena.

Resorts and sights – west to east

In the Eo estuary in the far west, **Castropol** has a lovely, boaty feel to it. **Figueras**, closer to the Eo's mouth, is a good spot for food and a bed. There are Atlantic-facing beaches. East towards Luarca is a series of unspoiled fishing villages, white with black slates, among them Viayelez, Ortigueira and Vega.

Midway along the western coast, **Cabo Vidio**, with lighthouse, offers a grand view of cliffs and inset beaches. Hawks hang over the cliff edge; autumn crocuses flower here; winter winds rock parked cars. The best beaches are **El Aguilar** and **Concha de Artedo**.

At **Cudillero** the road winds down a tight valley with just a row or two of cottages on either side, opening up to a substantial fishing port cheerful with fish restaurants.

Lastres, east of Gijón, is another fishing port. A little inland the Mirador de Fito offers fine rural views.

The grey but friendly little town of **Llanes** is an excellent base for exploring the Picos de Europa. There are pretty coves near by at **Celorio**.

Luanco, situated on the cape north of Gijón, is tops for Asturian fish dinners. The road winds down through a defile of fishermen's cottages, to fishing harbour, bars and restaurants.

Ribadesella is a town on a pretty rivermouth with a beach and the cave of **Tito Bustillo** (see page 89). Like Llanes, it is a good base for exploring the Picos de Europa. From Villanueva nearby there is low tide access to the sea caves of **Cuevas del Mar**.

Costa Verde fisherman with his catch

A corner of deserted Veigas, 18th-century time capsule

Walk Taramundi

Taramundi is a deeply rural area of hills and valleys, woods and meadows just within the western limits of Asturias and south of the delightful Eo estuary. Historically it has been desperately poor. In the mid-1980s the local community decided, against the odds, to open their forgotten countryside to visitors. They built a small hotel, provided a few rooms to let, and put up wooden signboards to steer their visitors around a network of paths and lanes.

Another age-old feature of the area, since time immemorial, has been the production of hand made steel blades, tools and, especially, clasp-knives in tiny forges in individual homes and one-man workshops. Power for flour-milling was, and still is, provided by small streams pelting down the valley bottoms. The little mills, in the last half century, have also produced a faltering supply of electricity, replaced only over the past ten years by the mains.

All these peculiarities combine with a sense of nature abundant on all sides to make this one of Spain's most pleasing areas for walks or strolls – no skills needed at all, since it is virtually impossible to get lost.

The most obvious walking circuit is to drop down from Taramundi on its hillside, cross the little river of La Salgueira and ascend to the right. Take a left-hand turn for Esquios and ascend for about 3km to the knife workshop of Manuel Lombardia. Now follow the path straight along the wooded valleyside, clothed with oak, birch and chestnut, as far as Veigas.

Veigas is an almost perfectly preserved 18th-century hamlet, without plastic or concrete, but now almost entirely empty.

To return by the same route provides beautiful and markedly different perspectives. Most walkers, however, continue the walk by taking the track on to Texois.

Texois is a remarkable combination of flour-mill, generator and forge. Far larger than most, the forge has a water-powered oak-beam hammer, on record since the 17th century. The site is believed by locals to have been in use since Roman times.

Now return by lane to Taramundi, as signposted.

The total walk takes 4–5hrs, or 3hrs only if to Veigas and return.

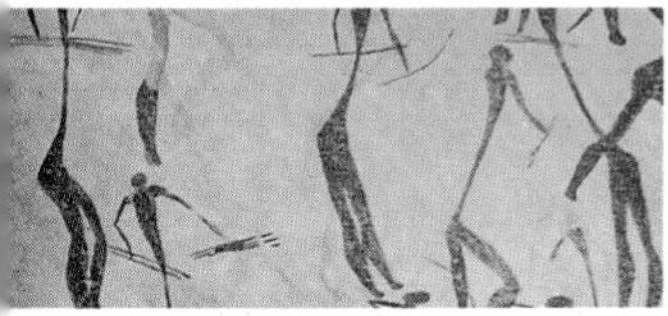

■ Northern Spain possesses an extraordinary and wonderful phenomenon – scores of painted caves, decorated by their palaeolithic inhabitants, between 25,000 and 10,000 years ago, with a brilliant array of naturalistic animals. .....■

Altamira was discovered in 1868 by a local man following his dog. He told the Santander lawyer and antiquarian, Marcelino Sanz de Sautuola. Ten years later Sautuola came to investigate, eyes fixed firmly on the ground in the manner of the ardent excavator. It was his bored daughter María, waving the lantern about, who first saw the great painted ceiling. '*Mira, papa*,' she called, '*bueyes pintados*!' – 'Look Daddy, painted oxen!'

Early theory held the cave paintings were a form of sympathetic magic as an aid to hunting. It is now known, however, that the animals most frequently hunted were not those most frequently painted. Present speculation suggests that the paintings were somehow connected with fertility – particular animals, regardless of their gender, possibly repesenting male and female. There are certainly painted signs and even depictions of parts of the human body which have explicit sexual reference. Respectable scholars have suggested that Altamira was not only an inhabited cave but a sanctuary concerned with fertility rites.

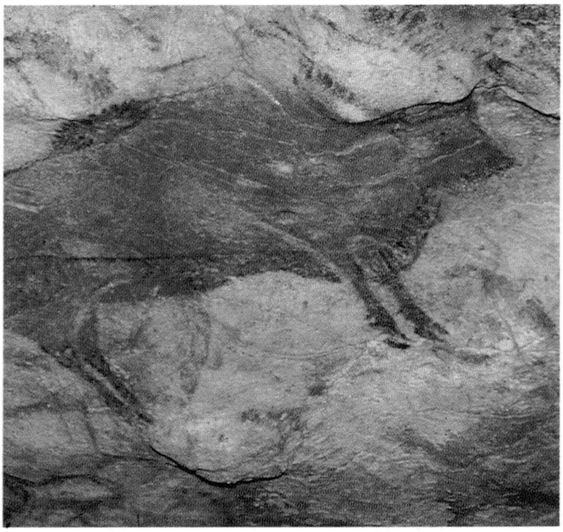

One of the famous Altamira bison

Altamira is the name everybody has heard of. This is the series of caverns near Santillana del Mar where a herd of bison painted in red ochre dating from around 12,000BC was discovered in 1879. Despite the painstaking presentation of the first analysis of the paintings by Marcelino Sanz de Sautuola, many of Europe's scholars promptly declared them a fake. Their authenticity has now been long established and more than 80 other painted caves have been discovered right across the Basque Country, Cantabria and Asturias. The observation and sure technique displayed in the paintings remain astonishing, but their meaning, or at least the intention of the painters, remains elusive.
Most of the paintings are of animals, with bison predominating, and horses, deer and wild goats in lesser numbers. Many engravings are of deer. There are also representations of wild boar, aurochs, elk and wolves.

The gallery of the bison, once part of the main entrance cave but now shielded by a specially built rock wall, is one of the most staggering sights of Spain. Up to two metres long, moving, mooing, curled up and even looking at their own tails, the deep red beasts spread over the ceiling, accompanied by a few animals of other species. Taking advantage of bosses and protrusions in the rock surface to gain effects of realism and animation, the ceiling gives the strong impression of being a single composition. The galleries beyond contain large numbers of line paintings, engravings and signs, and even, in a deep recess not shown to visitors, a weird human mask.

Atmosphere changes caused by visitors began to threaten the paintings and the cave was closed in 1977. It reopened in 1982, but now admits only 10 to 40 visitors a day, depending on atmospheric conditions. Groups of five spend ten minutes in the bison gallery, 20 in the rest of the cave. Write at least six months in advance to: **Centro de Investigación de Altamira**, Santillana del Mar, Santander. The 90,000 who come each year without getting in get some enjoyment from the rural situation, a small museum and a nearby cave with stalactites. If you arrive early and a place has not been taken up, you may even get in on the same day.

Puente Viesgo The cave of El Castillo, south of Torrelavega and near Puente Viesgo (300 maximum each day – first come, first admitted), makes the liveliest substitute for Altamira. There are striking and important representations of animals and human hands, and formalised shapes or signs which may stand for women or for female sexual organs. When El Castillo has had its complement of visitors other caves in the complex may be opened.

Pindal This magically sited cave runs inwards from a cleft above the sea, full of early primroses and violets in spring, blackberries in summer. The main painted surface, with three clear animals – one arguably a wild boar – and a row of strange signs which may be hunting implements or human figures, lies some 260m deep into the cave. There is also the rarity of a painted fish, not shown to visitors for conservation reasons.

Another cave at Ribadesella in Asturias, discovered in the late 1960s, may disappoint non-specialists since many of the paintings are faint. This is Tito Bustillo. There is, however, a great variety of animals, including two fine horses, one in bold head-and-shoulders outline. Multiple images are curiously superimposed, and there is a set of red ochre signs, or drawings, universally accepted as representing the human vulva.

The hand of palaeolithic man on a cave wall

Picasso's huge monochrome painting entitled *Guernica* is often claimed to be the greatest painting of the 20th century. It was the result of a commission for the Spanish (Republican) Pavilion in a Paris exhibition during the Civil War. Picasso accepted the commission, but started on the picture only after the bombing of Gernika. He was determined the painting should not hang in Spain while Franco ruled, and it spent many years in New York, entering the Prado collection only in 1981

▶▷▷ Durango

Durango is a busy main road town with pretty corners, especially by the old town gate with bridge and church of Santa Ana. There is an attractive drive south to the pass – and shrine – of Urkiola. Elorrio, to the southeast, has many heraldically emblazoned mansions.

▶▶▷ Fuenterrabía (Hondarribia)

Looking into France at the mouth of the Río Bidasoa, Fuenterrabía is a charming spot. La Marina, the lower town, centres on the *alameda* in Calle de San Pedro. Above is the castle of Charles V, now a parador. Noble houses run up the hill; the Calle Mayor, running away down the far side with wide eaves and stone houses, is even more attractive. The beach faces the river mouth.

▷▷▷ Gijón (Xixon)

Now a large town, lively but ugly, Gijón wants to be considered the capital of Asturias. It has a fine (crowded) beach, a pretty fishing district and a sculptural monument by Eduardo Chillida on a cliff west of town.

▶▶▷ Guernica (Gernika)

An undistinguished market town near a lovely estuary, Gernika, to give it its Basque name, was one of four sacred places where Spanish monarchs swore to uphold Basque rights. On 26 April 1937, Franco's German allies attacked Gernika from the air in Europe's first mass air attack on a civilian target. The remains of the sacred tree of the Basques stand under a cupola beside the Casa de Juntas or Batzar-Etxea (open to the public), where the Basque parliament holds occasional meetings.

Palacio de Revillajigedo in Gijón

Carving in Oviedo cathedral

▶▷▷ **Navia, Valle de**
The ascent of the Navia valley from the coast leads into deep Asturias (follow the western bank). Shortly beyond Coana, a conical green hill is densely covered with ruins of a Celtic settlement. Soon the hills climb sharply higher, the river itself mostly dark reservoir. Hamlets are white or grey, amenities almost non-existent.

▶▷▷ **Oñate (Oñati)**
Though close to industrial Mondragón, Oñati is massively monumental, with the former Basque university (16th-century), the church of San Miguel and its tombs, the town hall and old town. Once headquarters of the Carlist pretender, modern Oñati is deeply committed to Basque separatism.

▶▶▷ **Oviedo (Uviéu)**
Persist with Oviedo. Despite its initial greyness, it has a fine old town, lively with students, under the single spire of a famous cathedral.The **cathedral** has 14th-century cloisters. The building itself is mainly Flamboyant Gothic but contains the early Asturian 'Cámara Santa' where the rich treasury includes the cross supposedly carried by Pelayo at the Battle of Covadonga (see page 92). From the cathedral take La Rua and Cimadevilla towards the town hall. One street before the arch, the fish market is on the left, surrounded by restaurants. Through the arch and down right is Fontán, a fruit and vegetable market centred round an old arcaded square. Dark and threatening palaces abound. The **archaeological museum** has early Asturian carved stonework. The **Museo de Bellas Artes** has 19th- and 20th-century Asturian painting.

▷▷▷ **Pasajes (Pasaia)**
Effectively the industrial port of San Sebastián, this one-time whaling community has three villages with different saints' days and a proportionately festive disposition. It retains pretty views across the river; French writer Victor Hugo lived in the village of San Juan, right on the water, while in exile in 1843.

The Basque Ignacio de Loyola (1491–1556), future saint and founder of the Jesuits, was born Iñigo López Recalde in the family mansion of Loyola just by Azpeitia to the south of San Sebastián. As a young soldier, he received a near-fatal wound in a battle at Pamplona. While recuperating, he devised the spiritual exercises that were to be so important both for the Jesuit order and the future of Catholicism. The large monastery at Loyola incorporates the room of the older house in which the saint was born.

Oviedo was springboard for the recapture of León in the Middle Ages, and so for the emergence of the kingdom of Castile. In 1934, as centre of the Asturian coalfield, it was site of a miners' revolution, bloodily suppressed by the young General Francisco Franco. Now recovering from the decline of coal, Oviedo is finding a new identity.

■ The Picos de Europa rise close to the north Atlantic coast. Essentially a gaunt limestone massif divided into three by a series of gorges and rivers, they culminate in great stone spires which rise to more than 2,640m, far more impressive than their height suggests. .....■

The medieval stone bridge at Cangas de Onis

The peaks are harsh and exposed, but the deep valleys are calm and sheltered, harbouring Mediterranean plants and a local architecture of stone and tile that looks as if it has grown from the green meadows. Some of the finest parts of the range – only 40km east to west and 20km north to south – are included within the Covadonga National Park.
The trouble with the Picos is that it rains or snows here half the days of the year. Mists linger for weeks. But those who achieve a clear view of these mountains never forget them.

Covadonga Back in the 8th century, only one small area and one people held out against the Moors – the stout Asturians, under their leader Pelayo, in the Picos valley of Covadonga in the northwest corner of the range. Here, the final refuge was a shallow cave. The story, devoutly believed by all Spaniards, is that Pelayo and his men, assisted by the Holy Cross and the Virgin of Battles, trounced 20,000 Moors sent after them in AD724. Pelayo became king; and the Christian Reconquest, or Reconquista, now began. As well as the cave and Virgin, there is a huge basilica, a choir school, a Civil Guards barracks and considerable numbers of tourist shops. The National Park extends high to the southeast, with a small road to two mountain lakes. The views are wonderful.

A round tour of the peaks
The tour includes some walking suggestions. Four-wheel drive vehicles may be hired for the high terrain.
Cangas de Onís Begin here, before the mountains start, in the northwest corner (easily reached from Oviedo or Ribadesella). There is a pleasant atmosphere, a medieval bridge and a chance to buy *cabrales*, the fierce cheese of the region. Covadonga is 7km into the base of the mountains.
Arenas de Cabrales Eastwards from Cangas, the soft valley soon narrows for a first real glimpse of rock. Just past Carreño, the Mirador del Pozo de la Oración offers views of Naranjo de Bulnes (2,519m), the majestic column of rock on which the Picos centre. Arenas is not so special, but the road south leads to the Cares Gorge, dividing eastern and western massifs.
There is a tremendous walk here from Poncebos through the gorge to Caín and on to Posada de Valdeón, with high path and bridges across the cleft.

The green valleys of the Picos de Europa provide good grazing

Panes Continuing east from Arenas, follow the Cares river to Panes, another point of entry to the Picos.

Desfiladero de la Hermida From Panes, a twisting limestone gorge climbs slowly south, eagles and vultures wheeling above. Tucked away by Lebeña is the 10th-century Mozarabic church of Santa María, with Byzantine-style roof and Moorish-style horseshoe arches on its belfry.

Potes Before Potes, the road enters the beautiful and wide Liébana valley with views up to the eastern Picos massif. (Conversely, there is a fine drive northwards to Potes, through the Cordillera Cantábrica from Cervera de Pisuerga.) Potes has a castle, and a holiday atmosphere.

Fuente Dé From Potes, drive up northwest to Fuente Dé, where a parador stands under a vast rock wall and a cable car ascends. There is a 1½-hour walk up from the higher cable-car station (taxing in its second half) through pure limestone to the Veronica refuge. Before the refuge, up round the corner to the right, there are staggering views of Naranco de Bulnes and its mountain cirque.

San Glorio Pass/Collado de Llesba Returning to Potes, ascend the ravishing San Glorio pass to the west. At the top, take the dirt road right to Collado de Llesba (1km), where you will find a sad-faced 'Monument to the Bear', views of the central Picos, and the Cordillero Cantabrica behind you.

Posada de Valdeón Continuing west, turn north at Portilla de la Reina. From the Pandetrave pass, there are more views of the central massif and at last a clear sight of the rock spires of the western group. Drop down into the valley of Valdeón, continuing to Caín for the southern entry to the Cares Gorge (see page 92).

Panderruedas Pass On the way up and west from Valdeón, this is another great viewing point for the western massif (climb for 5 minutes up to the right).

Desfiladero de los Beyos (Beyos Gorge). This limestone slit descends to Cangas, marking the western limits of the Picos.

Beach life in San Sebastián

The Iberian brown bear is a dwindling and desperately threatened species. The few survivors live almost exclusively in the Reserva Nacional de Somiedo, southwest of Oviedo. The reserve, which includes both the crest of the Cantabrian Cordillera and the deep lake of Salienca, also has a population of wolves and golden eagles.

San Sebastián is mad on festivals and sports, with rowing regattas (September), wood-chopping contests (any time), and bands composed of children, all smartly dressed in Napoleonic uniforms. The latter feature in the famous San Sebastián *tamborada* (January).

▶▶▶ San Sebastián (Donostia)

San Sebastián is an elegant seaside city, the leading resort on the north coast. Its greatest asset is its situation – a near-perfect circle of bay, the entrance guarded on either side by a single steep hill and with the pretty little island of Santa Clara right in the middle. An old town and fishing harbour are tucked in behind Monte Urgull, the guardian hill on the eastern side, surmounted by castle remnants and a gigantic statue of Christ.

A royal past Round the rest of the bay, in the late 19th century, there grew up a classic Belle Epoque resort. This was above all thanks to Queen Isabella II, who began to come here from 1845, when her doctors recommended sea-bathing to cure a skin complaint. By 1893 Queen María Cristina had built the royal palace of Miramar right in the centre of the bay, in brick and tile and with half-timbered gables, using an English architect to achieve a Queen Anne 'cottage' effect (nowadays it is used as a summer university). A casino – now the town hall, elaborate in brownish stone – went up in 1887. Visitors included Bismarck and Napoleon III, Sarah Bernhardt and King Leopold of Belgium. The Spanish court came here each summer.

Fashion and food San Sebastián is still elegant, with well-dressed citizens, its own designers and scores of small fashion shops. Main streets for these are Urbieto, the Boulevard (Alameda del Boulevard) and Avenida (the Avenida de la Libertad). By contrast, the old town is agreeably thronged with counter-culture dressers. Apart from its summer beach life, the other great feature of San Sebastián is the food – bars serve elaborate tapas and restaurants offer Spain's finest cuisine, largely based on fish. Behind this lies a unique phenomenon – more than 120 men-only gastronomic clubs, whose members meet to cook each other elaborate meals. The setting for these is rather like a restaurant – but one where all are free to enter the kitchen.

Churches Santa María, close to the fishing harbour, has a fine Churrigueresque façade. Gothic San Vicente, deeper in the old town, holds services in Basque.

Museums The provincial museum occupies the former Dominican monastery of San Telmo, in the old town. The permanent exhibition round the cloister concentrates on Basque life and painting. The Palacio del Mar (Palace of the Sea), above the fishing harbour, has an aquarium. Nearby is a small museum of seafaring.

Boats leave for the tiny hop to the island of Santa Clara from just beneath the information kiosk in San Sebastián's harbour (100m from the town hall). It's the top spot for Sunday afternoons in summer.

Walk San Sebastián: around the bay

Go left along the front from the town hall.

You soon pass the **Hotel de Londres y de Inglaterra**, marking the early arrival of the British in the resort and now with a casino. On your right all the way, crowded but lively in summer, with cafés and changing rooms tucked in beneath the road, are the sands of the beach of **La Concha**. This is interrupted by a spit of land, site of the royal palace of Miramar, and the continuation of the beach is known as Ondarreta. Locals regard **Ondarreta** as smarter than La Concha.

After the beach, up left behind the tennis courts, there is a funicular railway to Monte Igueldo.

On this western peak guarding the bay are viewing points and a fun-fair.

Continuing at sea-level, the walk ends at El Peine de los Vientos (the Comb of the Winds).

This consists of iron sculptures like alphabet spaghetti, by the distinguished Basque artist Eduardo Chillida.

Walk Monte Urgull

Start at the casino, leave the fishing harbour on your left and carry on round. Cross back through the old town.

The old town is an area for wandering – and, incidentally, enjoying tapas. Burned out in the Napoleonic wars, except for its churches, it is nevertheless highly atmospheric, especially the arcaded Plaza de la Constitución, which was once used as a bullring.

Climbing Urgull is a little more arduous (180m to the top), though the gravel paths pass through the shade of woods.

Part way up , there is a monument to British soldiers who died in 1813 defending the castle on top which now contains a military museum.

One of San Sebastián's quieter quarters: elegant houses along the Rio Urumea

Drive Alto Campoo

Just beneath the mountains in the deep south of Cantabria, west from Reinosa, take the high valley into the Alto Campoo (High Country).
At 5km is the sleepy village of **Fontibre**, with the source of the Ebro in a poplar-filled dip to the left. Park and walk down. The river runs out under loose stones into pools of milky blue.

Continuing, the road leads up past the skiing station of Braña Vieja towards the final watershed (a short walk from Fuente de Chico car park). Rivers descend from here in three directions: to the Atlantic north coast, to the Atlantic west (the Duero system) and to the Mediterranean (Ebro system). Magnificent!

One of the advantages of being a Spanish aristocrat in times gone by was that you were exempt from all taxes. The inhabitants of the north coast sought to make an unfair system fairer by spreading noble titles as widely as they could. In some places, the whole population was simply declared noble – a tax dodge to beat all others. Heraldry and aristocratic emblems are perhaps even more common here than elsewhere in Spain – Santillana del Mar is a case in point.

▶▶▷ Santander

Santander lies at the mouth of a wide bay. Rebuilt after a fire in 1941, the city offers good beaches (see El Sardinero below), and the agreeable ambience of a port, seaside and university town. Out on the promontory, in public gardens, is La Magdalena, the summer palace of King Alfonso XIII. You can visit the austere home of the great conservative scholar Marcelino Menéndez y Pelayo (1856–1912), opposite his 42,000-volume library and the Museo de Bellas Artes. The much remodelled Gothic cathedral is built over a 13th-century crypt. The new Festival Theatre is on the waterfront .

▶▶▶ Santillana del Mar

This beautiful village is composed of stone-built mansions, dripping with heraldic emblems and backing on to meadows. Look out for the home of the Marquis of Santillana and the Casa de los Hombrones. The Romanesque collegiate church of **Santa Juliana** has magnificent carved capitals in the cloister. Use the same ticket for the museum of religious art in the **Convento de Regina Coeli** on the far side of the main road.

▶▷▷ El Sardinero

Beach, resort and suburb of Santander, El Sardinero has a casino, hotels, restaurants, turn-of-the-century mansions and modern apartments. Good nightlife in summer, but the beach gets crowded.

Balconied old houses in Santillana del Mar

Bridge in the 'High Country' – Alto Campoo

▶▷▷ **Villaviciosa**

Villaviciosa is a surprisingly monumental little town tucked into Asturian countryside behind Tazones on the coast – where Charles V landed by mistake in 1517 on his first arrival in Spain. The house in which the future emperor stayed is Calle del Agua 31. The early Asturian church of **Valdediós** is sited in rural tranquillity 10km south with adjacent monastery under restoration.

▶▶▷ **Vitoria (Gasteiz)**

As home of the tumultuous Basque parliament since the 1980s, Vitoria is often on Spanish TV screens. The modern town is surprisingly calm and bourgeois in appearance. The old town, on a hill above, is striking.

In the **new town** are the pleasing Parque de la Florida and the neo-classical new cathedral, the Basque parliament and the arcaded 18th-century Plaza de España, built to accommodate the town hall. Here, the Plaza de la Virgen Blanca, surrounded by glazed balconies, starts to ascend the hill.

Once you are in the **old town**, steps lead up to the church of San Miguel, with a large portico and carved tympanum. The Virgen Blanca (White Virgin) stands outside in a kind of sentry box of black marble and tinted glass. To the right, an arcaded walking street, Los Arquillos, passes through the middle levels of a Renaissance building on the hillside. Behind it, and beneath the hilltop church of San Vicente, is the historic Plaza del Machete. The hilltop has two palaces, and it ends with the agreeable Gothic old cathedral. Dropping down steeply on the far side of the hill are several restored medieval mansions, among them El Portalón.

There are antique shop-fronts in the Calle (or Kalea) Correria, an archaeological museum and museums of fine art – and of playing cards.

▷▷▷ **Zumaya (Zumaia)**

In this Basque town, the house and studio of the Basque painter Ignacio Zuloaga (1870–1945) is joined to an ancient chapel in what was once a halting place for Santiago pilgrims.

Vitoria's Plaza del Machete gets its name from a genuine machete, a kind of straight-edged scythe for hacking at undergrowth. In the good old days of the Basque rights, or *fueros*, every 1 January, the mayor of Vitoria would take up his stance here facing the town's representative in the national parliament. The latter had to swear to defend local rights under pain of beheading by the official machete. The ceremony ceased with the loss of Basque *fueros* in 1841.

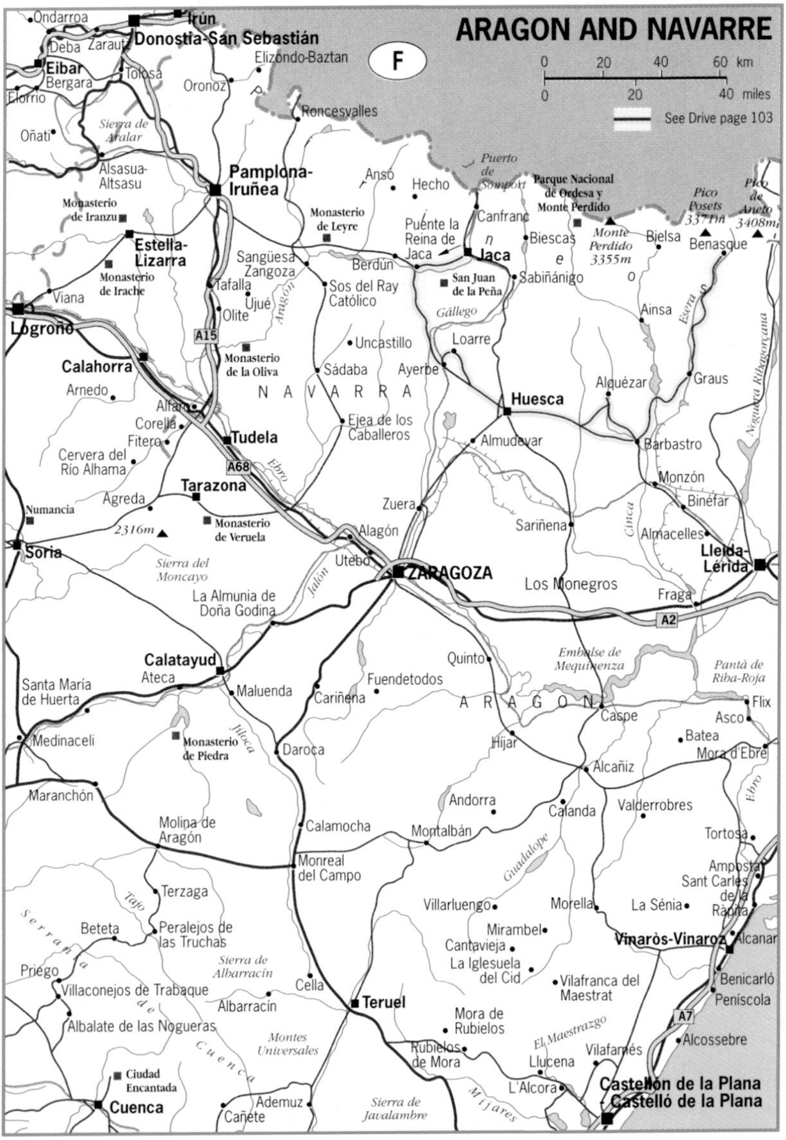
ARAGON AND NAVARRE
F
0 20 40 60 km
0 20 40 miles
See Drive page 103
Ondarroa
Irún
Donostia-San Sebastián
Deba
Zarautz
Eibar
Bergara
Elorrio
Tolosa
Elizondo-Baztan
Oronoz
Roncesvalles
Oñati
Sierra de Aralar
Alsasua-Altsasu
Pamplona-Iruñea
Monasterio de Iranzu
Estella-Lizarra
Monasterio de Irache
Viana
Logroño
Monasterio de Leyre
Ansó
Hecho
Puerto de Somport
Parque Nacional de Ordesa y Monte Perdido
Pico Posets 3371m
Pico de Aneto 3408m
Canfranc
Puente la Reina de Jaca
Jaca
Biescas
Monte Perdido 3355m
Bielsa
Benasque
Sangüesa Zangoza
Berdún
San Juan de la Peña
Sabiñánigo
Tafalla
Ujué
Olite
Sos del Ray Católico
Gállego
Aragón
Uncastillo
Loarre
Ainsa
Esera
Noguera Ribagorçana
A15
Monasterio de la Oliva
Calahorra
Arnedo
Sádaba
Ayerbe
N A V A R R A
Alquézar
Graus
Huesca
Alfaro
Corella
Fitero
Tudela
Ejea de los Caballeros
Almudévar
Barbastro
Cervera del Río Alhama
A68
Ebro
Monzón
Tarazona
Binéfar
Agreda
Numancia
Monasterio de Veruela
2316m
Zuera
Sariñena
Cinca
Almacelles
Alagón
Soria
Sierra del Moncayo
Utebo
Jalón
ZARAGOZA
Lleida-Lérida
Los Monegros
La Almunia de Doña Godina
Fraga
A2
Calatayud
Ateca
Quinto
Embalse de Mequinenza
Pantà de Riba-Roja
Santa María de Huerta
Maluenda
Fuendetodos
Cariñena
A R A G O N
Flix
Caspe
Asco
Medinaceli
Monasterio de Piedra
Jiloca
Daroca
Híjar
Batea
Mora d'Ebre
Alcañiz
Ebro
Maranchón
Andorra
Calanda
Valderrobres
Molina de Aragón
Calamocha
Montalbán
Tortosa
Guadalope
Monreal del Campo
Amposta
Sant Carles de la Ràpita
Terzaga
Tajo
Villarluengo
Morella
La Sénia
Serranía de Cuenca
Beteta
Peralejos de las Truchas
Mirambel
Cantavieja
Vinaròs-Vinaroz
Alcanar
Sierra de Albarracín
La Iglesuela del Cid
Priego
Villaconejos de Trabaque
Cella
Vilafranca del Maestrat
Benicarló
Albarracín
Teruel
Peñíscola
Albalate de las Nogueras
Mora de Rubielos
A7
Montes Universales
El Maestrazgo
Alcossebre
Rubielos de Mora
Llucena
Vilafamés
Ciudad Encantada
Mijares
L'Alcora
Castellón de la Plana
Castelló de la Plana
Cuenca
Ademuz
Sierra de Javalambre
Cañete

ARAGON AND NAVARRE

Too often imagined as an empty space between the Basque Country and Catalonia, Aragon and Navarre (Aragón and Navarra in Spanish) together occupy some of the most dramatically beautiful – if challenging – of Spanish landscapes.

The land Both regions come tilting down from the high Pyrenees. To the west, in Navarre, the mountains are often moist and misty, subject to Atlantic weather. Aragon is higher and more 'continental' – hotter and colder by turns and very much drier in summer. From the Pyrenean foothills, the land stretches out southwards, with vines and fruit and what might be called temperate farming. Next, the basin of the River Ebro runs through, west to east, agriculturally rich but often dreary in appearance. In Navarre, the Ebro area is known as La Ribera (the river-bank), and it marks the southern border of the region. Aragon stretches on far to the south of the Ebro, gaunt, sometimes tremendous, sometimes threatening, to reach such mountain ranges as the Montes Universales in the southwest and the formidable Maestrazgo in the southeast.
Physically, the visitor perceives Aragon and Navarre as one – and linked in their northern reaches by the passage of the Pilgrims' Way to Santiago de Compostela. Historically, the two regions could scarcely be more different.

Aragon's past Aragon, larger and usually more important in Spanish affairs than Navarre, had its beginnings high in the Pyrenees in a pocket of resistance to the Moors. Little by little the infant kingdom advanced from Jaca, through Huesca and Tarazona and finally to Zaragoza, retaking the city in 1118. Zaragoza up to that time had been the major centre of Moorish civilisation in northern Spain; Moorish subjects, now known as Moriscos, stayed on and constituted the majority of the population until expelled in 1609. The result is that while the northern part of the region has its fine Romanesque and, later, European-influenced Christian buildings, the south is Spain's grandest repository of the Mudéjar, the immensely evocative architectural forms created by Moriscos, working for Christian masters.
Almost from the start, Aragon looked east, forming a dynastic alliance with Catalonia (1137) and sharing in Catalonia's medieval empire. It produced Ferdinand of Aragon, husband of Castile's Isabella, then gradually over the centuries was forced into submission to a centralised Spain. Nowadays, though Zaragoza flourishes, the rural areas of Aragon are seriously depopulated. The people are vigorous and friendly, loud-voiced, and famous for calling a spade a spade.

Navarre's independent spirit Where Aragon looked east to Catalonia, Navarre, by contrast, looked north and west, to France and the Basque Country. Though much of the population was originally Basque, that identity is not so visible today, except in the northwest. Always aloof from the Spanish mainstream, Navarre was in fact

Roofs and towers of Calatayúd. This largely Mudéjar town once guarded the Aragonese frontier

Ferdinand of Aragon (1452–1516) was a teenager when he married Isabella of Castile. The two together became the strongest force the post-Roman peninsula had seen. They captured Granada, the last bastion of the Moors, in 1492, set up the Inquisition and laid the foundations of modern Spain. One of Ferdinand's last great coups was the annexation of Navarre. Foxy and devious, Ferdinand was hailed by Machiavelli as a 'new prince' who had risen from weakness to become 'for fame and glory, the first king of Christendom'.

ruled by a French dynasty from 1234 until its annexation to Spain by Ferdinand of Aragon in 1512. From then on, it struggled to hold on to its local rights and freedoms, launching a series of bloody civil wars in the 19th century under the banner of Carlism, a reactionary, romantic creed. The Carlists were still one of the strongest forces supporting General Franco in the 20th-century Spanish Civil War. Conservative, temperamentally rugged and full of the relics of a battling past, Navarre has one visitor 'spectacular' above all others – Pamplona's fiesta of San Fermín with the world-famous running of the bulls.

▶▶▷ **Albarracín**

This small town on the edge of the Montes Universales, an independent state from 1165 to 1333, is one of the most strikingly sited in all Spain and remarkably unspoiled. Arriving from Teruel, you see the whole façade of the town rising vertically before you in a concave crescent, brown ochre to strawberry in colour. Streets are narrow with overhanging first storeys. The walls are impressive; so is the high silhouette of the small cathedral. There are numerous cave paintings in the sierra to the south.

▶▷▷ **Alcañiz**

A messy town in parts, Alcañiz has an old quarter running back from the River Guadalope to the impressive Plaza de España. Look out for the Renaissance town hall and the baroque façade of the town's huge collegiate church. The castle, now a parador, was one of the leading centres of the Knights of Calatrava.

▷▷▷ Alquézar

A few kilometres north of Barbastro, Alquézar is noted for the beauty of its setting and its collegiate church, on the site of a Moorish *alcázar* (fortress).

▷▷▷ Alsasua (Altsasu)

This Navarrese town is an historic centre of commerce at a meeting place of mountains. The landscape of harsh, rocky cliffs above green pastures and ancient woods, offers memorable approaches.

▷▷▷ Barbastro

Barbastro is undistinguished except for its cathedral – on the site where Petronila of Aragon married Ramón Berenguer IV of Catalonia in 1137, establishing Spain's grandest medieval alliance. There's a huge 16th-century retablo by Damián Forment.

▶▶▶ Baztán

The Arcadian Baztan valley – the valley of the Bidasoa river – green with meadow and forest, runs down from the low peaks of the western Pyrenees, becoming steeper and more dramatic as it nears the sea. The towns of Aranaz, Lesaca, Vera de Bidasoa, Yanci and **Echalar** once formed the famous local alliance of the Cinco Villas. Echalar is the most impressive with huge harmonious homesteads, mighty stones around their doors and windows. The town of **Elizondo** has fine old mansions along the river, heavy with the armorial bearings of emigrants returned from the Americas.

▶▷▷ Benasque

This pretty, stone-built town, northeast of Huesca, with such historic buildings as the Renaissance palace of the Counts of Ribazorga and the 13th-century church of San Marcial, is now expanding rapidly as a centre for skiers.

▶▶▷ Calatayúd

This dilapidated but engaging Mudéjar town lies below a ruined castle and the grey cliffs bounding the valley of the River Jalón. After centuries of neglect, attempts are being made today to restore its notable brick-patterned churches, Santa María and San Andrés. The age-worn, part-arcaded Plaza de España is a delight. Elsewhere, in lanes in the old town no wider than an arm-span, walls bulge ominously. Leave the main road here for the outstanding 12th-century **Monasterio de Piedra**, about 28km to the south (see page 107).

▶▷▷ Daroca

Daroca, once a well-to-do medieval craft centre, has shrunk back within the great but ruinous walls and towers surrounding it, a dwarf in giant's clothing. Glimpses from the main road above are a temptation to enter by the upper gate and pass downhill along a winding cobbled street, with another fine gateway, carrying the imperial arms of Charles V, at the Jiloca river exit far below. The collegiate church of Santa María and the church of San Miguel are the main monuments. **Maluenda** has a notable Mudéjar tower and church.

The poet and epigrammatist Martial (AD40–104) was born in Bilbilis, a recently excavated Roman city 3km from Calatayúd. He prided himself on his Celtic Iberian descent although, like Seneca and Lucan, also born in Spain, he made his literary reputation in Rome. The author of over a thousand bawdy, clever, astringent verses, he has been a model for epigrammatists through the ages. He coined the phrase *rus in urbe* for 'the country in the town', an ideal lying behind many a leafy suburb.

Retablo: the Spanish word for altarpiece, often far larger in Spain than elsewhere. The classic retablo rises in several storeys behind the altar, each storey containing panels filled with statuary or painted scenes. Much of Spain's most powerful religious art is to be found in its often magnificent retablos.

The watery setting of popular Monasterio de Piedra

In almost all the cities, towns and villages of Aragon, from Alcañiz to Huesca, from Teruel to Zaragoza – and often, too, in neighbouring Catalonia and Navarre – it is worth tipping one's head backwards now and then to admire the immense eaves protruding from the older buildings. Sometimes, as in the alleys of Daroca, they practically meet, forming a broad umbrella overhead. Aragonese eaves are generally wooden, and often elaborately carved, almost on the scale of a Chinese temple.

▶▶▷ Estella (Lizarra)

Some of the old parts of Estella, much praised by early pilgrims, are close to collapse today. But there are two splendid monumental sites. The Romanesque church of San Miguel has a magnificently sculpted north façade, now enclosed in a protective glass porch. Further west and across the river (take the pilgrims' Calle de la Rua, one house-width in along the southern bank), the Plaza de San Martín is flanked by an early palace of the kings of Navarre (12th century). San Pedro, with fine carved cloisters, is at the top of yet another monumental stairway.

A short way north, following signs to San Sebastián and turning left soon after Abárzuza, the monastery of **Iranzu** is sited in a beautiful and calming valley (fine Cistercian church; great 13th-century kitchen). On the main road towards Logroño stands the equally fine monastery of **Irache** with a magnificent Cistercian church, in the barest and sparest of Romanesque.

▷▷▷ Fitero

The honey-coloured Cistercian monastery of Fitero offers a Gothic church behind its Romanesque doorway, often closed.

The key is kept in the Casa Parroquial opposite. The slightly tatty neighbouring spa, **Baños de Fitero**, on the edge of the sierra, is said to be sovereign for rheumatism. Waters issue forth at 11° Celsius.

▶▶▷ Fuendetodos

The solemn, stone-built village where the artist Goya was born in 1746 lies in country of forbidding vastness and aridity. The Goya house (closed Mondays, open other days at 11.00hrs) is not so humble as its plaque maintains. The Museo de Grabado (Museum of Etching) shows the complete Goya *Caprichos* and *Disasters of War*, making an unforgettable impact.

Inside the restored Goya house, main attraction in the artist's birthplace, Fuendetodos

High on its crag, the castle of the kings of Aragon at Loarre

Drive Mountains and plain

See map on page 98.

This drive will take a minimum of two days but could be used as the basis for a week or so of travelling.

Starting at Jaca (perhaps after a visit to the Ordesa National Park, see page 111), drive west on the main road to Pamplona.
After 10km divert left to the monastery of **San Juan de la Peña**.

Return to the main road and continue west. From Puente la Reina de Jaca, drop south on the N240. From Ayerbe, divert left to Loarre and follow signs to 'Castillo de Loarre'.
Here visit the splendid castle-eyrie of the kings of Aragon, one of Spain's great military buildings.

Continue to Huesca (see page 106).
You could possibly spend a night here, but certainly an hour or two for visiting the old town.

Thence, take the N240 to Barbastro.
There is a potential side-trip to Alquézar (see page 101).

From Barbastro, the C138/9 leads to Graus.
The route is mainly through peach orchards, shortly picking up the lower reaches of the River Esera. **Graus** is faded but very pleasing, a town that time (and guidebooks) have forgotten. The once-grand Plaza de España has wide Aragonese eaves and traces of ornamental painting on the façades. The town is gathered under a rounded sandstone cliff and a large grey basilica.

Continue along the Esera valley to Benasque.
The valley opens and closes, at times forming a dramatic gorge. It leads out eventually into a broader, grassy valley, with Benasque at its head. To the southeast of Benasque, the ski resort of Cerler is reached by a pine-flanked road with magnificent views. All the highest Pyrenean peaks – Aneto, Maladeta, Posets and El Perdiguero – are close to Benasque.

Spanish Flora and Fauna

■ Spain enjoys the largest area of wild, uncultivated land in all Europe. Some of the continent's rarest creatures including wolves, bears and the magnificent bearded vulture, survive here. There is great regional variation. .....■

There are nine national parks on Spanish soil, four of them in the Canary Islands. Mainland Spain's five are: Covadonga in the Picos de Europa; Ordesa y Monte Perdido and Aigüestortes i Estany de Sant Maurici in the Pyrenees; Tablas de Daimiel in Castilla-La Mancha; and Doñana in Andalucía.

The north coast The northern provinces of Cantabria, Asturias and Galicia are cool and green. Beyond the pockets of industrialisation, the economy is based on fishing, small farming, timber and hazelnuts. Much meadowland has degenerated into weed beds, but the late appearance of intensive farming methods has helped the preservation of wild flowers. Orchids, speedwell, saxifrages and columbine are common. In the fastnesses of the Picos de Europa there are over 40 recorded species of orchid. Rare butterflies also survive here. Some primary beech and oak woods still exist (particularly in the Sierra de Ancares), and newly planted chestnuts stand on hillsides clothed with broom, gorse and heather. The planting of eucalyptus and pine as cash crops by ICONA, the official nature conservation body, has come in for heavy criticism on the grounds that the trees impoverish the soil and are of only short-term financial benefit.

Northern Spain still has deer, wolves and a few Iberian brown bears, now severely reduced in numbers (the majority of sightings has been in the Reserva Nacional de Somiedo, see panel page 94). Wild boar flourish here as in most wild places in Spain, though they are rarely seen. Easier to spot is the chamois, once endangered but now making a successful comeback. There are capercaillie in the woods, and in the sky – particularly among the deep gorges and ravines of this area – you might see eagles (golden, Bonelli's, booted and short-toed), as well as vultures (Egyptian and griffon). The rare eagle-owl shelters in caves and rock holes.

The rivers contain sea trout, brown trout and salmon, with otters to hunt them. The wetlands area around the Bay of Santoña, between Bilbao and Santander, is an important stopping place for migratory birds like spoonbills, avocets, plover, greenshank and curlews. The Cíes islands, off the northwest coast, are a breeding ground for shags, guillemots and gulls.

Tongue orchid (Serapias lingua). *Many orchids grow in Spain's northern mountain regions*

The Pyrenees The Spanish Pyrenees have been accessible only since this century and especially since the skiing boom of the last 20 years. The environmental pressures that other areas have had to resist for decades are new dangers for this region of mountains, lakes, waterfalls, trout streams and flower-filled meadows. The slopes of the Val d'Aran are prized for their profusion of orchids and rare butterflies. The Parque Nacional del Valle de Ordesa shelters gentians, edelweiss, anemones, alpine roses and violets; there are roe deer, wild boar, eagles, vultures, foxes and ermines. The Parc Nacional d'Aigüestortes i Estany de Sant

Maurici has chamois, otters, eagles, grouse, capercaillie and the rare lammergeyer.

Central Spain The central area of the *meseta* is a landscape of open wheatfield, vineyards and sheep tracks through barren plains. There is little diversity of flora and fauna, though the common sight of white storks nesting is always a pleasant one. The mountain ranges around the *meseta*, though, are a different matter. The sierras of Gredos, Guadarrama, Ayllón, Béjar and Peña de Francia have the usual complement of wild boar, lynx, wolves and roe deer, as well as imperial eagles, vultures and kites. The Serranía de Cuenca to the east is rich in orchids.There is an abundance of smaller mammals such as rabbits and hares. Hunting (mostly of red and fallow deer) is a popular activity in the Parque Natural de Monfragüe. The Tablas de Daimiel, an area of lagoons formed by the Río Guadiana, once supported a huge variety of birdlife, but is now endangered by water extraction (see page 195).

Mediterranean and Andalucía All the variations of topography – and flora – from near-desert to high mountain are represented in this area. The Sierra Nevada is always snow-covered, despite being within striking distance of the Mediterranean.

Mediterranean wetlands provide an important refuge for wildfowl and migrating birds – stone curlews and marsh harriers, spoonbills and glossy ibis, as well as smaller warblers and shrikes. They find their way to Aiguamolls de L'Empordá in Catalonia, to the Ebro delta, to the Valencian Albufera and to the Coto Doñana in the province of Huelva. All these areas are under threat from the pressures of high-tech farming, industrial waste and tourism. Regional autonomies are responding by designating some key areas as *parques naturales*, so providing an element of protection. Whether this will be enough is an open question.

The lammergeyer, also known as the bearded vulture, is noted for dropping bones from a huge height in order to smash them so that it can eat the marrow. Already rare, this bird is, sadly, becoming rarer.

Nesting white stork, a common sight in central areas

Time out for a game of bowls in Jaca

Legend claims that King Ramiro II of Aragon, thoroughly displeased with his nobles, summoned them one day to see the forging of a bell whose voice would ring across the kingdom. Welcoming them instead to a gloomy chamber in his palace, virtually a cellar, he promptly cut their heads off. The cellar is still to be seen within the late 17th-century Universidad Literaria, now housing the provincial museum in Huesca. There is a dramatic painting of the scene (visits during office hours) on the first floor of the town hall.

▶▶▷ **Huesca**

Modern Huesca is a standard provincial city, but old Huesca at its centre contains a rich ensemble of Aragonese art and architecture. The sculpted portals of the cathedral lead into a bare hall of stone, with nave and two side aisles and a fine Damián Forment retablo in alabaster. In the handsome *ayuntamiento* (town hall) across the square is a famous painting of the Bell of Huesca (see panel).

▶▶▷ **Jaca**

Jaca, a fresh little Pyrenean town, was the city from which the tiny Kingdom of Aragon launched its comeback against the Moors. Soon, it became first point of call for Santiago pilgrims taking the eastern route from France. Today, it is the centre of an important skiing region in the Pyrenees above.

The cathedral and its diocesan museum (entered via the cathedral, open 11.00hrs) are musts of the culturally inclined. The cathedral portico contains a fine sculpted tympanum of the Wheel of the Trinity and archaic lions. The carved Romanesque capitals of the south porch (especially Abraham and Isaac, right of the door) are naïvely powerful. The diocesan museum has an excellent collection of Romanesque paintings and sculpture. On the western edge of town is a huge citadel, open to the public, with deer grazing in its moat.

▶▶▷ **Leyre**

The monastery of San Salvador de Leyre, burial place of the kings of Navarre and the spiritual centre of the kingdom during the 11th century, lies beneath the limestone cliffs of the Sierra de Leyre (hang-gliding) above the vast blue reservoir of Yesa (watersports). The 11th-century crypt and Romanesque church are surrounded by modern monastic buildings, including a hotel. Vespers with Gregorian chant are at 20.00hrs and full service at 22.15hrs.

▶▶▷ **Maestrazgo**
The ancient domain of a knightly order (see pages 218–19), the Maestrazgo is a rugged territory of rock and gorge with evocative, unspoiled medieval townships such as La Iglesuela del Cid, Cantavieja, Vilarluenga and, especially, Mirambel. Driving is slow and arduous, but the rewards are immense. The easiest entry is from the south through Teruel, via impressive Mora de Rubielos or neighbouring Rubielos de Mora.

▶▷▷ **Nuévalos (Monasterio de Piedra)**
Beyond the reservoir that threatens to engulf red-roofed Nuevalos, the Monasterio de Piedra is one of Aragon's most popular spots. Below the monastery, paths follow the Río Piedra, cool, arboreal, full of waterfalls.

▶▶▷ **Olite**
Olite sits on a plain – a surprising choice for the greatest castle of the kings of Navarre. Though heavily restored, it is a fine place to explore, with galleries, courtyards and views of the town below. It includes a parador.

▶▷▷ **La Oliva**
The Cistercian monastery of La Oliva was founded in the 12th century, in the lower valley of the Río Aragón, rich now in fruit trees and poplars. It was a major cultural centre for Navarre. The church has a Romanesque façade, fine Gothic cloister and chapterhouse.

▶▶▶ **Ordesa y Monte Perdido, Parque Nacional**
see page 111

▶▶▷ **Pamplona (Iruñea)**
The city best known in modern times for its bull-running festival was once the fortress-capital of Navarre and an important stage in the Santiago pilgrimage. It was here (marked by a plaque) that the young Basque nobleman, Ignatius Loyola, fell wounded in 1521 during the defence of Pamplona against the French. He went on to found the Order of Jesuits, and to achieve sainthood.
The city today has a smart modern quarter and a private university. The walled old town contains a Gothic cathedral; the neo-classical façade is disappointing but the cloisters, the Puerta de la Sala Preciosa, and the star vaulting in the Barbazan chapel more than compensate. See also the Museo de Navarra, the *ayuntamiento* (town hall), and the twin-towered church of San Saturnino.

▶▷▷ **Puente la Reina**
Puente la Reina is sited at the river-crossing where pilgrims arriving via the Somport pass finally converged with those entering Spain via Roncesvalles. It is a surprisingly dour little town where ancient trades jostle with modern tourist shops and up-to-date hairdressers. The twin-aisled church of El Crucifijo contains a noted 14th-century German crucifix. The narrow main street, or Calle Mayor, with handsome mansions and the sumptuous baroque church of Santiago, leads to the arched bridge of the pilgrims, for pedestrians only.

Pamplona's bull-running festival, made famous by Ernest Hemingway, among others, is held each summer in honour of the town's patron, San Fermín. With the whole town out to cheer them on, the runners, dresssed in white and red, begin by singing the hymn of San Fermín. As the starting rocket goes off and the bulls are released from their pens, young bloods are soon squeezing under or vaulting over the barricades, into the crowds, to escape the horns. Afternoons of the week-long fiesta are devoted to bullfights and evenings to heavy junketing.

One of the waterfalls along the Piedra river

FOCUS ON *The Pyrenees*

■ For most of history, the Pyrenees have proved a substantial barrier between France and Spain, often regarded as one of the key reasons for the great differences between the Iberian peninsula and the rest of Europe. .....■

In the present century, with the immense pull now exerted by wild places, and the consequent development of Pyrenean tourism, the mountains have come to seem almost a unifying factor.

The highest peaks of the Pyrenees – Pico de Aneto (3,408m), Pico Posets (3,371m) and Monte Perdido (the Lost Mountain, 3,355m) – rise in their year-round snow-cover in the Aragonese province of Huesca. Today, ski resorts in the high valleys provide for winter visitors. There are magnificent national parks to explore on foot in summer, one in Huesca (**Ordesa y Monte Perdido**, see page 111), one close by in the Catalan province of Lleida (**Aigüestortes i Estany de Sant Maurici**, see page 130). Tucked into the folds of this lofty terrain, there is an extraordinary and unexpected wealth of largely medieval art and architecture. At the same time, it must be acknowledged that the intrusions of skiing and ski facilities are considerable and often discouraging.

The *Chanson de Roland*, a medieval epic poem of chivalry, describes the retreat of Charlemagne's army into France through the Pyrenees. The poem tells how the rearguard is attacked by Moors but the leader, Roland, chivalrous to the end, refuses to sound his great horn, Oliphaunt, until it is too late. His army is cut down. In fact, the diasaster was inflicted not by the Moors but by the Basques, hostile then as now to interference from outsiders.

Travellers' trials One major point about travel in the Pyrenees – Catalan and Navarrese as well as in Aragon itself – is that the valleys on the Spanish side run down north to south. Roads up and down are good; but east–west roads between one valley and the next,

Pyrenean church, Linas de Broto

where they exist at all, are usually slow and tortuous and generally ignored by locals.

The easiest way to understand the shape of the Pyrenees in Aragon is to consider the main valleys in order, starting in the west near Jaca, true capital of the locality, then moving eastwards to Benasque, fast emerging as a second focus.

To Ansó and Hecho Entering Aragon from Navarre, the first route northwards from the N240 doubles back into Navarre to ascend the **Roncal valley**, famous for its cheeses. Next, north of depopulated but dramatic little Berdun, twin valleys ascend to Ansó and Hecho. Unusually, they are linked towards the top by a good cross-wise road. Both little towns, **Ansó** and **Hecho**, are remarkably attractive, with solid stone houses, high wooden balconies, immense eaves and the occasional conical chimney. But Ansó in particular is now growing very rapidly. Cross-country skiing is the speciality here.

Puerto de Somport This pass above Jaca is a main point of access for France. Snow sometimes blocks the pass but an all-weather tunnel is now planned. The border itself, beyond the pass and lower down, is now open 24 hours a day, thanks to an EU directive. Starting from Jaca, the road winds up the valley of the River Aragon, offering extensive panoramas of peaks and, very often, swirling cloud. The pass itself is bleak and may be windy. The well-established ski-resort of **Candanchú** is at a high altitude here, as also the more recent but fast growing Astún. Canfranc, accessible by train, is lower down on the Spanish side.

Going north The River Gallego ascends next – from **Sabiñánigo**, which is industrial but has an interesting art gallery. Moving north up the valley, there is soon a turn-off right to an intriguing scatter of Romanesque churches – at Olivan, Oros Bajo, San Juan de Busa, Súsin and Lárrede. Carrying on north up the main road past Biescas, where the C140 diverts right towards National Ordesa Park, a much improved road carries one up and over into France (the valley from this point is known as Tena; border closed in winter). It passes the attractive settlement – now a skiing centre – of **Sallent de Gállego**. A side road to the right, climbing steeply up the formidable little gorge of Escalar, leads to the strange high-level spa of **Balneario de Panticosa**, known to the Romans for its medicinal waters. High rocky peaks rise round a small lake, with a dreary cluster of hotels. There is skiing here and at **El Formigal**.

From Barbastro A fair step southeast, **Barbastro** (see page 101) is starting point for two more valleys. The Cinca Valley leads up via Ainsa to Bielsa and beyond, with, finally, a high-level parador and entry to the Monte Perdido end of Ordesa National Park. The dramatically lovely valley of the Esera also leads up from Barbastro, past sleepy Graus (see **Drive**, page 103) and on towards the mountain cirque above Benasque, highest point of the whole Pyrenees.

The Somport Pass, historic pilgrims' crossing point from France

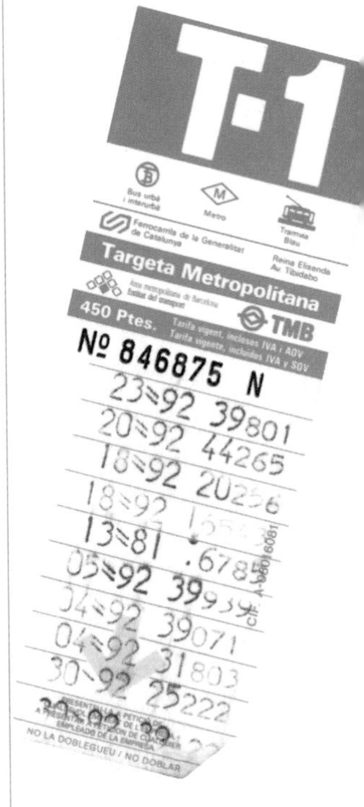

In the Ordesa National Park

Birthplace of Ferdinand of Aragon (1452), Sos del Rey Católico lies in wild sub-Pyrenean country. It has steep stone streets, fine arched doorways and a tunnel under the church of San Esteban offering a dramatic glimpse of the crypt.

▶▷▷ **Roncesvalles**

Roncesvalles was for centuries the main crossing point in the western Pyrenees. The village below the pass has a monastic 13th-century church containing the tomb of its founder, Sancho the Strong of Navarre; a Pilgrims' Way museum; and a later building over the supposed site of Roland's tomb.

▶▶▷ **Sangüesa (Zangoza)**

Despite its stinking pulp mill, Sangüesa is a charming, rather serious little town. Here pilgrims who had followed the River Aragon from Jaca crossed it for the last time. The church of Santa María on the river bank has one of the most graceful carved façades in Spain (12th–13th centuries). Behind the wide-eaved town hall is the Castillo del Príncipe de Viana (palace of the Prince of Viana).

▶▶▷ **San Juan de la Peña**

This extraordinary monastery, burial place of Aragonese royalty and nobles, is sited under a huge overhang of rock. It was originally built in Mozarabic style with horseshoe arches and painted frescos. A Romanesque church was built on top, taking advantage of the rock for its roof, with a tiny open cloister and exquisitely carved capitals. A narrow forestry road to the right at the top of the cliff gives one of the best of all Pyrenean panoramas.

▶▷▷ **Tarazona**

Tarazona, historic Mudéjar town under the Sierra de Moncayo, has a fine brick-patterned cathedral tower and brilliant *celosía* plaster tracery in its cloister windows (the cathedral is temporarily closed for restoration at the time of writing). The 18th-century bullring is an octagon, its perimeter made up of ancient houses.

Walk Ordesa National Park

This national park is one of the glories of the Pyrenees. Established in 1918 and extended in 1982, it embraces the mountain country round El Monte Perdido (3,355m) which rises on its northern flanks. Four valleys, Pineta in the east, Puertolas and Añisclo in the south and Ordesa in the west, run up towards the inhospitable high ground. This is great walking country.

Enter the park from Torla (where there are hotels and camping sites). Maps and information are available from the shop by the car park if the national parks office is shut. Walks of various levels of difficulty and duration start here.

For a long but easy walk, head straight up the valley to Cascada de Cola de Caballo (Horsetail Falls). There are astounding views of cliffs and many earlier waterfalls.

Return the same way (total distance 20km).

For a more rigorous outing (6–8 hours for moderate walkers) follow the signs for Senda de Cazadores. The hike starts with 1½ to 2 hours' walking straight up a crag; steep but safe.
Follow the cliffside Faja de Pelay path left at the top. Head slowly down towards Cascada de Cola de Caballo.

Return down the track as above.

<< Less dramatic but greener and softer than the high Pyrenees in Aragon, the Pyrenees of Navarre are cut through by the valleys of Irati, Salazar and Roncal – as well as Roncesvalles and Baztan, closer to the sea. Salazar is most famous locally for its hard round cheeses, good for picnics. **>>**

Walk Señorio de Bertiz

This is a compact but diverse botanical garden, situated at Oronoz, at the beginning of the Baztan Valley on the C133 road. The garden was created by a wealthy Navarrese who, being childless, willed it to the government of Navarre.

You can simply walk or, for a longer, more rugged stroll, take the path behind the garden.
This takes you into the 25sq km of densely wooded natural park immediately behind.

There are two unmarked walking trails, one over a hill and the other beside the river.
All minor paths lead to one or other of the trails.

Gardens open: 09.00–14.00 and 16.00–20.00hrs. Open access to the park.

Torla, gateway to the Ordesa National Park

Teruel has its own Romeo and Juliet legend, the 'lovers of Teruel'. Way back in the 13th century, Isabel de Segura fell in love with penniless Juan Diego Martínez de Marcilla, but was forced to marry another. Returning from the wars, Juan Diego met her secretly but died of love. She kissed his corpse at the funeral next day and promptly died herself. They were buried in the same grave, in the church of San Pedro, their hands allegedly entwined. Today, their mummified corpses may be glimpsed (in separate tombs) in a specially built mausoleum near the church.

Gustavo Adolfo Bécquer, romantic 19th-century writer, stayed in Veruela and celebrated the area.

▶▶▷ **Teruel**

Much fought over during the Civil War, Teruel is far from attractive from some vantage points. But its astonishing Mudéjar towers, the most impressive and bizarre in Spain, and the magnificent *artesonado* ceiling of its cathedral, have helped establish it as a World Heritage site (1988). The finest and most intricate of the five towers are those of San Martín, San Salvador and the cathedral.

▶▷▷ **Tudela**

Tudela, Aragon's main settlement along the Ebro river, is a somnolent agricultural centre, trailing a Moorish past. Tumbledown brick mansions bear Mudéjar patterning; the doorway of the old mosque survives within the cathedral cloister. The cathedral itself is splendid.

▶▶▷ **Ujué**

High on its crag, Ujué is tremendous – church and ruined castle rising over what appears a ghost town from without, commanding huge, wild views. On the Sunday following St Mark's Day, 25 April, thousands of barefoot, black-clad penitents process round the church.

▷▷▷ **Valderrobres**

Remote and tiny Valderrobres retains a castle of the kings of Aragon and an impressive 12th-century church.

▷▷▷ **Veruela**

North of the Sierra de Moncayo, this 12th-century Cistercian monastery combines charm with solidity. A gateway through stout external walls leads to the façades of the church and abbots' palace. Within, the handsome two-storey cloister is Gothic below, Renaissance above.

▷▷▷ **Viana**

Cesare Borgia died in battle in this Navarrese border city. The church of Santa María has one of Spain's best Renaissance portals.

Not a great deal happens in downtown Tudela

▶▶▷ **Zaragoza**

Lying on the west bank of the Ebro, Zaragoza (Saragossa in English) was a major Roman city and later spent 400 years as capital of Spain's most northerly Moorish kingdom. It still contains one splendid Moorish palace, the Aljafería. During the Reconquista, Zaragoza became the capital of the new Aragonese regime and a leading city in emergent Spain. Later, it gained fame from its heroic resistance to Napoleon's forces during two great sieges in 1808–9.

El Pilar The place to start sightseeing is in the large open rectangle which forms the effective centre of the old city, separated from the river only by the Basilica of El Pilar. A huge brick building, 18th century in its present form, El Pilar has high corner steeples and central dome, all flashy in ceramic tiles and heavy with statuary. Within, it is huge and creamy coloured with vast fluted pilasters. An inner church or shrine shelters the immensely revered image of the Virgin on the very pillar (El Pilar) on which she is said to have appeared to St James the Apostle in AD40. The faithful kiss the pillar itself through a small gap in the back of the shrine-structure. There are ceiling paintings here by Goya and his brother-in-law Francisco Bayeu (not too easy to make out). In the main church, note also the expressive retablo by Damián Forment.

Other sights Off the same square are the cathedral (closed for restoration since 1984) and the Lonja (Exchange). Excavations of the Roman forum in front of the cathedral have recently been opened to the public in a kind of 'underground-garage' display.

The **Lonja** is built in tiny bricks, with bands of severe ornament under mighty eaves. The interior – open only for exhibitions but a must if open – displays magnificent reliefs and brilliant stone ornament.

The **Aljafería** is about 15 minutes' walk to the west, a castle much modified and restored over the ages but centred on a Moorish courtyard and its original mosque. Ferdinand and Isabella contributed a grand stairway and fine *artesonado* ceiling on the first floor.

Zaragoza's cathedral is on the site where the Great Mosque of the Moors once stood

Once you know, it seems so obvious ... Caesar Augusta ... Zaragoza (by way of Moorish Sarakusta). The Roman emperor gave his name to the city on the Ebro in AD25.

In the 11th century, Zaragoza was ruled by the super-civilised Beni-Hud dynasty, becoming a haven for scholars and poets. El Cid, who still enjoys something of a false reputation as a Christian hero, in fact served for five years, from 1085, as mercenary leader for the Beni-Huds, winning great victories against the Christians and capturing the Count of Barcelona – not once, but twice. It seems quite likely he spoke Arabic as well as Spanish.

Las Ramblas, favourite strolling place of Barcelona's citizens

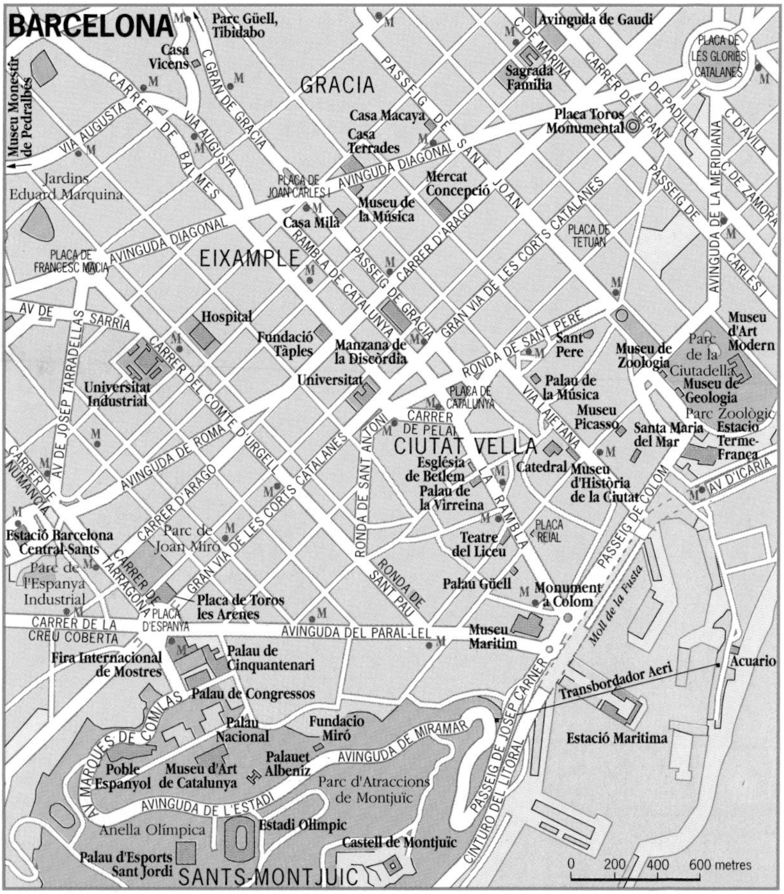

BARCELONA

Catalan Barcelona – seaboard city, capital of a nation of six million, sophisticated, glamorous and fast-moving – is, for many people, Spain's top city, leaving Madrid in the shadows. The essence of Barcelona, as natives explain it, is that it is intensely Catalan (give or take a huge immigrant population from Andalucía and the rest of rural Spain) and simultaneously open to the world.

The history of the city is written eloquently into its various districts, starting with the earliest and probably most famous – the Barri Gòtic (Gothic quarter), just behind the harbour. Up one side of it goes the wonderful strollers' avenue called Las Ramblas, full of flower stalls and cafés in the dappled shade. Within 100 metres of the Ramblas, you find yourself in a stone-built warren of churches, palaces, cathedral and Roman remnants, the first Barcelona. Somehow it mostly survived two episodes of destruction by central Spain – first in 1652 and again in 1714. (The Franco period, 1939–75, was another hard time for Barcelona, with repression of the language and Catalan identity itself.)

Inland from the Barri Gòtic lies the Eixample, the ample 19th-century extension laid out on a grid system. This was the building ground for the Catalan Modernista architects, the band whose works are cumulatively the most brilliant of Spain's 19th- and 20th-century artistic achievements. It is here that most Modernista buildings are found, including, of course, Gaudí's Sagrada Família.

On its southern side, the city is bounded by the great green hill of Montjuïc, site of some of the finest museums. It also holds the handsomely revamped Olympic Stadium and other buildings erected for the 1992 Olympics, as well as Mies van der Rohe's brilliant Pavelló Barcelona. The 'Olympic Village', closer to the centre, now adds considerably to the city's housing stock. Other outlying areas also came in for Olympic restructuring, and these, with a brand new ring road system and a vigorous programme of *Nou Urbanisme* (new urbanism) – meaning mainly open spaces filled with lively modern sculpture – have brought Barcelona into a fresh phase in the 1990s.

Decorative detail on a Modernista building

▶▶▶ Barri Gòtic

For descriptions of the main churches and museums in the Barri Gòtic see within the alphabetical listing on pages 117–23.

But nobody should visit this city without a few hours of simple pottering in its medieval heart. Starting in Plaça Nova or the Plaça de la Seu (the cathedral square), dive down the Carrer del Bisbe Irurtia through the Portal del Bisbe, its towers going back to the Romans, and by the bishop's palace, with a right turn into picturesque Plaça Sant Felip Neri or a glimpse, left, into the cathedral cloister. The little lane then passes between the Casa dels Canonges and the elaborate Renaissance façade of the Palau de la Generalitat, home base for an autonomous Catalonia. Once into the Plaça Sant Jaume, you see that the Ajuntament (Casa de la Ciutat – Town Hall) is just opposite the Generalitat: thus the city government faces the would-be nation-state – not always in friendship.

The Plaça del Rei, tucked in round the northern side of the cathedral, is even more impressive. As well as the Museu d'Història de la Ciutat, brought here stone by stone to complete the ensemble, it contains parts of the former royal palace and a noble Gothic hall, the Saló de Tinell, where Columbus reported the success of his first voyage to Ferdinand and Isabella. The Plaça Ramon Berenguer el Gran, with its equestrian statue of Berenguer III, Count of Barcelona, offers fine views of the Roman walls from outside the Barri Gòtic.

Spain's Golden Age came in the 17th century; Catalonia had achieved its own four centuries earlier. Chief figure of Catalan literature is the Franciscan friar Rámon Llull (1232–1315), polymath, traveller, missionary and Arabist. One of the first to write in the language of common speech, Llull penned lively novels as well as learned essays and spiritual works. Intellectual Catalonia lives in his shadow.

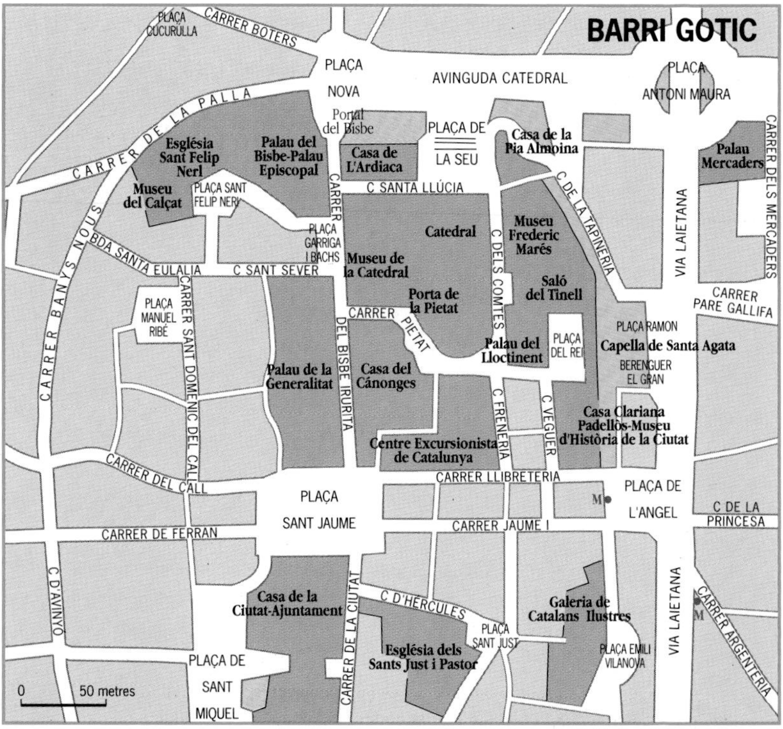

Casa Amatller/Casa Batlló/Casa Lleó Morera
see **Manzana de la Discòrdia.**

▶▶▶ **Casa Milà** or **La Pedrera (the Stone Quarry)**

Passeig de Gràcia 92

Gaudí's triumphantly peculiar block of flats is a massive construction, combining the weight and dignity of stone with surging organic flow. The bristling ironwork of the balconies is by Gaudí's collaborator Josep Maria Jujol. There are guided tours (starting on the hour during normal museum opening times) and sometimes exhibitions on the first floor.

▶▷▷ **Casa Terrades** or **Casa de les Punxes (House of Spires)**

Diagonal 416

This large, spiky building by the Modernista architect Puig i Cadafalch mingles Rhineland castle turrets with a kind of Oxford college neo-gothic.

▶▷▷ **Casa Vicens**

Carrer de los Carolines 18

On rising ground above the Eixample, this is an early Gaudí work, combining flamboyant ceramic tiles with strongly Moorish forms.

▶▶▶ **Catedral La Seu**

Plaça de la Seu, Barri Gòtic

This mainly 14th- and 15th-century Gothic building only acquired its present façade and spire – built to original designs – in the late 19th century. Yet the medieval ambience is deeply impressive. The interior, with its height and multiplicity of chapels, is also effective. Note carved choir stalls (14th- to 15th-century), choir screen (16th-century) and cloister (15th-century) – a release from sombre gloom. Santa Eulàlia, potent local martyr, is buried in the crypt.

Getting about
The Barri Gòtic (see page 116) is for walkers. For most other destinations, the metro is simplest and fastest. A range of tickets is available for multi-trips either on metro alone or public transport generally; there are also passes ranging from one to five days. The Plaça de Catalunya is the transport centre – start the journey from here to Tibidabo by local train, finish by bus and funicular. For Montjuïc, take the metro to Plaça d'Espanya and climb or use the escalator; or take the funicular from Paral-lel metro station.

Roger de Flor is sometimes considered a pirate, more often a Catalan hero and patriot. At the head of a mercenary light infantry force called the Almogàvers, he adventured across the Mediterranean between 1302 and 1311, taking first Sicily, then Athens and a chunk of the Greek mainland. The Catalans stayed in Greece for most of a century. They took Corsica and Sardinia later in the 14th century, then Naples in 1423. This remained a Spanish possession until 1714.

The Gothic calm of Barcelona's cathedral

Walk The Ramblas

See map on page 119.

The Ramblas is the city's favourite *paseo*. Formerly a dry river bed, it is really a series of five interconnecting avenues stretching from the corner of Plaça de Catalunya all the way (2km) to the Columbus statue and the port. It is a walkway crowded with open air cafés, newspaper kiosks, shoppers, pavement artists and entertainers.

Begin at the Rambla de Canaletas.
If you want to ensure your return to Barcelona, they say, you must drink from the iron fountain here.

Pass the recently restored 17th-century baroque church of Església de Betlem on the corner of Carrer del Carme and the rococo Palau de la Virreina.
This palace of the vicereine of Peru now houses a postal museum and exhibition centre.

You have now reached the Rambla de les Flors.
Flower stalls fill the street. On your right is Barcelona's famous 19th-century covered **Mercat de la Boqueria**, a cornucopia of fruit and vegetables, meat and fish. Look down, in the Plaça de la Boqueria, to find the mosaic pattern designed by Joan Miró. Look up at the corner of Casa Bruno Quadras for the green Chinese dragon holding a lamp.

Continue to the Café de l'Opera on the same side.
Opposite stands the shell of the **Gran Teatre del Liceu**, Spain's most prestigious opera house, destroyed by fire in 1993. Performances now take place in the Palau Sant Jordi on Montjuic.

Walk on towards the port.
The famous **Hotel Oriente** (site of a 17th-century monastery) is no longer luxurious but it retains its faded charm and glass-domed dining room. The near end of Carrer Nou de la Rambla is distinguished by the **Palau Güell**, the Modernista mansion of Gaudí's foremost patron. You are now in the district known as the Barri Xines (Chinese Quarter). There are few Chinese here but ample evidence of Barcelona low life. Avoid after dark.
Behind the Rambla on the other side, is the Plaça Reial, ringed with cafés, palm trees and lamp-posts designed by Gaudí.

Time for refreshment at the end of the walk

▶▶▷ Fundació Antoni Tàpies

Carrer d'Aragó 255

The entire career of Catalan and international artist Antoni Tàpies, is represented here – from the distorted realism of his beginnings to later abstraction and use of intriguing surface textures. The airy building is an early Modernista factory by Domènech i Montaner. The sculptural tangle of wire on top of the building aroused great antagonism when the Foundation was opened in 1990.

▶▶▶ Fundació Joan Miró

Plaça Neptú, Montjuïc

The cool white building by Josep LLuís Sert (with fine views, from the rooftop, of the city below) encloses a colourful riot of work – paintings, tapestry, ceramics, *objets trouvés* – by Joan Miró (1893–1983), one of Barcelona's favourite sons. Miró's work leading up to the Civil War is distressed and distressing. Much of the rest seems playful, despite the artist's avowed pessimism. The Foundation, an active art centre, also holds outstanding exhibitions.

▶▶▷ Hospital de la Santa Creu i de Sant Pau

Avinguda de Gaudí

Puig i Cadafalch's hospital proves that Modernista buildings can really work – though you may be surprised to see the fanciful elaboration of specialised departments around the pleasant open patio. You can visit the public courtyards.

▶▷▷ Liceu, Gran Teatre del

Ramblas (Sant Pau 1)

A famous Rambla Landmark before the 1993 fire, this was Spain's leading operatic venue, often featuring such Catalan talents as José Carreras and Montserrat Caballé. Until restoration is complete, performances take place in the Palau Sant Jordi.

Striking tapestry in Fundació Joan Miró

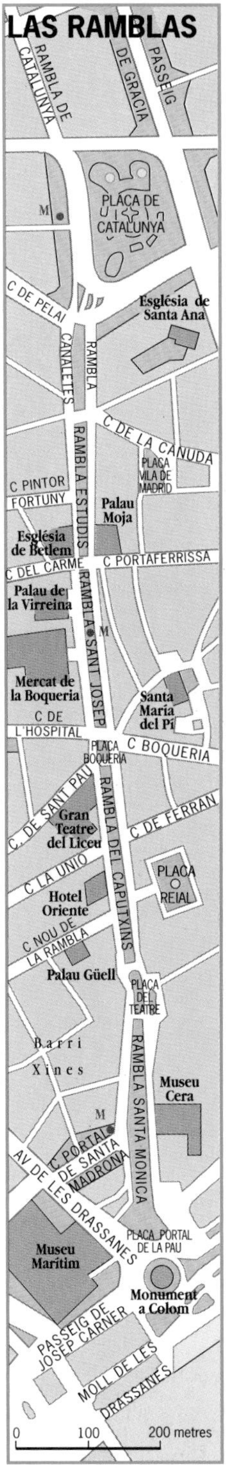

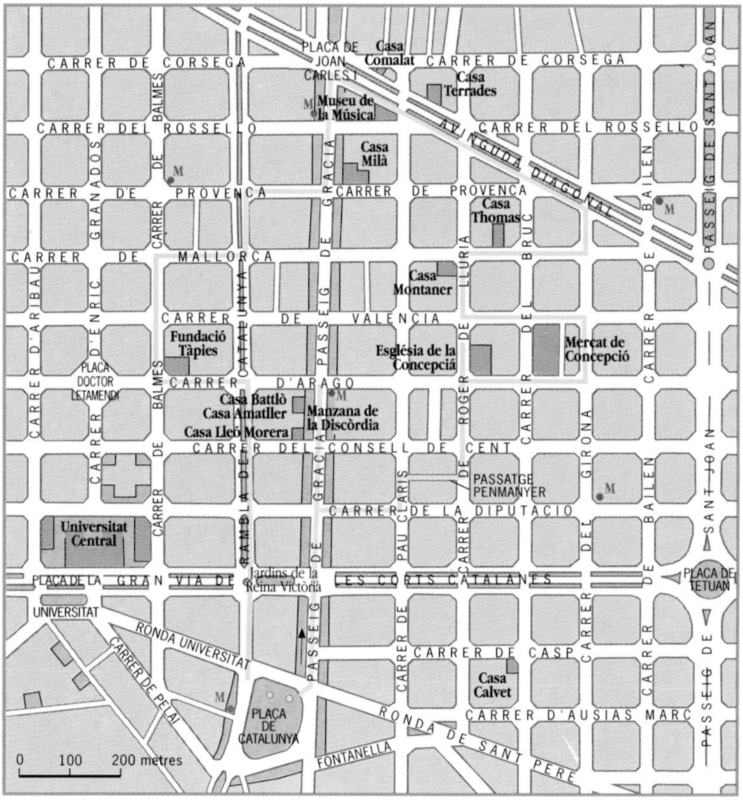

Walk Eixample

Leave Plaça de Catalunya, top right, by the broad Passeig de Gràcia.
Nos 35, 41 and 43 are the famous **Manzana de la Discòrdia**.

Return two blocks, then go left down Carrer de la Diputació, up Pau Claris and cut through pretty Passatge Penmanyer. Continue left up Roger de Llúria.
There are pretty Modernista fronts at nos 72, 74 and 80.

Go back a block and left down Carrer d'Aragó to Mercat de Concepció, up Girona and left down Valencia, right and up Roger de Llúria.
Casa Montaner, designed by Domènech i Montaner, is on the next corner.

Go right down Mallorca.
Modernista Casa Thomas is here.

Turn left up Girona and left into Avinguda Diagonal.
Casa Terrades is on the right, and the **Museu de la Música** is left at no 373, a fascinating building.

Turn left down Passeig de Gràcia
Gaudi's **Casa Milà**, is at no 92.

Right here down smart Provença, left down Rambla de Catalunya, with a diversion through Balmes and back down Aragó.
Fundació Tàpies is here at no 225.

Finish the walk down Rambla de Catalunya.

▶▶▶ **Manzana de la Discòrdia**
35–43 Passeig de Gràcia
Manzana means both city-block and apple. Here, buildings by each of the three great Modernista architects, in styles that vary hugely, distinguish this extraordinary block. Domènech i Montaner's **Casa Lleó Morera** is at no 35; its richly decorated interior is the headquarters of Barcelona's tourist board. Puig i Cadafalch's **Casa Amatller**, with stepped gables, ceramic decorations and mock-medieval stairway is at no 41. And Gaudí's **Casa Batlló**, at no 43, has an amazing sinuous roofline.

▶▶▶ **Museu d'Art de Catalunya**
above Plaça d'Espanya, Montjuïc
This palatial relic of the 1929 Exhibition now holds Catalonia's incomparable collection of Romanesque art. Mainly from Pyrenean churches in such remote areas as the Vall de Boi, these exceptional works were rescued from imminent threat of destruction and theft earlier in this century. They include frescos, painted wooden panels, altar frontals and wooden statuary. There are also Gothic, Renaissance and baroque contributions.
For opening times see Travel Facts, page 266.

▶▷▷ **Museu d'Art Modern**
Parc de la Ciutadella
'Modern' here means mainly late 19th- and early 20th-century Catalan, with painters like Fortuny, Santiago Rusiñol, Ramon Casas and Isidro Nonell, reflecting local life and artistic aspiration. Though no match for Modernista architecture, their work is interesting.

▶▷▷ **Museu Frederic Marès**
Plaça de Sant Iu
The private collection of a professional magpie (opened 1946), this museum right by the cathedral contains Roman, Carthaginian and Moorish bits and pieces, good religious paintings and sculpture (especially the Romanesque) and a dense array of hat-pins, door knockers, knives, pipes, fans, binoculars...

Barcelona has staged three major international events and has used each of them to make improvements to the city. For the 1888 Exhibition, notable Modernista buildings were erected. The 1929 Exhibition produced the much-praised Mies van der Rohe Pavelló and the huge Palau Nacional on the hill of Montjuïc where the Museu d'Art de Catalunya is installed. The 1992 Olympics have given the city new sports venues, an Olympic village, a reopened shoreline, new ring roads, and sculpture in parks and public places – the so-called *Nou Urbanisme*.

Stadium for the 1992 Olympic Games

▶▶▷ Museu d'Història de la Ciutat

Plaça del Rei

This museum site shows the compacted layers of civilisation – Roman, Visigothic, Christian, Moorish, Carolingian – of old Barcelona. It also includes mid-19th-century ground-plans for the Eixample.

▶▶▷ Museu Marítim

Plaça Portal de la Pau

This new museum has been assembled in the vaults of the Drassanes, medieval ship-building sheds close to the Columbus monument. Centrepiece is a gilded replica of *La Real*, flagship in the battle of Lepanto, 1571.

▶▶▷ Museu-Monestir de Pedralbés

Baixada Monestir 9

This beautiful Catalan-Gothic monastery houses part of the Thyssen-Bornemisza collection (see page.54) with religious masterpieces from Fra Angelico to Titian.

The British writer George Orwell reached Barcelona in December 1936 to join the Republicans in the Spanish Civil War. 'It was the first time I had been in a city where the working class was in the saddle,' he wrote in *Homage to Catalonia* (1938). No formal modes of address were used; hardly anyone was well dressed. Orwell found it 'queer and moving' and renewed his determination to fight.

▶▶▷ Museu de la Música

Diagonal 373

A collection of musical instruments, and memorabilia of Catalan composers Albeniz and Granados, occupies a fine Modernista building by Puig i Cadafalch.

▶▶▶ Museu Picasso

Carrer Montcada 15–19

Housed in a Catalan-Gothic palace, this collection provides a full view of Picasso's early years. From the first studies of doves and a bullfight through to portraits of his family, the childhood works are enthralling. Teenage paintings such as the prize-winning *Science and Charity* (1897) are at least a match for anything produced by adult artists working in late 19th-century realistic/sentimental mode. The museum includes Picasso's early Parisian night-life studies, and the best of his Blue Period with its sadly alienated figures. The *Harlequin* of 1917 is also here. Works from his maturity and old age include the long series called *Las Meninas*, a deconstruction of Velázquez's greatest work.

For opening times see Travel Facts, page 267.

Colour and history in the Museu Marítim

▶▶▷ Palau d'Esports Sant Jordi
Showcase for athletes, and venue for rock musicians, the new sports stadium on Montjuïc, work of the Japanese architect Isozaki, is put forward as a late 20th-century companion to Gaudí's masterpieces.

▶▶▷ Palau Güell
Carrer Nou de la Rambla
Gaudí's chief patron, the industrialist Count Eusebi Güell, commissioned this mansion (1886–8) in a narrow street off the Ramblas. The interior, open to the public, is crammed with intriguing details and furniture.

▶▶▷ Palau de la Música Catalana
Sant Pere Més Alt
Art nouveau fans will love this effusive Modernista concert hall by Domènech. It combines the work of master-craftsmen in all the decorative arts.

▶▶▷ Palau de la Virreina
La Rambla 99
This was the rococo palace of the wife of a viceroy (or virreina) of Peru, now an exhibition hall/arts centre.

▶▶▶ Parc Güell
The happier side of Gaudí's genius is evident in the curious buildings in this park on a flank of Tibidabo (see below). Don't miss the cursive benches, in ceramic collage, by Josep Maria Jujol.

▶▷▷ Poble Espanyol
Montjuïc
Replicas of representative buildings from all over Spain were built for the 1929 Universal Exhibition. This is now a lively evening entertainment centre.

▶▶▶ Sagrada Família
Gaudí's unfinished Expiatory Temple of the Holy Family is Barcelona's number one sight. Some visitors find it majestic, to others it is ridiculous. Gaudí took over the project in 1883 and worked on it obsessively until he died, struck by a tram, in 1926. The eastern end, with four honeycomb pinnacles and a cascade of organic sculpture representing the Nativity, went up under his direction. Elements of the western end have been erected since, amid bitter criticism. Should Gaudí's ideas, never set down on paper, be interpreted by others? The debate continues. There is a museum in the crypt.

▶▶▷ Santa Maria del Mar
Plaça Santa Maria
Grandly solid – though definitely scruffy from outside – the high-rise interior of Santa Maria del Mar establishes it as the most ambitious of Barcelona's Gothic churches.

▶▶▷ Tibidabo
With fun-fair, basilica and views of the city far below, this mountain-top (512m) behind Barcelona makes a jolly outing for adults and children alike.

The wonderland of Parc Güell

Parc Güell was intended as open space for a building project which never happened. A few houses were built, though, and Gaudí lived in one of them – rather dingy but open to the public.

'Tibidabo', Latin 'Unto you will I give...', recalls Satan's promise to Jesus in the Wilderness.

Shopping

The city divides itself readily into three main shopping areas: the Ciutat Vella or Old Town, where the emphasis is on souvenir items and traditional crafts; the smart avenues of the Eixample, particularly the Passeig de Gràcia; and the Avinguda Diagonal and northwards to the Sant Gervasi district.

Design Barcelona prides itself on being at the diamond-sharp cutting edge of style. Design is an obsession here. To test the truth of this statement, start at **Vinçon**, Passeig de Gràcia 96, purveyor of the seriously designed household artefact – everything from lights and kitchen furniture to ashtrays. For those interested in furniture, **B D Ediciones de Diseño** at Mallorca 291–3 displays work by (relatively) old masters like Charles Rennie Mackintosh and Mies van der Rohe and contemporary designers like Javier Mariscal (creator of the Barcelona Olympics mascot, Cobi).

For design in fashion the **Bulevard Rosa** arcades in the Passeig de Gràcia and on Diagonal are a good place to start. You will see established names like **Loewe** and **Adolfo Dominguez**, but for younger, more radical fashion, try **Jean Pierre Bua** at Diagonal 469.

Food and fun goods The best food market is undoubtedly **La Boqueria** in the Ramblas. Good delicatessens, of which there are many in the city, include **Gran Colmado** at Consell de Cent, 318. Buy chocolate and ice cream from **Escribà** at Rambla 83, with a tiled Modernista façade.

The flea market (Monday, Wednesday and Saturday) is at Los Encantes at the Plaça de les Glòries. Calle Bisbal in the Old Town near the cathedral is good for novelties – puppets, papier-mâché masks, glass and ceramics, etc. Wax candles, a local speciality, are sold at Subira Cereria on Baixada Libertaria 7 (founded in 1761). For Basque berets, baseball caps, leather caps, etc, try the Carrer del Cal.

Note: department stores like El Corte Inglés and Galerías Preciados, are often open during the long Spanish siesta.

Tops for food shopping: La Boqueria market in the Ramblas

Snatching a snack in the Ramblas

See also pages 278–9

Visitors to Barcelona are guaranteed variety. The Catalan countryside supplies farm-reared meat and fowl, wild game, smoked hams and sausages, while the coastline provides a rich variety of fish and shellfish. Catalan cuisine is adventurous, with a ready use of herbs and spices and a mingling of sweet with savoury flavours.

Tapas bars Though not as ubiquitous as in Madrid, the choice is still enormous. **El Roble** on Lluís Antuñiz is good for seafood. **Cristal City**, on Balmes, sells books as well as tapas. At the other end of the scale, **Pinocho** is at stall no 66–7, in the Boqueria market.

Ciutat Vella The old town has the best choice of restaurants in a concentrated area. **Can Culleretes** at Quintana 5 is the oldest restaurant in the city and still going strong, with good reason. **Les Set Portes** (7 in Catalan) at Passeig Isabel II 14, **Agut** at Gignás 16, in the Barri Gòtic Quarter, and **Egipte** at Jerusalem 3, behind the Boqueria Market, are all good-quality, well-priced restaurants which serve Catalan food. **Els Quatre Gats**, a Modernista café at Carrer Montsió 3–5, was a favourite haunt of Picasso and friends.

Eixample Eating places in the Eixample area are generally more expensive. **Els Perols de l'Empordà** at Villarroel 88 serves the cuisine of the province of Girona. Try the *polleto de Bañoles*, chicken stuffed with sausages, cherries and pine nuts. **Eldorado Petit**, Carrer Dolors Monserdà 51 (to the northwest) is regarded by some as pretentious and others as the last word in tasteful eating. Stop for *merienda* (evening coffee and cakes) at **Mauri on** the corner of Carrer de Provença and Rambla de Catalunya.

Barceloneta The best fish and seafood restaurants are concentrated in this peninsula beyond the port. The choice is enormous but both **Can Majo** and **Can Costa** serve excellent fish in a lively atmosphere.

Spanish *cava* (champagne-style wine) is a regional speciality and Barcelona has a number of *xampanyeria*, or champagne bars. Try Xampanyeria at Provença 236. For cocktails as well as *cava*, 'Boadas', just off the Ramblas at Tallers 1, is central and long established.

Granjas are milk bars, the place to stop for a cake and coffee.

Nightlife

The bright lights of Plaça d'Espanya

Barcelona fiestas:
23 April is the day of Sant Jordi, Catalonia's patron saint, celebrated by the gift of a red rose from a man to a woman and a book from a woman to a man.
24 June, Sant Joan's day, is preceded by bonfires and fireworks the night before to mark midsummer.

The Poble Espanyol, the Spanish Village on Montjuïc, built for the 1929 trade fair, has recently become one of the livelier concentrations of night-time entertainments in the city, particularly at weekends. There are some good bars and restaurants and you can hear jazz as well as flamenco. Try the designer bar **Torres de Avila**, actually seven bars in one.

The distinguishing thing about Barcelona nightlife is that it begins in the morning – at weekends, at about 02.00hrs.
Those who prefer to be tucked up in bed by that time need not feel left out. A city of the size and sophistication of Barcelona offers a choice of entertainments including opera, ballet, modern dance, theatre and music-halls which begin and sometimes end long before the serious night revellers get going. Invest in a copy of the city's listings magazine, *Guía del Ocio*, to plan your entertainments.

Cabaret Music-hall entertainments don't require a subtle grasp of the language so try an evening at **Belle Epoque**, Montaner 246, or the slightly run-down but atmospheric **El Molino,** Vilà i vilà 99.

Late-night music and dancing If ballroom dancing is your passion, take your partner to **La Paloma** on Tigre or **Cibeles** on Córcega. As for discos and late night bar/dining/dancing places, you will find a concentration of them in the area north of Diagonal and Plaça de Francesc Macià and between Passeig de Gràcia and Muntaner north of Plaça de la Universitat.
Up and Down, Numancia 179, is where the smartest Barcelona families go – parents upstairs and young people down; then they share a taxi home. **Otto Zutz**, Lincoln 15, a designer night-spot on three floors, is open for members only after 02.00hrs – or so they say; but if your face and clothes fit, well ...
The **KGB**, Allegre de Dalt 55, has good live music and begins its evening activities earlier than most other clubs, around 23.00hrs. **Distrito Distinto** on Meridiana, on the other hand, is the place to end the evening – around 05.30hrs. **Divertido**, Moià 1, formerly gay, is now mixed but with a strong transvestite flavour. Xampanyerias or champagne bars are a speciality, serving excellent Spanish champagne-style cavas.

Accommodation

See also page 278

Barcelona has always been short of accommodation. Booking in advance or coming on a package tour is a good precaution against homelessness when you arrive.
Much of the new hotel building is in the luxury class. The Olympic Village has new hotels like the **Artes**, and up on the Diagonal are business hotels such as the top-range **Hilton**, **Princesa Sofía**, **Melià Barcelona Sarrià** and **Presidente**.
Hotels in the Eixample, with such exceptions as the 5-star **Ritz** and **Avenida Palace**, are generally smaller. Some such as the **Regente** and **Condes de Barcelona** are former Modernista mansions.
The Old Town has an increasing range of accommodation. There are 5-star luxury hotels like the **Meridien** (formerly the Ramada Renaissance) in the Ramblas. The **Oriente**, also bang on the Ramblas and much loved by old nostalgics, is still full of atmosphere but lacks double glazing (noise is the enemy of all who like to sleep in Barcelona). The Colón, opposite the cathedral, equally well loved, has been refurbished.
Aparthotels, like **Avenida Victoria**, on Pedralbes, are good for families who want to stay for a week or more.

• **Stroll** *There are any number of objectives for a stroll on* **Montjuïc**. *Take the metro to the Plaça d'Espanya. There are steps and an escalator up to the Palau Nacional, then an escalator to the Olympic Complex and the pretty little Jardins d'Acclimatació. You can then head along to the cooling Fundació Miró. Alternatively, arrive by funicular from the Avinguda Paral-lel or cable car from the harbour, and you are well placed for the fun-fair or a stroll around to the new Botanical Gardens above the cemetery on the seaside. Best of all on Montjuïc are the views of city and harbour.*

You can stay in old-style splendour in Barcelona

Catalonia's capital city is populous, bustling Barcelona

CATALONIA

Catalonia, that northeastern triangle of the Iberian peninsula – within Spain but by no means entirely of it – is in the deepest sense a true nation. Written 'Cataluña' in Castilian Spanish but 'Catalunya' in Catalan, the region has its own language, spoken everywhere, and its own history, customs, culture and achievements. Above all, it has its own aspirations, symbolised most recently in the Barcelona Olympic games of 1992. Not the most romantic part of Spain, Catalonia is continually among the most exciting. Its centre and symbol is the city of Barcelona (see pages 114–27).

The Catalan landscape is immensely varied. In the north are the Pyrenees, popular with skiers. The foothills give way southwards to orchard territory and then to bleak *meseta*. The Mediterranean east is defined by the rugged Costa Brava, heavily built up but still beautiful and wild in many places. After that the coast drops south through Barcelona to the tamer landscape and long sandy beaches of the Costa Dorada. The hinterland here yields the best white wines in the whole Iberian peninsula.

Catalonia was settled early by Greeks and Phoenicians. The Romans and Moors (briefly) followed; then the area was conquered by the Carolingian kings of France, so setting it off on its distinctive course. Autonomous from 874, it was taken into the Kingdom of Aragon in 1137 but retained remarkable independence, continuously resisting the centralising power of Madrid from the 17th century. Today Catalonia is the most solidly independent of the Spanish autonomous regions.

The Catalan national sense of identity is centred on Barcelona

The trees of Aigüestortes are pine, fir, silver birch and beech. Fauna include the chamois and capercaillie (the latter close to extinction), the ptarmigan and the black woodpecker with his shocking scarlet cap.

Take the road for Muntanya de Sal from Cardona and descend, if you should dare, by eroded salt steps towards salt lagoons amid strange colours and formations.

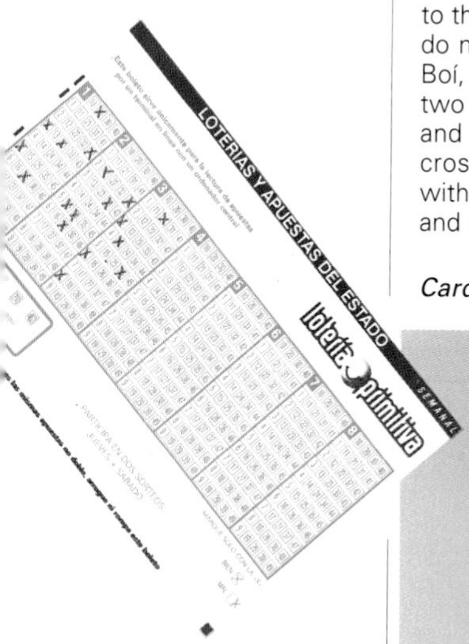

In the gazetteer entries below, where both Castilian and Catalan names are given, the Catalan appears in brackets after the Castilian.

▶▶▶ **Aigües Tortes (Aigüestortes)**

The 'Parc Nacional d'Aigüestortes i Estany de Sant Maurici', to give this enchanting tract of peaks and water its Catalan name, is one of two National Parks in the Pyrenees (see also page 111). 'Aigüestortes' means 'twisting waters' and 'Estany' means 'lake'. In the east, round Lake Sant Maurici, pines climb steeply from the lakeshore to meadows which in turn yield to scree and needle peaks. Of these the Encantat peaks to the southeast (2,747m) are most memorable. From Sant Maurici a trail leads westwards over the pass of Espot.

Getting there From the east, access is up the valley of the Noguera Pallaresa and through the village of Espot (train from Lleida to Pobla de Segur, then bus). From Espot, cars may drive as far into the park as the Sant Maurici lake. After that it is a matter of hiking or proceeding by jeep (for hire with driver or self-drive). From the west, follow the valley of Noguera Ribagorcana, then Vall de Boí, with magnificent Romanesque churches, to the village of Boí. Above Boí to the west the road is not so good, though some drivers do make it to the final car-parking point. For jeep hire in Boí, tel: (973) 69 60 36. Fit hikers can walk between the two last car points in about four hours or make it there and back in a long day. In winter, the park is open to cross-country and mountain skiers though only those with good experience should try. Park offices with maps and information are open at either end in summer.

Cardona's bulky castle, now a parador

Besalú, with its Romanesque bridge

▷▷▷ **Argentona**
Just inland from Mataró, north of Barcelona, Argentona specialises in earthenware, with an annual fair for waterjars. There is good municipal museum.

▶▶▷ **Bañolas (Banyoles)**
The lake here, 2.2km of straight water between winding banks, was the 1992 Olympic rowing course. There are boat tours and rowing boats to rent. The town has a pretty arcaded Plaça Major and an archaeological museum with prehistoric remains.

▶▶▷ **Besalú**
A delightful medieval town of creamy stone, Besalú stands beside the River Fluvia spanned by a fortified Romanesque bridge. From a profusely arched and arcaded main square visitors pass through narrow streets to the ancient Jewish quarter with Jewish ritual baths, or Miqwe.

▶▶▷ **Cadaqués**
This former fishing village, on Cape Creus, is lively but not noisy. Perhaps its small beach and artistic connections (Picasso, Magritte, Buñuel and Lorca all came here) have contributed to its slightly elevated tone. You can see surrealist Salvador Dali's house, with giant eggs on the roof, at nearby Portlligat.

▶▷▷ **Cardona**
A weird little Pyrenean foothill town, Cardona is dominated by a castle (now a parador) and an austere Romanesque church.

▶▷▷ **Cervera**
No 66 Carrer Major is where the marriage contract of Ferdinand and Isabella was signed in 1469. This town is also home to the university founded by Philip V when he closed Catalonia's other universities in the 18th century.

Two major bottled waters, Vichy Catalan and Malavella, are produced in the quiet, pleasantly jumbled town of Caldes de Malavella. A grand old spa hotel in Mudéjar style and remains of Roman baths, testify to its long tradition as a health spa.

It was only natural for the ancient Greeks to push on from Massalia (Marseilles) to Empúries and other spots in Catalonia. They were traders, and business was good in this rich agricultural area. When the Romans first came in through Empúries in the Second Punic War, under the command of the Scipio brothers, the intention was simply to defeat the Carthaginians. But victory gave the Roman Republic the immense mineral wealth of the peninsula, mainly from the Cartagena region in the southeast and from southwest Andalucía, today's Rio Tinto area.

Drive Behind the Costa Brava

See map on page 128.

This is essentially a drive inland from the Costa Brava, starting at Figueres and finishing at Girona. It crosses much fine scenery, takes in several of Catalonia's key shrines and a number of interesting natural phenomena. To complete it pleasurably in a day would require an early start; but there is a possible break-off point halfway, at Olot.

Starting from Figueres, take the N260 west for 26km to Besalú.
Olive groves in a semi-rural landscape give way to rolling plains of wheat fields and woods, with Pyrenean foothills rising ahead and to the right. Much in evidence in this peaceful and settled landscape is the stout and ample Catalan *mas* (farmhouse), many now restaurants.

Continue for 14km to Castellfolit de la Roca.
This pink-tiled village is built on the edge of a volcanic precipice.

From here the road to Ripoll ascends with fine views back over Olot and its volcanic countryside.
This is made up of lushly forested hills rising from flattish valleys.

After climbing to the Col de Coubet pass, take the road angling obliquely right to Sant Joan de les Abadesses.
The road descends through glorious country to the town and the upper valley of the River Ter.

On leaving Sant Joan, follow the main road south through a steeply wooded valley to Ripoll.
The magnificent monastery here has an even more spectacular place in Catalan history (see page 142).

From Ripoll, take the C150 directly back towards Olot.
The road rises steeply and enticingly, but all this western end of the arrowhead is hard driving.

Rejoin the original road for a brief stretch down to Olot.
The views are quite good enough for a second look.

After a stop at Olot, take country back-roads (not very good surface) for 33km, through Santa Pau and on to Banyoles lake.
Before Santa Pau, a path leads to the crater of Santa Margarida, 2km wide, for an optional detour.

After a winding hill crossing, descend finally to the peaceful lake of Banyoles and drive 20km to Girona.

The precipitous village of Castellfolit de la Roca

Empúries

■ When the torch for the 1992 Barcelona Olympiad came ashore in Empúries (Ampurias) the symbolism was entirely fitting. For this was one of the foremost settlements in the westwards drive of the ancient Greeks, ranking, for them, with their colonies at Nice and Marseille. .....■

Nowadays, though, **Empúries** is only a cluster of ruins beside the sea, much added to and partly built over by the Romans, with grey stone walls and remains of ancient streets running down to the intense green of pines and the glittering blue of the Mediterranean.

History The Phoenicians were here first, settling on an inshore island, now a knoll of mainland with a village a little way beyond the site. The Greeks arrived in about 600BC. By the 5th century BC their town was growing smartly, perhaps because of a lucrative trade in cereals, and in due course it became a proper Greek 'polis' or city state. Empúries was pro-Roman and anti-Carthaginian in the First Punic War. At the start of the Second Punic War, in 218BC, the Romans, led by the Scipios, landed here before moving south against Sagunto. From then onwards, Empúries was a powerful and important Graeco-Roman city. The religious buildings and city market stood on the same sites right through Greek and Roman times. The Romans added villas and public buildings along the summit of the hill. After the Romans, though declining, the town became a Visigothic bishopric.

The site Visiting the site is fairly simple, with a route clearly indicated and explanatory signs along the way. The path leads from the car park, and follows around the top of Cyclopean walls dating from the 2nd century BC. It takes in the main religious areas and temples, turns away left through the *stoa* or market and then leads up to the small explanatory site museum. The Roman villas lie above the museum (some excellent mosaics and a park-like atmosphere), with the Roman forum and other public buildings back along the ridge above the car park. The site terminates in a Roman gate and walls with remains of an amphitheatre beyond.

Tired sightseers can relax on the beach near the Empúries excavations

▶▶▷ Costa Brava

Spain's 'wild coast' of rocky inlets, pine covered hills falling sharply down to the sea and sheltered coves alternating with wide golden beaches, stretches from the border with France down to the town of Blanes in the south. The choice extends from lively high-decibel resorts to quietly secluded bays. But only a few kilometres inland, tourist Spain is left far behind.

Resorts and sights

The beach at **Aiguablava** is generally reckoned to be top of the league on this coast of ravishing beaches. It is small, with a marina, a couple of beach restaurants and a smart parador on the hill behind.

Bagur (Begur) is the central point for access to several fine sandy beaches in the area including Aiguafreda, Fornells and Aiguablava. This walled town, with its fine houses and lively market, is dominated by a commanding 17th-century castle.

The most southerly resort of the Costa Brava is **Blanes**, a busy, rather tatty industrial town (nylon manufacture) with a large beach, marina and fishing harbour. There are a few grand but decaying buildings in the old town. From the Marimurtra botanical gardens on the hill above the town there are spectacular views along the coast.

A cheerful and busy tourist resort (mostly self-catering accommodation), **L'Estartit** is the main centre for diving on the Costa Brava. Enthusiasts come for the caves, tunnels and coral reefs of the Illes Medés (Medés Islands) immediately off the coast, formerly the haunt of pirates. The area, with its coral, is now protected and visitors may see the coral beds and underwater life by glass-bottomed boat. The wide, gently sloping town beach is popular with families.

Lloret de Mar is a thrumming package tour destination

The system known as *pesca de la trayña*, or traina fishing, involves a ring of boats with lamps at the stern laying a net around a central illuminated boat. The fishermen confidently expect fish, particularly their chief catch, the anchovy, to be attracted by the lights and to gather innocently together to be caught – and it seems to be foolproof. The sight of boats fishing at night with lights is one of the most romantic of the Mediterranean.

A floral corner in well-restored Pals, one of the Costa Brava's most attractive spots

Popular Palamós was once simply a fishing village

with a good beach and esplanade. Bars, discos and fast food joints insulate the visitor from any experience that could be described as Spanish.

The resort of **Palamós** is low on charm, trafficky and hot in summer. There is a busy port near the old town centre at the top of an ear-shaped bay, with massed holiday apartment blocks. Less developed **Platje de la Fosca**, just to the north, offers two attractive beaches inside a large bay.

Pals beach stretches from Estartit southwards to Begur in a wide sweep of sand. The town itself, neat, floral and beautifully restored, is some way inland and deservedly popular.

Rosas (Roses) has a fortunate position at the end of a wide bay backed by mountains and a good sandy beach, but this cannot compensate for the ugliness of its tourist development.

Much famed in earlier times for its exclusive, discreet development, **S'Agaró** is in the throes of new building, albeit low rise, which will not improve it.

Formerly a spa and the centre of the cork producing industry, **Sant Feliu de Guíxols** is now a gentle commercial town and coastal resort. It has a charming promenade shaded with plane trees, a busy market and the ruins of an 11th-century monastery.

Benedictine monks built the walled monastery of **Sant Pere de Rodes** in the 9th to 10th centuries. Though partly destroyed in the 18th century, it still stands imposingly on a high peak in the last foothills of the eastern Pyrenees with far views along the coast. You can drive there, or walk (two hours) from the harbour town of El Port de la Selva. (The buildings are currently undergoing restoration.)

The long established, popular resort of **Tossa de Mar** has retained much of its character and charm, thanks to its position around a large semicircle of beach, backed by wooded hills, and to the Vila Vella (old town), with 12th-century walls, towers and lighthouse. Boats from here call at various points along the Costa Brava.

In the Jardí Botànic de Cap Roig (Cape Roig Botanical Gardens), enjoy wonderful sweeping views of quiet bays and rocky cliffs from high terraces, as winding, leafy paths lead from one thrilling *mirador* (look-out point) to another among carefully tended flower beds.

The town of El Vendrell (El Vendril), a rival to Valls in the construction of human pyramids (see panel page 148), is also the birthplace of cellist Pablo Casals, who is celebrated in the Casa-Museo Pau Casals, Calle Palfuriana. The Roman Arco de Bará (see page 147) is a short way south.

Several areas of the Ebro delta were set aside as natural park during the 1980s and bird life remains rich, including ducks such as shoveler, widgeon and mallard, as well as the rare and beautiful red-crested pochard. Marsh harriers and pratincoles are also seen.

Salou's beach, always crowded in summer

▷▷▷ Costa Dorada

The Costa Dorada (Golden Coast) stretches from the Ebro delta in the south almost to Barcelona, and then, if you believe the propagandists, on again to meet the Costa Brava. Most of the shoreline is fairly ordinary, hot and flat, with thrumming resorts and popular if rather uninspiring beaches. But it has two notable towns in Tarragona (page 146) and Sitges (page 143), and a magnificent hinterland, with good wines from the rugged district of Penedès, behind Tarragona, and the world-famous monastery of Poblet (see page 142).

Resorts and sights

The little seaside town of **Cambrils** has a good wide beach and rather a jolly old-fashioned esplanade.

Adjoining the Costa to the south, the **delta of the River Ebro** protrudes into the Mediterranean like a flattened arrowhead. Though very hard pressed by towns and agriculture (rice fields, fruit and vegetables) this is Spain's largest Mediterranean wetland.

L'Ampolla, the most southerly Costa Dorada resort, is a place of low-rise apartments and small hotels, with yachts and fishing boats. Views south of the Ebro delta resemble a mangrove swamp with telephone poles.

Salou is a concrete pleasure factory, living off its pubs and beaches. Always popular with local Catalans and with Spaniards generally, it is doubly crowded at weekends. It has lately improved its water and sewage systems following a health scare in the British press.

Industrial neighbour to Sitges, **Vilanova i la Geltrú** has good restaurants, an agreeable atmosphere and several interesting museums.

▶▶▷ Figueras (Figueres)

Spaniards, and Catalans, have great respect for their own birthplace, a tradition followed by Salvador Dalí. He endowed his birthplace, the busy little town of Figueres behind the Costa Brava, with an extraordinary surrealist museum of his own life and work. Full of visual jokes, inside and out, this museum in an artfully converted theatre is a complex blend of exhibitionism and deep seriousness. Don't miss the living room designed as 'The Face of Mae West', with the famous red sofa as her lips. King Juan Carlos opened an extension to the museum in 1994.

The visual humour starts before you even enter the Dalí museum at Figueres

▶▶▷ Gerona (Girona)

Girona, meeting-place of rivers, possesses an old town packed deep with treasures and full of shadowy medieval arches, alleyways and dark stairways. Old houses, recently restored and painted in ochre, orange and green, hang over the River Onyar, reflected in its waters. The city has a long history going back to the Celtiberians. It was called Gerunda under the Romans. Essential sights include the old Jewish quarter, a cathedral with the widest single Gothic span in Christendom, the Museu d'Art (a fine gallery of paintings and ceramics), Arab baths, and the archaeological museum within a former Romanesque monastery.

▶▷▷ Lérida (Lleida)

The Catalan provincial capital, Lleida looks grim from outside but will repay a visit. The skyline is dominated by La Zuda, a ruined Moorish fortress, and the Seu Vella (old cathedral), with a fine south portal and soaring Gothic cloisters. Below the cathedral lies the old town, the new 18th-century cathedral (with a collection of tapestries) and, opposite it, the magnificent Catalan Gothic Hospital de Santa María (archaeological museum here temporarily closed).

Walk Costa Brava patrol path

This is a coastal walk, following the old Cami de Ronda, or Civil Guard patrol path, between Cap Roig, Calella de Palafrugell and Llafranch. It can be started or ended at any of these points and takes a short hour in each direction, allowing for stops.

Starting from the housing development just beneath Cap Roig Botanical Gardens, follow the sign 'Al Cami de Ronda' on the Carrer del Cant del Ocells. Turn left at the sea, through a tunnel.

On approaching Calella beach keep as close to the sea as possible, hitting the road again at Hotel Mediterraneo and following it down along the arcaded front of Calella de Palafrugell.

Keep to the coast again round the cape to Llafranch.

Views all the way are varied and often dramatic, a true Costa Brava blend of red rock, green pines, blue seas – and with new development and older towns.

▶▷▷ **Montblanc**

The 14th-century town of Montblanc, like its monastery neighbour Poblet (see page 142), gains much from proximity to the attractive sierra of Prades (1,201m). Somewhat sunk into a melancholy tranquillity today, it retains massive walls and turrets, particularly impressive when approached from the west. The heirs to the kingdom of Aragon traditionally took their title from here as Dukes of Montblanc. The town contains several important churches; the most impressive is Santa María, with baroque façade and Gothic interior. Note also the patio of the Hospital de Santa Magdalena.

▶▷▷ **Montseny**

High and wooded, the Montseny sierra rises not far north of Barcelona, good for hiking, cycling or Sunday lunch among its restaurant-rich villages. There are lofty views of the mountains from the Girona motorway and from Vic to the north. The **Parc Natural del Montseny** has chestnuts, wild cherries, pines, bracken, great views and abundant birdsong. The towns of **Breda** and **Hostalric** are recommended stops.

▶▶▶ **Montserrat**

Montserrat, literally the saw-toothed mountain, is chief of the spiritual homes of Catalonia. The ancient Benedictine monastery, at 721m, was destroyed by Napoleonic invaders and rebuilt in forceful rather than attractive style beneath the rocks. The venerated 12th-century Virgin of Montserrat shelters in her great dark church. Her face is black, allegedly smoke-stained. The atmosphere is highly impressive, not least because the monks, even in the dark days of Franco, heroically took a stand for learning allied to Catalanism. There are rich collections in the museums here, open to the public. A cableway and funicular take you up the mountain for great views.

▶▷▷ **Olot**

This town at the centre of the Garrotxa volcanic area is famous for its late 19th-century school of landscape painting (County Museum of La Garrotxa, Hispici building). There is a Museum of Volcanoes in the park (closed Sunday pm and Tuesday). Look out for a splendid Modernista mansion, the Casa Sola-Morales at no 38 Paseo Blai. See also **Drive** page 132.

▶▷▷ **Peralada**

This ancient wine-growing settlement behind the coast produces a good champagne-substitute. The local grandee family owns the castle, with library, wine museum and crowd-pulling casino.

▶▶▷ **Peratallada**

Near neighbour of Pals (see page 135), the walled village of Peratallada is less restored, more rustic and more medieval in atmosphere. Its Romanesque church stands in fields outside the walls. Inside, enjoy the palatial castle façade, the arches rising over narrow streets and several good restaurants.

Catalan countrymen used to wear a kind of shortened stocking cap, bright red with a black band at the base. The best were made in Olot, where they are still produced – though mainly for 'folklore' purposes (for dance teams and local costume). Olot also has sculpture workshops, turning out brightly painted religious statues. These go mainly to South America, the Spanish market being close to saturation.

The red and black Catalan stocking cap is called a *barretina* and the red sash worn round the waist is a *faixa*.

The great monastery of Montserrat in its stupendous setting

The Catalan Pyrenees

In a real sense the Catalan Pyrenees begin – or end – with the Costa Brava, and especially with rugged Cap de Creus, where the monastery of Sant Pere de Rodes stands like a last outpost overlooking the sea. .....

From here, with little intermission, the ground climbs ever higher, up through the grand, green hills and lesser mountains known as the Pre-Pyrenees and finally to the main ridge and glacial cirques of the highest mountains. These lie along the border with France, rising ever higher as they move east-west. The Pyrenees reach their highest point just across the Catalan border and into Aragon (see pages 108–9).

The northern mountains The Costa Brava end of the Pyrenees (Pirineus in Catalan), already quite high enough to offer numerous ski stations, is crossed diagonally by the historic route from Perpignan to Lleida. There is plenty of interest along the way; just north of the border town of Puigcerdà lies Llívia, a little Spanish enclave entirely surrounded by French territory. Just north of La Seu d'Urgell lies Andorra, even more remarkable as a survival. All this is skiing territory and all along here to the south runs the splendid Cadí range, offering magnificent rock-wall views and the handsome split-peak of Pedraforca (2,497m). Pierced now by a north-south tunnel (access to Barcelona), the range is the centre-piece of the Cadí-Moixeró Natural Park.

Going south and west South again, the Pre-Pyrenees are a treasure store of Catalan Romanesque architecture and such historic splendours as the monasteries of Sant Joan de les Abadesses and Ripoll.

Next westward, and last before Aragon, come two quite lovely north–south valleys, the Noguera Pallaresa and the Noguera Ribagorcana, running up towards the highest ground and linked at the top by a narrow road over the high Bonaigua pass. This is the climax of the Catalan Pyrenees.

Between the two valleys lies the Parc Nacional d'Aigüestortes and the extraordinary Vall de Boí (see page 148), heartland of Catalonia's rural Romanesque architecture. Above again, lies the equally extraordinary Vall d'Aran decanting downwards into France, not Spain, with a language of its own. For beauty, walking and winter sports, this area is past compare. But it is also true that its inhabitants are rather dour, lacking the easier charm of other parts of Catalonia.

The wild spaces of the Pyrenees near the French border

FOCUS ON *Religious Processions*

Spain is a country where every small town celebrates its saint's day as well as the highlights of the Christian calendar. In an increasingly secular society, these festivals are more than Christian feasts – indeed, many of them date from pre-Christian times. They also mark the bonds of locality, community and tradition. .....

It is a great honour to carry the holy image

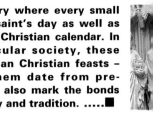

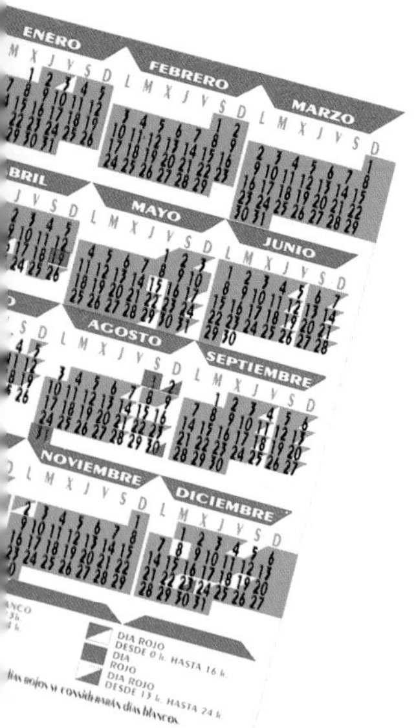

Semana Santa The Holy Week before Easter is the chief religious festival – celebrated with dour and dreadful sombreness in Old Castilian towns like Burgos and Valladolid; in Cuenca, Holy Week forms the occasion for a sacred music festival; for Sevillanos, it is almost a theatrical showcase of religious fervour.

In every case, the week begins with the blessing of palms on Palm Sunday, progressing to a climax of grief through Thursday night and emerging to triumphant joy on Sunday. Throughout the week, activity is focused on church services and street processions. Huge floats, or *pasos*, decorated with flowers and lit by candles, bear polychrome, life-sized statues in mute re-enactment of the events of Holy Week. Timetables of processions and services are usually printed in the local press.

The participants The bearers are members of various town brotherhoods, who have often paid for the privilege of carrying the floats on their shoulders. The penitents, many dressed in the pointed hoods and robes of the Spanish Inquisition, may walk barefoot beneath the weight of crosses or self-inflicted blows.

Often a *paso* will wait while muffled drums echo from another street. Suddenly the ululating cry of a *saeta* (literally an arrow), directed at Heaven from an onlooker moved by grief, pierces the air. Sometimes an oppressive and dreadful silence hangs in the incense-filled air, interrupted by a sharp rattle as the bearers resume their load and continue their dolorous progress. Yet the prevailing atmosphere is not one of lamentation. Locals will expound at length on the techniques of carrying the *pasos* and the subtleties of footwork involved. Youngsters emerge from town discos to see the progress of a *paso* and exchange a joke with a friend in the *paso* before ducking back into the party.

Corpus Christi This festival, like Semana Santa, is a moveable feast, generally falling at the end of May. It celebrates the triumph of good over evil and culminates in the procession of the Host through the streets, carpeted with flowers and scented herbs. Even young children stay up through the night to make these carpets, knowing their perfection will last only until the first step of the procession.

Christmas and Carnival Though never of much significance, Christmas is celebrated on 6 January. This is the Feast of the Three Kings, Los Tres Magos, and the occasion for the exchange of gifts. Carnival takes place in February before the austerities of Lent and is celebrated with variable fervour throughout the country. For many, it is the occasion for a great deal of dressing up and processions and general merry-making.

Romerías or pilgrimages often involve all the inhabitants of a small town or village. They set out to some remote and venerated place, usually a shrine to the Virgin, in a day trip that often has all the appearances of a village picnic. The *romería* in Ujué, though, is a notable exception. Pilgrims walk in chains through the night, flagellating themselves at the Stations of the Cross.

The most famous *romería*, to the shrine of Nuestra Señora del Rocío (Our Lady of the Dew) in the province of Huelva, takes place at Whitsun and is undoubtedly of pre-Christian origin. It has a strong southern – even gypsy – flavour as the vast cavalcade of people on horseback or decorated carts travels to the shrine at the southern extremity of the province. The journey involves camping out and is the occasion for as much music, dancing, drinking and horsemanship as pious religion.

Religion comes out on the streets

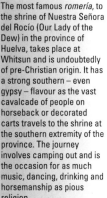

▶▶▶ Poblet
Poblet monastery ranks with Ripoll in importance but is much more attractive, its stone and architecture a golden testament to Catalan history and religious aspiration. Founded by Ramón Berenguer IV in 1150, the triple-walled monastery was largely destroyed in the 19th century but has now been restored and reoccupied by monks. Tours reveal cloisters and locutorio, kitchen, refectory and library. The huge church contains mock-Gothic, fake tombs of the kings of Aragon-Catalonia and a Damián Forment retablo, many of its lower figures decapitated in revolutionary periods. There is an 87m-long dormitory, and a good museum illustrating the reconstruction of the monastery.

Wilfred the Hairy, stout ally of the Frankish emperor Charles the Bald, was the key figure in the evolution of Catalonia, gathering several territories into an independent County of Barcelona in 878. Soon after, he founded the Abbey of Ripoll (where his remains reside in a casket of waxen smoothness, cantilevered from the wall of the north transept) and Sant Joan de les Abadesses in 885. He died in 897, founder of a dynasty which was to rule till the 15th century, when Catalonia was taken over by the Kingdom of Aragon.

▷▷▷ Puigcerdà
A frontier ski resort town, Puigcerdà is also popular with people from Barcelona who pop over the border to shop in France. The tiny Spanish enclave of Llívia lies 5km onwards, in France.

▷▷▷ Reus
Inland behind Salou and Tarragona, Reus is not a holiday-makers' town, though its central area has an attractive 19th-century atmosphere. The Plaça Prim contains an equestrian statue of local magnate Juan Prim, who became Spain's best 19th-century prime minister. This was the birthplace of Antonio Gaudí (see page 145) - witness the many fine Modernista buildings.

▶▶▶ Ripoll and San Juan de las Abadesas (Sant Joan de les Abadesses)
These two great Benedictine monastic foundations, both established in the 9th century by Wilfred the Hairy, are often called the cradle of the Catalan nation. The splendour of **Ripoll** is best illustrated by its now glassed-in portico, with its large, detailed and lively sculptured façade. Though worn by pollution, it remains one of Spain's great set pieces of early Christian art. Ripoll was a major centre of learning and transmitted much of Arab culture, especially mathematics, into northern Europe. The town, however, is on the dingy side.

Sant Joan de les Abadesses, 10km up the valley, is another gem. Wilfred's daughter Emma was first abbess of this foundation for high-born ladies. Don't miss the Romanesque church, Gothic cloister and the major works of sculpture inside the abbey. The town has an agreeable, arcaded baroque Plaça Major.

Diversity of olives in the market at Ripoll

▶▷▷ San Cugat del Vallés (Sant Cugat del Vallès)

Behind Barcelona's Tibidabo mountain lies the little monastery town of Sant Cugat. The church of the one-time Benedictine monastery is extremely handsome, with rose windows over the main portal, and triple apse.

▶▶▷ Santes Creus

Santes Creus monastery, in a tranquil valley of vines and fruit trees, is one of the many burial places of the kings and queens of Aragon. Their remains were moved here from an earlier site by Ramón Berenguer IV in 1158. The monastery's gateways, with ornamental plasterwork and complete with sundial, give way to a handsome, quiet square. The monastery is battlemented; on the church façade a Gothic window surmounts a Romanesque door. The traceried cloister is a delight.

▶▷▷ Seo d'Urgel (La Seu d'Urgell)

Today La Seu d'Urgell, seat of the archbishop (who happens to be joint ruler of Andorra) is essentially a point of passage on the way to Andorra, set in a landscape increasingly commercialised for skiers. The 12th-century cathedral is solid, a fraction militaristic, but elegant with a pretty gallery high on the exterior of the apse. Don't miss the 13th-century cloister and diocesan museum.

▶▶▷ Sitges

Sitges is a proper little seaside town built around an older nucleus on a knoll beside the sea. It is a resort where gay life (not too flamboyant) and family holidays exist comfortably side by side. The original old town, with baroque parish church, a diminutive square, fine mansions, whitewashed corners and a section of rampart, divides two very satisfactory beaches from one another.

The small northern beach of San Sebastián is backed by palms and cafés and 1920s apartments. The large beach to the south, the Playa de Oro, is divided into segments by breakwaters and backed by a fuller display of palms. Most of the restaurants and jollity are around the Carrer de Parelladas. Among several museums, one is a star – the Museu Cau Ferrat, up on the knoll, was once the home of the Catalan painter-playwright Santiago Rusiñol (1861–1931), and is stuffed with tiles, ceramics, iron work, glass and paintings galore, including five Picassos and two El Grecos.

▶▶▷ Solsona

The rather tatty little town of medieval alleys lies in a wide bowl in the pine-clad Pyrenees. One corner of it is formed by the combination of the bishop's palace with the Romanesque and baroque cathedral. The slender and much venerated Romanesque Virgin of the Cloister is displayed in the cathedral, well worth a coin in the light box. The diocesan museum has well displayed prehistoric galleries, polychrome Romanesque statuary in the cloister and a fine assemblage of Romanesque murals from local churches, as well as good Catalan Gothic religious art.

Church and beach at Sitges

Even before the Ancient Greeks, the Phoenicians and the Romans, the Costa Brava was surprisingly well populated. The megalithic peoples of 4,000 and more years ago left standing stones and a good supply of dolmens (at Fitor in the Gavarres hills, for instance, and La Cova d'En Daina, inland from Palamós). At Santa Cristina d'Aro, near Sant Feliu, is an 80-tonne granite block precariously balanced upon another.

The extensive cork oak forests of the Costa Brava hinterland have always produced much of Spain's cork exports. Now, however, with plastic largely replacing cork, and in the face of Portuguese competition, Catalan factories confine themselves mostly to cleaning, steaming and pressing high quality cork from Portugal. Local cultivation has declined, but the trees can still be seen.

Creative Catalonia

■ Would-be artists should move to Catalonia. There seems to be something in the air that inspires great achievements. 20th-century Catalonia has given us such international artistic giants as Miró and Tàpies, Dali and the young Picasso. .....■

The Romanesque The story starts, however, with Wilfred the Hairy, first count of independent Barcelona, and his 9th-century Monasterio de Santa María at Ripoll. By the end of the Romanesque period the monastery had not only acquired its great carved portals; it stood at the centre of international learning and Catalan self-awareness. Another great foundation, the later Cistercian monastery at Poblet in mid-Catalonia, was to be equally important. Meanwhile, in the Pyrenean valleys, Romanesque churches with tall-stacked towers were acquiring some of the most outstanding frescos in Spain. Catalan Romanesque mixes a local earthiness with Byzantine gravity and an Italianate sense of character (there was strong influence from Lombardy).

A flowering culture Architecture throve mightily during the Gothic period, when the Catalan speciality, distinct from the rest of Spain, was for vast single-span hall-churches. The cathedral in Girona has the widest Gothic vault in Christendom. This style spread beyond the Pyrenees into France. Meanwhile, Catalan intellectuals like the renowned 13th-century mystic, polymath and poet Ramón Llull were continuing to influence the pattern of culture in the whole of Europe.

The restored monastery of Poblet, founded in the 12th century

Cultural rebirth Spain's centralist centuries, especially under the Bourbons, were not good for Catalonia. But the 1840s saw the start of a great linguistic and literary revival known as the *Renaixença* (Renaissance). It was a period of literary creation, choral singing, lively folklore, all in Catalan. It led, in a clear succession, to the curious glories of Modernista architecture (see opposite).

Suppression and revival Catalan art also emerged, with artists like Ramón Casas and Santiago Rusiñol preceding Picasso and the other contemporary greats. Then all of a sudden the Civil War and the Franco dictatorship brought a renewed banning of the language and the suppression of Catalan culture. Far from disappearing, however, Catalan creativity went underground, ready to break out again on Franco's death in the joyful exuberance which characterises the region today.

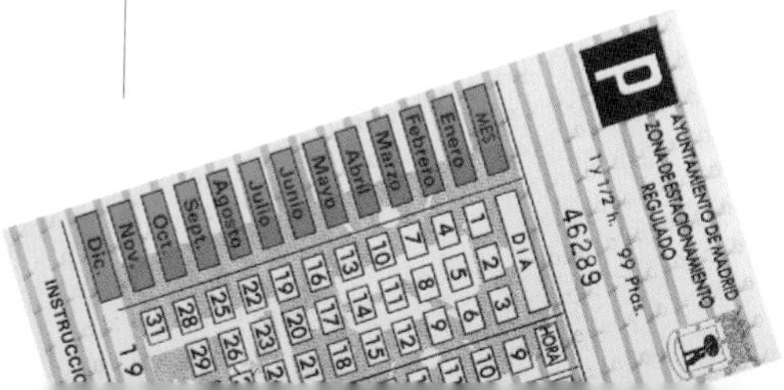

Gaudí and Co

Gaudí – Catalan architect extraordinary, fantasist and creator of the astonishing spiky and organic-looking church of the Sagrada Família, Barcelona's foremost picture postcard image – his is the name that everyone knows. .....

But we should not forget the 50 or so other Catalan architects – most notable among them Lluís Domènech i Montaner and Josep Puig i Cadafalch – and an army of hundreds of master craftsmen who supported these brilliant designers in every domestic manufacture from stained glass to ceramics, from furniture to door locks.

The Modernista movement The depth and richness of the movement transformed Barcelona itself, made a real impact on other Catalan towns from Olot in the north to Reus in the south, and reached out into Valencia and many non-Catalan provinces. The style was a close cousin to German Jugendstil and British, Belgian and Austrian art nouveau, based on a flowing organic line and a richly romantic use of colours and materials. But the motivating force behind the movement was Catalan cultural nationalism.

Domènech, Gaudí and Puig
Domènech made his mark first. As a 28-year-old architecture professor he called, in 1879, for a 'national' approach. He went on to define it in a long series of buildings, ranging from houses and hospitals to the Palau de la Música Catalana in Barcelona (see page 123). Preferring to build in brick with bright ceramic ornament, he leaned quite heavily on Gothic antecedents. Stained glass was a favourite Domènech medium. Antoni Gaudí, born in 1852, was conservative and rigid in his philosophy where Domènech was open and eclectic. He would certainly have repudiated the label Modernist. But his technical daring matched a soaring imagination and he gathered around him a tight network of disciples, all achieving unprecedented effects, even though in the service of a restrictive ideology. Concrete and wrought iron were his forte, the list of craftsmen who worked with him immense. Puig, the last of the great trio, was both younger and fractionally less inventive, more inclined to rely on historical precedent. But his range is also surprisingly great; and he went on to become head of the regional government which Catalonia briefly achieved at the start of this century.

Gaudí's extraordinary masterpiece, the Sagrada Família in Barcelona

Tarragona's cathedral

Names beginning with 'Caldas de' (Catalan 'Caldes de') – meaning 'the springs of' – are extremely common and imply both a profusion of local mineral waters and of many spas. The Romans appreciated such springs and built baths in, for instance, Caldes de Malavella and Caldes de Montbui in Catalonia.

▶▶▶ Tarragona

Leaving aside Barcelona, which is another thing entirely, Tarragona is by far the most agreeable of the larger towns along the coast of Catalonia. Open, airy, pleasantly modern in parts, it also possesses some of the best Roman remains in Spain – and a huge sense of antiquity – confined, but by no means entirely, within high city walls and an impressively tangled old town.

The city is a provincial capital. Despite some dreary apartment blocks on its southern approach the centre has a remarkable atmosphere, full of light and a sense of civilisation. This is best sampled on the Rambla Nova, a modern street which leads to a fine *mirador* (look-out point), the well-named Balcó del Mediterrani. Here, from beside the statue of the town's medieval hero Roger de Lauria, the slope falls away steeply beneath to the railway station, beach (cleaned and renovated) the harbour and, not quite in view, the remains of the Roman amphitheatre.

Publius Scipio, driving south from Empúries against the Carthaginians in 218BC (in the Second Punic War), adopted Tarragona as a Roman city. Later the emperor Augustus lived here. The poet Martial praised the city lavishly and Pontius Pilate was born here. It was the main Roman city in Spain, sharing in the imperial glory.

Chief ancient sites Pretori Roma (Roman Praesidium) is physically linked to the vaults of the Roman Circus (these two form the Museu de la Romanitat, see below). The separate Archaeological Museum is in a modern building linked to Pretori (combined ticket with old Christian necropolis, see below). The Archaeological Museum has fine sculpture and mosaics, including the famous Medusa head, which has become almost a

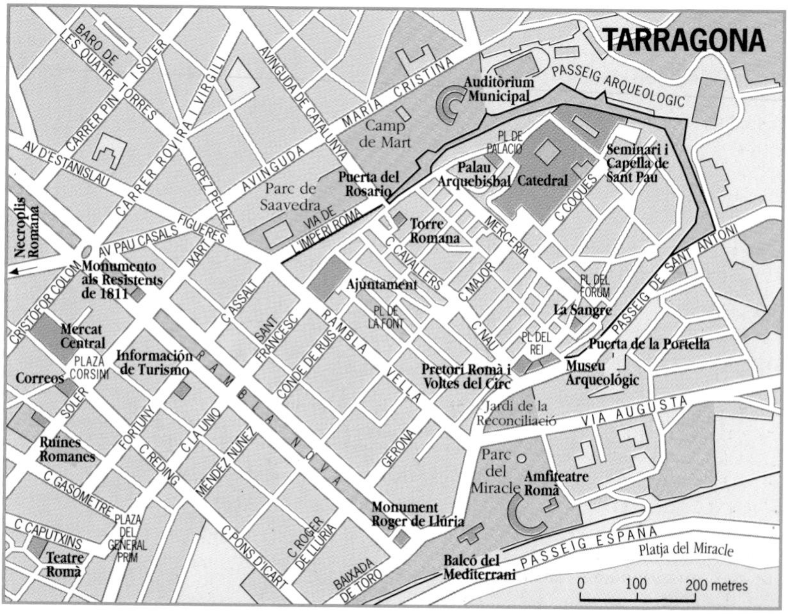

Roman aqueduct near Tarragona

stock image of Tarragona.

Passeig Arqueológic A walkway, round the outside of the inner wall, pre-Roman, Roman, medieval and 18th century. Open till midnight and illuminated.

Amfiteatre Romà, a short walk down towards the sea. Modern seating follows the old shape of the theatre, with the ruins of the Christian basilica of Santa Maria del Miracle superimposed.

Forum Divided by a modern street, this site beyond the Rambla Nova is extremely fetching, with golden brown columns, cypresses and geraniums.

A combined ticket is available for Museu de la Romanitat, the wall walk, amphitheatre and forum. No lunchtime closure.

Christian Tarragona Until Toledo took over in the 11th century, this was the seat of the Primate of Christian Iberia. The cathedral, real focus of the old town, is built on the site of the Roman temple of Jupiter and also succeeds a mosque. Broad stone stairs ascend to a time-worn square and the handsome sculpted portals of the cathedral, Gothic in style. Within, a magnificent retablo soars up in Gothic pinnacles.

The ancient Romano-Christian necropolis, on Avinguda Ramón i Cajal, out past the bullring, has a fine assortment of tombs and sarcophagi.

Around Tarragona On the road east towards Barcelona, the old via Augusta, look out for the funerary tower named after the Scipio brothers, with a pair of half-obliterated statues on its upper portions (at 16km, to left of road); and, at 20km, isolated now on a floral roundabout, the fine Arco de Bará, an impressive 2nd-century arch which once straddled the highway.

About 4km along the road to Lleida (north), there is a fine two-storey Roman aqueduct, one of Spain's best.

For reasons which remain unknown, Catalans love building human pyramids. Strong men, often assisted by a tight-packed crowd, put their arms on each other's shoulders to form a tight circle. A slightly smaller number climb to their shoulders, and so on up and up, in as many as eight or even nine diminishing tiers, with a young boy generally hoisted to the summit, where he gaily doffs his red cap at roof-height. Classically, the teams of *castellers*, or pyramid-builders, come from El Vendrell, Valls and Vilafranca de Penedès, but they travel all over Catalonia to give feast-day displays.

▷▷▷ **Tarrassa (Terrassa)**

Close to Montserrat but very much in the busy hinterland of Barcelona, this important textile town is little visited by tourists but tells much of the condition of non-tourist Catalonia. It has a handful of monuments of great interest and charm – notably the churches of Santa María, San Pedro and San Miguel containing ancient elements, including Visigothic horseshoe arches and Gothic paintings. There is also a varied and interesting textile museum, at Calle Salmerón 19.

▶▷▷ **Tortosa**

Situated close to the mouth of the Ebro, Tortosa has a long history both as a meeting place and point of division between the two distinct cultures of the peninsula, Moorish and Christian. Taken by the Moors in the 8th century, it was conquered for the Christians by Ramon Berenguer IV in 1148. The Moorish *zuda* (hill fortress), today containing a parador, offers fine views of the town and its setting and of the multi-buttressed, largely Gothic cathedral below. The 16th-century Collegi de Sant Lluís (temporarily closed for restoration) was built by Charles V for the sons of Moorish converts. In the river is a spiky steel memorial to those who died in the Battle of the Ebro, one of the fiercest battles of the Civil War. Visitors should be aware that the old town is in bad shape and can seem mildly threatening.

▶▶▷ **Vall d'Aran**

The Vall d'Aran is the high valley of the Garona (Garonne), with some of the best skiing in Spain. It was cut off from the rest of Spain each winter until the construction of the road tunnel from the south after the Civil War; the language is a mixture of old Gascon and Catalan and the local spirit is one of sturdy independence. The valley's capital is Viella (Vielha); prettier Artiés, 6km to the east, is best for food and accommodation.

▶▶▷ **Vall de Boí**

This beautiful high Pyrenean valley has recently become well known for its skiing. Its earlier and greater fame resided in its extraordinary collection of Romanesque churches.

▶▷▷ **Valls**

Valls specialises in human pyramids, which seem to be echoed by the lofty open stonework belfry of San Juan, the principal church. There are faded Modernista houses in the Carrer de la Cort and handsome 19th-century street lighting. The vaunted Jewish quarter, however, amounts to very little.

▶▶▷ **Vich (Vic)**

Pleasantly sited in a broad valley northwest of the Montseny range, the old Catalan city of Vic remains the busy centre of the area. Visitors should take in the quieter old town, especially the Plaça Major and the cathedral square, the Plaça del Bispe Oliva. In the latter, the 18th-century neo-classical cathedral with elaborate Romanesque tower is made extraordinary by the vast grisaille-to-sepia frescos, depicting scenes from the lives of Jesus's disciples, by the 20th-century Catalan painter Jose María Sert. Though not to all tastes, some find them strangely stirring. Opposite is Catalonia's leading episcopal museum, one of the most important in Spain. Its Romanesque collection of painted wooden panels and altar fronts and frescos, drawn in from the surrounding region, is spectacular. See particularly the Last Supper from La Seu d'Urgell. There is also notable Gothic work (by 15th-century artists Lluís Borrassa and Jaime Huguet in particular). Going further back in time, the town possesses the ruins of a 2nd-century Roman temple.

In 1991, Vic was the site of an anti-police ETA bombing in which several children were killed.

▶▷▷ **Villafranca (Vilafranca del Penedès)** and **Olèrdola**

Capital of the Penedès wine region, where wagon-loads of grapes can be seen bowling through the town at harvest time, Vilafranca is certainly worth a stop. A pleasant main road *rambla* opens into a square confusingly known as the Rambla Sant Francesc. Behind here is the old town – the town hall is half monumental-medieval, half florid-19th-century; the parish church is quite baronial and across from its main portal, in Plaça de Jaime I, is the local museum with various archaeological displays, housed in a fine building with Aragonese royal connections. In the same square there are other mansions, and a monument dedicated 'Als Castellers' – to the human pyramid builders (see panel page 148).

Olèrdola, above the Sitges road, has an ancient site with Romanesque church (Mozarabic elements) and castle.

The cluster of Romanesque churches in the high Pyrenean Val de Boi, including San Climente de Taüll, is one of Catalonia's most remarkable riches. Free-standing towers rise up to six storeys, with little arched windows in ones and twos and threes against the mountains. Rounded apses are sweetly decorated with the rings of blind arches known as Lombard banding. Inside were the famous frescos, rescued in the nick of time from theft, and the elements for the Museu d'Art de Catalunya in Barcelona.

Forget the nasty blocks put up for skiers in the '60s and the swarms of skiers' apartments which have followed – traditional Vall d'Aran architecture is one of the most distinctive styles in Spain. The villages are built in dark stone, with fly-away eaves and dark slates reaching up and up in pyramids, encircling the Romanesque church tower which rises in each.

Cathedral and bridge in Vic, an old Catalan city, now a busy industrial centre

The Christian reconquest of Spain threw up first the kingdom of León, and then that of Castilla, which surpassed its parent in power, creating in the process a landscape bristling with castles. These fortresses, strongest along the River Duero, stretched right down towards Madrid. The provincial capitals of Castilla-León – León itself, Zamora, Palencia, Burgos, Valladolid, Soria, Salamanca, Avila and Segovia – all have their roots in this expansion and together form a roll call of Spanish history. Two-thirds of the land is plain, the rest mountain; it comprises the largest single region in the European Community and one of the most sparsely populated. Its agriculture is suffering through competition from European neighbours. The villages are rather dour and enclosed.

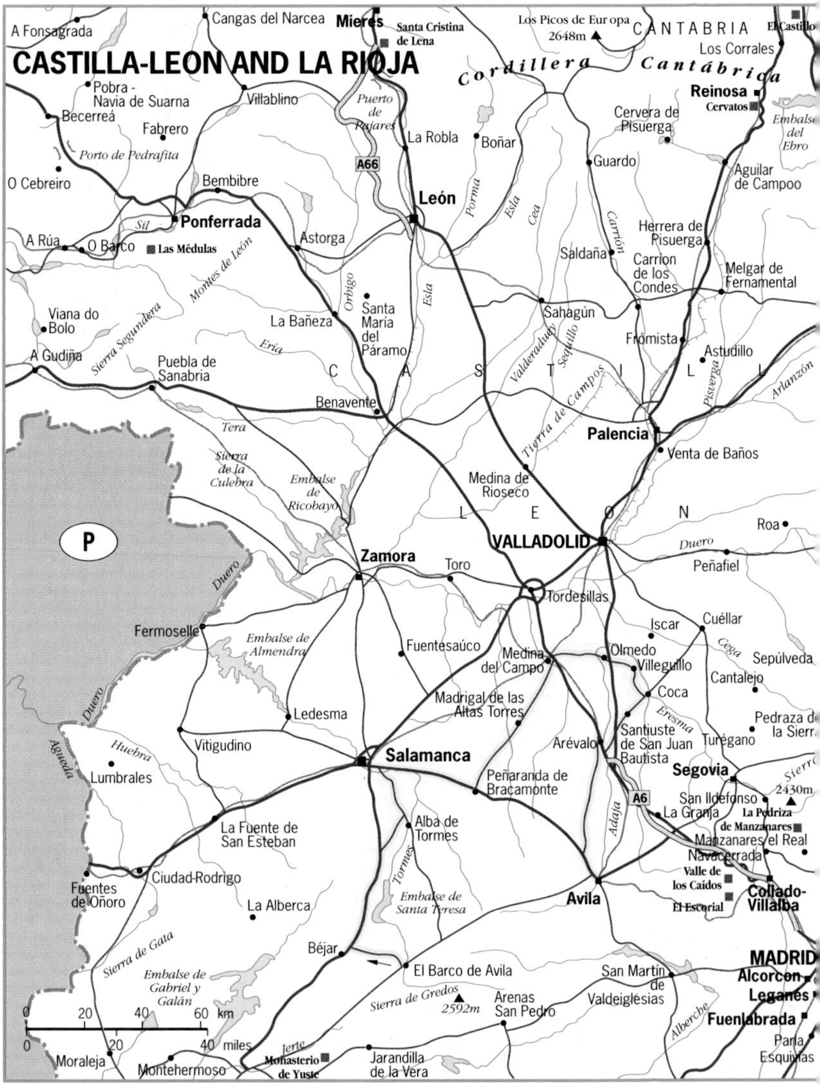

CASTILLA, LEON AND LA RIOJA

La Rioja, bordering Castilla-León to the east, is a different proposition. It too has its wide plains, its gorges and mountains, but it seems to have drawn a greater cordiality from the richer lands along the Ebro. It is, quite frankly, more sociable, an easier place to feel at home. One of Europe's smallest regions, it is noted for producing the best red wines of Spain. La Rioja is also famous for its excellent peppers. Fresh vegetables, in fact, characterise the cuisine of the area. This is another feature of contrast with neighbouring Castilla-León, where meat is the basis of regional cooking – roast kid, lamb or suckling pig, or spicy sausage.

One unifying aspect, however, is the Pilgrims' Way to Compostela, which passes through, linking the regions, in history, architecture and spirituality.

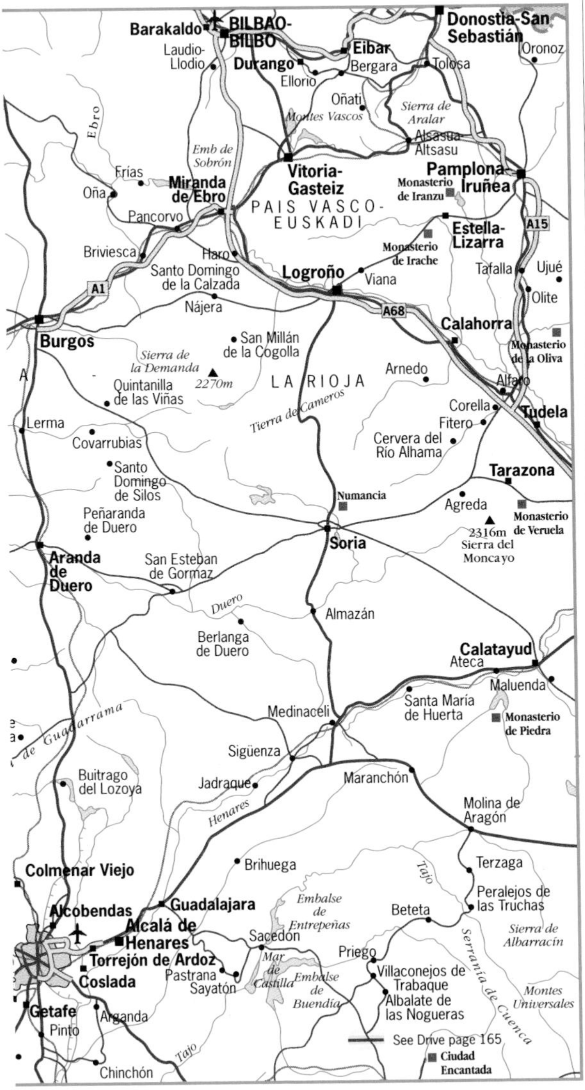

St Teresa's body, though treated with quicklime after death, gave off a smell of roses, provoking an investigation during which her left hand was removed. This eventually came into the possession of General Franco who clutched it on his own deathbed. The saint's heart was removed to gauge the effect of a vision in which she felt her heart and bowels had been pierced by a burning spear. Her left arm was also removed and small parts progressively trimmed for reliquaries. The practice was stopped by Pope Clement IX.

▷▷▷ **Agreda**

Agreda marked the early frontier between Castile and Aragon, as witness its castle and the fortified tower of the church of San Miguel. Later it was home to Sor María de Agreda, nun and confidante of King Philip IV.

▶▷▷ **Aguilar de Campóo**

Aguilar, dominated by a castle, a communications mast and a biscuit factory, is a satisfying town, with plenty of ancient mansions. The long arcaded main square leads up to the large (Gothic interior) collegiate church of San Miguel, with kneeling funerary couples. The heavily restored monastery of Santa María, on the exit to Cervera, is scheduled to become a national museum of Romanesque architecture (already open with local exhibits).

▶▶▷ **Alba de Tormes**

The town gave its name to the Dukes of Alba and later St Teresa died here. Though prettily situated on the River Tormes, it is now rather dismal. All that is left of the dukes is a huge tower, closed for reconstruction. St Teresa fares better. Visitors enter the convent church of La Anunciación under a fine Plateresque rendering of that scene. Opposite, behind a grille, is a reconstruction of the cell where St Teresa died, showing her on her deathbed. Further along the left-hand wall is her original burial place. She is now in a casket high above the altar, her arm behind a door to the left, her heart behind a door to the right. The index finger of St John of the Cross is kept in the museum of the Teresian centre opposite.

▶▶▷ **La Alberca**

This beautiful half-timbered village in the Sierra de Francia south of Salamanca has become very trippery. The district, once spectacularly poor and neglected, retains ancient architecture and customs. La Alberca has a little stream, a cobbled opening for a square, old trades actively pursued and a pretty stone cross. On the peak of La Peña de Francia above, reached by a road that winds round the mountain, is a monastery-retreat. Views are awesome.

▷▷▷ **Alfaro**

Lorries avoiding motorway tolls thunder through this easterly outpost of La Rioja, home of the Palacios *bodegas* (tastings and tours). In the quieter old town, there are grand mansions and the brick-built, Mudéjar-patterned collegiate church of San Miguel.

▶▷▷ **Almazán**

This is a pleasing walled town, with three gates, on the Duero. One of its three gates leads straight into the main square, with flower beds, statue of 16th-century local worthy, Diego de Laynez, and the classical 16th- to 17th-century palace of the Counts of Altamira. In one corner of the square is San Miguel, a Romanesque church whose octagonal tower is topped with patterned brickwork showing a clear Mudéjar influence. This is a Castilian meeting place of cultures.

▶▷▷ Aranda de Duero

This river-crossing on the Duero was a busy place until the main road by-passed it. It is still good for Castilian roast dinners and its church of Santa María has one of Spain's finest façades. Isabelline elaboration is tamed by harmony of composition; scenes from the Passion and Resurrection mingle with the richest dynastic heraldry.

▶▷▷ Arévalo

The home of Spain's best suckling pig is a sad mess, with the old town decayed and the modern town a straggle. But enter from the north and you will have a different impression, with bridge and surviving gate and the huge castle where Queen Isabella spent her youth.

▷▷▷ Arnedo

Arnedo is the capital of Rioja Baja (Lower Rioja), less interesting in itself than in its situation, under a line of cliff and hill with man-made caves and galleries.

▶▶▷ Astorga

Now only a medium-sized town, Astorga was one of Spain's earliest bishoprics and, later, an important stopping point on the Pilgrims' Way.The Romans called it Asturica Augusta. It has a fine Gothic/baroque **cathedral**, with a Renaissance retablo by Gaspar Becerrá, pupil of Michelangelo. Note especially the marvellous central porch, with carvings. The adjoining Diocesan Museum (open all week but closed in February), is also worth a visit. **The bishop's palace**, begun by Gaudí and finished by Ricardo Guereta, is Gothic-baronial without, Gothic-Mudéjar within. Never actually used by a bishop, it now houses the motley collection of the **Museo de los Caminos** (Museum of the Pilgrims' Way) and provides a fairly rare chance to see a Gaudí interior (closed on Sundays, except August).

Nobody knows where the Maragatos people came from, though recent studies argue for Phoenician origins. They lived – and this is certain – in village communities around Astorga and worked as muleteers, the men in bowler hats with curly brims, the women in long aprons and plentiful necklaces. These clothes still appear on feast days, as do Maragatos dances, but the tribe vanished with its way of life – the railway put the Maragatos out of business. But meals said to be Maragata style may be enjoyed in the village of Castillo de los Polvacares.

Scene from the life of Christ – Astorga cathedral

▶▶▶ Avila

Avila, birthplace of St Teresa, is a key to understanding Spain. The stern remains of military might, in the form of Europe's greatest medieval walls, and the reminders of religious intensity in the convents and churches that abound, combine to offer an awesome vision of Old Castile.

The past preserved Inhabited earlier by Celts, whose carved stone bulls or boars are found everywhere in the area, Avila became a much contested buffer-zone between Moors and Christians until King Alfonso VI, on retaking the city, ordered his son-in-law Ramón de Borgoña (Count Raymond of Burgundy) to build a definitive set of **walls**. Between 1088 and 1091, the count constructed a circuit of 2.4km, with 88 round towers and nine gates. The whole complex still stands. Following the old Roman line, the walls form a rectangle, running downhill to a river in the west. The apse of the city's rugged cathedral, an essential part of the defensive scheme, forms a protrusion in the wall on the higher, eastern side where it was most open to attack. The two most impressive city gates, with low arches for entry and high walkways above to join the towers, are also here.

The future St Teresa (see panel) was born here in 1515 and lived much of her life within sight of the medieval walls. Few notable contributions to the city have been made since her death. It has survived so well because it was so thoroughly bypassed by subsequent history. Spain's highest provincial capital, Avila is outstandingly bleak in winter, arguably the most fitting time to see this atmospheric city.

St Teresa (1515–82) was born into a family of Jewish background. When she was seven, she and her brother ran away from home in search of martyrdom. A monument – Los Cuatro Postes (Four Columns) – marks the spot where they were overtaken. She became a Carmelite nun at 18, spending over 20 years in the Convent of the Incarnation in Avila. She was a practical and energetic reformer, travelling ceaselessly and founding many convents in her own order, the Barefoot (or Discalced) Carmelites. The first, San José, was in Avila. She died in Alba de Tormes.

Within the walls The main feature is the early Gothic **cathedral**, rather dour outside with an unfortunate late 18th-century main façade. The interior is relieved by sculptural scenes on the Plateresque retrochoir, notably the *Massacre of the Infants*; by the strangely mottled

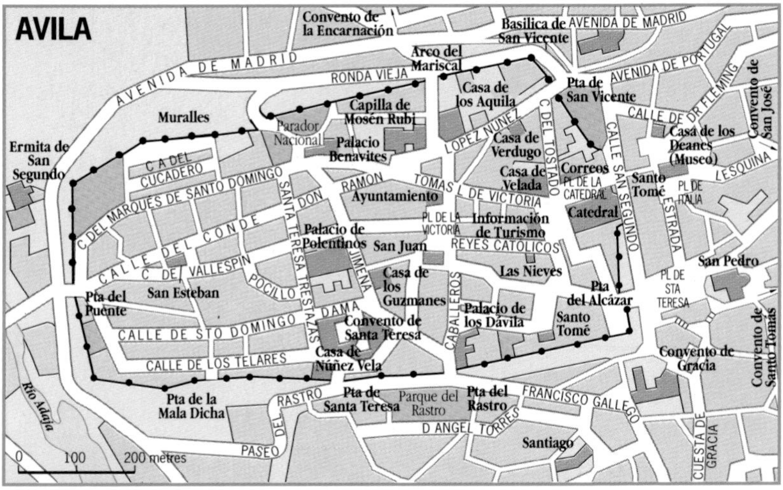

Carvings above a doorway of Avila cathedral. The city is a treasure-house of medieval architecture

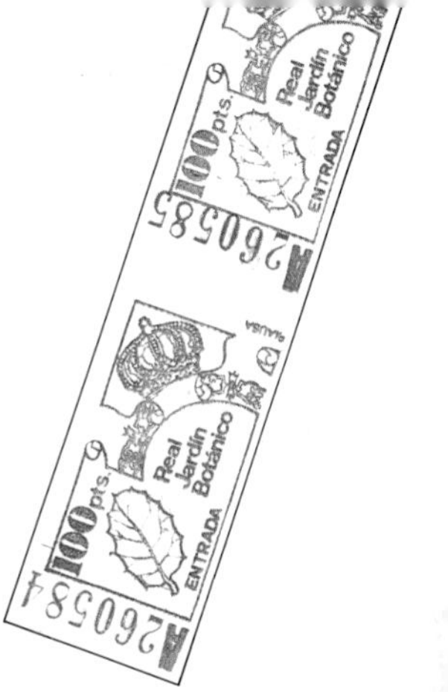

red and white stone of apse and transepts; and, in the ambulatory, by the alabaster tomb of El Tostado (the Toasted or Swarthy One), otherwise Bishop Alfonso de Madrigal. The cathedral **museum** includes the sacristy, where the leaders of the 16th-century Comuneros rebellion met, and there is a fine *Ecce Homo* by Luis de Morales.

Of the **palaces** within the walls, the best, including those of the Nuñez Vela, Guzman Oñate and Dávila families, cluster to the south. In the centre is the impressively vast Polentinos palace, with a further, less remarkable cluster, on the north side.

Outside the walls All the best religious architecture, and some of the more agreeable parts of town, are here. Beyond the northeast corner of the fortifications is the very fine Romanesque church of **San Vicente** (under restoration). It was built as a shrine on the site of a triple martyrdom (Vicente and his sisters Cristeta and Sabina), with colonnaded side gallery, a remarkably sculpted west entrance and, within, the carved sarcophagus of the saints. In the centre of this part of town is the Renaissance **Casa de los Deanes**, housing a good provincial museum, and the Romanesque church of San Pedro. Behind **San Pedro** is **St Teresa's birthplace**, now encased within a baroque church, and **San José**, Teresa's first-founded convent, with a small museum of the saint's life next door.

St Teresa in stained glass in the Convento de Encarnación

It is worth taking a car to the magnificent church and monastery of **Santo Tomás**, down on the south side of town, once used as their Avila residence by Ferdinand and Isabella. The poignant alabaster effigy of their only son, Prince Juan, dead at 19 years of age, looks up at a retablo painted by Pedro Berruguete. There is a series of three magnificent cloisters, one of which contains a museum with oriental art.

On the northern side of town is the **Convento de Encarnación**. Young ladies conducting visitors about the convent point out the very spots where St Teresa saw visions well remembered by posterity. The small museum is highly evocative both of her life and of that of her confessor, that other great Spanish mystic, San Juan de la Cruz (St John of the Cross).

The castle of Berlanga de Duero

▷▷▷ **Astudillo**

Astudillo (40km north of Palencia), with its 13th-century walls and Mudéjar church of Santa Clara is another reminder of the richness of Palencia, once residence of the Kings of Castile (see also Frómista, page 160).

▶▷▷ **Béjar**

A messy but interesting walled town under its own sierra (good views of the town from N630 to the northeast), Béjar occupies a promontory jutting down into an enclosed valley. Follow the promontory to its end for the Plaza Mayor and palace of the Dukes of Osuna, now a school.

▷▷▷ **Benavente**

Benavente, set at an important road junction and familiar to many travellers in northwest Spain, is unremarkable except for its hill-top parador, incorporating the one remaining tower of the ruined and rebuilt castle of Ferdinand II of León.

▶▷▷ **Berlanga de Duero**

Berlanga is one of a huge chain of Christian fortresses, built along the Duero valley from Soria to Valladolid, marking the first stage of the Reconquista. (Others are at Gormaz, Peñaranda and Peñafiel.) Its curtain walls and turrets, seen from the south, rival those of Avila. The town is dour, with arcades and a large collegiate church.

▷▷▷ **Briviesca**

The heir to the Spanish throne receives the title of Principe de Asturias (Prince of Asturias). The practice was established by the Castilian Cortés, meeting in this little Burgos town in 1388. Briviesca is otherwise known for its convent church of Santa Clara and the shrine of Santa Casilda just outside.

▶▶▶ **Burgos**

The best approach to Burgos is along the Madrid road. Arriving this way, you get an early view of the open stonework of the cathedral towers, rising in knobbly, thrilling eccentricity under the castle hill.

Early prominence Fernán González, count of Castile, pronounced himself independent of León in the mid-10th century, thus becoming, in the Castilian-centred view of Spain, a national hero. His descendant Fernando (Ferdinand) I became first king of Castile, then of León as well. Alfonso VI was the last king to rule from Burgos, shifting the court to Toledo in 1085 soon after the capture of that city. Rodrigo Díaz del Vivar, better known as El Cid, and rather notionally a vassal of Alfonso, was born a short way north at Vivar del Cid. He is as much a presence in the city as Fernán González.

In 1221 Fernando III, El Santo, laid the first stone of a Gothic cathedral which was to be among the finest in Spain. Successive kings and queens used the nearby Monastery of Las Huelgas as a residence when in Burgos. Isabella I commissioned family tombs in the Cartuja de Miraflores, Burgos' other great monastery.

Up to the present The city was headquarters of the Mesta and gathered in wool from all Castile for dispatch down to the coast and so by sea to Flanders. This trade collapsed during the 16th century. Despite declining wealth, the city always remained a military and religious capital. Franco used it as his Civil War headquarters from 1937 and, later, its military courts played a large part in his suppression of the Basques, notably in the famous Burgos trials of 1970, when international protest prevented the execution of Basque dissidents. As well as its Gothic monuments, the city retains a distinctly conservative feeling.

Visiting Burgos The old town rises on the north side of the agreeable little River Arlanzón. Only the municipal museum, which is fairly central, and the two great monasteries, Las Huelgas (1km) and the Cartuja de Miraflores (4km), are on the south side, best visited by car. For the rest, Burgos is very much a walker's city. Approaching the old town across the Santa María bridge, with the attractive riverside *alameda* called the Paseo del Espolón, the city's favourite strolling place, to the right, pass under the Arco de Santa María, a splendid 11th-century gateway. This brings you directly to the cathedral.

The cathedral The exterior of the cathedral is a festival of spires, towers and pinnacles. More or less dead centre in the interior – and beside an impressive choir carved by Felipe Vigarni (*c* 1500) – El Cid and his wife Jimena lie under a simple slab. A replica of their marriage settlement and a trunk belonging to El Cid are displayed in the cloister museum. In the first chapel to the right on entry is an early image of Christ, made of leather and supposedly with human hair. Both hair and nails are said to grow.

Gil de Siloé, possibly of Flemish origin, was one of the immensely talented group of architects and sculptors on whose services the Catholic Kings, Ferdinand and Isabella, were able to call. Others were Juan Guas and Simón de Colonia. Gil de Siloé was responsible not only for the exquisite royal tombs in the Cartuja de Miraflores at Burgos, but also for the decoration of that other masterpiece, the Constable's Chapel in Burgos Cathedral. His son Diego was one of the greatest architects of the Spanish Renaissance.

On the city walls of Burgos

From an early date, the royal families of Spain's tiny Christian kingdoms were almost obsessed by the desire to live, at least during their later years, in pious monastic settings. They founded numerous monasteries and stayed in them during the peripatetic course of medieval rule. This tradition was carried on by the Habsburgs – Charles V at Yuste, Philip II at El Escorial – and even, to a lesser degree, by the Bourbons, whose palace at La Granja incorporated a monastery. Las Huelgas, a royal foundation at Burgos, is an earlier member of this same series.

Spires and pinnacles of Burgos cathedral

An architectural highpoint is the magnificent double-stairway descending to the north transept from a high outer door, the so-called Escalera Dorada (Golden Staircase) of 1519–23 by Diego de Siloé. At the east end of the cathedral is the late 15th-century Capilla del Condestable (Chapel of the Constable), by Simón de Colonia, magnificent in Isabelline Gothic and with the fine tomb of the constable and his wife.

Castle, churches and Casa del Cordón
The **Castillo**, where both El Cid and Edward I of England were married, was blown up during the 18th century and finally demolished by the French in 1813. At the base of the castle hill there are several Romanesque and Gothic churches, including **Santa Agueda** where El Cid supposedly forced Alfonso VI to swear a great oath that he had not killed his brother at Zamora. Lower in the city, close to the main shopping street of Calle Santander, stands the handsome mansion where Columbus reported to the Catholic Kings after his second voyage. Its door is surrounded by a stout stone cord – whence its name, the **Casa del Cordón**.

Monasterio de las Huelgas Las Huelgas was founded by Alfonso VIII in 1187, at the request of his queen, Eleanor of England, after victory against the Moors at Navas de Tolosa. Its Sala Capitular still holds the tent-flap of the Moorish leaders, as also the banner from the battle of Lepanto. The church served as mausoleum to the early kings of Castile. There is a museum of textiles containing important grave-goods. Even more impressive are the monastery's Mudéjar remnants, including the chapel of Santiago. Here, the moveable arm of St James's image was used by Ferdinand III to dub himself a knight, no other mortal being worthy.

The Cartuja de Miraflores The church (open to visitors) contains a fine retablo by Gil de Siloé and two of Spain's finest funerary monuments, both commissioned by Isabella la Catolica and both also carved by Gil de Siloé. These are the tombs of her parents, Juan II and Isabella of Portugal, and of her brother, the Infante Alfonso.

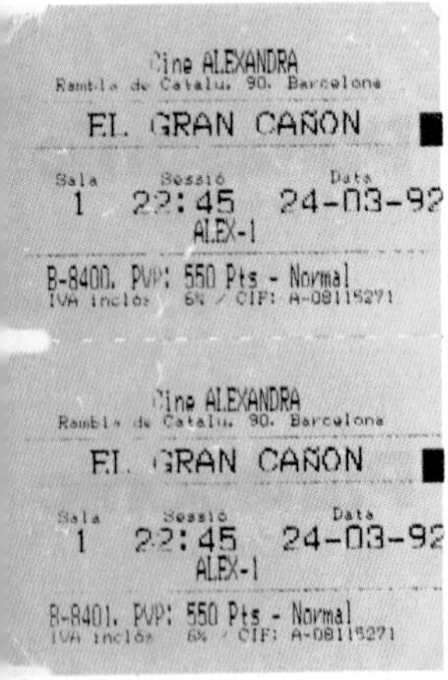

▶▶▷ Carrión de los Condes

Carrión, in rolling wheat country between Burgos and León, has retained two pilgrims' churches with Romanesque carving – Santa María del Camino and the more elaborate Santiago with a fine frieze topping its west façade. The former monastery of San Zoilo to the west has admirable Renaissance cloisters.

The Infantes of Carrión married the daughters of El Cid and then behaved in a surprising manner. They beat them up and stripped them naked and left them in an oakwood – all this according to the epic poem of El Cid's deeds. The Cid caught up with the Infantes and killed them. Well, he would, wouldn't he?

▷▷▷ Cervera de Pisuerga

Though on the bubbling Río Pisuerga, this is a disappointing village, except for the fortified church of Santa María del Castillo (with cloisters), on a great rock in the village. The neighbouring parador has fine views into the mountains of the Reserva Nacional de Fuentes Carrión.

▶▶▷ Ciudad Rodrigo

A place above all for strolling and relaxing, Ciudad Rodrigo rises over the Río Agueda just a few miles from Portugal. Twelfth-century walls still enclose the old town – and their whole circumference can be walked, offering fine country views and glimpses into streets still somewhat scarred from the Napoleonic Wars. The French held the town; the Duke of Wellington besieged and finally took it in 1812. He became Duke of Ciudad Rodrigo, a title still held by his descendants. The castle, once belonging to Enrique de Trastámara, is now an ivy-covered parador. The cathedral has fine choir stalls and an interesting rebuilt nave. Of the two palaces in the Plaza Mayor, the one from the 16th century now does duty as town hall. This square also sees the climax of wild bull-running festivities at Carnival time. The favourite local bar is called El Sanatorio.

Drive Historic Castile

This varied drive is seen as a continuation of, or prelude to, the Extremadura drive on page 186.

Picking up the route at El Barco de Avila, strike north.
Divert 5km left to scruffy, well-positioned **Béjar** (page 156).

Return up N630 towards Salamanca.
Angle right for **Alba de Tormes** with its St Teresa connections (page 152).

Hence to Salamanca and out towards Avila on N501.
At Peñaranda de Bracamonte, you go north across the flat plain to visit **Madrigal de las Altas Torres** and **Medina del Campo** (page 165).

Leave Medina on the Olmedo road. Jink very briefly right on N403, following signs to Llano de Olmedo, Villeguillo, and so to Coca (page 160). Return via Santiuste for Arévalo and finally south for Avila on a fast minor road.

Ciudad Rodrigo

The romanticised legend of El Cid (*c* 1043–1099) as Christian hero of the Reconquest has reached posterity through a wonderful epic poem. In reality, the Cid (Arabic for leader) was a minor aristocrat named Rodrigo Díaz de Vivar, born at Vivar near Burgos, who became an over-powerful military chieftain. Banished by his king, Alfonso VI, he took service with the Muslim ruler of Zaragoza, winning him great victories. Later he helped Alfonso take Toledo (1085), lost favour once again and finally carved out a private territory for himself in Valencia. His horse was named Babieca, his sword Tizona and his wife Jimena.

▶▶▷ Coca Castle

A castle of extraordinary elaboration, white and pink and set in pine woods roughly midway between Segovia and Valladolid, Coca is a true phenomenon. It was built for an archbishop of the ecclesiastically powerful Fonseca family in the late 15th century and swarms with turrets like swallow nests, so numerous they seem at least partly ornamental. The castle is deeply moated.

▶▷▷ Covarrubias

This well-preserved, not to say prettified little township in the green Arlanza valley, is nowadays no stranger to tourism. With the tomb of Fernán González (see Burgos, page 156) in its Gothic collegiate church, the visitor is very close to the heart of old Castile. The church has a rich museum and the tower of Fernán González still stands.

▶▷▷ Frías

With its castle tower alarmingly perched on a crag-and houses hanging by their fingertips in Cuenca style, Frías rises above the Ebro just west of the Sobrón *embalse* (reservoir). The village's 13th-century bridge springs from Roman foundations.

▶▶▷ Frómista

Here, in a tiny town on the Pilgrims' Way to Santiago, one of the finest Romanesque buildings in all Spain was erected around 1066 – the church of San Martín. Roof-levels stack up from a triple apse (reflecting triple aisles) through transepts to the nave, their heavy tiles creating an almost Byzantine effect. Capitals are profusely carved; there are no fewer than 315 carved corbels and a mass of tightly controlled decoration. This is a fully achieved masterpiece.

The turrets and towers of Coca Castle

▶▶▶ Gredos, Sierra de

The Gredos mountains, some of Spain's loveliest, begin to rise at the western edge of the Comunidad de Madrid area. Their lofty central section falls mostly into the province of Avila and they run on westwards, more and more remote – some would say more beautiful – right into Extremadura.

The range itself centres on the Pico de Almanzor (2,592m), the highest point of a north-facing cirque, or corrie, rising over a high lagoon. The peaks may all be seen from the upper terrace of the first-ever parador, personally sited by Alfonso XIII in 1928, a little way northeast of the cirque. This side of the range, though good for serious walking, is a little bleak and cold except in high summer. The Río Alberche flows laterally along it, then swings down round the Madrid end of the range. The southern side, with the valley of the Tiétar (see page 186) following it east to west, is far warmer, with crops like tobacco and red peppers; the mountains rise above, sometimes to straight, sometimes to jagged crests. Summer settlements at the head of the Tiétar valley dwindle away with distance from Madrid.

Towns like Arenas de San Pedro (with the castle of Alvaro de Luna) and the village of Guisando above it have an interesting vernacular architecture of jutting upper storeys and wooden balconies. This reaches a climax further down the valley in Villanueva de la Vera and especially Valverde (see page 186). Crossing the main pass above Arenas (fine castle at Mombeltrán), the old Roman road is clearly visible and may be walked above Cuevas del Valle.

The high mountains are magnificent walking terrain, but difficult tracks require experience. Maps are in short supply and guides – like the useful *Andar por la Sierra de Gredos*, by Jorge Lobo, no 30 in the Penthalon 'Aire Libre' series – tend to be in Spanish only. Mountain refuges are fairly plentiful. Many fine walks may be made upwards from the Tiétar valley, from spots close into the sierra like Casillas in the east and from Guijo de Santa Barbara above Jarandilla in the west.

Walk A taste of the Gredos mountains

This is an undemanding stroll (though with some gradients) which can be combined with a trip to San Martín de Valdeiglesias and the Toros de Guisando (see page 202).

To reach the start, take the road north from San Martín for Avila and at the point of entry to El Tiemblo, turn left up an unpromising-looking asphalt road, which later turns into a good dirt road. Ascend some 10km and park where the road doubles back over the bridge, or go a little higher straight up.

Walk in increasingly lovely country, with pine, oak and chestnut, and mountains rising above.

In Arenas de San Pedro

Going to mass in León's San Isidoro basilica

When the Romans came to Spain, the peninsula was still rich in gold, silver and other valuable minerals. The Romans mined prodigiously, nowhere more so than at Las Médulas, in the wild Bierzo mountains of León. They used a combination of water and slave labour to wash away whole mountainsides, creating an enormous empty amphitheatre riddled with red rock spires unaccountably left standing. Galleries the size of cathedral naves disappear into the hills; tunnel mouths gape darkly in the middle of cliff faces.

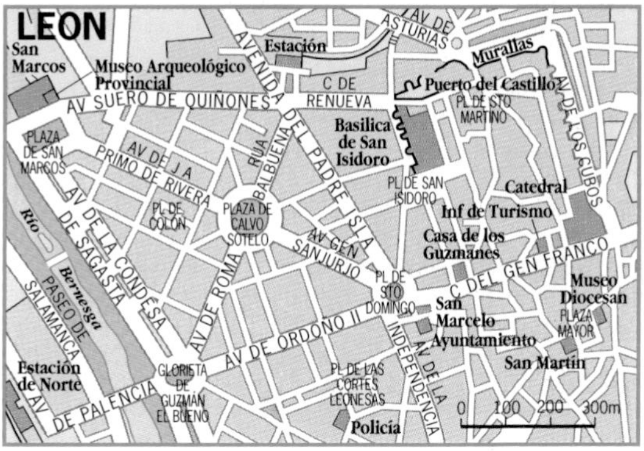

▶▶▶ **León**

Capital of a province of plain and mountain, and now with a full-ranking university, León has a strongly individual character. The city's huge importance in early Spanish history has left it with three of Spain's most remarkable monuments: the Romanesque royal pantheon of San Isidoro, a great Gothic cathedral and the pilgrimage hospital of San Marcos, now a parador.

History León was founded by the Romans; its name derives from 'Septima Legion'. Occupied by the Visigoths and then rather briefly by the Moors, it became chief city of the Christian advance across the Cantabrian mountains into the wide frontier zone of the northern *meseta*. In 998, Almanzor, on a summer raid from Córdoba, destroyed the city utterly, pulling down the Roman walls. But the Christians soon rebuilt it. In the following century Ferdinand I of emergent Castile combined the two young kingdoms by marrying Sancha of León. With the Santiago pilgrims, French influence was now not only pouring in but was also welcome. The cathedral of León was built almost entirely in French style during the 13th century. Meanwhile, the vast and monumental hostel of San Marcos was assembled by the Knights of Santiago. Later, when the tide of history brought Castile to the fore, León disappeared from prominence at least until the present generation.

City exploration The town is small enough to explore on foot. Its main contemporary focus is the Plaza de Santo Domingo and adjacent Plaza San Marcelo, with the patioed Renaissance Casa de los Guzmanes, now the Diputación, on the site where Guzman el Bueno was born. Opposite is the Savings Bank headquarters, built by Gaudí in something close to Scottish baronial style (see also **Astorga**, page 153). From here the pilgrim route led along La Rua, now a shopping street. Following it, then bearing left, the visitor comes to the pleasing if dilapidated Plaza Mayor with the old town hall, the bar-district or Barrio Húmedo, and substantial 14th-century city walls.

The cathedral Started in 1205, the cathedral's two unmatched but evocative spires rise above a great rose window. The richly carved triple doorway beneath, though widely praised for its scenes from the lives of Christ and the Virgin and for its Final Judgement, is not so well preserved as some elsewhere (see **Huesca**, for example, page 106). And the statue of the Virgen Blanca (White Virgin) at the centre is a substitute for the real thing, now sheltered in a chapel behind the altar. The transcendent glory of the cathedral, however, is its glass, light flooding through in gorgeous blues, reds, purple and a seemingly omnipresent golden yellow. Different colours dominate at different times of day and one of the great experiences of Spain is to be inside the cathedral when cloud gives way outdoors to sunlight.
The walls themselves were kept minimal so as to provide maximum window space, 1,800sq m of glass in 125 window openings, mainly dating from the 12th to 16th centuries. There is a two-tiered choir with *trascoro* (retrochoir) by Juan de Badajoz. The cathedral museum is housed in the 14th-century cloister. It has a Crucifixion by Juan de Juni and early oriental silks.

The glowing interior of León cathedral

The French sculptor Juan de Juni, influential on his Castilian successors, made a first appearance in about 1533 in León, where his retablo of the Virgin and St John, in the church of Santa Marina, was much admired. By 1541 he had made his way to Valladolid, which then embarked on the great tradition of sculpture so well displayed in its Museo Nacional de Escultura. He is buried in the convent of Santa Catalina.

Panteón (royal mausoleum) and San Isidoro Virtually part of the city walls, León's Basilica of San Isidoro was reconstructed late in the 11th century to house the relics of St Isidore, the great early Christian polymath of Seville, whose bones had been negotiated away from the Moors. The earlier building which it replaced had as its porch (now at lower level and reached by a separate entrance) a crypt-like space which still survives. Until disturbed by the French in the Napoleonic wars, it was the resting place of 23 kings and queens, 12 royal children and a variety of aristocratic retainers. Its vaults are supported by columns with massive capitals, wonderfully carved with mainly Visigothic motifs. Some smaller capitals, one showing the raising of Lazarus, are among Spain's earliest Romanesque sculpture. The structure dates from about 1060.

Even more extraordinary are the frescos which cover the vaults, painted about a century later. Massively imposing, they spread over all surfaces, designs adapted to ceiling shape, and featuring the Last Supper, scenes from the Passion, and many more from the Bible and Apocrypha. The depiction of country pursuits, in the Annunciation and in a country calendar made up of round medallions, is especially touching. This is unquestionably one of Spain's great works of art. Don't miss the treasury/museum upstairs.

Wool was the life-blood of Castile and sheep fairs or markets were central to the organisation of stock rearing. The greatest fair of all was held at Medina del Campo (see opposite). Mass was conducted from a balcony in the flank of the collegiate church of San Antolín in the Plaza Mayor, and only then could dealing begin. The burning of much of Medina by the troops of Charles V greatly embittered the Comuneros, or Commons, who were as interested as the next man in maintaining income from wool. It was during this reign that the wool trade began its slide to ruin.

San Marcos Inevitably one is struck first by the façade, 100 majestic metres of it, in a double-decker arrangement, composed of windows, columns, niches and medallions and every other device of the Plateresque. Above the main door rides a fantastical Santiago Matamoros (St James the Moor-slayer), while above him, in turn, a decorative gable protrudes high above the skyline with imperial arms and a statue of Fame. Behind the main entrance a grand stone stairway, now part of the parador, ascends, with many hotel rooms in the old part of the building and a modern wing tucked discreetly in behind.

There is a fine Renaissance cloister, giving access to the provincial museum. This houses a miniature masterpiece, the so-called Carrizo ivory, a small and affecting 11th-century Crucifixion. The church on the right-hand end of the façade, heavily decorated with pilgrim shells, is unfinished but contains, at upper level (ask at the hotel if it is closed) a finely carved, raised choir. The whole building, one of Spain's finest, has had the good luck to survive many vicissitudes and even, at one point, proposed demolition.

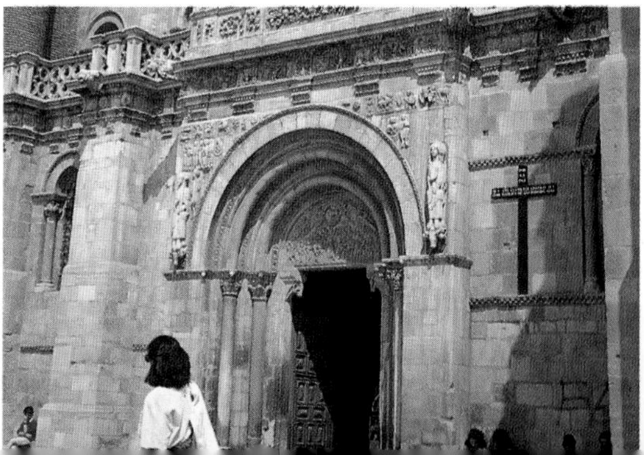

Finely decorated entrance to San Isidoro

▷▷▷ **Lerma**

The Duke of Lerma (1550–1625), favourite of King Philip III, built himself a monstrously ungainly palace here at the top of the town from which he took his title, a modest accumulation of churches, convents and cobbled streets.

▷▷▷ **Logroño**

Modern Logroño, capital of La Rioja, is centred on the Espolón, a one-block city park distinguished only by a statue of General Espartero, local hero and 19th-century military dictator. Pilgrims to Santiago, crossing the Ebro here, filed along La Rua, now one block in behind the river. The large church of Santiago is along here, with St James' horse – an obvious stallion – prominent on the southern façade. If you take, instead, the pleasantly arcaded Calle Portales past the cathedral, you will soon pass General Espartero's stout stone mansion, now the provincial museum.

Haro, capital of the Rioja Alta, is pre-eminently a wine town, with the *bodegas* of houses as famous as CUNE (also written CVNE, the Compañía Vinicola del Norte de España), Federico Paternina and the Bodegas Bilbainas. Several are open for visits. Shops in town, like Casa Quintín, display the local brews available.

▶▶▷ **Medinaceli**

From its height Medinaceli controlled the crossing of the southern route out of Soria and the east–west route between Zaragoza and the old cities round modern Madrid. The Romans built a fine triumphal arch, still standing though with worn inscriptions. Almanzor, Moorish scourge of Christians, died here in 1002. It is a lovely place, all stone, with walls and castle remnants, ivy and huge trees in monumental settings. The mansion of the Dukes of Medinaceli stands on the arcaded Plaza Mayor. Art galleries and ceramics shops are plentiful.

▶▷▷ **Medina del Campo**

Medina's Plaza Mayor was the site of the medieval wool trade fairs which were the centre of the Castilian economy. Queen Isabella died in the fine house over the arch in the corner of the same side (beside the gabled *ayuntamiento*). Pink Castillo de la Mota, across the main road, is one of Spain's grandest castles.

Passing the time of day in Medina del Campo

The red wines of La Rioja are probably more admired in other countries than in the region itself. They come in four grades: Garantía de Origen (the newest and cheapest), then on up through Vino de Crianza (at least three years old) to Reserva and the very expensive Gran Reserva (specially selected, seven years old or more). The wines are matured either in French oak or in American oak, with its strong vanilla flavour. Tastings are not as common as in France, though there are bodegas open to the public in Haro, Alfaro and a few other places.

▶▷▷ **Medina de Rioseco**

The stately churches of this rather decrepit town, north of Valladolid, testify to former wool wealth. Gothic Santa María stands under a baroque tower; the church of Santiago has weathered better than the streets around.

▶▶▷ **Nájera**

Nájera is on the Pilgrims' Way in La Rioja. Here, in the monastery church of Santa María la Real, are the tombs of kings and queens of Castile, León and Navarre.

▶▷▷ **Olmedo**

This former strong-point on the plain retains an impressive quantity of its town walls and gates. The Casa Consistorial and adjoining church of San Julián have been restored to make a pleasing complex.

▶▷▷ **Oña**

Oña, set on a bend in the gorge of the Río Oca, is burial place of the descendants of Fernán González. It has an abbey, three-decker Plaza Mayor and Roman bridge.

▶▷▷ **Pajares, Puerto de**

This pass from León into Asturias is one of the steepest points of interchange between the high *meseta* and the north coast's verdant strip. There is a ski station here, at Valgrande.

▶▶▷ **Palencia**

Palencia, on the Río Carrión, an important point on the Santiago pilgrimage, is centred on its beautiful late Gothic **cathedral**. In the handsome retablo of the Capilla Mayor the Renaissance statuary of Felipe de Vigarny combines with painted panels by Juan de Flandes and Juan de Valmaseda. Beneath is a crypt, with Visigothic columns, capitals and arches. The cathedral museum houses fine Flemish tapestries and a much-prized *San Sebastián* by El Greco. **San Miguel,** one of several notable churches, is said locally to have been the marriage place of El Cid and Jimena (but see also **Burgos**, page 158).

Far vistas on the Puerto de Pajares

▶▷▷ Pancorvo, Desfiladero de

Just east of the village of Pancorvo, the N1 highway and the railway make their way through an impressive ravine, staked out with a Moorish castle.

▶▷▷ Pedraza de la Sierra

This pretty walled town lies north of the Sierra de Guadarrama. It is an archetypal Sunday lunch spot, full of *hornos de asar* – Castilian-style, wood-fired meat rotisseries. Many of its houses have been restored, a service originally performed for the castle by the Basque painter Ignacio Zuloaga. The parador (restaurant only) is named after him.

▶▶▷ Peñafiel

This small potato and cereal town on the banks of the Río Duratón has one of the most astonishing castles in the whole Duero region (14th to 15th centuries). From below it appears like a battleship riding the crest above the town. From inside, the keep feels like the ship's bridge and the walls are genuinely ship-shaped.

▶▷▷ Peñaranda de Duero

Hardly a mouse stirs in Peñaranda, a little Duero town suffering serious agricultural decline. But a castle and city walls survive in parts and the collegiate church stares across the Plaza Mayor at the palace of the Dukes of Avellanada.

▶▷▷ Ponferrada

An industrial town with important monuments, Ponferrada lies at the end of a rewarding stretch of the Pilgrims' Way, running south from Astorga through extraordinarily lovely country and with a string of pleasing stopping points.

On approaching Ponferrada from the west, take the side turn for the 10th-century Mozarabic **Santo Tomás de las Ollas**, with nine horseshoe arches in its apse and good views *en route* of Ponferrada on its mountain-ringed plain, complete with coal-tip. In the town a tremendously crenellated castle guards the crossing of the river Sil.

▶▷▷ Puebla de Sanabria

Modest but beautiful medieval houses lead upwards in this little hilltop town to a Romanesque church and 15th-century castle. The town is the main point of access to a large lake/reservoir, extremely popular in summer.

▷▷▷ Quintanilla de las Viñas

The main attraction of Quintanilla itself is the Visigothic church close to the village, with its strange and unexplained carvings. The Río Arlanza rises nearby (take the C113) in fine scenery.

The great art of Castile is sculpture. Santo Domingo de Silos is the epicentre of Romanesque; Burgos has tremendous work from the time of the Catholic Kings. Valladolid came into its own in the 16th century with Juan de Juni and, above all, the emotional work of Alonso Berruguete, his subjects always in passionate movement. After Berruguete comes the great if sometimes excessive Gregorío Fernández – see the work of both men in churches and cathedrals and in the Museo Nacional de Escultura in Valladolid.

The castle at Pedraza de la Sierra

The Pilgrims' Way

■ The face of Europe changed in the 9th century when the Catholic church let it be known that the tomb of St James the Apostle had been discovered in Santiago de Compostela, in far Galicia, in the northwest corner of Spain. .....■

The pilgrims wore wide hats against the sun and rain and carried a leather pouch or scrip, a stout stave and often, mysteriously, a cockleshell (in the ancient world, this had been the symbol of Venus).

The story told how the Saint had come to Spain on a long ministry after the death of Christ. Returning to Jerusalem he was beheaded by Herod. When burial was refused, angels conveyed his body by boat to Padrón in Galicia and took it on to the place we now call Santiago de Compostela. The hermit who found St James (Santiago) was guided by a star, to a 'field of stars', in Latin *campus stellae*, whence the name Compostela. Or possibly the name comes from *compostum*, a Roman burial place, for there was in fact a tomb and it seems to have been Roman.

Theodemir, the local bishop, authenticated the remains as those of St James and the claim was accepted by the king of Asturias. The presence of the holy corpse began to exercise a mesmeric fascination in Europe.

Journeying for salvation Pilgrimages had been important in the ancient world. Among Christians, the greatest was originally to Jerusalem. Now Santiago became another sacred goal, possibly along the route of a far more ancient and magical pilgrimage to the 'world's end' at Finisterre on the Galician coast west of Santiago. When the Holy Sepulchre fell to Islam in 1078, making travel there impossible, Santiago became the European Pilgrims' Way *par excellence*.

Most of the earliest pilgrims were French and the route was often called the Camino Francés, the French Way. Later pilgrims came from all over Europe. The enterprise was difficult and dangerous and the pilgrims travelled in large groups.

Upon arrival at Santiago they spent at least a night in prayer and song and gained remission of their sins according to a complicated sliding scale. All social classes were represented; some were criminals or murderers, seeking redemption; some were making the pilgrimage in proxy for wealthy folk at home. They flowed in an incessant stream from the 9th to the 16th centuries and now, once again, in modern times.

How they came The main routes out of France, spelled out in the world's first guidebook, written by the French monk Aimeric Picaud in the 12th century, led across the Pyrenees, either by the Somport pass and down to Jaca, or across the more westerly pass at Roncesvalles and so down to Pamplona. The routes met at Puente la Reina and flowed across northern Spain in a broad stripe, finally crossing the Bierzo Mountains into Galicia and so to Santiago. There was a north coast route as well; Christian pilgrims from Muslim Spain used the old

Via de Plata, the Roman route through Mérida, Salamanca and Zamora.

Hopes of a Christian Reconquest of the Iberian peninsula were matched by a new story – that St James in person had helped the Christians to victory in the (apparently mythical) battle of Clavijo in 844. By the 11th century, when Reconquest first began to seem a real possibility, St James the Pilgrim had become St James the Moor-slayer (Santiago Matamoros), riding triumphantly over his turbanned victims on a thousand church façades in Christian Spain.

Pilgrims' Way architecture From the early days, the pilgrimage brought its own architecture. The monks of Cluny in France were heavily involved, subsidised by the Spanish kingdoms. Relying on the normal Romanesque round arch, churches of much greater size were now built (and some very pretty small ones too). The large ones had galleries along the nave and transepts, to handle the great numbers of pilgrims. Best of all was the sculpture, simultaneously assured and innocent. Indeed the architectural delights of the Camino de Santiago are one of the main reasons for a modern pilgrimage.

The Plaza Mayor in Salamanca. This historic city was on the Roman Via de Plata, a route used later by Christian pilgrims

Waiting for customers: cafés on Salamanca's Plaza Mayor

The stone from which the old city of Salamanca, and much of the new, is built comes from nearby quarries, deep pits in flat ground. At first the stone is soft and buttery in appearance, easily cut. It only hardens on exposure to air, then little by little a minor miracle occurs: the tiny traces of iron in it slowly oxidise, giving the golden city a soft red hue at sunset.

▶▶▶ **Salamanca**

Up from the Roman bridge across the Río Tormes, down from the Plaza Mayor to the twin cathedrals and the university, all-of-a-piece in golden stone, Salamanca is one of Europe's greatest and most agreeable of show-pieces. If almost a third of it had not been blown apart during the Napoleonic Wars, producing a district long called Los Caídos (the Fallen Ones), the accumulation of splendour might have been positively overwhelming. The atmosphere is lively with young people, yet rather different from that of Spain's other major university cities. For here there is not just a meeting between youth and a respectably inclined provincial city society. The city is also unmistakably part of a province that is still strongly agricultural. The local economy is based on cattle-breeding, with large landholdings, traditional if rather battered villages, and the complement of gypsies that is usually associated with stock-rearing in Spain.

History Salamanca is also a very ancient place. Captured by Hannibal in 217BC, it retained its importance under Rome and the Visigoths. The Moors captured it in the 8th century, and during the early centuries of the Reconquista, it fell into the vast no man's land south of the Duero and was twice sacked by Almanzor. Like Avila, it was walled and repopulated by Count Raymond of Burgundy late in the 11th century. And here, in 1218, Alfonso IX of Castile founded the university. It was, however, centuries a-building and was supported to wonderful architectural effect by the Catholic Kings, Ferdinand and Isabella. They also provided funds for a great Gothic cathedral which was simply pinned on to the side of the existing Romanesque structure. By now the city had also acquired a huge array of churches, convents, palaces and towers.

Salamanca was occupied by the French in the Napoleonic wars. Wellington defeated them nearby at Arapiles (the Battle of Salamanca in English), but promptly retreated, leaving the city to be sacked.

General Franco used it as his headquarters during the early part of the Civil War, removing to Burgos after an assassination attempt. Today the city is busy and active with the university now seeking to regain the leading place which it lost along the way to Madrid and Barcelona.

Finding your way All of central Salamanca can be walked. Starting at the Plaza Mayor, down the old main street or Rua Mayor, go off right to the university, passing several notable Gothic and Renaissance buildings *en route*. Alternatively, carrying straight on down the Rua Mayor, the visitor soon reaches the city's twin cathedrals and then, by walking a little eastwards, rather uphill and down, a series of outstanding churches and convents. Each of these routes is discussed below, starting with the Plaza Mayor.

Plaza Mayor Salamanca's beautiful main square is the centre of the city, spiritually, practically and for recreation, the place where everybody meets for a drink and a chat, where cattlemen still make deals and where civil and religious celebrations are centred. Three residential storeys rise serenely, with small wrought-iron balconies, shutters and the most regular of windows, above an arcaded ground floor with shops and cafés; the grander and more florid *ayuntamiento* (town hall) is on the north side, topped by clock and belfry. Medallions of Spanish heroes and would-be heroes are carved in the squinches, including General Franco, who is often ink-splattered. The square was built in the second quarter of the 18th century. Three members of the Churriguera family were involved, proving that not all their works involved the wild excess associated with their name. Andrés García de Quiñones designed the *ayuntamiento*. These names can go down in a special hall of fame, since this is undoubtedly Spain's most admired Plaza Mayor.

Off the main street Start down the Rua Mayor, then angle right at the **Casa de las Conchas** (House of the Shells). This extraordinary mansion of the late 15th and early 16th centuries was encrusted all over by its owner, a knight of Santiago, with the stone scallop shells symbolic of the pilgrimage to Santiago. It has very fine Gothic wrought iron, the shield of the Catholic Monarchs at the top of the façade and a notable Plateresque stairway. The next building of note that you will see is the twin-spired, baroque **Clerecía**, a church built for the Jesuits starting in 1617. From here it is a short step south to the university.

The University You will start – there is no other way – in the Patio de Escuelas, containing a statue of Fray Luis de León, mystic and university teacher, standing before the main university **façade**, a Plateresque front to the slightly earlier cloister of the old university or Escuelas Mayores within. This façade, with a medallion of the Catholic Monarchs, a portrait of the pope, statues of Hercules and Venus and any quantity of heraldry and

The Roman road that led from Seville to Merida and all the way north to Gijón is traditionally known as the Ruta de Plata or Silver Way, and is vigorously promoted by tourist offices along the route for its association with silver. Alas, the reason for the name is quite unclear, though it could be something perfectly simple like the way the old road shone in moonlight. Plenty of silver came from Spain, though. Records show that Rome received 141,325 kg of it between 206 and 198BC.

Local crafts market in Salamanca

gorgeously elaborate shallow carving, is arguably the finest in Spain. Scholarly argument suggests it is intended as a humanistic dialogue on the nature of Sacred and Profane love, the former winning out, of course, along with Learning and the Monarchy. It also includes a skull with a frog on top of it, a symbolic coupling of death and sexual sin ominous for the young scholar.

Important rooms give off the cloister within, including chapel and *paraninfo*, the main formal hall of the old university. It was here, at the start of the Civil War, that university rector and philosopher Miguel de Unamuno became involved in a confrontation with Franco's General Millán Astray, who finally shouted 'Death to intellectuals. Long live death!' Unamuno retired to his home, notionally disgraced, to die there shortly afterwards. Next door is the lecture room used by Luis de León and with its original furniture. From here he was taken to imprisonment by the Inquisition, returning five years later with the phrase 'As we were saying yesterday...' These words were invoked again by Unamuno in the 1920s after a period of internal exile under the dictator Primo de Rivera. A beautifully carved staircase leads to the first floor, still containing the university's once world-famous library.

On the far side of the Patio de Escuelas is the cloister of the Escuelas Menores, with thrilling mixtilinear arches. Another doorway gives into a room now containing the **Salamanca Sky**, a considerable portion of the original library ceiling moved here for safe-keeping when the original began to crumble. This strange painting, with the serpent Hydra and astrological signs, shows that the university – visited by Columbus – placed as much faith in astrology as in astronomy.

When you won your doctorate in Salamanca you were allowed to daub your initials, entwined with a 'V' for 'Victor', in red paint on almost any suitable wall. The courtyard of the Palacio de Anaya is full of them (as also the walls of the seminary at Baeza in Andalucía). During the Civil War, Franco appropriated the symbol for the Nationalist cause.

Salamanca's twin cathedrals The **Catedral Nueva** (New Cathedral) on the cathedral square is a festive concourse of pinnacles and domes. Juan Gil de Hontañon worked here as well as at Segovia. Within, there is late Gothic vaulting and the regulation chapels, but rather fewer artworks than might be expected. The best moments are external – the whole north side and skyline and the west façade, grandly Plateresque, with relief carvings of scenes from the life of Christ.
Crossing the interior of the New Cathedral, you step through a common wall into the **Catedral Vieja**, the Old (12th-century) Cathedral, immensely impressive, with cloisters, frescos and a magnificent painted retablo of the 15th century. Again the finest feature of all is external – the strangely fish-scaled, elongated pyramid of the Torre de Gallo, or Tower of the Cock, immediately recalling the towers of Toro, Zamora and Plasencia.

On from the cathedral The imposing **Palacio de Anaya**, opposite on the right as you leave the New Cathedral, belongs to the university.
Now it is worth descending eastwards to the **Convento de las Dueñas** (Dominicans). Not only do the nuns sell sweetmeats – at a price – the convent also has a strange and impressive cloister, architecturally harmonious but incorporating in its capitals and other ornamentation a ghastly accumulation of portraits of death, dismemberment and agony, human, animal and fantastical.
Shortly beyond comes the Dominican church of **San Esteban** (16th century, with cloister and a magnificent 17th-century western façade showing the stoning of San Esteban). Like the façades of the University and New Cathedral, this is best seen in evening light. The three together make a series unmatched in Spain.
Past San Esteban to the left, the visitor will come to the small and pleasing Romanesque church of **Santo Tomás Cantuarensis**, the first in Europe to be dedicated to the martyr of Canterbury.

The dramatic outline of Salamanca's twin cathedrals, across the Río Tormes

Salamanca province is bull-breeding country *par excellence*. You will see many of the wild black cattle grazing under the holm oaks and cork oaks in the sometimes park-like countryside. The ranches, called *fincas*, are often very large. Their entrances are marked by stone pillars which sometimes bear the brand-mark of the *finca*. The homesteads frequently have both a chapel and a small bullring where the behaviour of the animals is studied as an aid to breeding. This is where young toreros first learn their skills.

The monastery of Santo Domingo de Silos

The first syntactically complete Castilian sentences known to scholars, in the form of a small verse, are written in the margin of a Latin manuscript from San Millán. It is rather like a photograph of the language at the moment of its birth. The first known Castilian poet, Gonzalo de Berceo, was a monk at San Millán. Fragments of Basque, already an ancient spoken language, are recorded here in association with early Castilian, showing the debt of the new language to the older.

A maid at the inn in Santo Domingo de la Calzada fell in love with a young German pilgrim. When he rejected her advances, she planted the hotel silver in his knapsack and told the authorities. He was arrested and hanged. On their return from Santiago, his parents found their son still alive on the gibbet and interrupted the judge's dinner with the news. 'If it's true,' he scoffed, 'this cockerel on my dish will crow.' It did, and the young man was promptly rescued. A cock and hen, changed annually, have been kept in the cathedral ever since.

▶▶▷ San Millán de la Cogolla

The hermitage of San Millán (6th-century Riojan ascetic) is reached through halcyon country with mountain views, high above the remote little town. The church is split into two naves by a row of Romanesque and Mozarabic arches. In one of two burial caves hollowed in the rock lies a green jade statue of the saint, with plaited beard. This church is called San Millán de Suso (San Millán of Up Above). Later the community moved down into the valley, founding a vast and far less sympathetic monastery, San Millán de Yuso (Down Below).

▷▷▷ Santa Maria de la Huerta

This monastery, just over the Castile-Aragon border, has a vaulted 13th-century refectory, 15th- to 16th-century cloister and florid 18th-century church.

▶▶▷ Santo Domingo de la Calzada

It was the lifelong labour of Santo Domingo to build a *calzada* (causeway) here for pilgrims traversing the plains of La Rioja. The 12th- to 13th-century cathedral of this agricultural town is celebrated for its cock and hens (see panel). It also houses the saint's shrine-tomb and a fine Damián Forment retablo.

▶▶▷ Santo Domingo de Silos

Not to be confused with Santo Domingo de la Calzada (see above) or the Santo Domingo who founded the Dominican order, also local, the 11th-century saint of Silos rebuilt a monastery sacked by Almanzor. It lies in challenging mountain country south of Burgos, the oldest surviving parts dating from 1042. The cloister with its small paired columns is delightful; the carved capitals (possibly incorporating Moorish workmanship) constitute one of Europe's finest assemblages of Romanesque sculpture, with representations of everything from flamingos and lions to cavalry battles. The corner reliefs give a moving account of Christ's life and resurrection. The monastery, though dissolved in the 19th century, is once again a religious community; visitors are welcome at Gregorian plainsong services.

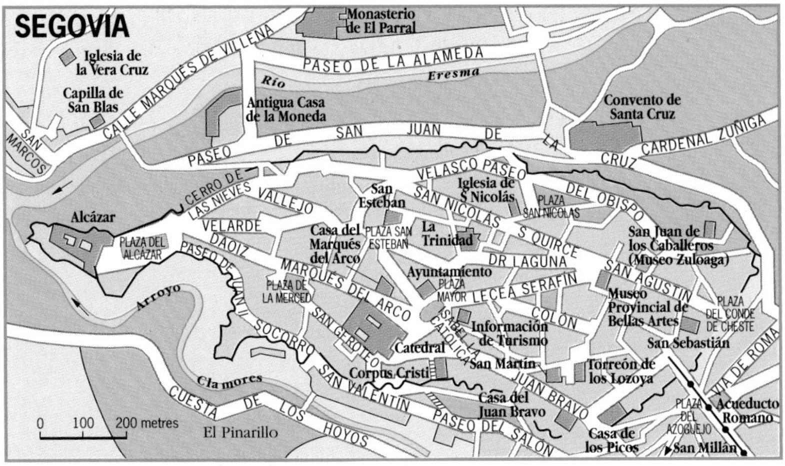

▶▶▶ Segovia

Gracefully ornamental in appearance, even a little frilly, Segovia is fun where neighbouring Avila is stern. The look of its architecture seems to carry over into its engaging present-day ambience. Segovia's best-known monuments are its lofty Roman aqueduct, one of Spain's main icons, the almost equally famous ship-shaped medieval *alcázar*, remodelled in 19th-century Gothic fantasy, and the pinnacled 16th-century cathedral which towers, more lovingly than threateningly, above the town. Segovia also offers a fistful of good Romanesque churches, a smaller number of palatial mansions, one of Spain's best military churches (Vera Cruz, which once belonged to the Knights Templar) and the bad-taste resting-place of St John of the Cross just nearby.

There are many good restaurants and a rather narrower choice of accommodation, most visitors being day-trippers. Segovia nevertheless makes an excellent base for touring in Castile and the Guadarrama mountains.

History Roman, Visigothic, Moorish in its time, the town was refortified – like Avila – by a triumphant Alfonso VI in the late 11th century. Most of the walls and three of the five gates survive. It was a favourite stopping-place for the Trastámara kings of Castile and it was here that Isabella was proclaimed Queen in 1474. Its greatest wealth came with the Mesta (see panel, page 176) and the wool-boom of the 15th and early 16th centuries, but after this, like the rest of Castile, Segovia entered a steep decline. Nowadays some sense of liveliness has returned.

The Roman aqueduct brought water from 15km south, reaching the height of 28m on a double tier of granite arches. Built with amazing exactitude (and pincer-holes for the lifting of each block), the last stretch is now well within the city, in the Plaza de Azoguejo, traffic pouring through its arches. Close by is the large and attractive Romanesque church of San Millán, early 12th century, with external galleries and carved capitals.

The summer palace of the Bourbon dynasty at La Granja de San Ildefonso lies 11km south of Segovia. The interior, now housing one of Spain's leading tapestry collections, was restored after a fire in 1918. The gardens combine the formality of Versailles with a mountain setting and magnificently monumental fountains – turned on at 18.00hrs in spring and summer 'when there is water'. In the attractive little town, which once produced the great mirrors and windows of the Spanish royal palaces, the 18th-century Royal Glass Works has been reopened as Spain's National Museum of Glass.

The Alcázar With slated turrets that might have been an inspiration to Gaudí, this old Castilian fortress stands on the furthest westward point of the hilltop site. Inside, there is a surfeit of suits of armour, splendid 15th-century Mudéjar ceilings (rooms 3 and 5) and great views out through modern plate-glass windows – a good safety precaution since at least one royal prince has fallen to his death here.

The cathedral Right on top of the hill stands the sandy-golden cathedral, last of Spain's Gothic constructions, and one of its finest, at least from outside, with pinnacled apse, and added Renaissance domes. It is mostly the work of father and son architects, Juan Gil and Rodrigo Gil de Hontañon, fresh from their triumph in Salamanca. It also incorporates the cloister of an earlier cathedral. There is a museum off the cloister, with church treasures, pictures and tapestries.

The Honourable Council of the Mesta, established by Alfonso X in 1273, was the immensely powerful association of sheep owners who held sway in much of medieval Castile and other parts of Spain, controlling the drovers' roads or *cañadas* along which the enormous merino flocks were moved with each change of season. The Mesta helped keep Spain a ranching country which preferred stock-rearing to cultivation. There was a law that any land where once the flocks had grazed remained Mesta territory.

Further exploration From the adjoining Plaza Mayor, starting in Calle Isabel la Catolica, the evening *paseo* drifts downhill to the aqueduct, passing the Romanesque church of San Martín, a statue of the Comunero leader Juan Bravo executed here, the tower of the **Lozoya palace** and finally, after a specially good viewing point, the **Casa de los Picos**, covered all over with ornaments like cross-cut mace-heads. Romanesque **San Esteban** with its tall tower stands closer to the cathedral.

There is also an outer circuit, or *ruta monumental*, offering specially fine views of the *alcázar*. This takes in the **Convento de Carmelitas Descalzas** founded by San Juan de la Cruz and, with a brief diversion, the Templar church of **Vera Cruz**. Its nave runs in a circle round a kind of two-storey central column containing a chapel on the first floor where entrants to knighthood watched over their armour all night.

Segovia's spectacularly positioned Alcázar was rebuilt in the 19th century after a fire

▶▷▷ **Sepúlveda**

The Río Duratón, on its way down from the Sierra Guadarrama to the Duero, loops between steep banks, with a grey stone town on its northern side. Climb to the Romanesque church of San Salvador for views. The beauty-spot villages of Ayllón and Riaza are within striking distance.

▷▷▷ **Sobrón, Embalse de**

Spaniards, being fond of artificial lakes and dams, make much of the Embalse de Sobrón, where once the Ebro ran north of Pancorvo, northwest of Miranda de Ebro. (See also Frías, page 160.)

▶▶▷ **Soria**

Soria was a frontier town, marking the limit of the Christian advance against the Moors. This, and its place in the poetry of Antonio Machado give it a special resonance for Spaniards. The town climbs steeply up a side valley of the Duero. There are fine Romanesque monuments, particularly San Juan de la Rabanera and Santo Domingo. Note also the grandiloquent Renaissance Palacio de la Gomera.

▶▶▷ **Tordesillas**

It was in this decayed Castilian town on the River Duero that the Treaty of Demarcation was signed in 1494. Spain was given all Latin America except Brazil, which went to Portugal. Here too Queen Juana II of Castile, mother of Charles V, was confined during 40 years of madness. The star of Tordesillas is undoubtedly the Monasterio de Santa Clara, a former royal palace of the 14th to 15th centuries, which emerged from restoration in 1990 as one of the finest Mudéjar buildings in all Spain. Guided tours only.

Antonio Machado (1875–1939) was a French teacher from Seville who made his emotional home in Castile, especially in Soria, where he lived from 1907 to 1913 and which he celebrated in lean, lyrical poetry. Later, after the death of his much-loved wife, he lived in Ubeda in the province of Jaén. Here too he is much remembered. He died in 1939, in Colliure in the south of France, a refugee from Franco. Many consider him a finer poet than the more dramatic Lorca.

Walk Laguna Negra

Laguna Negra, the Black Lagoon, is a natural lake, backed by sheer cliffs.

To get there from Soria, 16km along the Burgos road take a right turn after Cidones, then follow signs. Alternatively, dropping south from Logroño on the N111, pass through extremely remote country. Shortly after Villanueva de Cameros, take the road to Villoslada de Cameros, and then south through Montenegro.

There is a 5-minute walk up to the Laguna from the road's end (angle left in the first clearing).
For the fit and active only, there follows an enthralling walk-cum-rock scramble right round the lake.

Numantia (modern Numancia), 5km from Soria on the Logroño road, was an Iberian settlement which resisted Roman conquest. The Romans devoted 20 years to an economic blockade. When defeat became inevitable in 133BC, after a year's tight siege by Scipio Aemilianus, the inhabitants killed themselves. The site was later built over by the Romans and has now been carefully excavated.

'Rome was not built in a day', most Europeans say, when speaking of the need to continue steadily with a chosen course. Spaniards, recalling the wars and sieges of northwest Castile, more often use the phrase: 'Zamora was not taken in one day'.

▶▷▷ Toro

Toro is becoming known outside Spain for its sturdy red wines. Like nearby Tordesillas, this is an ancient town built on the high northern bank of the Duero. It has its old mansions (many outside the early walls), a ruined castle, and above all the 12th-century collegiate church of Santa María la Mayor, one of Spain's most admired Romanesque buildings with finely carved west door and three naves. It is given a curiously Byzantine aspect (see also **Zamora**, below) by its polygonal dome.

▷▷▷ Turégano

Easily visited from Madrid, Turégano is well provided with shops and restaurants. The castle, founded by Fernán González, enfolds the Romanesque church of San Miguel.

Valladolid see opposite.

▶▶▷ Zamora

Zamora, fortified by strong if stubby walls, lies on a hill above the Duero, within 50km or so of modern Portugal. Here, to the mortification of El Cid who served him, King Sancho II of Castile was murdered, thus opening the way for his brother, Alfonso VI, strongman of medieval Castile. The old town is rather sporadically preserved but its monuments have a romantically medieval feeling.
The castle on the western extreme is now a school for the applied arts. Just next to it is the remarkable **cathedral**, with a 12-sided Byzantine-style dome like that at Toro. It also has a fine and solid Romanesque tower and a less appropriate 18th-century façade. There is a severely dignified cloister. Outside the city walls and beneath the castle is the tiny Romanesque chapel of **Santiago de los Caballeros** where El Cid is said to have been knighted.
Other sights include: the church of **La Magdalena** with fine doorway; the Renaissance palace of the Counts of Alba and Aliste, now a parador; a Holy Week museum with work by 19th-century local sculptor, Ramón Alvarez, and the pretty church of Santa María de la Horta. Zamora, by the way, is a good place for tapas.

Zamora seen across the Río Duero

Plaza de Zorrilla, Valladolid

▶▶▷ Valladolid

Valladolid was for centuries the chief city of emergent Spain, main centre of the court and birthplace of kings and queens. Columbus died here and Cervantes also spent time here. Today, it remains a large and active city, not especially beautiful overall but richly studded with major monuments.

In the Plaza de San Pablo, north of the cathedral, are two of Spain's greatest façades. That of **San Pablo** itself falls into two elaborate sections, the lower part Isabelline Gothic, the upper Plateresque. Round the corner to the right is the majestic portal and façade of the **Colegio de San Gregorio**, its many motifs dominated by the shield of Isabella and Ferdinand. Inside, round the cloisters, is the **Museo Nacional de Escultura** (Spain's National Sculpture Museum – for opening times, see page 266). Concentrating heavily on polychrome wood statuary, a Spanish speciality, this offers an unrivalled display. The main exhibit is the retablo from the Valladolid monastery of San Benito, greatest masterpiece of Alonso Berruguete. Nearby is the house where Philip II was born.

The **cathedral**, a gaunt work by Herrera, Philip II's architect for the Escorial, was finished off in Churrigueresque baroque. The cathedral museum, in a Gothic-Mudéjar setting, houses works by the major sculptors. Close by are the elegantly Gothic church of Santa María la Antigua, the University square and, just down Calle Librería, the **Colegio de Santa Cruz**, part of the university, with a particularly fine patio.

The Plaza Mayor, with arcades and statue, is the town centre. Close by is the surprisingly grand house occupied by Cervantes from 1603 to 1606, now a museum dedicated to Spain's best known writer.

The kings of Navarre, León and Castile supported the great Benedictine monastery at Cluny, in France, with tribute money paid in by the Moorish *taifa* kingdoms. They positively welcomed the French order, who soon established the Santiago pilgrimage on an international scale and built Romanesque monasteries along the route. The biggest, at Sahagún, is ruined. The Cistercians who followed in the 12th century were even more prolific builders, their monasteries now Gothic in style.

Extremadura acquired its name as the land 'beyond the Duero'. Since *duro* means 'hard', the name also evokes the toughness of frontier country. As the frontier against the Moors pushed further and further down into the peninsula, so the name at last became attached to a tract of country a good distance from the Duero and far enough south to share a border with Andalucía. Today's Extremadura is a genuine midway point between the lively good humour of Mediterranean Spain and the severity of Old Castile. Its people remain rural, often traditional, though also aspiring to modernise. Their greatest hope is to break the historic cycle of deprivation. The countryside they live in is intensely beautiful – that is, if you care for wild and sweeping landscapes – though a few districts are bare to a fault. Except in the mountains, Extremadura is very hot in summer.

The land Portugal lies to the west. The region's northern rim is formed by the Sierra de Gata and the last outposts of the Peña de Francia, both ranges pungent with cistus in late spring. The Sierra de Gredos creeps in

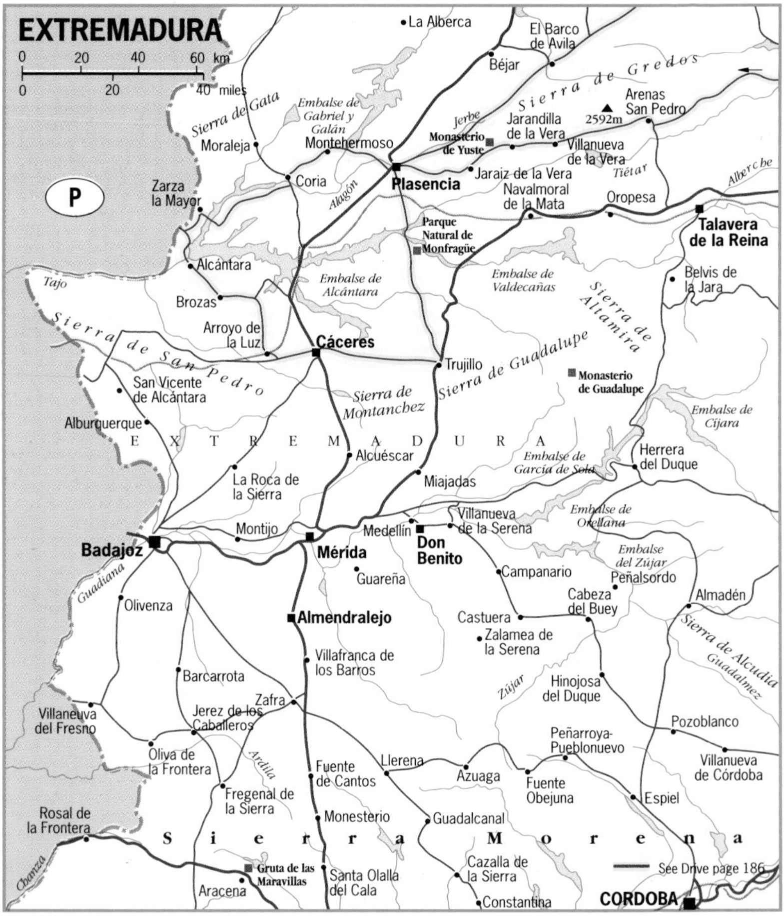

from the east, diminishing but still magnificent. From this mountainous beginning, open terrain runs away south. Mostly this is archetypal Spanish cattle-country, with holm-oak and sometimes cork-oak growing well spaced apart, throwing pools of shade on grassland that is tawny by summertime. Black cattle stand beneath the trees. Black pigs, though much prized, are nowadays considerably less visible. Red kites and other hawks are common; griffon vultures nest in the mountains and the Tagus gorge. Cotton, tobacco and other warm-country crops grow where valley land has been irrigated, usually as part of the post-Civil War 'Badajoz plan'. There are also grapes and olives.

The background The towns, such as Plasencia, Cáceres and Villanueva de la Vera, are often exceptionally lovely, well-matched by castles and monasteries. Two of the great orders of military knights – those of Alcántara and Santiago – were founded here, the latter in Cáceres. From here too came that fierce breed named the *conquistadores*. An extraordinary proportion of their leaders (see pages 188–9) were Extremadurans, taking with them to the New World a militant Catholicism and an untameable hunger for wealth. Survivors brought their riches home again, building palaces still on show today, such as the Pizarro residences in Trujillo. At the latest count, three Extremaduran towns, Cáceres, Guadelupe and Merida, have been declared World Heritage Sites.

Charles V abdicated in 1556, retiring to Yuste with his family portraits, 100 servants and a friendly clockmaker with whom he hoped to pass his time. He found it difficult, however, to refrain from seeking news and opinions, and Yuste became a place of pilgrimage for important folk and imperial servants. Ravaged by gout, Charles built a rampart for riding straight up to his first floor apartments in his litter. His winter bedroom, draped in black, gave on to the altar of the monastery church. He heard mass four times a day and fished in a pool beneath his living room – source of the malaria which finally killed him.

The El Bobo de Coria restaurant in Coria (at Calle Pizarro 6) recalls Juan Calabazas, the sad-eyed court fool and jester twice painted by Velázquez. He was born in Las Hurdes and taken into service by the Duke of Alba (who also held the title of Marquis of Coria). From Alba's retinue, Juan Calabazas passed to Philip IV and so to the canvas of Velázquez. The restaurant named after him serves excellent potato and spinach soup, and the wine is Pitarra, a little sherry-like and much admired locally.

▶▷▷ Alcántara

The extraordinary six-arched bridge across the Tagus gorge, rising almost 70m from the water and surmounted by a triumphal arch, looks as if it was built yesterday, not in 105AD. It was restored in 1860. The huge dam wall and hydro-electric installations above, though they do not diminish the phenomenon of *el kantara* (Arabic for bridge), do spoil the atmosphere. The little town above the gorge was once the headquarters of the Knights of Alcántara (see also page 219). It has a rather crumbling air from outside but is well kept and tidy within.

▷▷▷ Badajoz

Badajoz, an architecturally dull frontier town, nevertheless has some points in its favour, including the narrow streets in attractive flat-fronted 19th-century style. The 13th-century cathedral (17th-century façade) and **Museo de Bellas Artes** have paintings by Badajoz-born 16th-century painter, Luis de Morales. The Plaza Alta area is seedy and unfriendly.

Cáceres see opposite.

▶▷▷ Coria

This sleepy town, with almost a Portuguese air, rises above the Rio Alagón. The bank is commanded by a 16th-century cathedral with massive baroque tower and Plateresque filigree carving to either side of its main door. On the north side, stout Roman walls survive.

Guadalupe see page 184

▶▶▷ Jarandilla and Yuste

The emperor Charles V chose the monastery at Yuste above the Tiétar valley (see page 161) as his place of retirement. He built his palace/villa slap up against the side of the existing monastery. Approach from Jaraiz via Garganta la Olla for best views of this idyllic place. (At the monastery, there are guided tours only.)
While his palace was under construction, Charles lived nearby at Jarandilla in the castle of the Counts of Oropesa, now the **Parador of Charles V**. This makes Jarandilla, where there are also *hostales*, a natural centre for exploring the area. The old town below the road, with two churches and castle, is not spectacular, but there is a pretty stroll below to the 'Roman bridge' and strenuous mountain walks from Guijo de Santa Barbara above.

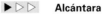

The Roman bridge across the Tagus at Alcántara

Cáceres

■ **Nowhere in Spain is there so dense a concentration of monuments as in ancient Cáceres. Confined within Moorish walls built up on Roman foundations, this is a hilltop town solid with Spanish grandeur – and with a mass of storks in springtime. The buildings, mostly Renaissance, are in a rough brown stone with heraldic crests, often curling towards the viewer at the top, and severe, if sometimes elaborate frontages. It is even more astonishing at night, with the details picked out by floodlighting. .....■**

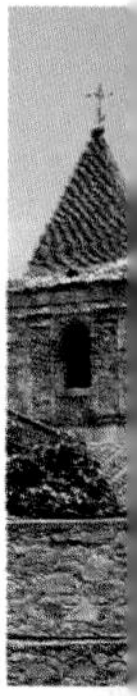

▶▶▶ **Cáceres**
The fine main square is built on a slope, with arcades and cafés, just underneath the ancient town. It is possible to enter the old town from here under the wide **Arco de la Estrella** (Arch of the Star). Turning immediately right inside the city wall you will encounter the **Generala** house, the **Palacio de los Golfines de Arriba** and several towers on the city wall. Left, left at the end, left again and up the narrow Calle Ancha (Broad Street!) past the parador in the 14th-century Ulloa palace, you come to an open square in front of the large church of **San Mateo** (14th to 16th centuries).
Immediately to the right is the magnificent **Casa de las Cigüeñas** (House of Storks). In 1477, the towers of the town were torn down on the orders of Queen Isabella (many of them were rebuilt afterwards), but here the original was allowed to stand. Diagonally to the right behind the viewer is the **Casa de las Veletas**, House of the Weather-vanes. This contains the Cáceres Museum and a fine Arab cistern. Down past San Mateo, tucked in under the large white church of San Francisco Javier, are more grand buildings: **Santa María**, used as the cathedral, the **bishop's palace**, **Palacio de los Golfines de Abajo**, and **Palacio de Carvajal**. The church of **Santiago**, where the Order of Santiago was founded, lies straight below outside the walls with an energetic retablo of the saint by Alonso Berruguete (1558).

Cáceres' walls enclose one of Spain's finest architectural ensembles

The massive walls of Guadalupe monastery

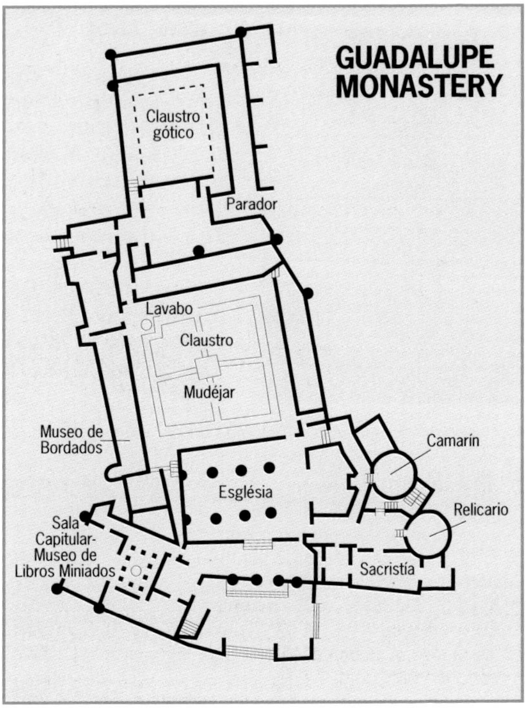

Right through Extremadura and western Spain, the storks arrive in February to take up nests left vacant over the winter months. In villages, these are usually on the highest available spot on the church. Cathedrals sometimes attract clusters of nests, and often they are to be found incongruously perched on disused factory chimneys. Nobody bothers the storks, who chatter with an odd rattling sound and wheel about the sky, long necks extended. When the nests are floodlit, as happens, for example, in old Cáceres, the disturbed birds peer down with a look of perpetual surprise.

▶▶▶ Guadalupe

The monastery of Guadalupe, in Gothic and Mudéjar styles, is one of the most beautiful monasteries in Spain. Set in a rugged sierra, it rises over a tiny town with cobbled streets and jutting, wood-beamed balconies.

It is said that a shepherd discovered the dark-faced image of the Virgin in the 13th century. The hermitage he built became a Hieronymite monastery, receiving rich gifts from Alfonso XI. It was both a stopping place for royalty and foremost of Spanish holy places to be linked with the discovery of America. Columbus named an island after Guadalupe; and Guadalupe's Virgin became Patroness of Mexico. Today the monastery stands as the centre of 'Hispanidad', the supposed common bond between Spain and her former American colonies.

Uncompromising towers give the building a military look. Close up, the façade is an array of swirling Gothic-Mudéjar tracery. The guided tour of the monastery (now Franciscan) includes arguably the finest Mudéjar cloister in Spain. The **Museo de Bordados** (Embroidery Museum) is a display of ecclesiastical wealth and elaboration in its vestments and altar frontals. In the sacristy hang scenes by the great Extremaduran painter Zurbarán, the only such series in Spain still in its original setting. Ascending high behind the altar, visitors are shown the Virgin of Guadalupe herself and may kiss the medallion on her back.

The monastery runs its own hostel around another, Gothic, cloister. There is also a parador, with charming patio, founded as a monastery hostel in 1402.

Modern bullring in Roman Mérida

▶▶▷ Jerez de los Caballeros

Jerez, a compact little town in the middle of the empty sierra, is full of churches, convents and mansions built by *conquistador* gold. Núñez de Balboa ('discoverer' of the Pacific) was born here. The 13th-century castle recalls Jerez's history as a frontier stronghold of the Templars and the Knights of Santiago.

▶▷▷ Medellín

The birthplace of Hernan Cortés, conqueror of Mexico (see page 188), is a village dominated by a castle, beside the river Guadiana. Cross the fine 17th-century bridge to the main square for the statue of Cortés and a stone said to mark the very spot of his birth.

▶▶▶ Mérida

Mérida was once the capital of Roman Lusitania. Many of the finest Roman monuments in Spain are to be found here. Just by the impressive 60-arched **Roman bridge** is the huge *alcazaba* (Arab fortress), built on Roman foundations and with Roman blocks. There is a Roman **theatre** (retaining a splendid backdrop of marble columns) and an **amphitheatre** (with a seating capacity of 15,000). The excavated **Casa del Amfiteatro** has engaging mosaics of wine-pressing.
The adjoining **Museo Nacional de Arte Romano** should not be missed. The **Temple of Mars**, further on and down the hill, has a shrine to the child saint Eulalia. The **Casa de Mitra** (House of Mithras), across town by the bullring, has more fine mosaics.

▶▷▷ Olivenza

Olivenza passed to Spain from Portugal only in 1801. Its tidy streets attest to its Portuguese past. The castle holds the local museum, and there are 18th-century barracks and an interesting bullring. Best of all is the agreeable atmosphere and the lonely countryside.

The lazy good looks of Manuel Godoy, caught admirably in a portrait by Goya (Real Academia de Bellas Artes de San Fernando, Madrid), transformed Spain's fortunes for the worse. The young guards officer caught the eye of the middle-aged Queen María Luisa and became her lover – and, at the same time, a friend and confidant to her husband Charles IV. Prime minister by the age of 25, he devised the treaty which gave Spain Olivenza. But he was supine before the French advance in 1808. He and Charles IV finally signed away Spanish independence to Napoleon.

Opened in 1986, the Museo Nacional de Arte Romano, incorporating a stretch of well-paved Roman road, is an essential stop on any Roman pilgrimage through Spain. Along with eloquent sculpture, glass, pottery, coins and astonishingly vivid mosaics, it lets you into many aspects of life in Emerita Augusta – theatre, the amphitheatre, and the mystery religions brought from the east by legionaries settled there.

Drive Along the Tiétar Valley

The valley of the River Tiétar, lying warm and protected from north winds by the Sierra de Gredos, is one of the loveliest in Spain.

Drive east to west into the district called La Vera. The road runs a little above the valley floor on the northern side, with village centres below the road that are easy to miss.

Villanueva de la Vera has an ancient town centre and main square, with jutting wooden balconies or protruding first storeys. **Valverde de la Vera** is still more spectacular with hugely projecting first floors. Beautiful **Cuacos** has a galleried main square and many seigneurial houses. All these villages are worth a stroll.

Drive Scenic Extremadura

See map on page 180.

This roughly circular drive will require at least two days and could easily be extended by a trip to the great monastery shrine of Guadalupe. Combined with the Castile drive (page 159), picked up in Barco de Avila, it would make a possible week's tour from Madrid.

Leave Madrid and pass to the south of the Sierra de Gredos by highway C501 and enter Extremadura along the Tiétar Valley.
Make sure you have enough time to enjoy **La Vera** and **Plasencia**.

Now drive west to Coria through open country. Take the road south, and after a few kilometres strike further west for Alcántara.
Garrovillas, *en route*, has an interesting plaza.

Head southeast to Cáceres via Brozas, following road signs. Take the N521 to Trujillo.
The reward in taking the main road lies in the impressive profile of that conquistador town.

Drive north now across wild cattle country from Trujillo to Plasencia again.
You pass the Monfragüe nature reserve where griffon vultures nest on crags above the Tagus.

Leave Extremadura on the N110.
The beautiful Jerte valley is best in cherry-blossom season.

Jarandilla, in the Tiétar valley, temporary lodging for Emperor Charles V

The main square in Trujillo

▶▶▷ **Plasencia**

The old town at the crossing of the Rio Jerte is full of noble mansions, ancient walls and towers, and hidden churches. Life is centred on the cafés of the **Plaza Mayor**. The chief monument is the cathedral, or rather the two (both unfinished) **cathedrals**. The one in use is newer, soaring grey Gothic within and entered by a fine Plateresque door. The adjoining old cathedral is now a museum with exhibits in the nave and lovely Romanesque/Gothic transitional cloister, where you can see the joins in the composite building. The town's ethnographic museum is outstanding.

▶▶▷ **Trujillo**

Trujillo produced the *conquistador* Francisco Pizarro (see pages 188–9) and still lives in his shadow. The main square, with steps and road leading up and down to different levels, is dominated by a large bronze of Pizarro, plumed and helmeted, astride a helmeted horse. The mansions in the square express the wealth of the *conquistadores*. The palace of Francisco Pizarro's brother Hernando – Palacio del Marqués de la Conquista – is diagonally across from the statue, grandly solemn, but with a Plateresque window and balcony let into the corner and a swashbuckling shield above, literally wrapped round the edge of the building (open to visitors, a little sporadically). On the lower side of the square, with gracious balconies, is the palace of the Marqués de Piedras Albas. Behind the Pizarro statue rises the large, lichen-encrusted church of San Martín and just below this, with more fine balconies, is the Palacio de los Duques de San Carlos (now a convent, parts shown to visitors). There are other palaces and mansions; it is also well worth climbing up to the old Moorish castle above.

▶▷▷ **Zafra**

With delightful arcaded squares and narrow white streets, with window grilles in southern style, Zafra is dominated by the nine-towered castle where Hernán Cortés of Medellín stayed as a guest before departing for Mexico. It is now a parador, named after him, with a marbled Renaissance patio at its centre.

Air-cured mountain ham, cut thin and raw, is one of Spain's great delicacies. *Jamón serrano* is the generic name for it and often refers to the ham of the unglamorous white pig. The black pig, or black-foot, *pata negra*, is an Iberian native, traditionally reared on acorns, roaming free in Extremadura and western Andalucía. The best *pata negra* hams are known by place-names – *jamón de Montánchez* in Extremadura, for instance. From Andalucía the best known are *Jabugo* (Huelva) and *Trevélez* (Granada). Ask the price first when ordering in bars; a good ham comes expensive.

FOCUS ON *Conquistadores*

■ Ten years after Columbus' discovery of America, the only Spanish settlements in the New World were in Cuba and Hispaniola (modern Haiti and the Dominican Republic). Yet by 1540, the brutal heyday of the *conquistadores* was over, replaced by a generation of settlers. .....■

A significant number of those who set out for the New World in search of gold came from Extremadura. The reasons are obvious. As service in the armed forces may appear attractive to the modern unemployed, so the lands across the Atlantic beckoned irresistibly to those trapped in the poverty and hopelessness of rural life in this deeply deprived region of Spain.

Although Cortés defeated the Aztec Empire and established his own from the Caribbean Sea to the Pacific Ocean, the difficulties of administration and the political intrigues against him were too much. He returned to Spain where, in his own words, 'old, poor and in debt', he died in 1547.

Conquest of Mexico Vasco Núñez de Balboa made the first settlement in Panama in 1508 and within five years had pushed through to the Pacific Ocean. Yucatan and its Mayan civilisation were discovered by Hernández de Córdoba. Inspired by this, Hernán Cortés sailed from Cuba for the mainland with 11 ships and 600 men. He came from a poor but respectable family in Medellín, had arrived in Hispaniola at the age of 19 and quickly established a power-base there. Now on the mainland, with the help of an Indian mistress, he defeated what opposition he met, set up a capital at Veracruz and marched into Mexico.

The Spanish party were open-mouthed at the wealth they saw. Initially they were welcomed and housed in a palace in the Aztec capital. When one of their party was killed they seized the occasion to demand that Montezuma, the Aztec king, should pay allegiance and tribute to Charles V. Montezuma was held hostage and later killed.

Pizarro and the Inca Empire The next stage was the defeat of the Inca civilisation and the conquest of Peru. The chief protagonist in this venture was Francisco Pizarro of Trujillo. Born illegitimate in around 1475, he spent his early life as a swine-herd. It is likely he had a spell fighting in Italy before he left for Hispaniola. In 1524, already wealthy and well into middle age, he formed a partnership with Diego de Almagro and Hernando de Luque to explore the west coast of South America.

Early difficulties led to a request for reinforcements from Panama, but Pizarro was ordered to return. His response, so the story goes, was to draw a line on the ground with his sword and invite those who wished to continue with him to step over the line. Of the 13 who crossed the line, some were to reap an eventual reward of untold wealth and honour, though many, like Pizarro, eventually died a violent death.

They knew already that an Inca Empire existed and it was equally clear that the resources of the original syndicate were inadequate. Pizarro returned to Spain to

get funds from Charles V. In the process he was made governor and captain-general of all he conquered. He returned, joined by his four brothers, and in 1531, Pizarro, Almagro and 168 Spaniards, set out to defeat a mighty empire of millions. Like Cortés with Montezuma, Pizarro knew his easiest tactic lay in capturing the emperor/sun god Atahuallpa. He succeeded in this, and held Atahuallpa hostage; the condition for his release was that the room in which he was imprisoned should be filled with gold and silver. But after fulfilling the condition, Atahuallpa was accused of the murder of his brother, baptised and then garotted.

Predictably, rivalries and dissensions arose between Almagro and Pizarro, which ended with Almagro's death – at the hands of Pizarro's brother – followed by Pizarro's, stabbed in his palace by Almagro's son.

At the end of the era of conquest, some 15,000 Spaniards had taken part, leaving the mother country to cross the Atlantic in their tiny ships. Many never came home again, casualties of hardship and disease.

Pizarro still rides – in bronze in Trujillo

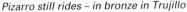

Old Castile is the heartland north of Madrid; south, east and west is the autonomous region of Castilla-La Mancha, once known as New Castile. With the Community of Madrid, it makes a shield-shaped territory right in the centre of Spain.

The Community of Madrid is well-populated, but with mountains and plenty of appealing and historic spots. Castilla-La Mancha, though spoiled in parts by industry, an over-enthusiasm for reservoirs, and some ugly roads, remains one of the most exciting parts of the whole peninsula, wild and varied in landscape. It ranges from the pine-forested Serranía de Cuenca in the east, with the weird rock formations of La Ciudad Encantada,

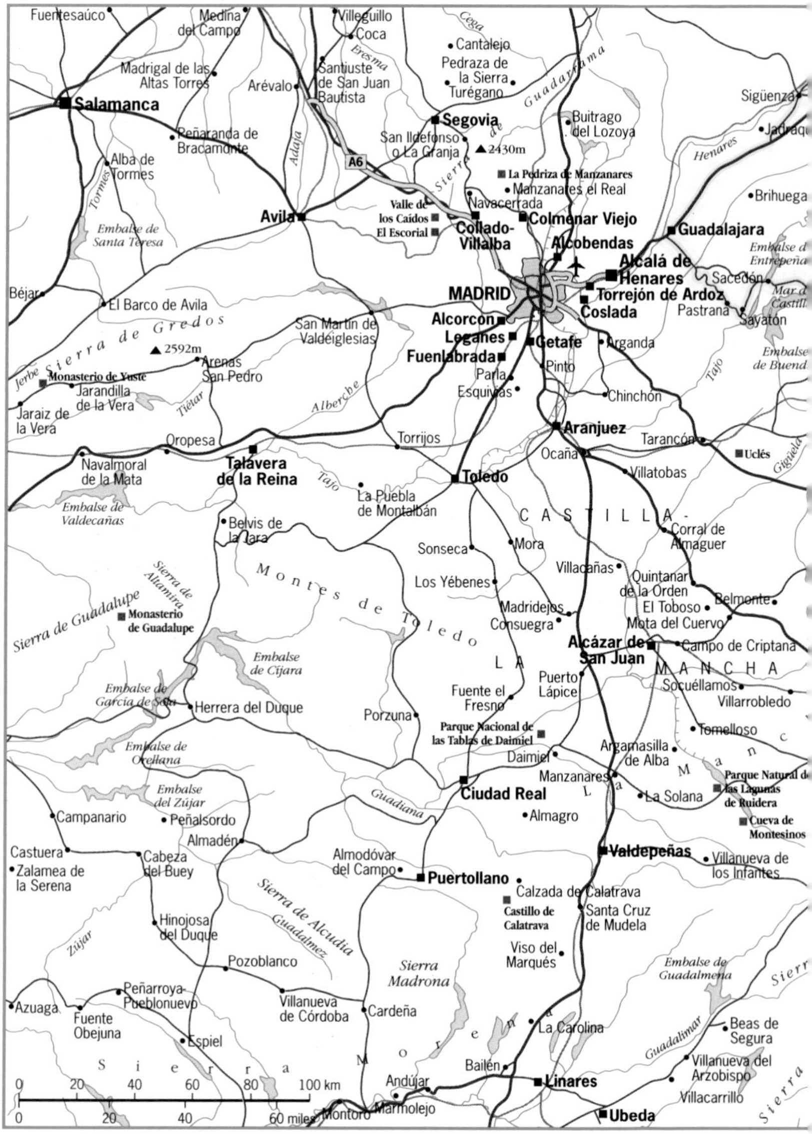

CASTILLA-LA MANCHA AND THE MADRID REGION

through the flatness of La Mancha, to the empty Montes de Toledo in the west. The Madrid region is bordered by the Guadarrama Mountains to the north; Castilla-La Mancha is set apart from Andalucía by the Sierra Morena.

Leaving aside Toledo, which often seems close cousin to such stern spots as Avila, Castilla-La Mancha is an affable, relaxed part of Spain. However, over 500 castles, Moorish and Christian, bear witness to its warlike past. The military orders, Knights of Calatrava and Santiago, ruled huge tracts of the new territory. There are also monasteries and aristocratic palaces, surviving alongside a vernacular architecture.

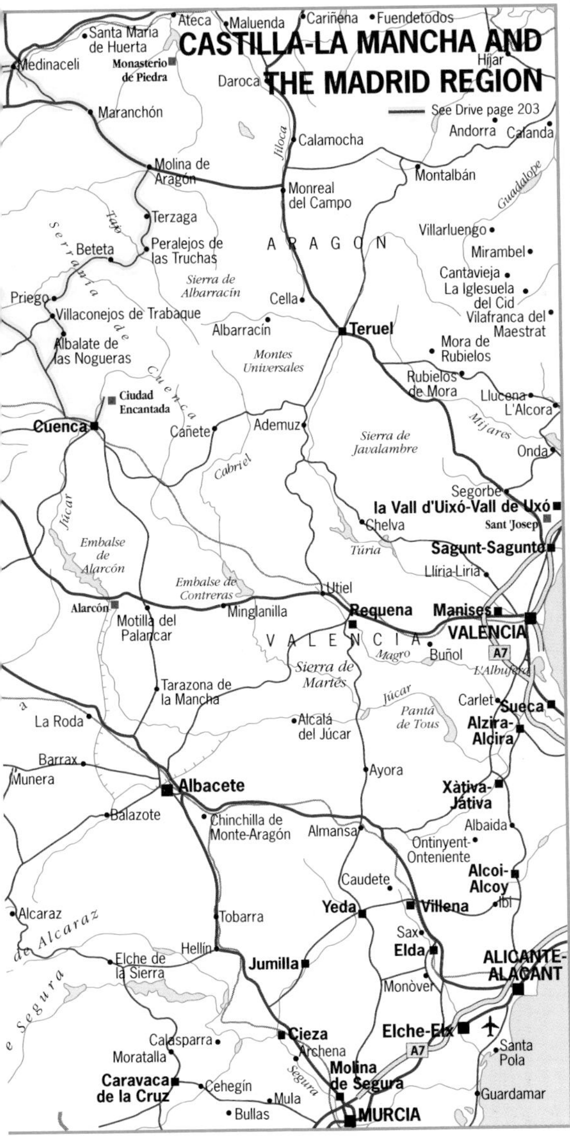

Francisco Jiménez de Cisneros, cardinal and archbishop of Toledo, was one of Spain's mixed blessings. He founded a great university at Alcalá and commissioned the Polyglot Bible, a huge cultural achievement which compared Greek, Hebrew and Latin texts. In Toledo he made it possible for the Mozarabic form of service to be preserved in perpetuity. But it was his severity that provoked the Moors of Granada into a hopeless rebellion; and after the death of Queen Isabella I, Cisneros squandered resources on Crusades against North Africa, as requested by the queen in her will.

Palace in Alcalá de Henares

▶▷▷ **Alarcón**

A fierce twist in the gorge of the Río Júcar offered the Moorish kingdom of Toledo the site for an impregnable castle – impregnable, that is, until 1184, when Hernán Martinez de Cevellos used two daggers to scale the walls. The site and the castle (now containing a parador) still combine to make a stirring impression. A village with three churches is contained within the walls.

▷▷▷ **Albacete**

Always a nerve centre in Spanish communications, Albacete, on the La Mancha plain, is famous for the manufacture of knives, but has little of historic interest. There are a number of Modernista houses (one by the cathedral in green tiles) and a recently restored medieval inn.

▶▶▷ **Alcalá de Henares**

Just 31km east of Madrid on the Barcelona road, industrial Alcalá de Henares with its crop of apartment blocks, has at its venerable core the fine Renaissance façade of the university founded here in 1498 by Cardinal Cisneros. Closed for centuries, the university has recently been reopened. Cervantes was born here (a 1950s version of his house in Calle Mayor contains editions of his works) and here Queen Isabella gave birth to Catherine of Aragon, who married England's Henry VIII. The university façade, by Rodrigo Gil de Hontañon, is a 1540s replacement of the brick original. The swans in evidence are a pun on Cardinal Cisneros' name (*cisne* means 'swan'). The bird became the personal emblem of Cisneros. Do not miss the Gothic-Mudéjar Capilla de San Ildefonso where Cervantes was christened, or the university's Patio Trilingüe, named after the trilingual or Polyglot Bible produced here at Cisneros' orders.

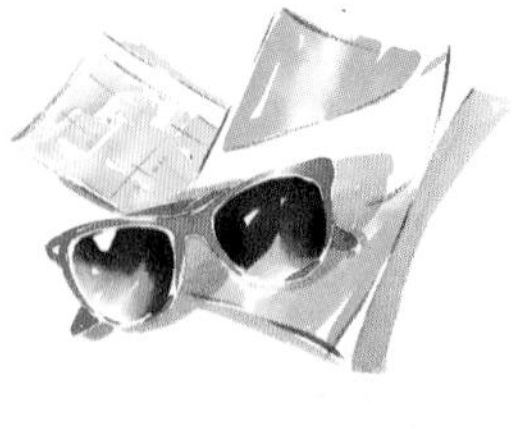

▶▷▷ **Alcalá del Júcar**

This tiny township in the Júcar gorge, with castle perched on top of a great cake of cliff, extracts effortless drama from its troglodyte houses and cliff-side site.

▶▷▷ **Alcaraz**

Alcaraz is marked by earlier grandeur, with castle ruins and a handsome Calle Mayor running along the steeply sloping hillside. The largely Renaissance Plaza Mayor reflects the style and spirit of local architect Andrés de Vandelvira, born here in 1509. There is a fine Plateresque doorway at the Plaza Mayor end of the Calle Mayor.

▶▶▷ **Almagro**

The historic home of the Knights of Calatrava lies white and peaceful in the plains of New Castile. Its extraordinary main square has long sides formed by what seems an infinite extension of glassed-in balconies, two storeys high, riding over stone arcades. The Corral de las Comedias is a uniquely surviving theatre of the Golden Age; churches and noble houses abound; the Fugger banking family retained a large warehouse now known as the Palacio Fucar. The convent of the Calatrava order, with Gothic church and calm Renaissance cloister, is also a survivor. Lace making and aubergine pickling are modern specialities.

▷▷▷ **Almansa**

The small plains town of Almansa is gathered round a rock with a crenellated fairy-tale castle. This was built by the Infante Don Juan Manuel. Below is the fine church of the Asunción and Renaissance Casa Grande next door.

▶▶▷ **Aranjuez**

Aranjuez, with its shady groves of trees beside the Tagus, is site of a major Bourbon palace and an easy day-trip from Toledo or Madrid. The palace exterior mainly reflects the taste of Charles III. So do parts of the interior (guided tours only), especially the porcelain room, housing the work of the Royal Porcelain Factory in Madrid. Both Charles IV and Queen Isabella II have left their mark here also. Note the 203 Chinese drawings presented to Isabella, some showing scenes of torture. The palace has fine chandeliers and mirrors.

The delightful formal Jardín de la Isla, just behind the palace, was originally planted by Habsburg Philip II. Acres of forest-parkland a little west along the river contain the royal boathouse, now rebuilt as a museum to show the royal barges, and a 'cottage' palace, known as the Casa del Labrador – the House of the Working Man.

Prince Karl of Austria was toe-to-toe with Philip of Anjou in the War of the Spanish Succession. Hostilities had opened all across Europe in 1702. In 1705, Karl's British and German forces landed in Barcelona and Valencia. They twice succeeded in taking Madrid but in 1707 were decisively beaten at Almansa by French troops under the Duke of Berwick. It was the beginning of the end for Karl in this particular contest, though he went on to be Holy Roman Emperor. Philip of Anjou was confirmed as Philip V of Spain and reigned, with a brief interruption, right up to 1746.

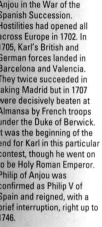

The palace at Aranjuez, one of the rural refuges of the royal family in former times

Belmonte: castle and crenellated walls

▷▷▷ **Belmonte**

Belmonte was guarded by an impressive castle on a hill overlooking the plains of La Mancha. From the castle, walls run down the hillside; several gates remain. Open to the public, the castle retains fine Mudéjar ceilings. (See also page 199.)

▶▷▷ **Brihuega**

This attractive village in the bee-keeping Alcarria region sits high above the River Tajuña. It has Gothic churches, Moorish town walls, the 12th-century Castillo de Piedra Bermeja and an 18th-century cloth factory.

The raw material of royal jelly is 'polen' or *pan de abeja* – bread of bees. Used by Alcarria locals to stir into milk or water, it is reputedly very good for prostate problems, stress control and as an aphrodisiac. Doesn't taste too nice, though.

▶▶▷ **Caídos, Valle de los**

As much as the Alcázar of Toledo (see page 206), the Valley of the Fallen, a few kilometres northeast of the Escorial, is a monument to the victorious Nationalists of the Spanish Civil War.

Following his victory in 1939, Franco set his political prisoners to work hollowing a monstrous cavern from the rock at the foot of a pine-clad valley of the Sierra de Guadarrama. The result was a tunnel-like church of a grandiosity to match that of the Escorial (see page 200). Franco himself is now buried on one side of the High Altar, José Antonio, theorist of Spain's Falange party, or national socialists (see page 45), on the other. On a rock above the cave-shrine there rears a cross 125m high (a tiny funicular ascends to its base).

To combine a visit here with the Escorial will greatly enhance an understanding of Spanish history between 1939 and Franco's death in 1975.

▶▷▷ **Calatrava**

This ruined and romantic castle of the Knights of Calatrava looms immense over a southerly pass out of La Mancha. Within encircling walls, the castle itself rises in a final crag, with a convent church tucked in behind.

Walk Parque Nacional de las Tablas de Daimiel

A visit to this national park is a chance to see the last of the once extensive wetlands of La Mancha, temporary home to a huge population of migratory water birds. This final outpost, formed by the confluence of the Guadiana and Cigüela rivers, is, alas, under threat. Excessive water pumping for the fields and vineyards of La Mancha, and the failure of an emergency scheme to divert more water in the direction of the Tablas, has dried up the area. Where once it was rich in birdlife all the year, now there is only a guarantee of water from January to June, naturally the popular months to visit.
Best in spring, but avoid Holy Week and weekends.

About 10km along a winding road north of the village of Daimiel, park at an Information/ Reception Centre. A terrain of rushes and small elevated islands among water courses now reveals itself. Paths and large railed bridges made of railway sleepers link islands and mainland, with observation points, a hide overlooking the one small permanent lagoon and another peeping into an enclosed aviary. There are numerous varieties of ducks, herons, etc.

A well marked walk circuit to Isla del Pan takes 2 hours; to Permanent Lagoon 30–40 minutes; and to 'Prado Ancho' 1½ hours.
Open: 08.00. Closed 18.30 in winter, 20.30 in spring, 21.00 in summer.

Walk Ciudad Encantada

At 36km northeast of Cuenca, well signposted via Villalba de la Sierra, La Ciudad Encantada (Enchanted City) is an extraordinary rockscape set at 1,400m among pine woods.

A 3km circuit of gravel path is laid out among the rocks (white arrows out, red arrows home), perhaps 1½ hours for a leisurely circuit including diversions.

Huge individual clumps or long parallel ridges of rock have been eroded near their bases leaving forms that rise up like hammers, inverted clubs or lines of aircraft carriers. The owners of this private patch of land (20 sq km) have posted up fanciful names such as 'The Theatre' and 'The Tortoise' alongside each of the main phenomena. This is a popular excursion site.

The flat, watery expanses of Las Tablas de Daimiel

La Mancha and the rough land round about has always been partridge-shooting territory. Nowadays, this has become something of a mania, both for Madrileños and well-to-do foreign tourists. Don't be surprised to meet men with guns and body-warmers lumbering towards you out of the winter mists.

Water and balconies: unspoiled Chinchón

▷▷▷ **Chinchilla de Monte Aragón**

Some 12km south of Albacete, on a rocky outcrop above the plains of La Mancha, stand the ruins of a 15th-century castle, once a stronghold of the Marquis of Villena, Grand Master of the Knights of Santiago. The little town which grew up around the castle is now somewhat decayed but still attractive with a pleasing main square – La Plaza de La Mancha – a town hall, and the 15th-century church of San Salvador. The castle (good views) is reached by a very narrow road, passing ruined houses and some cave dwellings.

▶▶▷ **Chinchón**

Chinchón, within easy striking distance of Madrid, is justly famous for its Plaza Mayor, the genuine, archetypal, arcaded Spanish square, nestled in a valley, with town rising above. Above the ground-floor arches rise two or three storeys of wooden balconies. These are used for viewing bullfights, but many have turned themselves into restaurants, with tables set along the balconies. On Sundays, delicious smells waft upwards to the grand stone church of La Asunción, which contains a Goya *Virgin*. The pleasant stone-and-brick, 17th-century Augustinian convent is now a parador. The region produces garlic and anísette.

▷▷▷ **Ciudad Real**

Ciudad Real, the Royal City, received its title in 1420, but was founded about 200 years earlier by Alfonso X, the Learned, as a check on the power of the Knights, with territory near by at Almagro and beyond. Interesting sights include: the large and bare cathedral, with Renaissance retablo; the adjoining house of the *conquistador* Hernán Perez de Pulgar (1451-1531), now used for exhibitions; the Provincial Museum, well demonstrating the rich archaeology of the region; and the Elisa Cendrera Museum, a glimpse into the lives of the turn-of-the-century bourgeoisie. The church of Santiago has an elegant, Gothic interior, San Pedro a swirling rose window, and best of all is the horseshoe Mudéjar arch of the Puerta de Toledo. Otherwise, the city is unattractive.

Crossing the gorge to old Cuenca

▶▶▶ Cuenca

Cuenca, capital of its province, is the supreme picture postcard town. The medieval town clings to the summit of two deep gorges formed by the Huécar and Júcar rivers passing far below. Some houses are built into the vertical side of a gorge – thereby earning them the description *Las Casas Colgadas* ('the Hanging Houses') of Cuenca. The pleasant modern town beneath is almost a separate entity.

Architecturally, Cuenca is a modest town, but note the **mansions** in the Calle de la Correduria and Calle Alfonso VIII, built by *conquistadores* home from the Americas, and the cathedral at the very heart of the old town in the Plaza Mayor. The **cathedral** (largely Gothic interior and ill-judged Renaissance façade) was founded by Alfonso VII. A few steps to the south is the cluster of buildings officially designated as **Las Casas Colgadas**. This strange and lovely architectural ensemble, heavily restored, houses the outstanding **Museo de Arte Abstracto Español**, a collection of Spanish abstract paintings and sculpture owned by the Juan March foundation. Painters include Millares, Rueda, Saura, Tàpies and sculptors Chillida and Serrano. A restaurant next to the gallery serves local specialities.

For best views of the Hanging Houses you should cross the gorge by the footbridge (Puente de San Pablo) to the left of the gallery and look back at the town. The bridge was originally constructed for the benefit of the Dominican monks of the monastery of San Pablo on the other side.

The **Diocesan Museum** near the cathedral is certainly worth visiting for its paintings, the cathedral treasury and a fascinating display of early carpets, their production formerly a local industry. The **Cuenca Museum** opposite is dedicated to prehistory and archaeology.

Osiers grow dense and reddish-coloured in valley bottoms north of Cuenca. Harvested in February/ March, the osier-bark is stripped by steaming and then dyed in primitive-looking pits. This picturesque trade is much diminished; whether it wil live or die is an open question.

The Romans knew Cuenca as Conca. It was part of a marriage settlement to King Alfonso VI by the Moorish ruler and was at one time headquarters of the Knights of Santiago. In subsequent centuries it was fought over by the French, the Carlists and during the 20th-century Civil War.

Quixote Country

■ In Don Quixote de La Mancha and Sancho Panza, his earthy squire, Miguel de Cervantes immortalised not only two extraordinary characters but also the landscape of La Mancha, from which the Knight of the Rueful Countenance took his name. And it was on this strange, flat plain, not so very far south of Madrid, that many of the couple's adventures came to pass. By far the best known, of course, is Quixote's tilting at the windmills, which lifted him up, complete with his horse Rosinante, and dumped him down again. .....■

Windmills of La Mancha – Don Quixote's 'giants' are still a prominent feature of the landscape

But there is more to the Knight than windmills and more landscape to the story than just the plain, extraordinary as it is. Much of the tale in fact takes place in the surrounding mountains and, in the final chapters, ranges as far as Aragon and Barcelona.

The Quixote route The 'official' (and signposted) Quixote route can be done in a single day. It sticks to the northern part of La Mancha and concentrates quite heavily on windmills.

The route starts at Consuegra, just to the west of the NIV, the main traffic artery between Madrid and the south. From here, it drops a little south to Puerto Lápice, then continues, eastwards, along the line of the N420.

At Consuegra windmills stand along a crest above the town, gaunt against the sky, stone-built and white-painted, with four great latticed sails.

Unlike Consuegra, **Puerto Lápice** (pronounced Lapiche) actually gets a mention in the book. It has a wonderful old *corral* – farm building with courtyard – done up as the inn on the Seville road which features so heavily in the Don Quixote story. There is a bar with *tinajas*, the enormous storage jars that are typical of this major wine-growing area.

Next stop, **Alcázar de San Juan**, offers 15th- and 16th-century monuments, but is essentially a railway town. **Campo de Criptana** has an impressive cluster of windmills above the town, though some are modern constructions. Up to the northeast is **El Toboso**, home of the lady, imaginary or otherwise, to whom Don Quixote plighted his troth. Visitors are shown 'Dulcinea's house', a handsome old dwelling furnished in the style of the period. There is a 'Cervantine Centre' with a collection of editions of *Don Quixote*. The route continues on through Mota del Cuervo (ruined windmills stand in fields of litter above the town) and finishes in **Belmonte**, rather dubiously attached to the Quixote legend but with a fine castle on a hill.

Off the beaten track Those with time will be well repaid by extending the route deeper into the country. From Mota del Cuervo, for instance, you could drop south to Tomelloso and nearby **Argamasilla** where, according to another doubtful legend, Cervantes was held in prison and began the work. The countryside around, however, is pure La Mancha.

South to the hills South again, but still within the territory of the story, are the lagoons of Ruidera, set in rough, wild country (see page 202) and the strange and prominently featured cave of Montesinos (reached from Ossa de Montiel or 3km from the southernmost lagoon). By now, you are among the Campos de Montiel (fields of Montiel), the first place actually mentioned by name in *Don Quixote*. Beyond, almost at once, come the thoroughly Quixotic mountains of the Sierra Morena.

Almost every town on the Quixote route has its statue of the melancholy knight

Miguel de Cervantes certainly got married and lived some while in the small Manchegan town of Esquivias. But did he use it as subject matter for his great novel? Names very similar to those of the characters of Quixote have allegedly been found in parish registers, now vanished, and there are some wonderful old houses, deeply dilapidated, with Quixote-style *corrales*. One, said by scholars to have belonged to the Quixote prototype, Alonso Quixada, and so perhaps the original of Quixote's house in the novel, is being turned into a museum and is described as Cervantes' own marital home. The family home of Cervantes' wife, Catalina Palacios, is nearby.

El Escorial

■ San Lorenzo de El Escorial is the most extreme of all the monastery-palaces and pantheons built by Spanish royalty. Vast in hard-edged granite, it rises from the southern slopes of the Sierra Guadarrama on a site chosen by Philip II, who had promised his father Charles V a mausoleum and had vowed to dedicate a monastery to St Lawrence in gratitude for a victory. In its ostentatious, penitential gloom (relieved by a collection of artworks and religious relics, and a magnificent library), it symbolises Habsburg Spain. .....■

At the heart of the Escorial are the private chambers of Philip II. A recess off his austere bedchamber, where he died in 1598, gave on to the high altar of the basilica.

Highlights Beneath the pompous basilica, with kneeling sculptural groups of Charles V, Philip II and their families, the gaudy Royal Pantheon contains the remains of virtually all the Spanish kings and queens from Charles V on. In the adjoining Palacio Real (royal palace), the Salas Capitulares or Chapter Rooms offer paintings by Flemish, Italian and Spanish masters. There is a museum of architecture also. The Bourbon rooms are charmingly decorated with tapestries, some Goya-based.

The rooms of Philip II and his daughter Isabella, have terracotta floors, tiled dados and creakingly ancient furniture. You will see the sedan chair in which Philip was brought here to his deathbed. The library, under ceilings by Tibaldi and Carducho, contains a sumptuous display of manuscripts.

The monastery and town can be visited on a day-trip from Madrid, by train or tour-bus. Visitors average 5,000 a day.

EL ESCORIAL

1. Palacio Real
2. Mascaroon Courtyard
3. Sanctuario
4. Panteon de los Reyes
5. Coro
6. Biblioteca
7. Convento
8. Apartamientos de Felipe II
9. Sala de la Trinidad
10. Old Church
11. Basilica
12. Throne Room

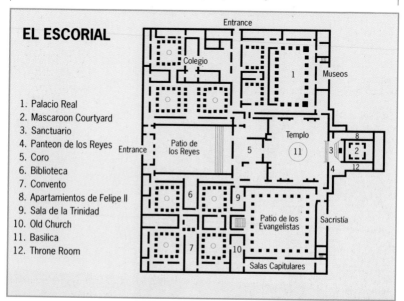

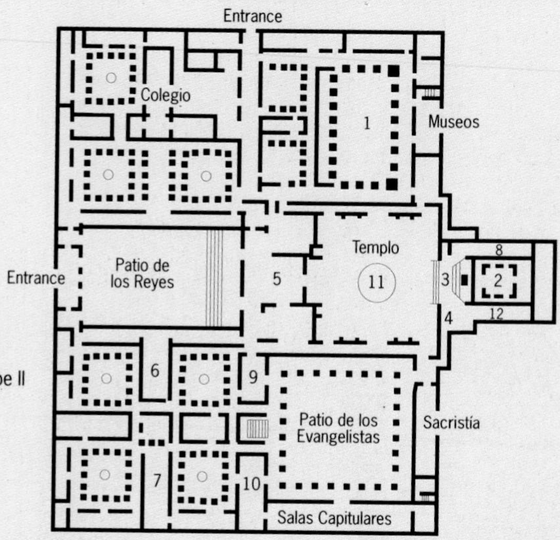

▶▷▷ Guadalajara

The capital of Guadalajara province is remarkable for one monument – the amazing **Palacio del Infantado** – the ducal palace of the Infantados, part of the important Mendoza family. Here Juan Guas' Plateresque façade is decorated with pyramidical stone protrusions, heraldry and 'wild men'. Inside are cloisters and Guadalajara's provincial museum.

▶▶▷ Guadarrama

The Sierra de Guadarrama (Guadarrama mountains) is only about an hour's drive from Madrid. Rocky and pine-forested, they angle up in a northeasterly direction from the Escorial, featuring the ski station of Navacerrada and attractive spots to visit. **Manzanares El Real**, on the southern approaches, boasts the region's most exuberant and decorative castle (15th century, restored). Nearby is the regional park of **La Cuenca Alta del Río Manzanares**, with the famous tumbled rockscapes of La Pedriza. Over the pass at Navacerrada is the sumptuously beautiful monastery of **El Paular**, founded in 1390 by Juan I of Castile. Further east, on the main road to Burgos, **Buitrago del Lozoya** retains an old walled precinct with medieval houses and a Picasso museum endowed by Picasso's own hairdresser, a loyal son of the village.

▷▷▷ Mar de Castilla

This inland 'sea' of artificial lakes was created by the damming of the River Tagus. Beside the three largest reservoirs of Entrepeñas, Buendía and Bolarque there is growing tourist development catering for fishing and watersports enthusiasts.

▶▷▷ Molina de Aragón

Stern walls and a keep, four stalwart towers aloft – Molina's much fought-over border status between the kingdoms of Aragon and Castile is still evident. The town, both new and old, lies far below. There are mansions and churches with ancient façades, some crumbling, others shored up with rather functional restoration. A murky river passes through, spanned by a Roman bridge of huge red sandstone blocks.

▷▷▷ Montes de Toledo

Venison and wild boar feature on menus in this region – with little sense of surprise or special luxury. The sparsely populated Pico Corocho de Rocigalpo rises to 1,447m – genuine huntsman's territory

General Franco probably opened more reservoirs than any other man in history, sometimes with devastating consequences for Spain's landscape. It was an essential part of his agricultural programme, and compulsory land purchase was rather easy for dictators. The story goes that on his deathbed his hand fell into his chamber pot. 'I bless this reservoir...' he mumbled – supposedly his last words.

Walking in the Sierra de Guadarrama

Lake San Juan, San Martín de Valdeiglesias

The tempestuous one-eyed Princess of Eboli from Guadalajara married the Duke of Pastrana, many years older than herself, and had 13 children by him. She was also the lover of the Spanish king Philip II, among others. In course of time and devilish intrigues, she fell out of favour. Escaping death, she was nevertheless kept under house arrest in the Palacio de los Duques de Pastrana. For one hour each day, she was allowed to sit on a balcony overlooking the square – a routine remembered in the square's name, Plaza de la Hora.

▶▶▷ **Pastrana**

A charming town of quiet streets and grey mottled roofs, Pastrana lies in the Alcarria hills above the Río Tagus. It was once held by the Knights of Calatrava, then given by Charles V to Ruiz Gómez da Silva, who later became the Duke of Pastrana and built a silk factory here. The stern but grand ducal palace (under restoration) occupies an entire side of the lovely town square. The nearby late Gothic collegiate church has a treasury with fine 15th-century Brussels tapestries commemorating the war fought against the Moors in North Africa by King Alfonso V of Portugal.

▶▷▷ **Priego**

Perched on the lip of a valley on the edge of the Serranía de Cuenca, the town of Priego looks rather down-at-heel by contrast with its wonderful position. There is no evidence of wealth gained from its famous wickerwork and ceramic handicrafts.

▶▷▷ **Ruidera**

Las Lagunas de Ruidera (the Ruidera lagoons) are a succession of narrow natural lakes in marshy land along the Pinilla river (dammed further downstream). All are popular in summer. Nearby is the Cueva de Montesinos, where Don Quixote had extraordinary visions.

▶▷▷ **San Martín de Valdeiglesias**

Barely an hour's drive from Madrid, this agreeable little town marks the eastern beginnings of the Sierra de Gredos. From here, take the Avila road, and follow signposts for **Toros de Guisando** to see these four stone bulls, believed to be Celtiberian, in a meadow/enclosure by the road.

Drive Sigüenza circular route

This route describes a two-day drive, either a circle based on Sigüenza or a scenic two-day extra to the direct route between Zaragoza and Madrid. Stop overnight in Cuenca.

From Sigüenza, follow the road east to Medinaceli (a corner of the neighbouring province of Soria). Leave Medinaceli by the old Madrid road, turning left for Maranchón, and cross the railway tracks.
The route now goes through barren rolling countryside and depopulated villages.

From Maranchón, head south to Molina de Aragón. Leave the town by C202 signposted to Terzaga and follow the Alto Tajo tourist route.
This part of the route is through agricultural villages and the wild ravines of the Serranía de Cuenca.The landscape becomes more wooded and mountainous to **Peralejos de las Truchas**, a fishing and hunting settlement. Pass through the Tajo (Tagus) gorge and on to **Beteta** (castle on top and old town below). Continue down the course of the Beteta Gorge — Hoz de Beteta – to **Priego** then southwards to **Villaconejos** (with its troglodyte dwellings).

Follow the road southwards towards Albalate de las Nogueras and join the N320 towards Cuenca.
Cuenca has both its famous 'Hanging Houses' and a parador, in a former monastery. Make a detour to the extraordinary rock formations of the **Ciudad Encantada**.

Leave Cuenca as you entered, by the Madrid road, then northwards on the N320 around the reservoirs of the Mar de Castilla.
At Sacedón, there is a sign to Buendía, one of the holiday resorts on the lake and somewhere to relax or indulge in watersports.

Continue on the N320 out of Sacedón across the Entrepeñas reservoir, turn left to Sayatón, then right to Pastrana.
It is worth spending some time in this delightful medieval town.

From here follow the N320 to Guadalajara. Head back to Sigüenza to make a circle or westwards to Madrid.

Quiet Sigüenza comes to life at fiesta time

Among Toledo's large and cultured Jewish community there were many scholars. They and colleagues from all over Europe were employed by Alfonso X, the Learned (1252-84), in his Translators' School in Toledo. The idea was to translate works from Arabic for the general benefit of Christian Europe. The Arabs, and with them the Moors, were not only skilled philosophers, mathematicians and navigators, but it was they, with their capture centuries earlier of much of the Byzantine Empire, who had become the guardians of the texts of Ancient Greece. Translations were also undertaken at the monastery of Ripoll in Catalonia.

▶▶▶ Toledo

Toledo may be a tourist trap, but it is unmissable: compact, awesome, often described as mystical. Certainly El Greco made it seem so, painting it in livid colours under a livid sky; and Cervantes referred to Toledo's 'rocky gravity'.

Toledo's past The history of the peninsula is encapsulated here: Romans, Visigoths (they made Toledo their capital), Moors (for whom it was a frontier city of great learning and cultivation), and Jews (who in early days lived here in some numbers, at peace with Moors and Christians). Alfonso VI of Castile conquered it in 1085. For a while, the tradition of scholarship persisted under the Christians, and Alfonso X (the Learned) maintained a school of translators here, salvaging Greek, Latin and Arabic texts for emerging Europe. Toledo's Jews, who were central to this process, were eventually to be persecuted at the instigation of Vicente Ferrer (who was later sanctified), and finally expelled in 1492.

As well as scholars, Toledo produced silks and fine-tooled, damascene daggers and swords. 'The Greek', El Greco, was its finest painter. It was, and remains, chief city of the Spanish Church, seat of the Primate, and so far as Spain had a capital, Toledo was it, until Philip II moved the court to Madrid in 1561. Between then and the coming of the tourists, the only power Toledo retained was spiritual. Its most bitter battle was the siege of the Alcázar, held by the Nationalists, in the Civil War.

Economic decay from the 16th century on ironically helped to preserve the historic buildings and Moorish atmosphere of Toledo, which today attracts tourists in such numbers.

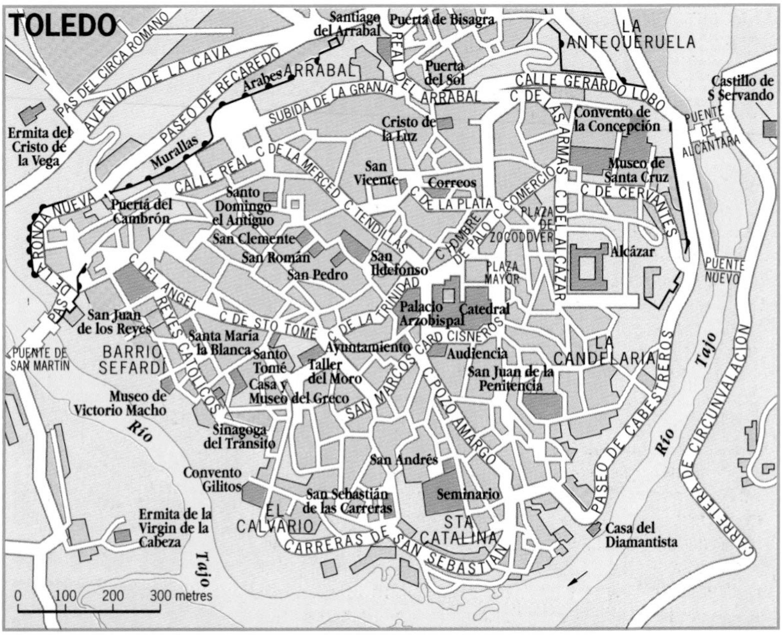

Toledo's 'New' Bisagra Gate, with its twin towers and imperial symbol

El Greco's *The Burial of the Count of Orgaz*, shows the miraculous appearance of Saints Augustine and Stephen who lower the count, a benefactor of the Church of Santo Tomé, into his grave, still wearing his damascene armour. A line of Castilian gentlemen looks calmly on. The upper portion of the painting stands for heaven, with the Virgin waiting to welcome the soul of the dead man. This is portrayed as a baby ascending through a shape like a birth canal. Non-Spaniards have come to see this work, with its gravely bearded, aristocratic faces, and swooning sense of divinity, as somehow epitomising an aspect of Spanishness – though the artist was born in Crete.

Sightseeing Toledo lies draped over high ground in a tight loop of the Tagus gorge. For motorists, there is a road around the outside, the Carretera de Circumvalación, or Ronda, which offers fine views. (El Greco painted the city from close to the site of the parador, reached from this road.) It is best to park outside the city and walk up by the 14th-century Mudéjar Puerta del Sol on the north side. From Madrid, there are also buses, trains and day-trip coaches by the hundred.

The point of departure inside the city is the roughly triangular Plaza de Zocodover (the 'Zoco'), site of ancient horse fairs and now of a Tuesday market. The most visited sights can be walked by making a rough semi-circle, starting from Zocodover down the Calle Comercio.

The Cathedral Toledo's cathedral was founded by Fernando III, el Santo, in 1227. Entry is to the left of the main façade (under a single tower and with the *ayuntamiento* opposite, designed by El Greco's son). The cathedral interior, centre of Spanish Catholicism, is lit darkly by stained glass and is dense with works of art. There is a shrine to the Visigothic San Ildefonso, featuring the rock on which the Virgin set foot when she presented him with a chasuble. The magnificent choir contains scenes of the capture of Granada, by Rodrigo Alemán. The vast retablo opposite includes (half-way up on the left, on the pillar) a representation of the shepherd who guided the Catholic troops to their great victory at Navas de Tolosa. Behind the sanctuary is the *Transparente*, a super-baroque work of wings and plunging figures, lit by the sun's rays through a round window. At the southeast corner of the cathedral is the Mudéjar chapel where the ancient Mozarabic order of service is still in use. The cathedral sacristy contains an

El Greco came to Toledo in 1576 or 1577. He quickly found work with the church, and the success – despite occasional rows over commissions – that always eluded him with Philip II. He never moved again. It is tempting to suggest that he identified personally both with the dramatic landscape of the city and with the rarified spirituality which he portrayed. If this seems particularly Castilian, so be it – Domenicos Theotocopoulos, the Greek, had come a long way from his native Crete.

The Nationalist defence of the Toledo Alcázar was one of the great epics of the early months of the Civil War. The story has it that the son of the Nationalist officer in command, Colonel José Moscardó, was captured by the Republicans, who threatened to kill him. Moscardó spoke to his son on the telephone, exhorting him: 'If it be true, commend your soul to God, cry Viva España and die like a hero.' An uncanny echo of Guzmán el Bueno (see page 237). Moscardó's battered operations room, even his telephone, can still be seen in the Alcázar.

impressive collection of Italian and Spanish masterworks, centred on El Greco's *Expolio, Christ Stripped of his Robes*.

In the tiny church of Santo Tomé, just a minute or two from the cathedral, is El Greco's huge painting, *El Entierro del Conde de Orgaz (The Burial of the Count of Orgaz)*. The crowds are often daunting.

Casa y Museo del Greco (El Greco's House and Museum) This agreeable 16th-century building is set out as if it really were El Greco's – with studio, kitchen, etc. It contains paintings by the artist, and in the museum the famous *View and Plan of Toledo*, a major source of information on the city in the artist's own day. See page 267 for opening times.

Santa María la Blanca The Judería, or Jewish Quarter, contains the stunning little church (originally a synagogue) called Santa María la Blanca, built in Almohad style in the 12th century. Snowy white within, it rises on graceful horseshoe arches to raised geometrical patterning.

Sinagoga del Tránsito This fine, 14th-century synagogue is elegant in Mudéjar style. It was built by Samuel Leví, treasurer to Pedro I (who finally had him executed). Leví's name is also remembered in a narrow medieval street nearby.

San Juan de los Reyes (St John of the Kings) The monastery church built by Isabella and Ferdinand is a grand display of Isabelline Gothic, encrusted with royal monograms and with their yoke-and-arrow symbol (borrowed by Franco for Spanish Fascism). Outsize stone shields tilt at a rakish angle on the walls. The cloister is delightful; the church's outer façade is hung with chains removed from Christian captives of the Moors.

Close in below, the San Martín bridge spans the Tagus. Its gatehouse bears the arms of Charles V.

Other central sights The **Alcázar**, rebuilt in 16th-century form after the Civil War, is a fascinating museum of the 68-day siege of the fortress, and a monument to the Nationalist cause (see panel). Don't miss it, whatever your views.

The **Museo/Hospital de Santa Cruz**, an airy hospital of the late 15th and early 16th centuries, with Plateresque façade and patio, is just under the Alcázar. It has an impressive collection of paintings by El Greco and others. See page 267 for opening times.

North of Plaza del Zocodover Crossing over to the Old (Moorish) and New (16th-century) Bisagra gates on the north side of town, it is well worth passing by the ancient mosque now named **Cristo de la Luz**. This small building, with its many echoes of the Great Mosque of Córdoba, may be Toledo's oldest. Beyond the gates, the **Tavera monastery/museum** has sundry works of art and curiosities including Ribera's *Bearded Woman*, often, alas, away on loan for exhibition.

Wine-tasting in a Valdepeñas cellar

▶▶▷ **Sigüenza**
From the *alameda* at the bottom of town, past the Plaza Mayor and cathedral to the castle at the top, little Sigüenza is a delightful, old-fashioned provincial town. The **cathedral** is the chief monument, a composite of Romanesque, Gothic, Plateresque and even 20th-century. The **cathedral** museum has one good painting each by El Greco and Zurbarán; the sacristy ceiling bears over 300 carved heads by Covarrubias.

▶▷▷ **Talavera de la Reina**
Wellington's forces defeated the French at Talavera in 1809; otherwise this drab, busy town means only ceramics. These rely on multi-coloured floral patterning and naturalistic designs such as lolloping large-eared rabbits. There are many commercial showrooms as well as a local ceramics museum.

▶▷▷ **Uclés**
The remarkable monastery here, 16th- to 18th-century in its present form but founded in 1174, was a key site for the Knights of Santiago (see pages 218–219). The refectory retains busts of the Masters.

▷▷▷ **Valdepeñas**
Workaday Valdepeñas handles the wines produced in this part of La Mancha. There are numerous *bodegas*, and *tinajas*, enormous amphora-like wine storage jars, stand by the roadsides.

▶▷▷ **Villanueva de los Infantes**
In the Campos de Montiel, this little town, with its extraordinary collection of monuments, is a good example of how history once touched New Castile, then passed it by. The Plaza Mayor has a huge parochial church, arcades and wooden balconies. There is a lovely little patio and enough shields and escutcheons to fill a book of drawings – literally: one has been published locally.

Ever since Renaissance times, the liveliest pottery in Castile has come from Talavera de la Reina and nearby Puente del Arzobispo. Using light greens, browns, yellows and often red for flowers, the potters decorate their wares with cheerful scenes of rural pursuits and nature generally. Floral designs, often rimmed in blue, are also traditional. There are masses of pottery shops in Talavera itself, and Talavera ware, along with a great deal of junk pottery, is commonly sold elsewhere in shops and markets. Some of the dishes are huge and intended for walls; others are small enough and cheap enough for domestic use.

In the chapel of San Juan y Santa Catalina in Sigüenza's cathedral, the delicate 15th-century effigy of Martín Vázquez de Arce shows him as an armed knight at ease, one leg folded over the other, reading a book, no doubt religious. Known as El Doncel, normally meaning a page-boy or even virgin but here perhaps 'young person of delicate beauty', this is Spain's most famous funerary statue.

Between Catalonia in the north and Andalucía in the south, there lies a tract of coastal Spain composed of the autonomous regions of Valencia and Murcia and popularly known as the Levante, the land of the rising sun. The two 'autonomies' are very different, for the Valencia region, the official 'Levante', is historically intertwined with Catalonia and speaks its own language, Valenciano, virtually Catalan. Murcia is more Spanish.

Spain's food bowl The whole of the area, with once-poor Murcia now beginning to come into its own, is Spain's chief market garden. This rich and fertile *huerta* (garden) has been one of history's choicest prizes. El Cid

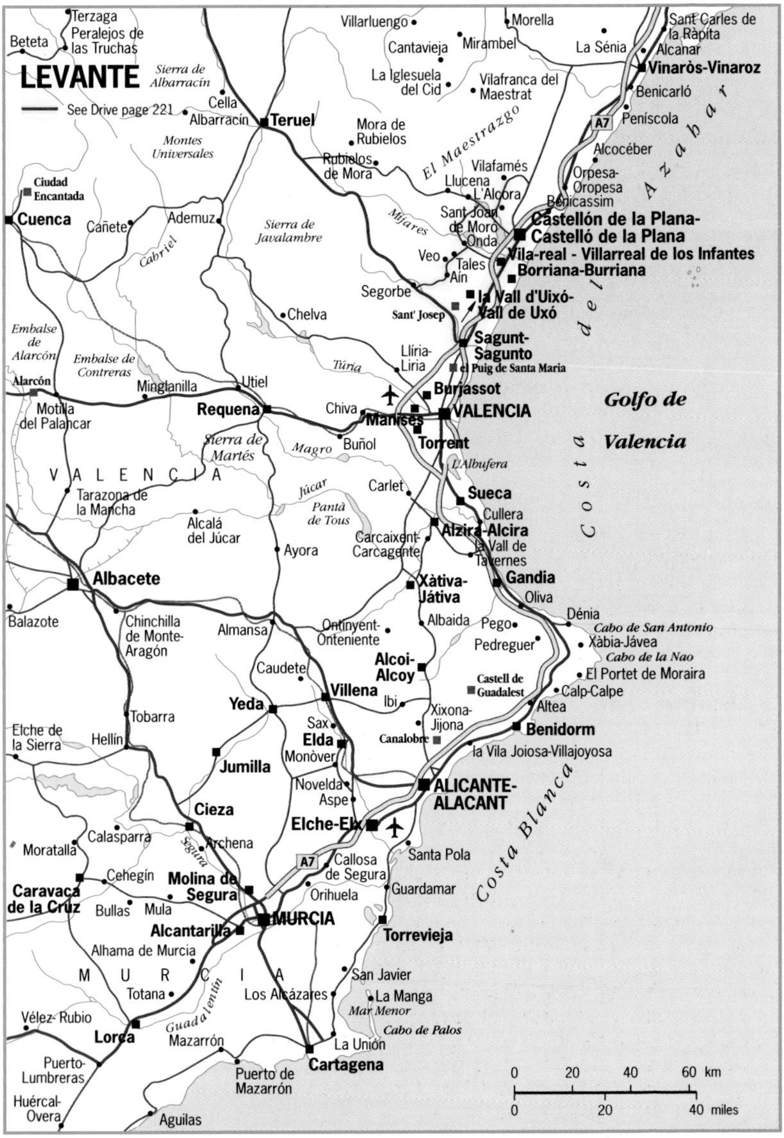

Women of Morella in the Maestrazgo

captured Valencia in the 11th century and founded a private kingdom here, but both the city and its famous *huerta* soon reverted to the Moors who held on for two more centuries. The present-day system of irrigation still owes much to the Moors. The basic crops, now as then, are oranges, vegetables – and rice (paella is a dish from Valencia). But the *huerta* is also a very messy area, full of light industry and litter. One pleasing relief is the Albufera lake, south of Valencia, though itself badly threatened by pesticides and encroaching building.

Tourist attractions There are three important costas. The Costa del Azahar or Orange Blossom coast, undramatic but much used by families, lies mainly north of Valencia. South and mostly round the corner of Cabo de la Nao lies the packed mass-tourism Costa Blanca, centred on Benidorm, a very well run resort. The Murcian coast (or Costa Calida) has a semi-inland sea, the Mar Menor, with new resorts emerging around it.
Valencia, Spain's third city, is unfashionable among tourists, largely, one suspects, for reasons of ignorance, but it has fine old buildings at its heart and a very pleasant atmosphere. Architecturally, Murcia is one of Spain's most baroque cities. Behind, round and between the two big cities are hosts of interesting places, ranging from Sagunto, the tragic site of one of the great sieges of the Punic War, to Játiva and Gandia, home of the Borgia family. And behind all of them rises the magnificent sierra, gaunt above the sea.

Local produce in Castellón de la Plana

Caravaca is the site of one of Spain's most exciting miracles. It seems that the local Moorish ruler was curious to hear the Christian Mass. A priest whom he was holding captive prepared to perform the ceremony, but suddenly remembered he had no cross. Quick as a flash, two angels arrived to remedy the deficiency. This celebrated cross disappeared during the Civil War, but the Pope made good the loss with the gift of a fragment of the True Cross. This is now embedded in the cross currently on display in Caravaca.

▶▷▷ Alcoy

North of Alicante (see page 214), in pleasant sierra with pine and fruit trees, Alcoy is a textile town with an industrial history. During the first Republic of 1874–5 it declared itself independent and so remained for several months. The town hosts Spain's best 'Moors and Christians' festival, and is home to the sugared almond.

▶▷▷ Caravaca de la Cruz

A hill town in inland Murcia, Caravaca de la Cruz is dominated by the pink, baroque Real Alcázar – Santuario de la Vera Cruz – a restored 15th-century Templar castle with a 17th-century church within it. The church was built to house a miraculous cross delivered by angels. The town has some fine rumbustious 'Moors versus Christians' parades.

▷▷▷ Cartagena

Cartagena, on the south Murcian coast, has been an important mining and naval town since the Carthaginians first exploited its deep water harbour and dug out minerals from the surrounding area. A densely jumbled town with a lively bustling air, it is now home to the Spanish Mediterranean fleet. Little remains of its tumultuous past except the old fort and ruins of a Romanesque church on the hill above the town, the arsenal established by Charles III, and a submarine designed in 1888 by a local officer, Isaac Peral.

▷▷▷ Castellón de la Plana

Castellón de la Plana is a small provincial capital, set in a lap of dead flat land (La Plana – the plain) with orange groves, between the mountains and its busy port, El Grao. Castellón itself was largely destroyed during the Spanish Civil War, but though rebuilt during an undistinguished period of architecture, it has a pleasant open feel. Some pretty 19th-century houses survive near the centre. In the Plaza Mayor, the cathedral, with octagonal free-standing belfry, was under reconstruction at the time of writing.

FOCUS ON 

■ South of Valencia lies the Albufera, a large freshwater lake divided from the Mediterranean only by a sandbank. Though shrunk to a tenth of its original size, it remains rich in ducks, herons, fish and eels. Parts are dense with reedbanks; parts are fringed by rice fields. This lake is at its best on misty mornings (good for wildlife) and at its most scenic at sunset. .....■

The Albufera lake, rewarding for wildlife enthusiasts – and for duck-hunters

Boat trip Boats ply for hire from **El Palmar** and **El Saler**. The trip from El Saler lasts about 30 to 40 minutes, at an all-in price for the boat – a traditional wooden craft, long and lowish, once punted, now motorised. The trip is highly recommended for views of the lake and its birdlife ... and also, alas, for a vivid glimpse of the fragility of the ecosystem. Though now subject to restriction, devastating out-of-scale building has occurred to the north and on the protective sand-spit, La Dehesa; the waters, once clear, are green. Mechanisation has arrived: the rice harvest used to come home by boat; now nobody would dream of using anything except a truck or tractor. The best months for wildlife – as also for duck-hunters, so keep your head down – are from September to March.

Old and new Around the lake, particularly on the southern side, there still survive a sprinkling of the original lakelanders' *barracas* – long, thin thatched houses with long, thin gardens, beautifully kept. Coastal apartment blocks all too often tower above them. A little south again, behind the dunes that back the beach, there is the very pleasant **Parador Nacional Luis Vives**, a haunt of golfers who come for the course which backs right on to the hotel.

Walk Gardens of Valencia

This is a walk of about 3½ hours combining two of Valencia's most pleasant and interesting open spaces, the Viveros Municipales (Vivero Park), sometimes known as the Jardines del Real, and the Jardín Botánico (Botanical Gardens). They are linked by a stroll along the bed of the diverted River Turia.

Start at the Tourist Information Office, Calle de la Paz 48. Turn right to cross Plaza Alfonso el Magnanimo, then left through Plaza de Tetuán. Now cross the fine old 16th-century bridge, Puente del Real, over the course of the Turia.
Diagonally to the right now is the city's most expensive housing, diagonally left the entrance to **Vivero Park**, southern in style and graceful. A 20-minute stroll takes you to the far end of the park.

Return to the same entrance, cross beneath the embankment road by foot tunnel and turn right along the course of the Turia.
Some parts have been newly planted, others are older; some areas are football pitches.

Alternatively, follow the road along the far bank.
You pass handsome medieval city gates, the **Serrano Towers**.

If you are at the lower level, emerge opposite the Corte Inglés department store and walk away from the river at right angles along Calle Beato Gaspar Bono.
The entrance to the **Botanical Gardens** is at the end of this long defile. Quiet and mature, founded in 1802, the gardens embody much of the Enlightenment quest for a scientific understanding of the flora of Spain and her dominions. *Open*: Tuesday–Sunday, winter 10.00–18.00hrs, summer 10.00–21.00hrs; closed in bad weather.

Return down Carrer Quart, becoming Cavalleros, cross the cathedral square and back to Calle de la Paz.

Valencia, Spain's third city, is rich in parks and gardens

Costa del Azahar

The Costa del Azahar (Orange Blossom Coast) runs south from just below the mouth of the Ebro towards the major city of Valencia, then on again to meet the Costa Blanca. It consists of a fringe of often flattish shoreline, backed in many parts by orange groves. The mountains behind, unimpressive in the north, become increasingly dramatic as they near Valencia. Though one of the less stylish Spanish Costas, some of its beaches are excellent and its generally calm atmosphere makes it suitable for families. Camping is popular in the area.

Alcocéber Midway down the Costa, Alcocéber has five beaches. The town beach is good; La Romana and La Tropicana, further south, are both outstanding, though not smart.

Benicarló This fair-sized town towards the Costa's northern end has a small but busy beach, a fishing port, a parador and a lively restaurant scene in summer. Wide streets and old buildings give it charm – note in particular the fine 18th-century church.

Benicasim Pleasant and well placed among palms, Benicasim is a northerly seaside suburb of Castellón de la Plana (see page 210) – an agreeable spot for family holidays.

Cullera South of Valencia, Cullera is definitely mass-tourism, with many French visitors. It lies under a rocky hill and castle, with a wide beach and many apartment blocks.

Grutas de San Josep (St Joseph's Caves) Follow road signs to 'Grutas' from Vall de Uxó (just north of Sagunto). The grotto experience involves a boat trip along an underground river (you will see caves and rock formations artfully lit), followed by a short walk along a gallery and a boat trip back again (45mins).
Open: Monday to Saturday 10.50–13.00 and 15.10–18.00hrs; Sunday 11.15–13.00 and 15.10–18.30hrs. Extended in high summer.

Oropesa del Mar With a scrap of old town around a ruined castle inland, this resort north of Castellón de la Plana has a long beach to the north and a rounded cove-beach to the south.

Peñíscola see page 220

Vinaroz The most northerly port and minor resort on the Costa del Azahar, Vinaroz is tatty but cheerful. The fishing fleet brings in giant prawns and scampi, irresistible to seafood lovers.

The true Valencia orange is as much a symbol of the Levante as the rice that goes into paella. Orange groves punctuate the rich market-garden land or *huerta* behind the coast, and lorries full of the chilled fruit go pounding off to northern Europe. As well as being skilled hi-tech horticulturalists, Valencianos are well known as some of Spain's shrewdest and most internationally minded traders.

The fishing harbour in Benicarló

In Spanish *turrón*, in Valencian *terró*, in English 'nougat' – Spain loves this Arabic sweetmeat, made of almonds, honey, sugar and white of egg. It comes in two forms in Spanish sweet shops: *blando* (soft), and the hard kind more familiar to northern Europeans, known as *duro* or *imperial*. The little town of Jijona, above Alicante in a region of almond orchards, is the nougat capital. Factories cluster thickly here, and there is a delicious smell. You can visit the El Lobo factory, just before the bridge on the northern exit from Jijona.

▶▶▷ Costa Blanca

The Costa Blanca (White Coast) of Alicante province is a phenomenon. In the north its offerings range from huge headlands and inaccessible coves, through the pleasant villa territory of retired foreigners to the mass pleasure-domes of Benidorm. At its southern extreme it has some of the most dense and dismal villa/apartment developments in all Spain.

Alicante Elegant Alicante, with its tree-lined squares and boulevards, bustling modern centre, magnificently baroque *ayuntamiento*, wide clean beaches and colourful waterfront Esplanada de España, is the undisputed capital of the Costa Blanca. For sightseers there is the Castillo de Santa Barbara (said to have been built by Carthaginians), with fine views; the 17th-century church of San Nicolás; and a small but interesting collection of 20th-century art in the Museo Asegurada.

Altea Though centred still on its pretty old town on a hill, Altea has now become a major tourist venue.

Benidorm Arguably Spain's capital of mass tourism, Benidorm is now almost a city behind its two long, crowded and excellent beaches. Having opted early for the high-rise solution, it pursues this course with great professionalism. Once very British in atmosphere, it is now international. It has the best water park on the Costa.

Calpe The mighty upthrust rock here, the Peñon de Ifach (Penyal d'Ifac) is now a natural park. The ascent on foot takes one hour. An isthmus of high-rise blocks links it to the mainland, with beaches to the north and south, and fishing harbour under the rock.

Benidorm, high-rise holiday mecca

Quiet beach near Jávea

Dénia A self-catering holiday centre, Denia has the excellent Las Marinas beach to the north. To the south, rocky and very pretty Les Rotes leads to Cabo de San Antonio and the resort of **Jávea**. Here, the hoop of sandy beach is overlooked by a parador with Roman ruins in its garden.

Moraira Many people from northern Europe retire to this cheerful town. Just to the north is the beautiful holiday cove of **El Portet**.

Torrevieja As well as a white Andalucian-style kitsch development, Torrevieja has salt pans, a semi-natural park with passing flamingos and a beach to the south of town.

Villajoyosa This weekend retreat of Alicante townees, centred on a small promenade with agreeable old houses, remains attractive despite a recent surge of apartment blocks.

▶▷▷ **Costa Calida**

Costa Calida (the Warm Coast) is the coastline of the Murcian region, hitherto the summer playground of locals, now known for the Mar Menor (Lesser Sea), with its pulsating resort of La Manga.

Aguilas Sailing and windsurfing are the attractions of this resort. The best beaches are southwest of town.

Gandia This southernmost resort on the Costa is backed by a forest of apartment blocks, and noisome with heavy through-traffic. It is the birthplace of San Francisco Borja (St Francis Borgia), who became the second head of the Jesuits. Group tours to the Palacio de los Duques de Gandia (ducal palace) on the hour, 10.00–12.00hrs and 17.00–19.00hrs May to September.
See also **Játiva** (page 217).

Mar Menor A large expanse of shallow water protected from the sea by sandbanks and with just one small entry to the Mediterranean, the Mar Menor and its resort of La Manga is now one of the concrete playgrounds of the Med. Strong winds make this an energetic paradise for windsurfers.

The Canelobre caves are a great destination for outings from Benidorm, reached via the village of Busot. At 700m, they are claimed as the richest stalactite caves in southeastern Spain. Coloured lights illuminate the rock formations; concerts are sometimes held here. Visit the caves April to September, 10.30–19.50hrs; October to March, 11.00–17.50hrs. Don't expect to find yourself alone.

■ Elche is a busy, commercial town, densely packed with small squares and fountains and old buildings. It is famous for its groves of date palms – and for shoe manufacture. The date palms, around 200,000 of them, radiate out from the middle of town. Though much reduced since they were planted by the Romans, they remain the largest palm plantation in Europe. The best place to enjoy them is in the captivating Parque Municipal (Municipal Park). .....■

Another palm park is the privately owned **Huerto del Cura** (Priest's Garden), on the east side of town. Here, many of the trees in a well maintained garden are named after celebrity visitors. The US palm, presumably for the ambassador, stands next to the late Señora Franco. At 150 years old, a famous seven-branched palm tree, known as the Palmera Imperial, leans perilously, much buttressed and supported by iron hoops.

<< The unusual sight of palm trees with their branches trussed in black polythene, shooting into the sky like tall spears, is a common one in Elche. Their fronds, protected from sunlight by the plastic, are being bleached for the Palm Sunday processions. Palm fronds are thought to divert lightning and are left to decorate balconies long after the religious celebrations are over. **>>**

Mystery of Elche The 17th-century Basilica de Santa María, baroquely beautiful in golden stone surmounted by a tower and two domes of brightest blue, was built for the performance of the famous Elche medieval mystery play about the death, or dormition, of the Virgin (played by a small boy) and her coronation as Queen of Heaven and Earth. The action unfolds over two days, 14 and 15 August, but the dress rehearsal of the whole play takes place the day before.

Next to the basilica are the sloping walls of the Moorish **fortress** and, within a short walking distance, the **Palacio de Altamira**, now an archaeological museum. Another archaeological museum is just out of town at Alcudia, where the beautiful 5th-century BC Iberian head of La Dama de Elche (now in Madrid) was discovered.

Some of the Elche palm trees

The cliff-top eyrie of Guadalest

▶▷▷ Guadalest

This little town, 12km inland from Benidorm and within the walls of a one-time Moorish fortress, is famous for its lace. For many visitors, an excursion here is a first intimation of the beauty and historical riches of the coastal sierra.

▶▶▷ Játiva (Xátiva)

This is the site of one of Spain's great Moorish fortresses, the **Castillo Major,** with accumulated castle building of centuries now rising along a high ridge where *huerta* meets sierra. The views are tremendous. The old town beneath the mountain has many fine façades and doorways. Two Borgia popes were born here; their statues stand outside the grand Renaissance Colegiata (collegiate church), which is itself a step away from the fine municipal hospital. Halfway up the mountain, the whitewashed chapel of St Felix contains fine Flemish primitive paintings.

▶▷▷ Lorca

Lorca is famous for the manufacture of ceramics and textiles. The old town on a hill is dominated by a castle with views of the modern town, spreading out into the *huerta* below. Much of the old town was rebuilt in grand baroque style after it was partially razed by an earthquake in the 17th century. The Plaza de España has an arcaded town hall and the collegiate church of San Patricio; just above, on the Plazita del Cano, are the law courts together with archive buildings. It makes a fine ensemble.

▶▶▷ Morella

A rugged but delightful mountain village in the upper Maestrazgo region, Morella has steep streets topped by a castle on an immense rocky hill (great views). Skirted by its medieval walls and gates, it is the epitome of the fortified hilltop town. Look for the fine Basilica de Santa María de Mayor with good carved portals; pass through the old Franciscan monastery and museum to the castle.

Borja in Aragon produced the Borja family, who became dukes of Gandia, in Valencia, in 1485 and also dominated nearby Xátiva. They were known as the Borgias in Italy. Cesare Borja was imprisoned variously at Xátiva and Medina del Campo and died in battle at Viana in Aragon in 1507. His nephew, Francisco Borja, the viceroy of Catalonia, became second General of the Jesuit order and is better known to us as San Francisco Borja. His former palace at Gandia belongs to the Jesuits and is open to the public. In Valencia cathedral there is a magnificently spooky Goya painting of the saint exorcising demons.

■ The Maestrazgo is a fiercely beautiful area of mountain and medieval townships in southern Aragon and the northern corner of the Levante. Its name means the Dominion of the Grand Masters. The Knights Templar, Knights of St John and Knights of Calatrava were all active here and had possessions in what was for centuries a bitterly disputed frontier area between the Moors and Christians. Nothing in Spain more eloquently sums up the later stages of the Reconquest than the story of these Knights of the Church Militant. .....■

The trend began in 1064, when the pope of the day granted indulgences to all French knights willing to fight the Muslims in Aragon. So off they went, dreaming of their 'castles in Spain'. Soon after the First Crusade in 1097, the Knights Templar and the Hospitallers were established in the Holy Land. Both quickly became active in Spain. The Templars received their first land grant in the peninsula, in Catalonia, in 1149. Even before that, Alfonso the Battler, King of Aragon, dying without an heir in 1131, had willed his whole kingdom jointly to the Templars, the Hospitallers and the Holy Sepulchre in Jerusalem. (The astonished nobles of Aragon rejected the will and in Alfonso's place elected his brother Ramiro the Monk, obliging him to renounce Holy Orders to father a son and heir.)

The Templar network Accompanied by strange symbols and rituals and octagonal church-shrines modelled on the Holy Sepulchre in Jerusalem, the network spread rapidly through Spain. One of the best Templar churches is **Vera Cruz**, outside the walls of Segovia. The lovely little church of **Eunate**, an octagon set in meadows beside the Pilgrims' Way in Navarre, borrows the Templar style, though probably it was a burial place for pilgrims erected by the Knights of St John of Jerusalem. Many Spanish castles, since refortified and reconstructed, have Templar origins. The most spectacular is that at **Ponferrada** in León. The Templars were interested in arcane knowledge; they were also strong supporters of the Jews and of the Moorish communities living in Christian territory.

Other Orders Meanwhile, several other, entirely Hispanic orders, came into being. When the Templars conceded they could no longer hold their fortress at **Calatrava**, south of Ciudad Real, the abbot of Fitero in Navarre, a former soldier, stepped in to mount a heroic defence. A new order, that of Calatrava, was founded in consequence in 1158. The new Knights, who followed strict Benedictine rules, eventually lost the castle to the Moors, recovered it in the next century and rebuilt it massively into a sacred convent-castle. To stand on its battlements as sunset strikes the sierra is an awesome experience. The Knights of Alcántara were formed in 1165 and the Order of Santiago was established in Cáceres in 1170. The Knights of St John meanwhile occupied a sturdy castle at Consuegra in La Mancha. Almost all held land in the Maestrazgo.

Threat and suppression The Templars became drastically over-powerful. Accused of everything from sodomy to Satanism, they were suppressed throughout Europe in a papal plot early in the 14th century. In Spain, those who would not disown the Order were tried for heresy in the Old Cathedral in Salamanca. These events were the signal for the Hispanic Orders, including the new Knights of Montesa in Valencia, to expand into the vacuum. They continued to battle for Christendom along the borders but they, too, grew over-powerful. Their dominions were huge; they dominated the nomadic routes of the sheep flocks, and their military forces were uncomfortably strong.

Their come-uppance came with the Catholic Kings. In 1476, the death of the Marquis of Villena, Grand Master of the Order of Santiago, created a vacancy at the top. As the chapter went into conclave to choose a successor – at their monastery-headquarters at Uclés in Castilla-La Mancha, rebuilt in the Renaissance – the young Queen Isabella arrived, hastening from Valladolid, and persuaded them, after a little arm-twisting, to elect her husband Ferdinand. He initially delegated the office, then took over in 1499. Meanwhile, he had been elected head of the Knights of Calatrava and of Alcántara. The Catholic Kings had scored another victory for the centre; from the reign of Charles V the Orders became purely ceremonial.

Salamanca's Old Cathedral, scene of Templar trials for heresy in the 14th century

▶▶▷ **Murcia**

Murcia, in the deep southeast, is a city apart, viewed askance by other Spaniards for reasons that are not apparent. Apart from its grimy outskirts and the erosion of its fertile *huerta* by ill-considered building, the city has much to recommend it for a short visit.

The cathedral displays an impressive mixture of rival styles. There is a grand baroque façade and fine carved Renaissance choir stalls. Though much of the interior is Gothic, Renaissance decoration runs riot in certain of the chapels. The tower (fine views from the top) is Renaissance-Plateresque below, Gothic above.

The nearby casino, formerly a gentlemen's club, in the old cloth-maker's street, the Trapería, is now open to all. Its fake Mudéjar and neo-classical rooms provide a fine civic amenity.

Away from the centre, the **Museo Salzillo** holds life-size polychrome figures for Easter processions created by the local 18th-century master, Francisco Salzillo.

Further strolls in the city will reveal Murcia's main street, the commercial Gran Vía, as well as many more baroque façades, pleasant river embankments and Spain's first-ever Jesuit college.

Francisco Salzillo's figures (*pasos*) are remarkable for their sweet-visaged portrayal of wild emotion. You can see the enormously long, multi-scene Nativity model which helped to make his name, in the Museo Salzillo in Murcia, where nativities are still made today, many for export.

▶▷▷ **Onda**

Overlooked by its high castle, formerly ringed by three walls (now under reconstruction) and known locally as the castle of 300 towers, Onda is a ceramics town. At the end of the Civil War, its citizens took refuge from advancing Nationalist forces in the complex of tunnels (now mostly fallen in) under the castle.

▶▷▷ **Orihuela**

Orihuela was once the capital of Murcia – witness the 14th-century cathedral and fine manorial buildings (mostly in a state of collapse). Another distinction is its extensive palm grove. Less pleasant is its evil-smelling river.

▶▶▷ **Peñiscola**

Now a centre of mass tourism, but easily the most remarkable place on the Costa del Azahar, Peñiscola is a rocky promontory jutting into the sea. Girdled with high walls, it is crowned by a castle, visible from afar. It was given its present form by the Spanish anti-pope, Pedro de Luna, alias Benedict XIII, in the 15th century. The white, Andalucian-style old town lies below the castle. The new town is a mass of hotels and apartments behind a long beach.

▷▷▷ **Puerto de Mazarrón**

This Murcian port, with rough sand and rock beaches and attractive neighbouring sierra, has an area of weird rock formations described by locals as a *ciudad encantada*, Cuenca style (see page 195).

▶▷▷ **Puig**

Just north of Valencia, the huge 13th-century monastery of Santa María in Puig is a major centre for pilgrimage and devotion, based on the 6th-century Byzantine stone relief of the Virgin and Child housed here.

Drive To the heart of the Levante

This is a drive into the Levante hinterland with its hard-edged ceramic manufacturing towns and spectacular mountain scenery.

From Sagunto take the N340 north. There is a possible diversion off this road to **Grutas de San Josep** (see page 213).

On the approach to the Castellón city limits, turn left towards Llucena del Cid. After 13km, turn right, passing local industry, through Sant Joan de Moró to the lovely town of Vilafamés. Retrace your route and turn right, towards L'Alcora.
Note the town hall in L'**Alcora**, with its baroque ceramic decoration.

Continue southwards through Onda, then inland towards Tales, past the tiny villages of Veo and Alcudia de Veo and then right for Segorbe shortly before Aín.
The drive now becomes spectacular – high, narrow and tremendous.

From Segorbe, take the N234 back to Sagunto.

▷▷▷ **Requena**
A pretty old wine-making town in a wide plain, Requena has a couple of charming 15th-century churches and a Moorish castle now housing a wine museum.

▶▶▷ **Sagunto**
The ancient town of Sagunto, much fought over by Romans and Carthaginians and enclosed by high walls, sits high and tremendous on the crest of a long hill overlooking the Levante *huerta*. The modern town and busy port lie below.
Sights include a Roman amphitheatre, the foundations of a substantial town within the castle walls (some of it under dubious reconstruction) and an old Jewish quarter.

▶▷▷ **Segorbe**
Segorbe stands high above the Palancia river. Its cathedral, over restored and neo-classical, houses an important art collection, including 15th-century religious panels.

Valencia see pages 222–3

▶▷▷ **Vilafamés**
North of Castellón, Vilafamés lies on the edge of a dense ceramic-manufacturing area and wild sierra. It has a fine high castle, pink stone houses, Renaissance town hall, baroque church and a 15th-century former palace, now housing a museum of contemporary art.

▷▷▷ **Villena**
A four-square castle – built in the 15th century for the Infante Don Manuel – presides over a modern town and fertile valley. Neighbouring castles are just south at Sax and at Petrer, guarding the way on down to Alicante and the coast.

The people of Segorbe are proud of their annual bull-running fiesta which takes place in the first week of September. Unlike Pamplona's, the bulls are run through unbarricaded streets.

In the back streets of wine-making town, Requena

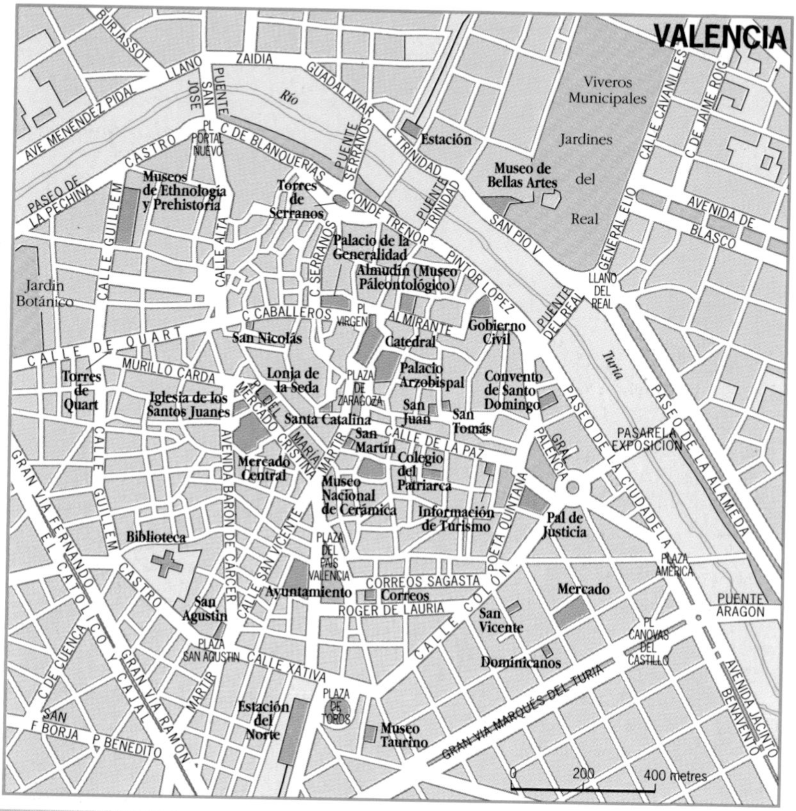

A short walk in Valencia's L'Eixampla district, not on the normal tourist trail, will reveal the charm of 19th-century bourgeois life in Spain – agreeable old houses, open octagons at street intersections, and considerable liveliness. There are many restaurants here, especially round Calle Ciscar, and some good small shops in Calle Salamanca.

▶▶▷ **Valencia**

Valencia is Spain's third city and capital of the Levante. It was founded by the Romans in 138BC and later became one of the chief cities of the Moors. After Valencia fell to the Christians in 1238, the Moors lived on as agricultural labourers and craftsmen till finally expelled in 1609. Generally politically liberal, Valencia was the seat of the Republican government of Spain in 1936–7; but it was also here, during the abortive coup attempt in 1981, that a rebellious general rolled his tanks out on to the street. The city's old town, which takes about 20 minutes to cross on foot, is confined by a bend of the now-diverted Río Turia. This empty watercourse is crossed by ancient bridges and mostly planted as a park. To the east of the old town lies L'Eixampla, an agreeable 19th-century extension. Modern Valencia is ranged round this nucleus.

Cathedral Valencia's cathedral is famous for its claim to possession of the Holy Grail, kept in the soaring Gothic chapterhouse (to the right on entry). The so-called Grail is an agate chalice. The museum beyond has splendid but neglected paintings, including Goya's brilliant rendering of St Francis Borja exorcising spirits. The cathedral retablo is by Juan de Juanes, one of Valencia's Renaissance heroes. The façade is baroque with Gothic and Romanesque portals north and south respectively;

and the octagonal 14th- to 15th-century tower, the Miguelete, offers fine views after a stiff climb.
Behind the cathedral is the 17th-century shrine of Nuestra Señora de los Desemparados. In front, recessed from the square, is the brilliantly decorative baroque tower of the church of Santa Catalina.

• *A stroll through narrow, picturesquely decayed streets reveals the market, in wrought iron and ceramic tiles. Stalls sell immense steel pans for paella-making. Immediately opposite is the Lonja (see below). Northwards now lie the Torres de Quart or Cuarte, two huge bastions flanking a city gate. Return down Calle de Quart, which turns into Calle Caballeros, with many 19th-century, and some earlier mansions. Left at the end of the road is the Presidencia or Palacio de la Generalidad (see below).*

Lonja de la Seda (Silk Exchange) Magnificently vaulted, this is one of Spain's finest buildings. Note the sinuous Gothic doorways with carving, some startlingly erotic.

Palacio de la Generalidad Valencia's ancient parliament building is the nerve centre today for the Levante region. It has two glorious *artesonado* ceilings.

Key museums
Museo de Bellas Artes With works by Valencia's notable Renaissance painters and many other Spanish masters, this is one of the best galleries outside Madrid.
IVAM. This major exhibition space now holds items from the (closed) Museo Nacional de Cerámica.
Colegio del Patriarca Another fine art collection is housed in beautiful buildings.

For parks and gardens, see **Walk** on page 212.

Valencia's Water Tribunal was founded by the Moors to allocate water supplies in the irrigated *huerta* round the city, and to punish those who took too much. It met at the door of the main mosque each Thursday morning. Though the mosque has been replaced with a Christian cathedral and the Moors with Christians, the Water Tribunal still meets on the very same spot on the same day of the week.

There are plenty of fiestas throughout the Valencia region. Las Fallas (the Bonfires), is the most spectacular. In the city of Valencia, in the week culminating on 19 March, St Joseph's Day, vast *papier-mâché* satirical figures are set alight amid a continuing explosion of fireworks. In villages which have a particular Moorish connection, like Alcoy, a good-humoured mock battle between Moors and Christians takes place in the streets. Some fiestas are new creations. Cartagena's battle between Romans and Carthaginians was instituted only in 1990.

Valencia's museum of ceramics is housed behind this extravagant entrance

So potent and exciting is the image of Andalucía – the dark, slender horseman, the sultry señorita side-saddle behind, the wild sounds and movements of flamenco, the heat, the wine – that many people use it, quite mistakenly, as a shorthand for the whole of Spain.

Visit Seville, Granada, Jerez, Córdoba and you will see that some part of this colourful and tantalising world really does exist. But Andalucía is many things besides.

First, there is the age-old poverty of Andalucía, born of a system of huge estates which left workers as badly off as Russian serfs. It is hardly surprising that left-wing parties have made their mark here.

Then there are the southern Costas, from the popular, populous, boisterous Costa del Sol, to the wilder, far less exploited Costa de la Luz, out west on the Atlantic.

Mountains are another key factor, for Andalucía has some of the most rugged and magnificent of Spanish landscapes including the mighty Sierra Nevada.

The Moors gave the region much of its cultural base, most apparent in the major cities – Córdoba, Granada and Seville. But lesser-known places, such as Ubeda and Baeza, are treasure-houses of Renaissance (Christian) architecture – while among the mountains are jewel-like white towns blending to perfection the Christian and Moorish heritage.

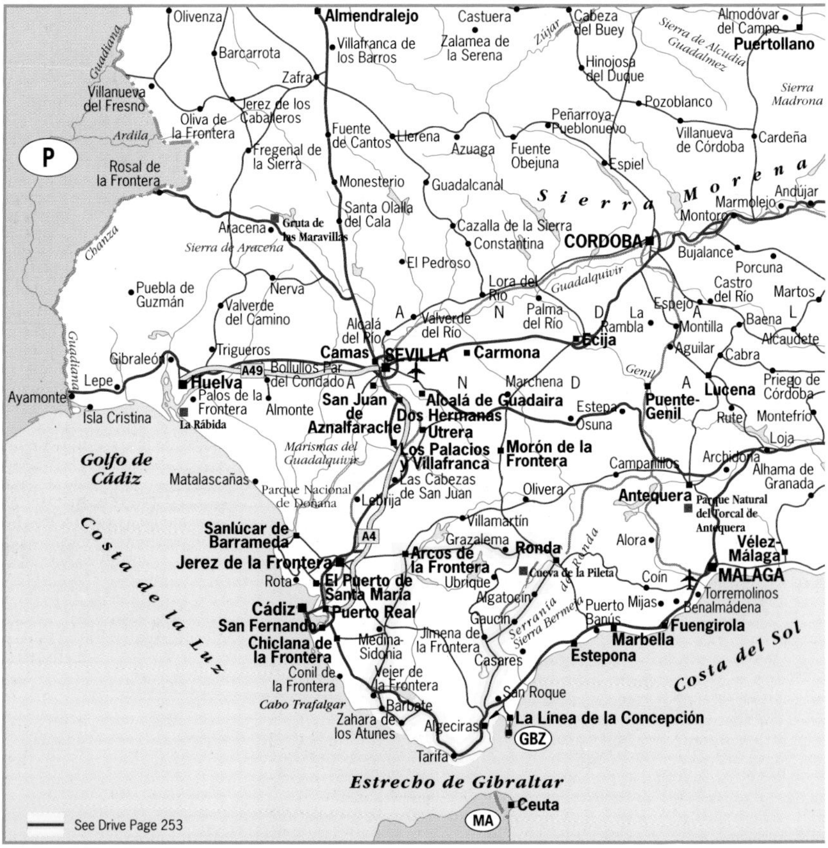

ANDALUCIA

Antequera, topped by its Moorish castle

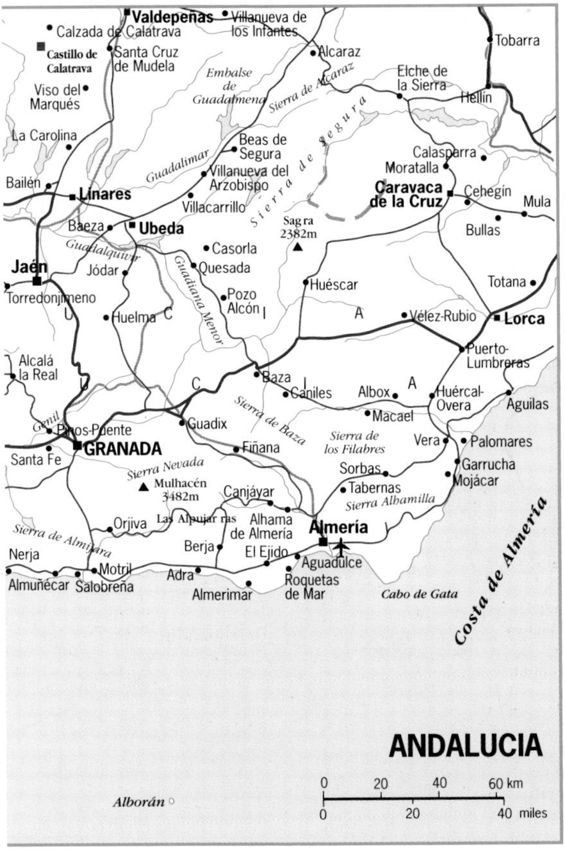

It is not just the street outside the Royal Palace in Madrid which is called Bailén, you'll come across this name in a good many other Spanish towns and cities. For Bailén was the site of a great military triumph for Spain – the first frontal defeat of a Napoleonic army anywhere in Europe. The event took place on 18 July 1808, just two months into the spontaneous war of national independence; it was the totally inexperienced General Castaños who got the better of Napoleon's veteran General Dupont and the 20,000 troops at his command. Spain has never forgotten.

▷▷▷ **Algeciras**

Algeciras, main point of departure for Morocco, stands opposite the Rock of Gibraltar. After 1968, when the Gibraltar border was sealed off, the heavy industrial investment required to compensate for loss of earnings did nothing for the town's looks. A pedestrian central area and pleasant park are the main features.

▷▷▷ **Alhama de Granada**

This town, high on the rolling terrain of Granada, was a key point in the Christian Reconquest against the Moors. The Catholic Kings themselves founded the parish church. Moorish baths remain as testimony to its long history as a spa town.

▷▷▷ **Almería**

Almería is a sun-baked town in an arid landscape, its summit dominated by a Moorish fortress. It reached the height of its fame in the 11th century under that most enlightened and cultured of Arab rulers, Motacín. Then, it is said, the town was all palaces and gardens and was the centre of learned discourse. The remains of walls and towers show that defence was an equal preoccupation. The old town falls steeply down from the *alcazaba* to busy, narrow streets of ochre houses leading to the 16th-century fortified cathedral. The modern town has a confident air, but suffers from heavy traffic.

▶▶▶ **Las Alpujarras**

This series of mountain crests with deep and fertile valleys drops away south from the highest points of the Sierra Nevada – wonderfully exhilarating country, now well organised for visitors. See **Drive** on page 252.

▷▷▷ **Andújar**

The old centre of Andújar has dignified mansions; the Gothic church of Santa María features an El Greco within and a handsome Renaissance façade without. Olive and sunflower oil are processed in the town today. Neighbouring towns, along the main road east of Córdoba, are historic Bailén and industrial Linares.

Gibraltar as seen from Algeciras

The White Town of Arcos de la Frontera

▶▶▷ **Antequera**

The castle which dominates Antequera not only offers splendid views; it also contains within its precincts the handsome 16th-century church of Santa María and a maze-like garden of cypress and cypress hedges. Below the castle, the town (largely modern) flows down the hill – a mass of white, studded with brown churches. Most impressive of all, however, is the huge, tumulus-covered dolmen of Menga, on the left at the town exit for Granada. The well-shaped stone slabs that comprise Spain's earliest piece of architecture (around 2500BC) are massive, one weighing 180 tonnes. There is a smaller dolmen adjacent and another 4km down the road. See also **Walk** on page 231.

▷▷▷ **Aracena**

Among the olive groves and almond orchards of the Sierra Morena, the small White Town of Aracena is built on the slopes of a hill with a ruined Moorish castle above. Beneath the hill, the Cuevas de las Maravillas have rock formations remarkable for their bizarre shapes and unusual colours, illuminated and reflected in the waters of subterranean pools. Guided tours of the caves are available.

▶▶▷ **Arcos de la Frontera**

Arcos de la Frontera, a half-hour drive inland from Jerez, is one of the most spectacular of the White Towns, offering fine vistas (and photographic angles) as you approach. Climbing steeply up one side of a hill it meets a dramatic precipice at the hill's summit. The main square is perched right on the edge, backed by the church of Santa María de la Asunción (with Plateresque west portal) and a handsome castle, converted into a parador. The drive down the even steeper slope on the far side requires steady nerves. Though the town is well used by American servicemen from the base at Rota, the whole effect of Arcos is charmingly medieval.

Christopher Columbus (Cristóbal Colón in Spanish) waited at the monastery of La Rabida in the province of Huelva while Ferdinand and Isabella pondered his plan to seek a new route to the Orient. Their decision to support him was finally announced in the small town of Santa Fe, near Granada. Columbus set sail from the old port of Palos de la Frontera, near Huelva, in August 1492. His subsequent American expeditions left from Cádiz (1493 and 1502) and the neighbouring port of Sanlúcar de Barrameda (1498).

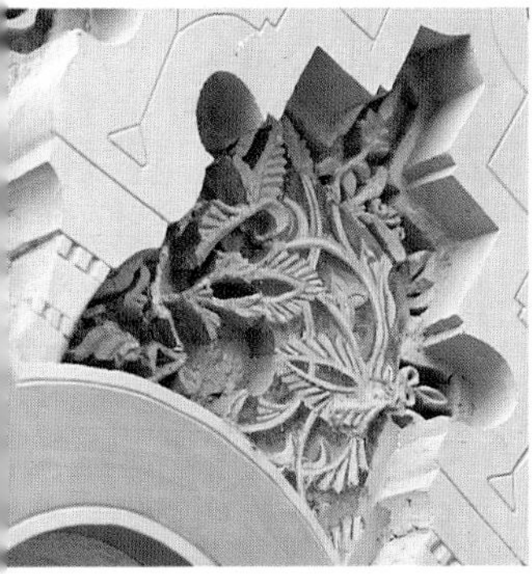

■ Baeza and its near-neighbour Ubeda, though slightly scruffy round the edges, are architectural delights. Situated in the upper valley of the Gualdalquivir, Baeza became the Christian capital of the area after its reconquest by Ferdinand III of Castile in 1227. Its early monuments were Romanesque. Its greatest glories came just at the end of the Gothic and the start of the Renaissance periods with the Isabelline style; a truer Renaissance style evolved under Charles V. Little has happened here since. .....■

Plaza de España to Plaza del Populo Start at the Plaza de España. Walking downhill through the Plaza de la Constitución, you pass the three-storey, arcaded front of the Corn Exchange (1554) to the left and, diagonally across, the two-storey Lower Town Hall. On the left, enter the Plaza del Populo, a miniature marvel. The fountain contains badly damaged but ancient Iberian lions. To the left is the gloriously escutcheoned Butchers' Hall and in front the equally fine 16th-century façade of the Casa del Populo, now containing the Tourist Office. To the right are two arches: the Jaén arch, built to celebrate Charles V's journey to his wedding in Seville and the Villalar, built as atonement to Charles V for the town's rebellion during the Comuneros movement.

From Plaza Santa María The Plaza Santa María is just below the cathedral; the important seminary of San Felipe Neri (1660) is behind you. Central in the square is a 16th-century three-arched fountain, badly worn. To the left is the Gothic façade of the Upper Town Hall, bearing the arms of Juana la Loca (Joanna the Mad) and Philip the Fair. The much-rebuilt cathedral is now essentially Renaissance, as conceived by Andrés Vandelvira. Within, note the beaten-metal, polychrome pulpit and arches of the old mosque in the cloister.

Descending past the seminary, on the left is the magnificently fanciful Isabelline Gothic façade of the Jabalquinto palace (late 15th-century). It confronts the stylish Romanesque church of Santa Cruz. Turn left here and on the right is the Old University (operative from 1544 to the 19th century).

The Jaén arch, one of two gates built for Charles V

■ Not just bird-watchers, but all who feel the slightest stirrings of interest in nature will wish to make the excursion to this greatest of surviving southern European wetlands. Here herons, egrets and spoonbills share the marshy spaces with flamingos, ducks and avocets. It is its position on bird migration routes, and the availability of water in a variety of marginally differing habitats, which make the area unique. Almost 130 species breed in the Doñana and many more pass through during migration. .....■

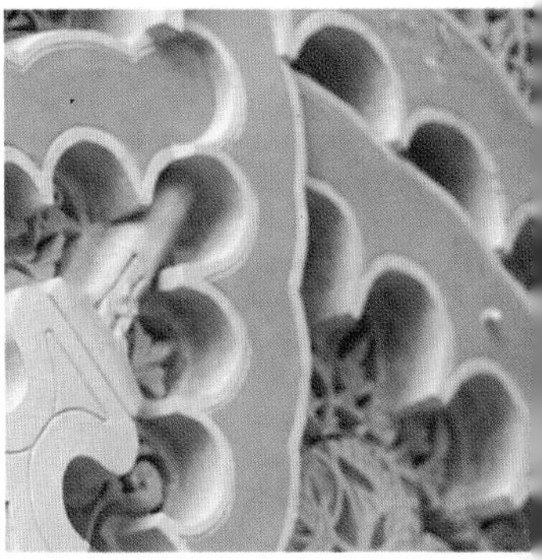

On the drier ground around the fringes, red deer are plentiful and lynx continue to hold their own. Seabirds throng the beaches on the far side of the ever-moving sand-dunes that divide the marshes from the Atlantic. Kites wheel overhead while, above them all, vultures sweep the sky. You might even see a very rare imperial eagle – recognisable by its white shoulders.

Getting there The official name of the area is the Parque Nacional de Doñana. In order to protect the extremely delicate environment, visits are by conducted tour only in large, high jeeps, at 08.30 and 17.00hrs (summer) 08.30 and 15.00hrs (winter). Pre-booking is absolutely essential – tel: (959) 43 0432 as far in advance as possible. The park is reached from Seville by taking the main road for Huelva and turning south at Bollullos par del Condado. Park entry is after El Rocío. Alternatively, you can take the bus to the resort of Matalascañas a little further on and backtrack from there. (You will need to stay the night, though – bus and park schedules combine badly.)

A unique wetland The Doñana is on an effective bridge between Europe and Africa. It is bounded to the east by the River Guadalquivir which flows out here into the Atlantic. The shifting dunes to the west restrain the water, creating permanent lagoons, some parallel to the coast and others further inland, and an area of marismas, or seasonal marshes. Around them are pine and scrub.

A question of survival Excessive water extraction is a major problem however, with high demands from tourism and agriculture. Growing pollution from industries higher up the Guadalquivir, from mining inland and from pesticides used locally have made the difficulties more acute. In 1986, 30,000 birds died of pesticide poisoning. In 1990 proposals to extend Matalascañas led to pitched battles between ecologists and local residents. Meanwhile lagoons and marisma are visibly retreating. The survival of the Doñana is immediately at stake.

In 1588 Philip II of Spain was an unhappy man. The dark forces of Protestant heresy were gathering strength in the Low Countries and in England; and the English pirate Francis Drake had just destroyed the Spanish fleet at Cádiz. Philip began to assemble another fleet, an 'invincible Armada' of 130 ships. It set sail on 22 July 1588, but the planned invasion of England was thwarted by the successful guerrilla tactics of the English navy combined with the foul weather, and nearly half the ships were lost. The Armada was the death knell of Spanish maritime power.

▶▶▷ Cádiz

No ephemeral tourist town, this, despite its modern blocks and the growth of hotels beside its beaches – Cádiz is the doughty repository of all ages of Spanish history. Legend goes that it was founded by Hercules; historians verify that it has been settled for 3,000 years. Phoenician, Roman and Moorish by turns, it later enjoyed huge wealth as the transit port for Latin American commerce. In 1812, it was the birthplace of an early republican constitution which failed. At least the attempt reflected an open, liberal attitude among the town's citizens, which continues to this day.

The old town Sitting on a rocky peninsula, its jaw jutting into the Atlantic ocean, old Cádiz is mildly dilapidated but charming, rough and breezy on its Atlantic side and offering a pleasant esplanade along its inner, eastern edge. Its sights are not demanding: the **Museo de Bellas Artes** on the Plaza de Miña houses some excellent paintings by Zurburán and has a rich archaeological section documenting the city's past. The Municipal Historical Museum has an 18th-century scale model of the town in mahogany and ivory as well as reminders of the Cortés' (parliament's) bid for a democratic constitution in 1812, during the war against Napoleon. The nearby church of San Felipe Neri was where this constitution was first proclaimed and where the deputies gathered to debate. The public watched from the galleries and the press scribbled in a side chapel. At the altar, there is a sweet-faced Murillo painting of the Virgin (the Immaculate Conception), apparently modelled on the artist's younger daughter.

The cathedral On the outskirts of the old town, tucked in behind the southern beach, lies the neo-classical Catedral Nueva (new cathedral) whose origins lie in much earlier times; the tower looks uncommonly like a surviving minaret and the surrounding area is now being dug up as part of the excavations of a Roman circus. There is also a so-called 'old cathedral', which is the Renaissance-style church of the Sagrario.

Cádiz beach and harbour

▶▶▷ Carmona

Carmona, 30km northeast of Seville, rises high on a bluff. Like its great lowland neighbour, Carmona went through Roman, Visigothic and Moorish periods; both fell to Ferdinand III (el Santo), and both had Mudéjar palaces built by Pedro the Cruel. Carmona's palace, a ruin high on the clifftop, now has a parador, in modern Mudéjar style, within the outer walls (originally Roman, rebuilt by the Moors). The old town runs gently downhill beneath. San Pedro has a tower built in imitation of Seville's Giralda. Another church, Santa María, occupies the site of the former mosque, retaining its patio. There are fine, fortified gateways and, best of all, a short kilometre along the Seville road, an underground Roman necropolis (2nd century BC to 4th century AD), full of rock-cut shafts and chambers, domes, niches and carved reliefs. It held 900 families. (Guided tours: 10.00-14.00hrs, closed Mondays.)

Potato crisps are still made on the premises in a shop or two in most Andalucian cities – the comparison with factory-made is a revelation. Usually crisps go hand-in-hand with *churros* – deep-fried pipes and rings of batter, traditionally consumed along with a cup of chocolate, though coffee will also do. Many Spaniards start the day with *churros*.

▶▷▷ Casares

This pretty White Town sits beneath its Moorish castle just inland from the coast in the Sierra Bermeja, cattle country with cork oak and pines.

▶▷▷ Cazorla

A remote, high town, Cazorla is the favoured base of hunters and visitors to the Coto Nacional de Cazorla (nature park). The town is set in a magnificent landscape of rugged mountains and pine forests with fine views of the Guadalquivir valley. It has an excellent parador.

Walk El Torcal de Antequera

To reach the starting point, go south out of Antequera on the minor 3310 for Málaga (12km, signposted opposite the bullring), then 4km, right, up a mountain road.
Here the visitor encounters one of rocky Spain's most extraordinary rockscapes. Whole mountainsides ascend, constructed out of thin layers of rock laid sideways. Countless individual rock formations stand among the larger hills, some like piles of folded shirts, others like stacked plates or human vertebrae.

The road ends at an information centre.
You can learn about the formation of the bewildering rock shapes. A small display illustrates the pattern of waymarked paths in the area, with buttons to light up photographs of major formations *en route*.

The length of routes varies from 30 minutes to 2 hours.
The going is on earth and rock, quite easy but up and down. The area is good for wild flowers but often very crowded (less so on longer paths).

The White Town of Casares

Perhaps it is no wonder a city so large as Córdoba produced so many figures remembered by posterity – among them, during Roman times, the two Senecas, father and son, and Lucan, author of the *Pharsalia*. The Moorish poet, theologian and statesman Ibn-Hazm lived from 994 to 1064. Greatest of all were two Cordoban contemporaries, Averroës (1126–98), an Arab philosopher who wrested the philosophy of Plato back from the neo-Platonists, and the Jewish polymath Maimonides (1135-1204), who codified Jewish law and is commemorated with a statue in Córdoba's old Jewish quarter.

▶▶▶ Córdoba

If the name of Córdoba has a romantic ring, so it should. Along with Seville and Granada, this is one of the great trio of Moorish cities, and indeed the greatest of them all in its own day. Today, however, it is by far the quietest, and to many tastes the prettiest and most sympathetic. In the old quarter, narrow whitewashed streets, seldom higher than two storeys, burst with geraniums that seem to push their way through iron window grilles and positively tumble over balconies. Delectable floral patios may be glimpsed within. All is the purest essence of southern Spain. Add to this the magnificent presence of the Mezquita, the huge mosque that was the spiritual centre of the Moorish caliphate, and there is no doubt that the brew is rich indeed.

Historical background The conquering Moors, arriving in AD711, made Córdoba their capital. In 929, Abd al-Rahman III declared Al-Andalus an independent

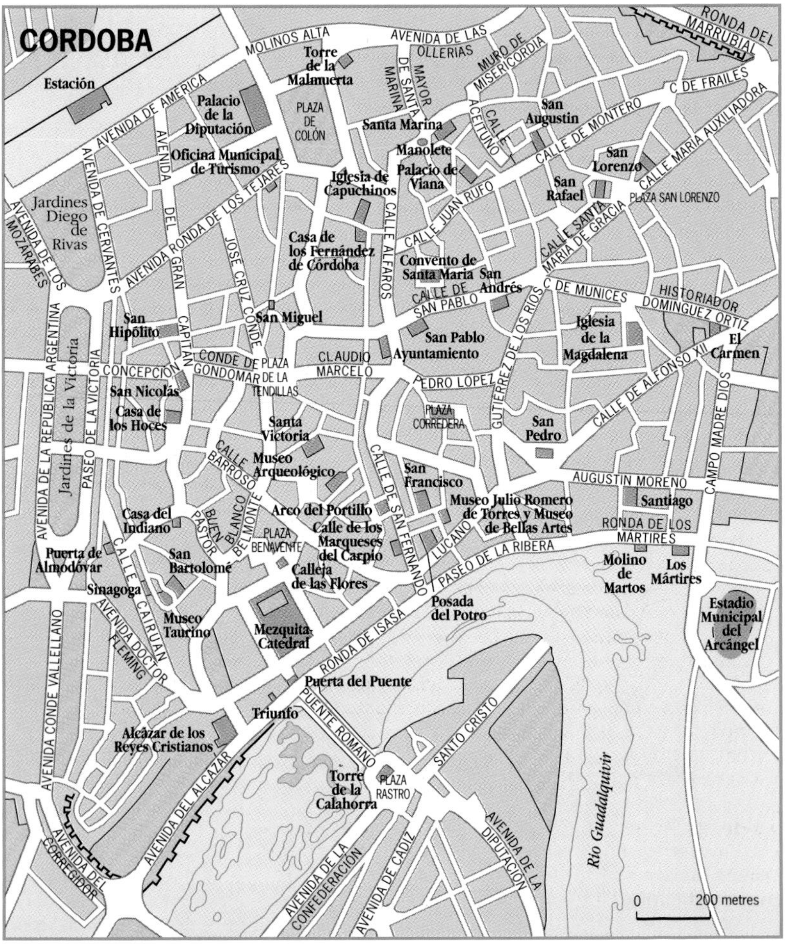

Córdoba is full of charming corners

caliphate, separate from Baghdad. Córdoba now rose to be the largest and most cultured city of Europe, before collapsing progressively from the early 11th century. It was retaken by the Christians in 1236. (For more history, see page 30.)

Mezquita

This is one of Spain's great buildings, unique within Islamic architecture, and with the added peculiarity of having a Christian cathedral inserted in its midst. Apart from the cathedral, the huge interior of the Mezquita, not high but covering an ample acreage, is a forest of two-tiered red-and-white striped horseshoe arches on gleaming columns. The effect, in the semi-darkness, is at first breathtaking, after a while meditational. Some believe the pattern is derived from Roman aqueducts, others that it was simply an engineering device to gain height; at all events, it was and remains quite revolutionary. The mosque, whose holiest sanctum is against the rear wall to the right, was built in three main phases as described on page 234. Part was then scooped out in the 16th century, and the Christian cathedral installed in its place, with devastating effect on the cool, columnar vistas of the mosque and bursting up through the roof like a surfacing whale. The Emperor Charles V was horrified when he saw it, despite having built a palace for himself inside the Alhambra.

Inside the mosque Visitors enter by the Puerta del Perdón (Gate of Absolution) with fine 14th-century bronze doors in Mudéjar style. A former minaret converted into a belfry stands just beside the gate on

No Spanish city has lovelier inner patios than Córdoba, glimpsed through doorways heady and heavy with blossom. The tradition is maintained by a competition for best patio, run in May each year.

the perimeter wall. Entry to the mosque itself is diagonally to the left across the old ablutions courtyard, the Patio de los Naranjos (Court of Orange Trees). If one could enter the door immediately opposite the Puerta del Perdón, however, this would lead directly into the oldest part of the mosque, built by Abd al-Rahman I in a single year, 786, mainly with columns earlier retrieved from Roman and Visigothic sites. Uneven in height, these are supported on bases of varying heights.

<<La luz que desde la catedral de Córdoba nos alumbra no es mortecina ni temblorosa. Es intensa. Penetrante, ilumina el camino. Propone el abrazo de las comunidades del mundo.>>

<<The light which shines on us from Córdoba cathedral is neither wasting nor wavering. It points the way forward penetratingly. It proposes the mutual fellowship of the communities of the world.>> King Juan Carlos, plaque on the Mezquita wall.

Walking straight forwards towards the rear wall of the mosque from Abd al-Rahman I's original construction, the visitor enters a section built by Abd al-Rahman II in 848 but interfered with by the later cathedral. This section contained a mihrab (prayer-niche), the symbolic sacred centre of this period, within an area of gloriously complex architectural display. Beyond this again is the most magnificent section of all, contributed by the last of the great caliphs, Al-Hakam II, in 964. Here arches become interlocked and multilobed, heavy with decoration. Ceilings of enormous intricacy, vaulted and with jewel-like ribbed domes, act as a prelude to the sacred mihrab niche of Al-Hakam's period, alas roped off from visitors, but decorated on the outside with mosaics made up of tesserae which were a gift from the emperor of Byzantium. The colours and patterning and the use of Arabic script create an effect which is piercingly beautiful.

Away to the left, on the east side (zone of first entry for the visitor), the military dictator Almanzor created a large extension, seven aisles deep and running the depth of the whole construction, from 987. The cathedral, jutting out into this as well, blends late Gothic and Renaissance work. The pulpits and choir stalls are highly praised but – to be frank – the cathedral's placing makes it an abomination.

The gardens of the Alcázar. The Moors loved the sight and sound of water

Alcázar
The old Umayyad castle, adapted by Alfonso XI and used by the Catholic Kings during the wars against Granada, has terraced water-gardens, Roman mosaics and a fine 3rd-century Roman sarcophagus. From its Torre de Leones (Tower of the Lions), there are golden views of the old city, the much-mended Roman Bridge and the defensive Torre de Calahorra on the far side of the Guadalquivir.

Barrio de la Judería
The old Jewish quarter of Córdoba clusters close to the key buildings of the Arab city: the mosque and caliph's palace (now Christianised as the cathedral and site of the archbishop's palace, with diocesan museum). This is Córdoba's inner sanctum of narrow streets and patios bright with geraniums. The former synagogue is here, in Calle Maimonides, a simple, high square building, in Mudéjar style, with Hebrew script instead of Arabic. There are now many restaurants, bars and tourist shops in the Judería. In the Zoco, a modern version of an Arab market-place, arts and crafts are sold by day, flamenco performed on summer evenings.

Key museums
Museo Arqueológico (Plaza Don Jerónimo Páez) An important and attractive collection of Iberian and especially Roman remains, set in the Renaissance Páez palace, itself worth visiting.
Museo de Bellas Artes (Plazuela del Potro) Less impressive than those in Seville or Cádiz, the Fine Arts Museum nevertheless has works by such masters as Luis Morales and Alonso Cano, as well as good Goyas.
Museo Julio Romero de Torres (Plazuela del Potro) The museum dedicated to local painter Romero, who painted the women of Córdoba in the early years of the 20th century, is a curiosity.
Museo Taurino (Plaza Maimonides) Spanish schoolchildren gaze at the bloodstained blouse of the legendary Cordoban torero Manolete, along with the head of the bull that killed him. There are many intriguing artefacts associated with bullfighting.

• ***Stroll*** *Away from the Mezquita area, a stroll through Córdoba should take in the Plazuela del Potro, listed by Cervantes among dens of thieves, and the arcaded 18th-century Plaza de la Corredera, once scene of bullfights. Northeast, the Palacio de Viana has been refurbished. There are half-a-dozen 13th-century churches, built under Fernando III – several are due north of the Judería.*

Excursion: Medina Azahara
The later caliphs built themselves a spectacular palace 8km east of Córdoba – the Medina Azahara. Destroyed at the fall of the caliphate, the site has been excavated and partially restored. Visitors descend towards the central terrace with caliphal apartments physically reminiscent of the Mezquita. Note the uniquely early cursive stone and vegetal wall-cladding. Bottom left of the large site are the remains of a mosque.

Córdoba is a walking city. It generally feels safe, though normal precautions are always in order. There is no airport. Road and rail connections to Madrid and other parts of Andalucía are now good.

Ox-tail often features on Andalucian menus not literally as *rabo de buey* but as the more glamorous *rabo de toro*, or bull's tail. Sometimes it's true. The carcases of bulls killed in the *corrida* are indeed sold off afterwards – and not just the tail, either.

Undeveloped beach near Mojácar

Palomas, where the Americans lost a nuclear bomb and could not find it for a month, is just to the north of Garrucha.

▷▷▷ Costa de Almería

This Costa is a very strange affair, with a dusky, North African feel to the northern part of it, especially round Garrucha and Mojácar, followed by the almost oppressive wildness of the Cabo de Gata. The south is ushered in by plastic greenhouses galore, horrible to look at, though richly filled with vegetables for the markets of northern Europe. West from the capital city, Almería (see page 226), plastic greenhouses become enlaced with large, mass-tourism resorts. The Costa ends with a grim and grey corniche.

Resorts

Aguadulce is a fair-sized resort 9km west of Almería, with large-scale development behind the beach and below the main road. The grey sand beach is quite wide and the whole front is made pleasant by palm and pine. West of Almería, an apron of flat land, filled largely with plastic greenhouses, spills out towards the sea. To the west of this is the rather swagger development of **Almerimar**. With its water-sprinklers, golf courses and young palms, this is an attempt at gracious holiday living.

Once a dismal fishing village, **Garrucha** has prospered and thrown up a substantial seaside town.

Hilltop **Mojácar**, once very Moorish in appearance, is now a mass of low development. Building now comes right down to the shoreline, enhanced by a parador. South lies the much wilder country of **Cabo de Gata**, with good beaches, though difficult to reach. One of them, Isleta del Moro, is now becoming very popular. Cabo de Gata itself has a lighthouse, salt pans and a sadly romantic old fort.

On the apron of land west of Almería, **Roquetas** is an important resort, low-rise and with a large accumulation of 'villas'. Its atmosphere is better than its looks.

▶▶▷ **Costa de la Luz**

Resorts

Just across the River Guadiana from Portugal, **Ayamonte** is a busy port and a low-key resort. A new road bridge now connects Spain with Portugal, replacing the river ferry boat.

Isla Cristina, a little tuna-fishing town close to the Portuguese border, is friendly if rather decrepit. A long sandy beach runs east, backed by pine and dune.

Matalascañas is a new concrete-style resort, with a lovely beach but immediately abutting the Coto Doñana (see page 229). Locals and ecological protesters clashed here in the early 1990s.

El Puerto de Santa María is famous for fresh fish and sherry. Buy your seafood at a *cocedero*, or take-away, and eat it in a neighbouring bar. Mansions, castle, bullring or a ferry to Cádiz are alternative diversions.

On the northern end of the Bay of Cádiz, **Rota** has a long sandy beach backed by mostly low-rise tourist development. It is home to a large American naval base.

Sanlúcar de Barrameda was starting-point for major voyages of discovery in the 15th and 16th centuries (Columbus and Magellan). The 16th-century church of Santa María de la O stands next to the Renaissance palace of the Medina Sidonia family.

A beautiful old town with a slightly hippy feel to it, **Tarifa** has a grandstand view of Africa. Famous as the landing place of the invading Moors in 711, it has extensive walls, a gate with horseshoe arch and the seafront castle of Guzmán el Bueno. A huge beach continues westwards for miles. Its final stretch is reckoned Europe's top spot for windsurfing.

Protected from development by a military zone, **Zahara de los Atunes** lies north of Tarifa. Its wild and windy beach is typical of this stretch of the Costa de la Luz.

Tarifa, the Moors' gateway to Spain

Sanlúcar de Barrameda's speciality is manzanilla sherry, matured here in soleras, supposedly gaining savour from the salt sea breeze. As an accompaniment, try local (but expensive) *langostinos*, or king prawns.

Alonso Pérez de Guzmán received the title El Bueno, the Good, as a result of his behaviour at Tarifa in 1292. His own son was page to the Infante Don Juan, turncoat brother of the king, who had joined the Moors in their assault. When Don Juan threatened to kill the son unless Guzmán surrendered, the father threw down his own dagger in a gesture of defiance. The decision to sacrifice his son before his honour has traditionally excited intense admiration in Spain, though maybe times are now changing.

▶▷▷ **Costa del Sol**

The Costa del Sol, in the deep south of Spain, used to be the pack leader in mass tourism. In the late 1980s the tide of package holiday-makers ebbed, leaving the Costa in gloom and disarray. Since then, considerable efforts have gone into improvements all along the coast – beaches, promenades, hotels, have all been refurbished, and marinas and golf courses built.

Resorts

Despite its large grey castle and little white town behind, **Almuñécar** is an outsize resort. There are fine views eastwards of Salobreña and its castle.

Lower **Benalmádena** is effectively a westwards continuation of Torremolinos with a new marina (lots of nightlife here). The older part of the town, a little inland, is white and well kept, with plenty of British residents.

Out to the west of the real mass building of the Costa del Sol, **Estepona** is rather quieter and once again very British. There are plenty of apartment blocks but also a pleasant old town and a harbour.

Quite a city today, **Fuengirola** has massed apartment blocks and a promenade. There are some pleasant spots in town, while the beach, especially Los Boliches to the west, is wide and popular.

The pleasures of **Málaga**, mostly ignored by tourists, lie in its essential Spanishness on a coast populated with foreigners. It is a modern town and working port with a long and settled history. It has a Roman amphitheatre, a 9th-century Moorish fortress, an 11th-century former Moorish palace (now partly restored, not very convincingly, as a museum) and the Gibralfaro castle and gardens on the summit of the hill. (Anyone walking alone up to the castle should exercise extreme caution.) The 16th-century cathedral is grand and sumptuous; the Sagrario, abutting it, was formerly a mosque and much of its Arabic decoration remains on the exterior wall. Pablo Picasso was born in Málaga. See his work in the Museo de Bellas Artes (Calle San Agustin 6).

The Moorish castle overlooking Málaga

The marina at Marbella

Golf is the great sporting passion of the Costa del Sol, with 36 courses in operation in 1994 and four more almost completed. Some of the older ones enjoy great fame – Las Brisas, Sotogrande, Río Real, Torrequebrada – but green fees have often been high. New courses should bring prices down, improve public access and generally help players. Meanwhile, the Dama de Noche course at Puerto Banus is setting a new trend with floodlights.

Marbella's charms are fairly evident – well-kept apartment blocks, good restaurants, designer boutiques, an attractive marina (and a rather less impressive beach). The old town behind, rising above the Plaza de los Naranjos with its ceramic benches, offers castle walls and stately buildings as well as small white streets. The focal point of the old town is the Plaza de Naranjos. To the east, at Banana Beach, an oasis-like development of tented bars is increasingly focus for the town's nightlife. The coast on either side of Marbella has a reputation as the playground of Spain's smart set.

High above Benalmádena and Fuengirola, beautifully tended **Mijas**, with its small white streets and startling views, is a very commercialised but attractive hill village. The square bullring is an unusual feature. Visitors come for carriage rides and souvenirs. Plenty of foreigners stay for ever.

Nerja, east of Málaga, is for many the most attractive town on the Costa del Sol. White, well kept, low-rise, with plenty of green in its gardens, it offers good tourist amenities without the over-insistence of places like Torremolinos. The main attraction is the Balcón de Europa, a central viewpoint giving a fine eastwards panorama. At **Burriana** to the east, there is an excellent beach and coves. Behind is the rest of the agriculturally rich Axarquía region. The **Cuevas de Nerja** (Nerja caves) are a major tourist draw.

Even smarter than neighbouring Marbella, **Puerto Banús** is a purpose-built development, with a marina, a clever pastiche of an old town and expensive shops and restaurants. Anyone can come to gawp in Puerto Banús; only the wealthy stay.

Torremolinos As the name suggests, there is an old tower here, up on a point. There is also a scrap of old town heaving with tourist shops, Chinese restaurants and discos. Hotels and apartment blocks abound. The beaches are now good. At La Carihuela, to the west, fresh sand has been shipped in and there are 200 fish restaurants immediately behind. If Torremolinos can make it good again, so can the Costa del Sol.

FOCUS ON *Bullfighting*

■ Spanish newspapers cover bullfighting in their arts reviews rather than their sports pages. This is a clear indication of its status as an art form, more akin to opera than to wrestling for its *aficionados*. .....■

Most Spaniards regard the bullfight as a test of a man's intelligence and will against the formidable strength of the bull. In some respects, the contest is an atavistic Mediterranean ritual about virility and sacrifice, the 'death in the afternoon'; almost a transfer of potency from vanquished to victor.

Although there are increasing numbers of Spaniards who oppose bullfighting on grounds of cruelty, it comes second only to soccer as the most popular national sport. In the Middle Ages, the contest was between a man on horseback and a bull. By the 18th century, it had become a folk pastime. The rules of combat were introduced about this time.

Where to see it The biggest names in the bullfighting world can be seen at the Plaza de Toros (bullring) in Madrid or Barcelona (if tickets appear to be sold out, try a tour operator). The bullring at Seville, though much smaller, is still very prestigious, while a bullfight in Ronda, where the rules and rituals were first propounded, has a special resonance. These are the very special venues; many small towns, particularly in the south, celebrate their fiestas, and their Sunday afternoons, with a humbler bullfight.
It may be popular, but it is not cheap. The most expensive seats are in the shade – 'Sombra'. Those in the sun – 'Sol' – are cheapest and in between there are the 'Sol y Sombra'. The seats nearest the ring are called *barrera* (best avoided if this is your first bullfight), the *contra-barrera* are the next row, then come the *tendidos*, and right at the back, the *gradas*.

The Real Maestranza bullring in Seville

The black fighting bulls of Spain

The introduction The whole ritual begins with a brass fanfare as each matador in his traditional costume, the *traje de luces* (suit of lights), accompanied by his team of *banderilleros* and *picadores*, processes round the ring. Three matadors fight two bulls each in the course of the afternoon and each fight is divided into three distinct parts, their division heralded by bugle blasts.
The first stage lies in testing the bull's reaction to the cape and gauging his strength and temperament. This is done initially by the bullfighter's team. The matador first watches, then tests the bull himself with especially flamboyant passes. If, at this stage, the animal appears to have some weakness, it is replaced by another.

The fight When the bugles sound for the second stage, the *picadores*, heavy men on horseback, enter and wait on the edge of the ring. As the bull charges they extend their pikes to penetrate the bull's shoulder muscles, to test, damage and tire him. Next, it is the turn of the *banderilleros* to attract the bull's attention. Balancing practically motionless over the horns momentarily, they thrust ribboned darts into his shoulders as he charges. Finally the matador, the star of the show, makes a dramatic re-entry. His aim is to demonstrate his skill, courage, grace and poise through a series of clever feints and daring passes, and to establish his supremacy over the bull. As the animal lowers his head, almost mesmerised into submission, the matador advances for the final stage, the *estocada*; he positions the animal square on his legs and thrusts his sword between the bull's shoulder blades, straight through his heart.
In reality the end rarely happens as cleanly as the text books decree. More often than not, the matador makes several fumbling efforts to deliver the fatal blow, all the time sweating under the disapproving boos of the crowd. If, on the other hand, he has done well and killed cleanly, he may be rewarded by the president of the day with an ear of the bull, even perhaps both ears. If the performance has been spectacular, he may win the bull's tail. Then he will be chaired out of the ring on the shoulders of supporters.

The bullfighting season extends from April to October. Fights, or *corridas*, begin at 17.00hrs sharp between April and June and sometimes at 18.00 or 19.00hrs between June and October. It is a truism that the only thing that begins on time in Spain is the bullfight.

Bullfighters and their teams feel real fear before the start of the fight. You have only to watch them waiting in the tunnel before their first entry to understand how bad it is. Not surprisingly, they have developed all kinds of good luck rituals and beliefs. Here is an example. The *torero*, head of his team, always takes a room in a local hotel and uses it to be hauled and squeezed into his suit of lights, the brilliant garb he will wear at the *corrida*. Most *toreros* believe that if anyone goes into that room before they come back to collect their everyday clothes, then they are sure to be gored.

▶▶▶ Granada

In most people's minds the name of Granada is inseparable from that of the Alhambra. This magical fortress-palace – the name in Arabic means literally 'The Red One' – quite properly stands as shorthand for all that was most graceful and intricate, most extravagant and most accomplished in the long-lost Moorish civilisation of Spain. Modern Granada is by no means an empty cipher, but it is the Alhambra and the Generalife gardens that visitors come to see, discovering the rest of the town almost by accident.

While most of Moorish Spain succumbed to the Christian Reconquest, Granada somehow held out, remaining in Arab hands two centuries longer than anywhere else. Militarily formidable, though often paying tribute to the Christians, this mountain kingdom excelled in all the arts of peace – in silk and ceramics, in tile-making, and above all in architecture and the decorative arts. Ferdinand and Isabella finally conquered it in January 1492, after a ten-year war, and they chose the city as their own burial place.

The Alhambra stands high on a spur of mountain under the Sierra Nevada. A second hill, to the north, is occupied by the Albaicín, an ancient and intriguing residential quarter. The 'modern' city (post-1492) lies at the foot of the two hills. Today Granada is a commercial centre and university city, and is also a popular venue for conferences.

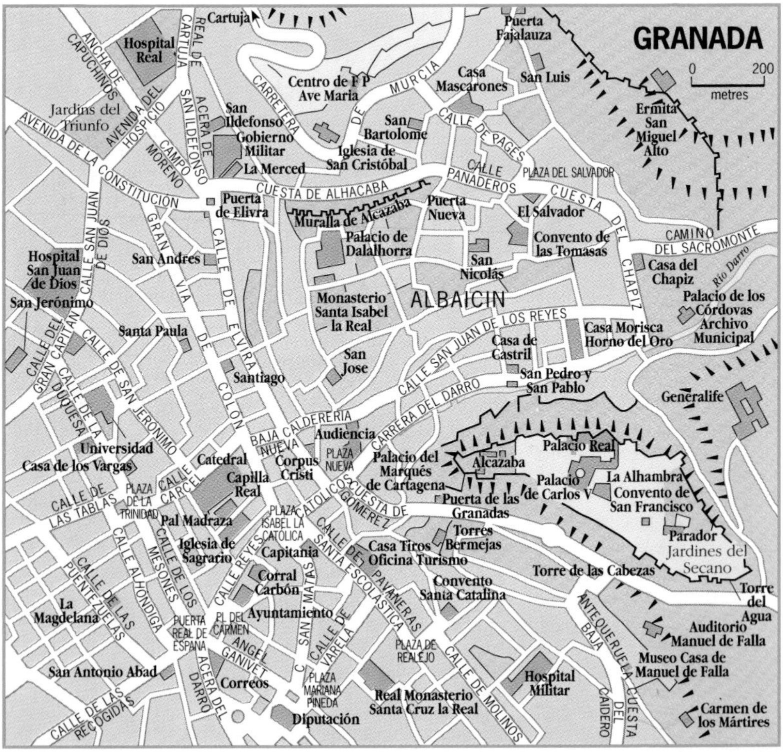

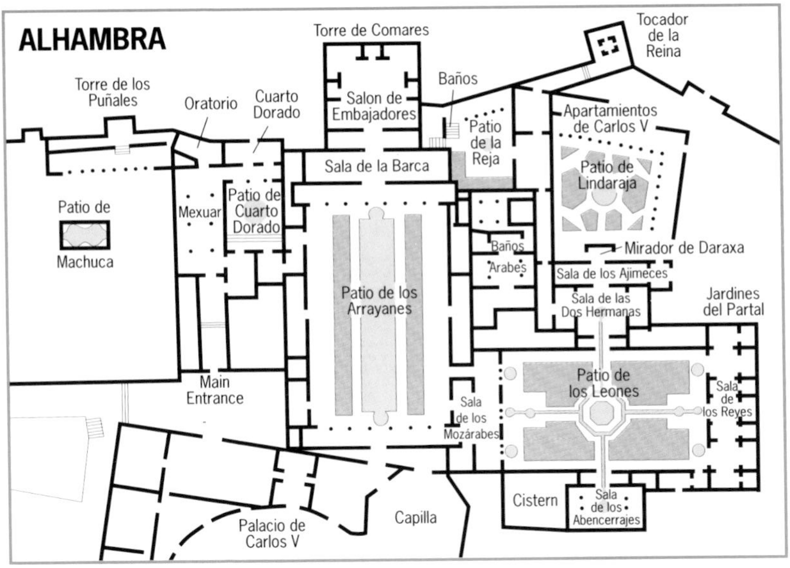

The Alhambra
The Alhambra came into being as a massive castle, built by the founder of the Nasrid dynasty in the 13th century. Later kings created palace buildings and the summer gardens of the Generalife above. It was an American diplomat, Washington Irving, who invented the ultra-romantic image in his *Tales from the Alhambra*, published in 1832.

Alcazaba (Fortress) The Alcazaba, oldest part of the Alhambra, stands on the tip of the spur above the River Darro. Entry was from beneath, through huge gates, still surviving. Modern visitors enter from above. There is a courtyard with several impressive towers.

The Palaces Various rulers built their palaces on different parts of the site at different times. The route of the tour, made freely at the visitor's own pace, necessarily ignores chronology.
The Mexuar (14th century), which was the audience room, is the first room entered, giving an anticipatory glimpse of the brilliant mixture of tilework and plasterwork, rich in Arabic script, that characterises the whole. Its oratory balconies, with a view over the Darro and Albaicín, have graceful paired windows *(ajimeces)*, of which there are many in the palace complex.
After the Patio del Mexuar and its Cuarto Dorado (Golden Room), the ensuing Patio de los Arrayanes (Myrtle Court) is serious and harmonious. Wooden galleries adorn one end. The other, over the river, is blocked off by the large Torre de Comares, a tower containing the huge and ornate throne room of Yusuf I (13th century). There is a long pool and a vista clear through the throne room and out to the Albaicín.
Next is the Patio de los Leones (Court of the Lions – 14th century), ranking with the myrtle court as focal point of the Alhambra. The rooms around its elegant

Flamenco is essentially about passion – deep, raw and spontaneous. It matters not a jot if the singer's voice is easy on the ear as long as it emerges from a state of inspiration, or *duende*, in which the audience, whether by clapping, stamping or remaining silent, is as important as the singer. In southern Spain it is not unusual for ordinary people who feel moved to give expression to ancient themes in song or dance. All that is required is the spirit and the audience.

The Alcazaba, the oldest of the Alhambra buildings

little pavilions with their groups of slender columns are all spectacular. The Sala de los Reyes (Royal Chamber) at the far end has Islamic ceiling paintings, a great rarity. The Sala de las Dos Hermanas (the Hall of the Two Sisters – actually two marble slabs in the floor), on the riverside, has one of the great ceilings of all times, an amazing honeycomb dome.

Palacio de Carlos V (Palace of Charles V) The Emperor Charles V plonked a palace of his own among the buildings of the Alhambra. Though out of place, it has great merit as an example of architecture of the High Renaissance. Within, there is a fine circular courtyard and an equally fine collection of paintings in the Museo de Bellas Artes on the first floor (open 10.00–15.00hrs, closed Mondays). The important Museo Nacional de Arte Hispano-Musulman is downstairs.

Palacio del Generalife
Walk up through the gardens of the Alhambra, or go direct by road, to the Palacio del Generalife just above, built in the 14th century by the Moorish rulers as a summer retreat. The gardens here are even finer then those of the Alhambra. Pavilions lean out over the Darro valley. Marigolds and custard-apple trees delight the eye. The whole is cooled by water in pools and fountains.

Other sights
Albaicín
This ancient hill across from the Alhambra is also full of Moorish remnants, including Moorish houses. The typical Albaicín homestead or *carmen* is an ancient house, set behind high walls in steeply ascending lanes, its garden full of jasmine, cypresses and orange trees. There is a magnificent view of the Alhambra from the church of San Nicolás, and a lovely walk down – but not at night – through the Plaza de San Miguel Bajo (turn right at the bottom of the square).

The brief and brilliant life of Federico García Lorca, born in Granada in 1898, ended with the bullets of Nationalist killers near the same city in July 1936, at the start of the Spanish Civil War. His lyrical and highly evocative poetry showed his sympathy with the gypsies of Andalucía, while such powerful and disturbing plays as *Blood Wedding* and *The House of Bernarda Alba* are still widely performed in many countries. A friend of leading musicians and painters, Lorca's homosexuality and Bohemian lifestyle made him a natural target for the Nationalists.

The beautiful Patio de los Arrayanes in the Moorish Alhambra palace

Reservoir in a wild landscape

Capilla Real
Isabella and Ferdinand ordered for their final resting place a splendid chapel in the style now known as Isabelline Gothic, profusely decorated, soaring in sinuous lines of masonry and vaulting. Behind a magnificent screen, the sculpted effigies of the Catholic Kings (on the right) lie close to those of their unfortunate daughter and son-in-law, Juana the Crazy and Philip the Fair. The coffins themselves are in a crypt below. Isabella's personal picture collection, with its strong allegiance to the Low Countries, is displayed in the sacristy to the side. Across the road, with baroque exterior, is La Madraza, a building of Moorish origin, sometimes open for exhibitions. The patio is delightful.

Cartuja
This stout Carthusian monastery on the northern side of town has a cloister, an impressive church and a sacristy in the most florid baroque imaginable. In the refectory there are many large paintings by the fine monk-artist Sanchez Cotán.

Catedral
Diego de Siloé worked on this large and airy building from 1528. The great artistic polymath Alonso Cano (see his work in the Prado as well as in Granada) contributed the main façade in the 17th century.

Corral Carbón
This balconied Moorish caravanserai (inn), set round a courtyard in the heart of town, later did duty as a coal store, whence its name (coal-yard). It now has an arts centre.

• ***Stroll*** *The lower town centres on the Puerta Real. On one side, climbing up the hill beneath the Alhambra from the nearby Plaza Mariana Pineda or Plaza del Carmen, there are interesting old streets. Even more intriguing is the triangle behind the cathedral, bounded on two sides by the Gran Vía de Colón and the Calle Reyes Católicos. It is full of animation and pleasant little squares.*

To get to the Alhambra, take bus (no 2) or a taxi. For the Albaicín take bus no 12 or 7, or taxi, to the top and then stroll down. Many buses start outside Galerías Preciados on the Carrera del Genil or just behind in the Plaza de Bibataubín. No 11 takes a useful circular route, 8 goes to the Cartuja. As in Seville, the major risks are bag-snatching and car-window smashing. Avoid walking in the Albaicín or Sacromonte areas at night.

Granada and the Alhambra lie under the Sierra Nevada (Snowy Mountains), highest range of mainland Spain. Skiing in the area has developed enormously in recent years, giving Granada an extra tourist season. There is a good road to the Pico de Veleta, Spain's second highest summit – a fine and cooling summer excursion which also offers an excellent restaurant, La Ruta de Veleta.

Sacromonte is an area of caves behind the Albaicín, where you can hear local gypsy families perform the indigenous, flamenco-style song-and-dance routine which they call Zambra. The shows are heavily commercialised, the dancing often poor, the ambience faked. If you feel you really have to experience it, go with a group or you will get hassled.

Sherry is made on the solera principle. The solera is a system of wooden butts – or, increasingly nowadays, stainless steel containers – all linked to one another and fed from the top with young wine year by year. The finished sherry is drawn from the bottom butt. Each solera always contains elements of the wine put into the system when it was originally laid down, often many years ago.

▶▷▷ Guadix

This town has two monumental buildings: the cathedral, begun by Diego de Siloé who built the cathedral at Granada, and a substantial Moorish *alcazaba* (castle). Visitors are often more interested in the gypsies of Guadix who live in caves – but caves with windows, TV sets, refrigerators and, occasionally, even a garage extension.

▷▷▷ Huelva

Huelva is one of Spain's most important commercial ports, and petrochemicals and concrete are also big business here. The city is therefore ignored by most tourists. However, there are important and attractive sites in the area, including **La Rábida,** connected with Columbus, delightful **Moguer** and **Niebla**, once a fine Roman and Moorish city, now down on its luck but still surrounded by Moorish walls and gateways.

▷▷▷ Jaén

Jaén is the rather tame capital of one of Andalucía's largest and wildest provinces. The old town, with a cluster of steep and narrow streets, is dominated by the immense Renaissance cathedral. High above is the hilltop castle of Santa Catalina, containing a parador with fine views.

▶▶▷ Jerez de la Frontera

The word 'sherry' being an English corruption of Jerez, the business of this town is evident. Long before you enter it, vineyards and sherry bodegas, or wineries, with names like Osborne or Harvey, signal its most important produce. The sherry producing region is a triangle formed by Jerez de la Frontera, El Puerto de Santa María and Sanlúcar de Barrameda. Most *bodegas* have guided tours and tastings on weekday mornings followed by invitations to buy a bottle or two. They may be closed in August however, in preparation for the September harvest and festival.

Jerez itself is substantial, with palm- and orange-lined avenues, some fine mansions and churches, including a Gothic-Renaissance cathedral, an 11th-century *alcázar* and remains of Moorish walls now planted with gardens. The town's name derives from the Moorish name 'Xeres'. 'De la Frontera' goes back to the time when Jerez was a Christian frontier town facing Moorish Spain. As much as for sherry, Jerez is famous for its horses. Each Thursday visitors flock to the Real Escuela Andaluza de Arte Ecuestre (Royal Andalucian School of Equestrian Art) for a vivid and musical display of horsemanship, one of the great tourist experiences.

▶▷▷ Osuna

A small white southern town, Osuna's plain outward appearance belies the splendour of its fine buildings – 16th-century mansions from the days of the Reconquest when the dukes of Osuna ruled over much of Andalucía. The Renaissance church, Colegiata de Santa María de la Asunción, has four paintings by Ribera and a fine pantheon of the Osuna family.

▶▶▷ **Ronda**

Ronda is the best known of the Andalucian White Towns and much visited by coastal tourists. Surrounded by mountains which once sheltered smugglers and bandits, the town sits on two sides of a dramatic 100m gorge with the River Guadalevín far below. The gorge is spanned by the Puente Nuevo, that is to say, the 'new' 18th-century bridge.

The old half of the town, the Ciudad, on one side of the bridge, is a delightful quarter of narrow streets and quiet squares. The Collegiate Church of Santa María la Mayor stands in one such square (Plaza de la Ciudad), its belfry formerly a minaret, with the sacristan's house hard by, made lovely by an arcaded façade. The grand houses are almost all Christian superimpositions on original Arab buildings following the Reconquest. The Renaissance Casa Mondragón, occupied for a short time by the Catholic Kings, Ferdinand and Isabella, is rich in patios and horseshoe arches. The 16th-century Palacio Salvatierra has a fine façade, and is decorated with a naively carved 'wild' couple, signifying 'primitives' from the Indies (*open*: 11.00–14.00hrs and 16.00–19.00hrs; guided tours on the half hour. Closed: Thursdays and Sunday afternoons). The old Moorish baths stand at the foot of the steep hill by the Puente Viejo, the old (17th-century) bridge.

The newer extension of Ronda, on the other side of the bridge, is called the Mercadillo, the market-place. Here the chief sights include the late 18th-century Plaza de Toros, the oldest and undoubtedly the loveliest bullring in Spain, with elaborate stone doorway and a wrought-iron balcony. The park behind the bullring, with its *alameda*, fountains and flower beds, has dramatic views over the gorge and the distant hills.

<<Dicen que hubo un torero
Que cuando hacia el paseillo
El sol perdia su brillo
Se llamo Pedro Romero.>>

<<They say there was a *torero*/his entry to the ring so fine/it did the very sun outshine/his name – Pedro Romero.>>

Lines written on the wall of the Pedro Romero restaurant opposite the bullring in Ronda. The restaurant was named after the famous bullfighter, whose grandfather, Francisco Romero, codified the rules of bullfighting early in the 18th century.

Ronda, spectacularly situated on two sides of a 100m gorge, is a popular tourist spot

Seville can now be reached by high-speed train as well as air. Road communications were improved dramatically at the time of Expo 92. Once in the city centre, most places can be reached by walking. For longer hops, buses are a little complicated, giving a clear edge to taxis (metered, not prohibitive). Agree the price of horse-drawn carriages beforehand.

▶▶▶ Sevilla (Seville)

With or without the 'Universal Exposition' – Expo 92 – and the wave of fame which it conferred upon Seville, the city is extraordinary. Seville's lovely situation on the River Guadalquivir, the old town centre, and, above all, the astonishing atmosphere of the place, ranging from the grief and lamentation of the Holy Week processions to the exuberant Feria (Fair) immediately afterwards, all add up to one of the most enchanting places to visit in Europe.

A full 115km up-river from the sea, Seville has been a major port for most of its history. It had an important Roman period, then came the Visigoths; and the Moors

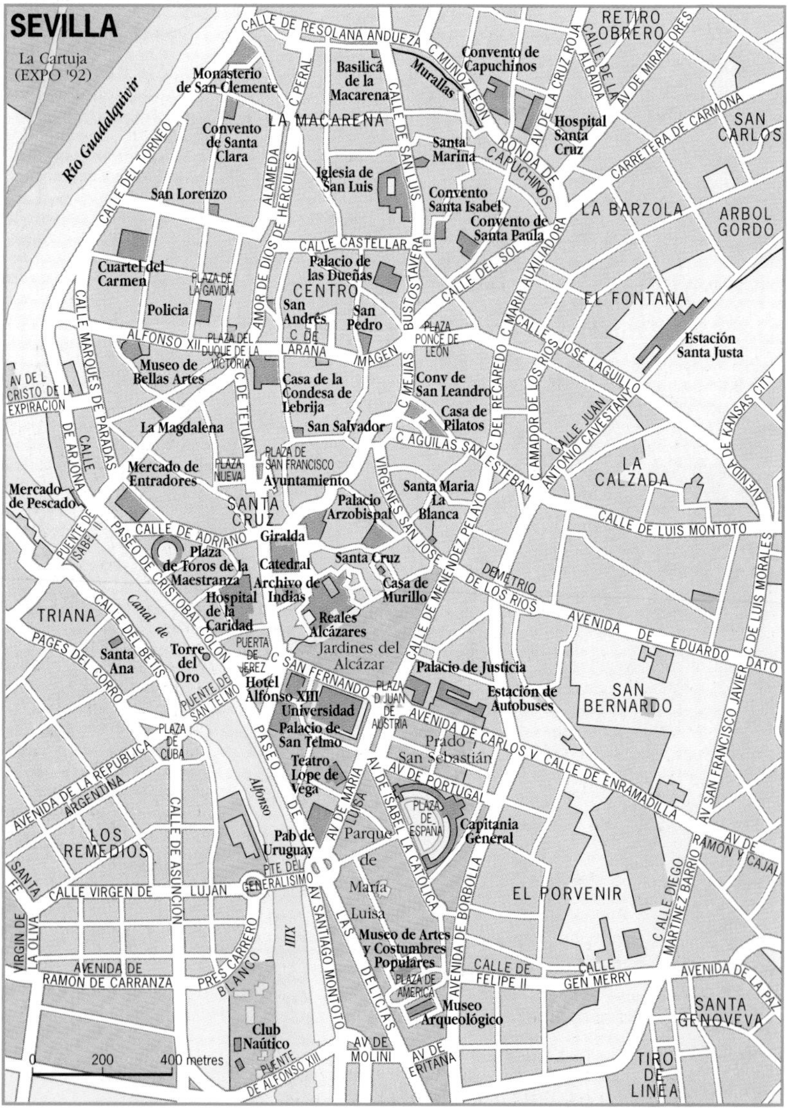

Seville's massive Gothic cathedral

arrived in 712 to stay more than 500 years. Moorish Seville was at its height under the Almohads, a new wave of invaders from Africa who put up stunning buildings. Many of these still survive. The Christians, winning the city back in 1248, made it their southern capital. From 1503 to 1717 Seville enjoyed a trade monopoly with the Americas, becoming the wealthiest place in Spain. Decline and decadence soon followed, with a return to good fortune only now occurring in the 1990s.

The Sights

Alcázar (Reales Alcázares) This palace in Mudéjar style, all ornamental patios, glorious tilework and sumptuously decorated chambers, is simply one of the most thrilling building complexes in Spain. The grandest room is the Salón de Ambajadores (Hall of the Ambassadors) with brilliant plasterwork and Mudéjar honeycombed dome. The once-private Patio de las Doncellas (maidens) and the Patio de las Muñecas (dolls) are a triumph of delicacy. The garden, still beautiful today, incorporates a fine Mudéjar pavilion.

Archivo de Indias Latin America was ruled from here. The paperwork of an unrivalled archive is kept in the Casa de Contratación (House of Contracting) or Casa Lonja (Exchange), built by Juan de Herrero, sombre architect of El Escorial. This department was responsible to the king for controlling the trade monopoly with the colonies. There is an exhibition, open to the public.

Barrio de Santa Cruz Close to the cathedral and *alcázar*, this former Jewish ghetto is an ancient area of narrow

Seville has the most awesome Holy Week processions in Spain. The two images which are most intensely revered are La Macarena, a Virgin whose face is streaked with crystal tears, and Jesús del Gran Poder, Jesus of the Great Power. Both take their names from parish churches where they reside during the rest of the year. A walk to either of them will take the visitor away from the main tourist trail.

As in other southern cities, security requires some thought. Leave cars empty (car-window smashing is rife); don't wear extravagant jewellery; don't carry passports or too much money in a handbag. The risk is snatching, not bashing.

whitewashed alleys and deep-set houses with graceful patios. Popular with tourists, its bars come highly priced. At its heart is the delightful Plaza de Santa Cruz.

Seville is good for tapas bars and eating out. The liveliest tapas hour is from 13.00 to 14.00hrs, with the evenings less frenetic. The Triana river bank and just behind is a good spot for tapas and restaurants, less welcoming after dark.

The traditional bitter marmalade of England and Scotland, often referred to as Seville marmalade, really does have a connection with the city. The municipally owned orange trees that grow in Seville's streets and squares are almost all of the bitter-fruiting variety which carries the city's name. When the oranges are picked – by municipal workmen – they are shipped to Britain and there converted into thick-cut marmalade.

Casa de Pilatos A miraculous blend of Mudéjar and Renaissance styles, with arcaded patio, and magnificent tile and plasterwork, this mansion is supposedly modelled on Pontius Pilate's home in Jerusalem.

Catedral Built in a spirit of pure triumphalism by Seville's Christian conquerors in the 15th century, this is the world's largest Gothic structure and third largest cathedral. Inside, note especially: the Capilla Real (Royal Chapel), gorgeous with royal funerary art; the huge tomb in which Columbus may (or may not) lie; the rich treasury and chapterhouse; and the fine grille before the high altar, scene of a ritual dance unique in Christendom. The old ablutions courtyard of the former mosque here (the Patio de los Naranjos) is reached from the street outside by a magnificent Almohad bronze door.

Expo and La Cartuja The Expo site, retained as a high-tech science park with many of the main pavilions still in use, lies on an island to the west of town, accessible by dashingly modern road bridges, a footbridge and cable-car. One original building on the site was the fine old Carthusian monastery or Charterhouse, La Cartuja, where Columbus stayed and left his personal archive. Kilns survive from an old ceramics factory here.

Giralda The Giralda, world-famous landmark and symbol of Seville, is the minaret of the former mosque, built to be the 'most beautiful tower on earth'. It now has a Christian belfry and outsize weathervane on top. Climb the long ramp for spectacular views.

Hospital de la Caridad Legend asserts, mistakenly alas, that the spectacular sinner-turned-penitent who headed this charity in the 17th century was the original for Don Juan. The hospital-church contains fine Murillo paintings and ghastly scenes of death by Valdés Leal.

La Maestranza (Plaza de Toros) Seville's whitewashed bullring on the river is one of Spain's most picturesque, particularly its arcaded interior.

Parque de María Luisa Tall trees from Latin America grace this fine park. Its dappled shade makes it the best of spots for carriage-riding.

Plaza de España In 1929, Seville celebrated a great Ibero-American Fair, precursor of Expo 92. Thanks to the Wall Street crash, this proved a damp squib, but left behind a trail of interesting buildings. The brick-built Plaza de España, decorated with bright ceramics and evoking all Spain's provinces, is both peculiar and appealing.

Torre del Oro The octagonal tower on the river, built by the Almohads and still casting a golden reflection in the

Ceramic decoration on the Plaza de España

water, is one of the trademarks of Seville. The nautical museum inside will not detain the visitor for long.

Triana Across the river from the old centre, Triana was once a gypsy quarter, haunt of flamenco singers. Some of that tradition persists, though there is plenty of contemporary town in place as well.

Universidad The former Fabrica de Tabaco (Tobacco Factory), the focus of Bizet's *Carmen*, now does duty, very amply, as the main building of the University.

Key museums

Museo Arqueológico (Plaza de América) The most interesting material here is Roman, no surprise considering that Roman Itálica, birthplace of the emperor Hadrian, is just nearby.

Museo de Arte Contemporaneo (Santo Tomás 5) This 18th-century building by the Alcázar has a collection of major modern artists (Miró, Tàpies, Chillida). Its younger, Andalucian artists are less convincing.

Museo de Artes y Costumbres Populares (Plaza de América) This is in one of the buildings in the María Luisa Park constructed for the 1929 Ibero-American exhibition. Find out exactly how to wear your mantilla.

Museo de Bellas Artes (Plaza del Museo) Strikingly installed in the refurbished Convento de la Merced, this contains a magnificent collection of Seville school art, featuring Zurbarán, Murillo, Valdés Leal, etc.

In its heyday, Seville enjoyed a flowering of the arts. Diego Rodríguez de Silva y Velázquez (1599–1660) served his apprenticeship in the city, and many of his early works were painted here. Alonso Cano and the great sculptor Juan Martínez Montañés both worked in Seville. So did the sombrely magnificent Zurbarán. Last in the great line was Murillo, whose over-sweet scenes are redeemed by unrivalled draughtsmanship. All these artists of Seville's great days are represented in the city's Museo de Bellas Artes.

Drive Alpujarras

Less a mountain range than a collection of fertile valley floors and steep slopes whose high ridges lean up hard against the Sierra Nevada to the north, the Alpujarras form an area of great physical beauty with impressive historical associations. It was here, after the fall of Granada, that the defeated Moorish ruler, Boabdil, was granted an estate. And here the last surviving Moors, openly Muslim though technically now Christian, staged their last, desperate revolt. Defeated and dispersed, they were finally expelled in 1609.

Approach by the fast new main road north from Motril or 'South from Granada'.
The latter phrase is the title of a classic book on the area by British author and Hispanophile Gerald Brenan.

Turn east at Venta de las Angustias for Lanjarón.
As entry-point to a thoroughly rustic area, **Lanjarón** may well surprise. It is a flourishing spa town with numerous hotels and restaurants. Patients are sent by their doctors to take the strong-tasting medicinal waters. They carry glasses of it up and down the streets in small baskets like candleholders.

Continue to Orjiva, turn left, before entry to town, on local road 421.

There is a winding climb to **Pampaneira**, a beautiful Alpujarra village with striking architecture.

Above Pampaneira, turn left and ascend the Poqueiro valley (poplars, chestnuts, eroded terraces once worked by the Moors) to the tourism-based but lovely villages of Bubión and Capileira.
There are views of the highest peaks in the Sierra Nevada.

Return to 421 and continue north to Trevélez.
Spain's highest village, **Trevélez** is a centre now not only for mountain hams but for horse-riding, camping, hostels and hotels.

The road loops to the south, soon much less frequented by tourists, passing via Juviles (unspoiled village architecture), Mecina Bombarón (magnificent views of the main Alpujarra valley), Yegen (one-time home of Gerald Brenan – his house is marked with a plaque) and finally rejoining the original, larger highway. At Ugíjar, turn right on a decidedly minor road, signposted Jorairátar and Murtas, and follow it round to the right for beautiful Yátor and Cádiar.
This stretch is fairly arduous driving. The road drops steeply to **Orjiva**, little country town and capital of the Alpujarras, then out via Lanjarón for Granada or southwards to Motril.

Drive White Towns

See map on pages 224–5.

This drive encompasses sea (both Mediterranean and Atlantic) and wild sierra. The route passes through some of the so-called Pueblos Blancos (White Towns), including Ronda, through cattle-raising ranchlands and the major port and town of Algeciras. In effect, it describes a wedge from the southerly point of San Roque north towards Ronda, then westwards to Arcos de la Frontera, south through Medina-Sidonia to Vejer de la Frontera. From there it follows the coast road along the Costa de la Luz to Tarifa before returning to San Roque. This is a two-day drive.

Leave San Roque by the C3331 in the direction of Jimena de la Frontera.
You drive through wooded country of cattle, cork oak and eucalyptus. **Jimena** has all the characteristics of a White Town. With pink-tiled roofs, wrought-iron balconies and grilled windows, it climbs steeply through narrow cobbled streets, falling a little short of the towered Moorish castle on the top.

Follow signs to Ronda on C341.
The road goes through green, cultivated land climbing into sierra. This is the old tobacco smugglers' route from Gibraltar past lovely Guacín and Algatocín. Climb to the 715m high Encinas Borrachas (Drunken Oaks) pass towards the town of **Ronda** high on its gorge.

Leave Ronda by the Seville road C339.
Within a few kilometres there is a possible diversion to Cueva de la Pileta.

Take the turning for Grazalema, and at El Bosque, turn left after the bullring in the direction of Arcos de la Frontera. Leave Arcos in the direction of Jerez, then turn south, following signs to Paterna and Vejer de la Frontera.
This is cotton, sunflower and cereal country with signs off to sherry towns.

After Medina-Sidonia continue southwards to Vejer de la Frontera. The coast road through Barbate de Franco leads to the small coastal resort of Zahara de los Atunes.
Cattle attended by egrets graze in fields hedged by prickly pear.

Return to the main N340 and head south to Tarifa with views of Africa. Then head northwards to Algeciras.

Precipitously situated Arcos de la Frontera, a challenge to drivers

Plaza Vázquez de Molina in Ubeda

The great mystical poet St John of the Cross died in Ubeda and is commemorated there by a sentimental statue entirely unworthy of him. One of the great figures of Spanish literature, he celebrated ascetic notions in a passionate, sensual poetry more easily associated with physical love.

Felipe González, Spain's long-serving Socialist premier of the 1980s and 1990s, began his career as a dashing young lawyer in Seville. Many of his political associates are also from Andalucía. One result has been a wave of government spending in the region. While outsiders shout 'Foul', locals believe their impoverished region is only now getting its just deserts. Spending on Expo 92 was phenomenal, with the bonus of a new airport and high-speed train for Seville and a motorway network for the south.

▷▷▷ Sorbas and Tabernas

These neighbouring towns lie in the northern region of the Sierra Alhamilla, bristling with solar energy installations. Sorbas, famous for ceramics, teeters on the edge of a grey stone cliff. Tabernas is a small flat-roofed town in gulch and canyon country, a perfect setting for the spaghetti (or paella) westerns once made there. Old movie sets are now used for cowboy shows for visitors from coastal resorts.

▶▶▷ Ubeda

Ferdinand III captured this town definitively from the Moors in 1234. Aristocrats flocked here and built their mansions. It owes the best part of its architectural glory, however, to three men: Francisco de los Cobos who enriched himself fantastically as Charles V's secretary; his relative Juan Vázquez who did the same in the same post; and the great local architect Andrés de Vandelvira.

The great set-piece of Ubeda is the Plaza Vázquez de Molina, a perfect grouping of buildings around an L-shaped space. At one end is El Salvador, built as chapel to the now mostly vanished Cobos palace. This has a sculpted front by Diego de Siloé. Its interior was completed by Vandelvira. Next to the chapel is the **Condestable Dávalos** parador, severe externally and with a lovely patio inside. Among other notable buildings in the square are the five-naved, pleasingly eclectic church of **Santa María** and opposite it, immensely dignified, the Vázquez palace, known as the **Casa de las Cadenas** (House of Chains), built by Vandelvira.

The town produces a startling green-glazed pottery, little known but beautiful.

▶▶▷ Vejér de la Frontera

Vejér, south of Jerez and Cádiz, has a double claim to fame – it is one of the most enchanting of the White Towns (with crenellated walls and ancient whitewashed houses) and it is virtually on the coast, meaning it can easily be paired with a visit to the growing resort of Conil de la Frontera or the wilder beaches of El Palmar and Los Caños de Meca.

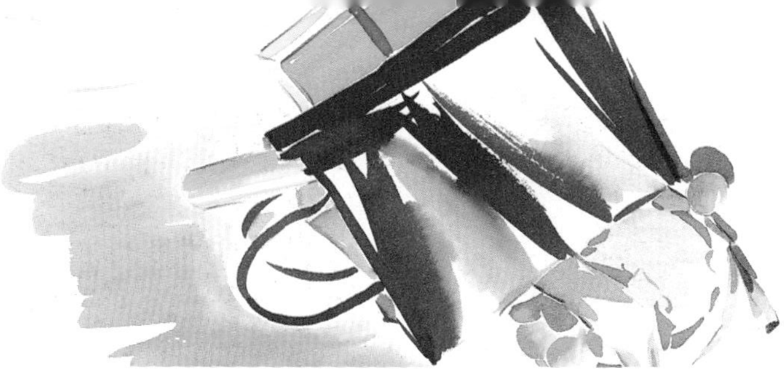

TRAVEL FACTS

Arriving

Entry regulations Foreign travellers to Spain need a valid passport – EU nationals (except those of Ireland and Denmark) may use a national ID card (British Visitor's passport in the case of the UK will not be acceptable after 1994). Passport-holders from the EU, Canada and New Zealand need a visa if they are staying over 90 days; Australians for stays over 30 days; US travellers for stays of over six months. Visitors from other countries will require a visa.
Always check with the consulate about entry regulations as they are liable to change, often at short notice.
For addresses of consulates and embassies see page 261.

By air The main airports for scheduled flights are Madrid, Barajas (tel: (91) 393 6000) and Barcelona, El Prat de Llobregat (tel: (93) 478 5000).
Iberia is Spain's national airline. Head office: Iberia, Velázquez 130, Madrid (tel: (91) 587 8787 or 587 4747).
There are Iberia offices in Sydney (Australia), Toronto (Canada), Dublin (Irish Republic), London (UK) and Washington, New York, San Francisco and Chicago (US).

By boat There are no scheduled boat connections between Spain and North America, although many cruise ships call in at Spanish ports.
Brittany Ferries tel: (0171) 836 5885), operate a ferry service between Plymouth (UK) and Santander (Spain). The ships sail twice a week in high season and once a week from late November to March. P&O European Ferries (tel: 01304 203388) sail twice weekly, year-round between Portsmouth (UK) and Bilbao.
Transmediterránea, Piazza Manuel Gómez, Moreno, s/n 28020 Madrid (tel: (91) 555 0049) operate a weekly ferry service from Genoa, Italy, to Málaga and a daily ferry between Morocco and Spain.

By car When comparing the costs of driving to Spain from northern Europe with other ways of getting there, take into account road tolls, fuel, extra motor insurance cover and overnight stops.
An alternative to driving down to Spain is to take the car with you on motor rail. Car sleeper trains operated by French National Railways (SNCF) run from northern France via Paris to the Spanish border.
There is also a service from Paris (Austerlitz) to Madrid.

By train Spanish National Railways (RENFE) operate international inter-city Talgo (fast, luxury) trains between Paris (France) and Barcelona (11½ hrs) and Paris and Madrid (13hrs). Information can be obtained from the following address:

It is usually cheapest , and often very chatty, to get around by bus

RENFE General Agency for Europe, 1–3 Avenue Marceau, 75115 Paris (tel: (1) 47 23 52 00).
For non-Europeans, a Eurail pass is offered by the continental rail systems. You must buy it either in your country of origin or from an agent in Europe (providing you have not been more than six months in the country where you wish to purchase the pass).

Beaches
Spain's premier beaches are those which have been awarded a Blue Flag by the Foundation for Environmental Education in Europe. Blue Flag requirements include the following:

- a high standard of water cleanliness
- good facilities for bathers (toilets, first aid, life-saving equipment, etc)
- daily cleaning of beaches during the busy season

For a list of Blue Flag beaches, contact EU offices in member countries.
Be sure, when swimming from any beach, to be careful of tidal and estuary currents. Spain's Atlantic coast demands *great* respect from swimmers.

Camping
There are nearly 800 campsites throughout Spain, most along the coast or close to the main towns and cities.
Advance bookings (advisable in summer) can be made directly with the site; or contact: Federación Española de Empresarios de Campings y CV, General Oraá 52, 28006 Madrid (tel: (91) 563 7094).
Camping is prohibited in certain areas. Always check with the local authorities first, and if you are camping on private property make sure that you obtain the owner's permission.
Tourist offices produce a *Mapà de Campings*, giving locations and telephone numbers for campsites throughout Spain. Sites are divided into four grading categories, with facilities ranging from (at least) refreshments, running water, first aid and postal services to the top Campings de Lujo category, including parking, electricity, children's play area, telephone, laundry, car wash, etc.

Children
Children take part in all aspects of life in Spain, including outings to bars and restaurants.

Babysitting Ask for information about babysitters at the local tourist office or at your hotel. Babysitters sometimes advertise in local papers, but you should check their credentials very carefully.

Entertainment Madrid, Barcelona, the coastal resorts and some other cities, have tailor-made entertainment for children in zoos, aquaparks and fun-fairs (eg Madrid's **Casa de Campo**, with a modern zoo, amusement park and open-air entertainment in summer). Many museums and other attractions offer reduced entrance rates for children.

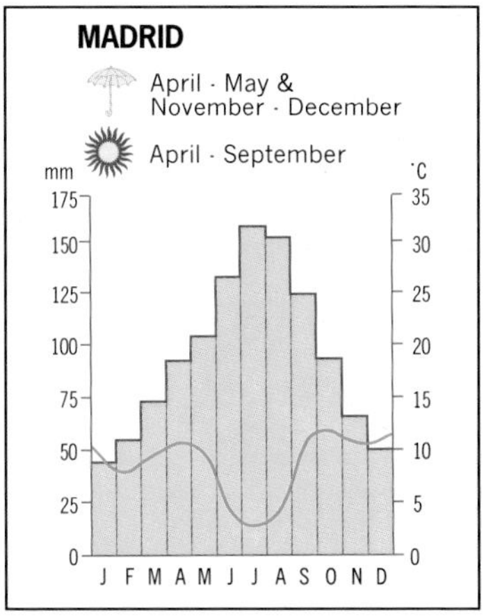

Climate
In northern Spain summers are warm with an average of eight hours' sunshine a day. Rainfall is highest in Galicia and the Cantabrian mountains.
Central Spain experiences scorching

summers while the winters are bitter, with heavy snowfalls and biting winds coming off the sierras. The Mediterranean coast in general has hot summers and mild wet winters. In the north summer heat is moderated by cool breezes off the sea and occasional thunderstorms. In the south a hot dry wind sometimes blows in from Africa.

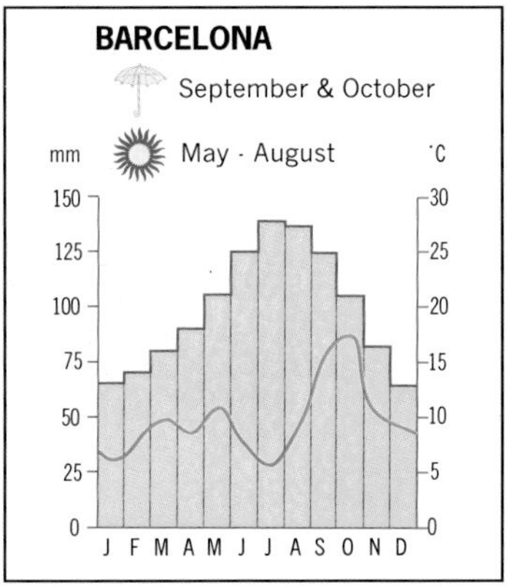

Crime
In urban areas there is a growing problem of drug-related crime. It is not of US or North European proportions, but obvious tourists are, unfortunately, special targets. Below are a few points to remember:
• Avoid dark, lonely and seedy areas.
• Keep an eye on your luggage.
• Don't wear handbags, cameras – anything with a shoulder strap – over one shoulder: it's best to hold them against your chest.
• Carry wallets and purses in the front trouser pocket.
• If you can, put your valuables, travel tickets and documents into a safety deposit when not needed.
If you're travelling by car:
• Make sure that you keep valuables out of sight. If the car has a boot keep luggage and bags in it.
• Always check, when you leave the car, that the doors are locked and that the keys are safe.
A growing problem in the cities of southern Spain and the Costas is *semáforos*: windows of cars are smashed at traffic lights by gangs of youths who grab anything valuable and make their getaway on mopeds.

Customs Regulations
There is no limit on the amount of pesetas or foreign currency you can take into Spain. However, it's best to declare any amount over 100,000 pesetas or the equivalent of 500,000 pesetas in foreign currency – you are allowed to take more than these amounts of money out of the country only if the excess was declared when you arrived.
Items brought into Spain for private use – such as portable videos and camping equipment – are not liable for customs duty. Spanish customs officials can issue a receipt in proof of any goods brought into the country.
EU citizens can now import any reasonable quantity of *tax-paid* goods into France for personal use. Duty-free limits are as follows (non-EU limits in brackets):

Tobacco	
Cigarettes	800 (200)
or Cigarillos	400 (100)
or Cigars	200 (50)
or Tobacco	1kg (250g)
Alcohol	
Still wine	30ltrs (2ltrs)
Spirits (22 per cent proof or over)	10ltrs (1ltr)
or Fortified or sparkling wine	60ltrs (2ltrs)
or Additional still wine	60ltrs (2ltrs)
Perfume	60ml
Toilet water	250ml

Disabled Travellers
Facilities for travellers with disabilities are not widespread, although the situation is slowly changing.

Travelling to Spain Brittany Ferries have specially adapted cabins on their ships to Santander: contact Brittany Ferries, Millbay Docks, Plymouth PL1 3EW (tel: (0752) 221321). For information on the accessibility of internal flights check with offices of Iberia, the Spanish national airline (see **Arriving**).

Money is best changed at a bank or exchange bureau

RENFE (Spanish National Railways) has wheelchairs available for transfers at main stations.

In Spain If you use an automatic car, check first with the rental company that automatics are available.
There is no national parking scheme for people with disabilities. There are, however, several provinces where parking is allowed in restricted areas – check locally.
As a general rule newer buildings are more likely to have ramps, wider doorways and large toilets.
Access guides are available for Barcelona and Madrid. Contact: ECOM, Avenida Gran Via de les Corts Catalanes 562, 08011 Barcelona, tel: (93) 451 5550, and Cruz Roja Española, Eduardo Dato 16, E-28010 Madrid, tel: (91) 537 0707).
ECOM, the federation of private organisations for the disabled, and **Cruz Roja Española**, the Spanish Red Cross, can also offer general advice.

Information General information on travelling abroad can be obtained from:

Australia: ACROD, P.O. Box 60, Curtin, ACT 2605
tel: (06) 282 4333
Canada: Canadian Rehabilitation Council for the Disabled, 45 Sheppard Ave E, Suite 801, Toronto, Ontario M2N 5W9
tel: (416) 250 7490
New Zealand: Disabled Persons Assembly P.O. Box 10–138, The Terrace, Wellington
tel: (04) 472 2626
UK: RADAR,12 City Forum, 250 City Road, London EC1V 8AF
tel: (0171) 250 3222
US: SATH, 347 5th Avenue, Suite 610, New York City, NY 10016
tel: (212) 447 7284

Driving
You can bring your car into Spain duty free for up to six months a year as a tourist. For a longer stay, apply to the Spanish customs administration for an extension.

Documents You will need to be at least 18 years old and have with you the original vehicle log book (registration document), evidence of motor insurance (talk to your insurers) and a valid driving licence.

Pink EU licences are acceptable, but national licences should be accompanied by either an official translation (from a Spanish consulate) or an international driving permit.

Rules and regulations Traffic in Spain travels on the right. Seat belts are compulsory and children under the age of 12 may not travel in the front seat unless the seat is fitted with a special harness. The blood alcohol limit is 0.8 per cent but the best advice is not to drink and drive at all.

In built up areas the maximum speed is 50kph (local speed limits can be lower). Outside urban areas the motorway speed limit is 120kph and 100kph or 90kph on other roads.

Accidents and breakdowns If you have an accident, your car and property could be impounded and you could be detained pending bail. Except in serious accidents a bail bond will usually be accepted by the police as a guarantee that you won't abscond and that you can meet any fines. You should speak to your insurance company before taking a vehicle overseas, so ask them about a bail bond at the same time. For emergency services, see under Emergency Telephone Numbers.

You should carry a warning triangle in case of breakdown and a set of spare lightbulbs for the car.

Roads Most motorways (*autopistas*) are toll roads (*peaje*). Tickets are issued on entry; payment varies according to the distance travelled and class of vehicle. There is also a growing number of non-paying *autovías*. The surfaces of main roads (*carreteras nacionales* – prefix 'N'– and *carreteras comarcales* – prefix 'C') are on the whole good. Off main roads surfaces can be rough and traffic slow.

Parking Urban parking can be a problem. If you cannot find a car park (*aparcamiento*), you must not park on busy roads, within 5m of the entrance to a public building, at a crossroads or intersection, on or near a tram line or within 7m of a tram or bus stop.

Garages are classified by the state into three categories according to the type of work they can deal with. They must display a blue sign giving their official rating and have set prices for common repairs.

Motoring associations The Spanish Motoring Club – Real Automóvil Club de España (RACE) has reciprocal agreements with the following associations:

Australia: Australian Automobile Association (AAA)

Canada: Canadian Automobile Association (CAA)

Irish Republic: AA Ireland Ltd

New Zealand: The New Zealand Automobile Association Inc (NZAA)

UK: Automobile Association (AA)

US: American Automobile Association (AAA)

RACE runs a 24-hour breakdown service from Madrid where there is an English-speaking service (tel: (91) 5933 333). If you have breakdown insurance or you are using a rental car, check on breakdown procedures before you start your journey.

Car rental If you're using one of the international companies such as Avis, Budget, Hertz, Eurocar or Kemwell, it's usually cheaper to arrange (and pay) for a car before you leave home.

If you choose to rent when you get to Spain, look for local firms in the phone book under 'Alquiler de Coches' (Car Rental) or ask at the Tourist Information Office. These companies usually offer very competitive rates. Spain's leading car rental firm is ATESA (Paseo de la Castellana 130, Madrid).

To rent a car you'll need your driver's licence – an international driver's permit is often more useful – and money up front for the deposit.

There may be a minimum age – often 21, sometimes higher – and a requirement that you've been driving for at least a year.

If you intend to use a car for more than 21 days it may be cheaper to lease rather than rent; your travel agent or the rental firm should be able to advise on the best option.

Fuel Two types of leaded petrol are available in Spain: Gasolina Normal (92 octane) and Gasolina Súper (97 octane). Unleaded petrol (ask for 'sin plomo') is becoming increasingly available.

Electricity
The electricity system runs on 220 and 225 volts. In some older buildings the voltage is still 110 or 125 volts. Plugs have two round pins, so you may need to buy an adaptor to use your own electrical equipment in Spain.

Embassies and Consulates
Most countries have an embassy in Madrid, and many also operate consulates in major cities and tourist resorts. Embassies in Madrid include:
Australia: Paseo de la Castellana 143 (tel: (91) 579 0428)
Canada: Nuñez de Balboa 35 (tel: (91) 431 4300)
Irish Republic: Claudio Coello 73 (tel: (91) 576 3500)
New Zealand: 3rd Floor, Plaza de la Lealtad 2 (tel: (91) 523 0226)
UK: Fernando el Santo 16 (tel: (91) 319 0200-0212 – 12 lines)
US: Serrano 75 (tel: (91)577 4000)

Spanish embassies:
Australia and New Zealand: 15 Arkana Street, Yarralumla ACT 2600 Canberra (tel: (6) 273 3555)
Canada: 350 Sparks Street, Suite 802, Ottawa (tel: (613) 237 2193)
Irish Republic: 17a Merlyn Park, Ballsbridge, Dublin 4 (tel: (1) 691640)
UK: 24 Belgrave Square, London SW1X 8QA (tel: (071) 235 5555)
US: 2700 15th Street NW, Washington DC 20009 (tel: (202) 265 0190)

Spanish consulates:
UK: 20 Draycott Place, London SW3 2RZ (tel: (071) 581 5921/5)
US: *Chicago*: Consulate General, 180 N Michigan Avenue, Suite 1500, Chicago, Ill (tel: (312) 782 4588); *Los Angeles*: 6300 Wilshire Boulevard, Suite 1530, Los Angeles, Cal (tel: (213) 658 6050); *New York*: 150 E 58th Street, New York City, NY (tel: (212) 355 4080)

Emergency Telephone Numbers
- **Fire** *(bomberos)*: in major cities 080, otherwise phone the operator.
- **Police**: in all cities 091, in other towns call the operator.
- **Ambulance**: contact the operator.

Radio Nacional de España broadcast emergency messages to tourists on 513 metres hourly at 5 minutes past the hour from 05.05hrs to 00.05hrs.

Etiquette
Remember that any attempt to communicate in the host country's language is always appreciated – even if it is only to apologise for not being able to understand!

Attitudes The Franco years saw the promotion of traditional Catholicism and conservative values and the repression of regional differences. Since the dictator's death, the democratic monarchy has encouraged liberalisation and development. The pattern of

Attitudes tend to change only slowly in the country

repression followed by rigorous reaction against it, is not, however, universal. But remember that what is accepted as the norm in resorts, on beaches, or in the big cities may be regarded as offensive elsewhere.

Dress One of the easiest ways to give offence is by dressing inappropriately. Beachwear can be scanty, but the rule of the beach does not extend to the street; and many churches still expect men to wear long trousers, and women to dress even more respectfully. A general rule of thumb is to wear smart but comfortable clothes; some hotels and restaurants are more formal and expect men to wear jackets and ties.

Church behaviour When visiting churches (or other religious buildings), remember that they are, first and foremost, places of worship – not tourist attractions; show respect for worshippers, and ask permission before taking photographs.

Regional differences Rural areas tend to be more conservative than towns, which in turn can seem staid compared with the cosmopolitanism of Madrid and Barcelona. Regional differences are also an important part of Spanish life and should be kept in mind. Some Catalans, for instance, see themselves as the commercial and industrial powerhouse of Spain, and look disparagingly on the more relaxed and perhaps less materialistic (certainly poorer) Andalucians.

Many visitors to Spain behave with little or no respect for, or even interest in, local life and traditions, so it is hardly surprising that in some places foreigners are regarded with suspicion and cynicism. Perhaps the real wonder is that so many visitors are still greeted with friendliness and genuine hospitality.

Health

Generally no inoculations are necessary for visitors to Spain, but an up-to-date tetanus jab is always a good idea. If you need special medical treatment or diets you should obtain a letter, translated into Spanish, from your doctor explaining the condition and the treatments and medicines required. Buy travel insurance which includes medical cover, so that you can take advantage of private health care. (If you already have medical insurance check if you are covered while travelling.)

Residents of the EU are entitled to reciprocal care from the Spanish state health service. However, the state service is quite limited: you must get treatment from a state hospital, state health centre or a

Rural life is a world away from the cosmopolitan cities and Costas

doctor who does work for the state health scheme. You will still have to pay for any prescribed medicines and for dental treatment.
Be aware that the sun can be dangerous.
• Use plenty of protection, checking that you have the correct oil or cream for your skin type
• Cover your head
• Drink plenty of non-alcoholic drinks
• Learn from the locals, who avoid venturing out at midday.

Hitch-hiking
Hitch-hiking is best on the main roads, although even there you are likely to find yourself waiting for some time for a lift. An additional problem is that in the Basque and Catalan provinces, separatist violence can make drivers suspicious and lifts scarce.
Motorway hiking is illegal and you can be fined on the spot – if you don't have the cash on you, your rucksack can be impounded or you could even be imprisoned.

Language
Castilian Spanish (Castellano) is understood throughout the country. But there are important regional languages which are used in local government and everyday life and are in fact 'official' in their own areas. The major regional languages are Catalan, Galician and Basque. **Catalan**, which is closely related to Occitan/ Provençal, is spoken in Catalonia and Valencia. **Basque**, the official language of the Basque country in northern Spain, is intriguing in having no connection with any other modern European tongue. **Galician**, spoken in northwest Spain, is influenced by Portuguese.

Castilian Spanish belongs to the Romance family of languages, and is closely related to French and Italian. As for pronunciation of Castilian, there are, of course, regional variations – in the south, for instance, a 'c' or a 'z' is pronounced 's', rather than the more usual lisping 'th' – but as a general rule every letter is pronounced, and the sounds are as follows (all vowels short):
A as in bar
E as in let
I as in marina
O as in lot
U as in rule
B as in boom
C before an 'e' or an 'i', a lisping 'th'; otherwise as in cattle
G before an 'e' or an 'i' as 'ch' in the Scottish 'loch', otherwise as 'g' in get
J as 'ch' in Scottish 'loch'
LL as 'li' in 'familiar'
Ñ as 'ni' in 'onion'
R always roll; 'rr' doubly so
Z as 'th' in 'thin'
The emphasis in Spanish is on the last syllable, except when a vowel is accented for stress, or if the word ends in 'n', 's' or a vowel, when the stress falls on the penultimate syllable.

Days of the week
Sunday domingo
Monday lunes
Tuesday martes
Wednesday miércoles
Thursday jueves
Friday viernes
Saturday sábado

Months of the year
January enero
February febrero
March marzo
April abril
May mayo
June junio
July julio
August agosto
September septiembre
October octubre
November noviembre
December diciembre

Numbers
one uno
two dos
three tres
four cuatro
five cinco
six seis
seven siete
eight ocho
nine nueve
ten diez
11 once
12 doce

Goats at a water-hole, an unchanging scene in rural Spain

13 trece
14 catorce
15 quince
16 dieciséis
17 diecisiete
18 dieciocho
19 diecinueve
20 veinte
30 treinta
40 cuarenta
50 cincuenta
60 sesenta
70 setenta
80 ochenta
90 noventa
100 cien
one hundred and... ciento
500 quinientos
1,000 mil

Basic words and phrases
good afternoon/early evening buenos tardes
good morning buenos días
good night/evening buenas noches
hello hola
goodbye adiós
yes/no sí/no
please por favor
thank you gracias
here/there aquí/allí
and y
today hoy
tomorrow mañana
how cómo
what qué
what time is it? ¿qué hora es?
where (is)? ¿dónde (es)?
with/without con/sin
go slowly lento
do you have?... ¿tiene...?
how much is it? ¿cuánto es?
I do not understand no comprendo
I do not speak Spanish no hablo español
Do you speak English? ¿usted habla inglés?
excuse me (to attract attention) ¡por favor!
(to apologise) ¡perdón!
help! (call for) ¡socorro!

Travel and sightseeing
airport aeropuerto
bus stop la parada de autobús
train station la estación de tren
fast/slow rápido/despacio
up/down arriba/abajo
entrance entrada
exit salida
push/pull empujar/tirar
timetable el horario
opening times horas de oficina
beach playa
left/right izquierda/derecha
straight on (todo) derecho

Eating and drinking
beer cerveza
bill la cuenta
breakfast el desayuno
lunch la comida
dinner la cena
waiter/waitress el/la camarero/a
bread pan
set menu el menú del dia
cheese queso
coffee café
cold frío
hot caliente
fish pescado
fruit fruta
meat carne
milk leche
vegetables verduras
wine, red/white vino tinto/blanco
water (mineral) agua mineral
water (drinking) agua potable

Lost Property
Report any losses to the local police – you usually need to advise the police to make an insurance claim. If you lose any official travel documents such as passports or visas advise the police and your embassy or consulate. If your travellers' cheques are lost or stolen let the issuing company know, as well as the police (keep a separate record of your cheques' numbers).

Maps
The Spanish National Tourist Office offers a useful free map of road, rail and air communications in Spain: *Mapa de Communicaciones*. It gives information on road rescue, local railway station and airport telephone numbers and border crossings, and also has city road maps of: Bilbao, Barcelona, Madrid, Seville, Valencia and Zaragoza. For driving you will need a proper road map, eg Michelin Spain and Portugal 1/1.000.000. ASETA, Estabanez Calderon 3, Madrid 20, produces a free guide to motorways – *Guía de Autopistas de Peaje*.
Local tourist offices can usually provide detailed town maps. Walking maps can be obtained from Servicio de Publicaciones del Instituto Geográfico Nacional, General Ibáñez de Ibero, 28003 Madrid.

CONVERSION CHARTS

FROM	TO	MULTIPLY BY
Inches	Centimetres	2.54
Centimetres	Inches	0.3937
Feet	Metres	0.3048
Metres	Feet	3.2810
Yards	Metres	0.9144
Metres	Yards	1.0940
Miles	Kilometres	1.6090
Kilometres	Miles	0.6214
Acres	Hectares	0.4047
Hectares	Acres	2.4710
Gallons	Litres	4.5460
Litres	Gallons	0.2200
Ounces	Grams	28.35
Grams	Ounces	0.0353
Pounds	Grams	453.6
Grams	Pounds	0.0022
Pounds	Kilograms	0.4536
Kilograms	Pounds	2.205
Tons	Tonnes	1.0160
Tonnes	Tons	0.9842

MEN'S SUITS

UK	36	38	40	42	44	46	48
Rest of Europe	46	48	50	52	54	56	58
US	36	38	40	42	44	46	48

DRESS SIZES

UK	8	10	12	14	16	18
France	36	38	40	42	44	46
Italy	38	40	42	44	46	48
Rest of Europe	34	36	38	40	42	44
US	6	8	10	12	14	16

MEN'S SHIRTS

UK	14	14.5	15	15.5	16	16.5	17
Rest of Europe	36	37	38	39/40	41	42	43
US	14	14.5	15	15.5	16	16.5	17

MEN'S SHOES

UK	7	7.5	8.5	9.5	10.5	11
Rest of Europe	41	42	43	44	45	46
US	8	8.5	9.5	10.5	11.5	12

WOMEN'S SHOES

UK	4.5	5	5.5	6	6.5	7
Rest of Europe	38	38	39	39	40	41
US	6	6.5	7	7.5	8	8.5

A hop field

Media
Major European and American newspapers are usually available in Madrid, Barcelona and the major resorts on the afternoon of their day of publication.
The two national state-run television channels are TVE1 and TVE2. Regional authorities also run local stations – Canal Sur, for instance, in Andalucía. There are also a number of private TV companies - Tele 5, A 3 TV and Canal Plus (subscription). Spanish radio broadcasts regular tourist emergency information.

Money Matters
The peseta is the Spanish currency, in denominations of 1,000, 5,000 and 10,000 (notes) and 1, 5, 10, 25, 50, 100, 200 and 500 (coins).

Banks are generally open Monday to Thursday 08.30–16.30hrs; Friday 08.30–1400hrs; and Saturday 08.30–13.00hrs. In summer, hours are often reduced.
Airports, large hotels and travel agents usually have bureaux de change (look for 'cambio').
Most hotels and major stores accept credit cards (check before trying to pay with one, however).
IVA – a value added sales tax – is levied on most items. Tax refunds are usually available on large purchases (refunds for EC nationals are restricted). Ask in the shop for information or contact the commercial office of the Spanish Embassy before you leave home (see Embassies and Consulates, page 261).

National Holidays
1 January (New Year); 6 January (Day of the Three Kings); 1 May (Labour Day); 15 August (Assumption); 12 October (celebrating the first voyage to America); 1 November (All Saints); 8 December (Immaculate Conception); 25 December (Christmas). The movable feasts of Good Friday and Corpus Christi are also national holidays.
There are also four holidays established by local authorities which vary between regions. Local tourist offices can give information on these.

Opening Times
Shops are usually open between 09.30 and 10.00hrs, close for lunch from 13.30 or 14.00 until 16.30 or 17.00hrs and then stay open till 20.00hrs. Most close on Saturday afternoons and Sundays, although in major resorts in summer shops may stay open seven days a week.The larger department stores don't usually close for lunch.

Museums Opening times vary throughout the country so check locally. The opening times of the national museums are given below.
Museo Arqueológico Nacional (Madrid): Tuesday to Saturday 09.15–20.30hrs, Sunday 9.30–14.30hrs; closed Monday.
Museu d'Art de Catalunya (Barcelona): usual opening times Tuesday to Sunday 09.00–14.00hrs.
Museo Nacional de Escultura Religiosa (Valladolid): Tuesday to Saturday 10.00–14.00 and 16.00–18.00hrs, Sunday 10.00–14.30hrs; closed Monday.
Museo del Prado (Madrid): Tuesday to Saturday 09.00–19.00hrs, Sunday 09.00–14.00hrs. Closed Monday.
Centro de Arte Reina Sofia (Madrid): Monday, Wednesday to Saturday 10.00–21.00hrs; closed Tuesday and Sunday pm.

Casa del Greco (El Greco's House, Toledo): 10.00–14.00 and 16.00–18.00hrs; closed all day Monday and Sunday afternoons.
Museu Picasso (Barcelona): 10.00–20.00hrs; closed Monday.
Museo de Santa Cruz (Toledo): Tuesday to Saturday 10.30–18.30hrs, Monday 10.00–14.00 and 16.30–18.30hrs, Sunday 10.00 –14.00hrs.
Museo Nacional de Arte Romana (Mérida): Tuesday to Saturday 10.00–14.00 and 16.00–18.00hrs (summer 17.00–19.00hrs), Sunday 10.00–14.00hrs; closed Monday.
Museu Dalí (Figueres): winter 11.30–17.30hrs, summer 09.00–18.30hrs.

For opening times of **banks** see **Money Matters**; **post offices**, see **Post Office**.

Organised Tours

Do not dismiss package tours as all sun and sea. Some can give you the benefit of expert couriers and guides with knowledge of the country and language, while taking the burden of planning and organisation from the traveller's shoulders. It is perhaps in specialist holidays (art, walking, sports, etc) that organised packages really come into their own. The Spanish National Tourist Office produces a regularly updated list of companies operating in Spain and a list of specialist holiday operators.

Pharmacies

Chemists' shops usually display a white sign with a green cross. Their opening hours are generally the same as shops (see **Opening Times**), but check locally. Outside 'shop hours' there is a special rota with a duty chemist (*farmacia de guardia*) which is displayed in chemists' shops and published in the local paper. Pharmacies sell a wide range of drugs and medicines, some of which are only available on prescription elsewhere in Europe.

Places of Worship

Tourist offices can give information on local places of worship and service times. The following bodies have information on services for different religious communities in Spain:
Catholic: Delegación Diocesana de Pastoral de Turismo, Avda General Perón 32, Madrid 28020 (tel: (91) 556 2976)
Other Christian faiths: Secretariado del Comité Cristiano Interconfesional, Conde de Barajas 1, Madrid 28012 (tel: (91) 266 1741)
Jewish: Central Synagogue, Calle Balmes 3, Madrid 28010 (tel: (91) 445 9843 or 445 9835)
Muslim: Mezquita de Madrid, Calle Anastasio Herrero 7, Madrid (tel: (91) 571 4040)

Police

There are three different police organisations in Spain dealing with different aspects of public order.
- **Policía Municipal**, whose main responsibility is urban traffic, are the local police. They are identifiable by their blue uniforms and the white checked bands on their vehicles.
- **Policía Nacional**, who wear grey uniforms and berets, deal with law and order and national security. Report crimes to the police station (*comisaría*).
- **Guardia Civil**, who are responsible

The Prado in Madrid, essential viewing for art-lovers

for border posts, policing country areas and the coast and highway patrols, wear olive green uniforms. There are also special Basque police in the Basque Country, recognisable by their red berets.

Post Office

There are over 6,000 post offices (*correos*) throughout the country. Opening times are usually 09.00–14.00hrs, Monday to Saturday. Stamps (*sellos*) are also sold at official monopoly tobacconists (marked with a 'T'). Post boxes are yellow.

Public Transport

Air Iberia and its subsidiary airline Aviaco operate an extensive network of domestic flights. Major cities are within easy reach of Madrid: Barcelona 55 minutes; Valencia 30 minutes; Bilbao 50 minutes; and Seville 50 minutes. Note that demand for seats is very high in summer.

Bus Spain has a good system of coach transport between major cities. The Spanish National Tourist Office produces a guide to domestic bus services. Check with local tourist information offices for details.

Some people prefer to keep to the old modes of transport

Taxis Although taxi fares differ between areas they are usually charged in the same way – an initial charge is made, plus mileage and surcharges for weekends, public holidays and nights. Taxi-drivers usually have a schedule of approved fares for journeys between cities and to airports and stations. City taxis are metered.

Rail The 3,000km of railway in Spain are run by the state-owned RENFE. The main types of trains which operated on the rail system are:
- Talgo and TER – fast inter-city trains
- Expreso and Rápido – long-distance but with stops at main stations
- Omnibus, Tranvía, Automotor – local stopping trains.

Fares, which are very reasonable by European standards, are available for first-and second-class travel. Discounted fares are available on Blue Days (*diaz azules*) – avoiding the holiday periods.
RENFE offer travellers from outside Spain a tourist card (*tarjeta turistica*) for first-and second-class travel and for various periods – 8 days, 15 days and 22 days – usable on any RENFE services, with no restrictions or supplements. There is also a 'Train cheque' (*Chequetren*) which is a travel voucher for one person or a family, entitling the holder to a 15 per cent discount on any ticket. RENFE operates a telephone railway information service. It is always wise to reserve a seat.

Subways Madrid and Barcelona have up-to-date and efficient subway systems. The Madrid subway runs from 06.00–01.00hrs. A metro tour card is on sale for unlimited travel for three or five days. The Barcelona subway runs from 05.00–23.00hrs on weekdays and 05.00–01.00hrs at weekends and on holidays. For cheaper travel buy a book of 10 tickets: *Tarjeta T-2*.

Senior Citizens

Saga is the leading international travel company organising package tours for people over 60. Contact addresses are:
Saga International Holidays, 120

Boylston Street, Boston, MA 02116, USA (tel: (617) 451 6808 or 482 0085).
Saga Holidays Ltd, The Saga Building, Middleburg Square, Folkstone, Kent CT20 1AZ, UK (tel: Freefone (0800) 300 500).

Information You can also get information and advice from the following national organisations:
Australia: Australian Retired Persons Association, 150 Queen Street, Melbourne, Victoria (tel: (03) 670 6275)
Canada: Canadian Association of Retired Persons, 27 Queen Street East, Suite 304, Toronto, Ontario M5C 2M6 (tel: (416) 363 8748)
Irish Republic: The National Federation of Pensioners Associations, 31 Parnell Square, Dublin 1 (tel: (01) 748221)
New Zealand: Senior Citizens Unit, Department of Social Welfare, Private Bag 21, Postal Centre, Wellington (tel: (04) 472 7666)
UK: Age Concern –
England: Astral House, 1268 London Road, Norbury, London SW16 4ER (tel: (081) 679 8000)
Scotland: 54a Fountainbridge, Edinburgh EH3 9PT (tel: (031) 228 5656)
Wales: 4th Floor, 1 Cathedral Road, Cardiff CF1 9SD (tel: (0222) 371 566)
Northern Ireland: 6 Lower Crescent, Belfast BT7 1NR (tel: (0232) 245729)
US: National Council of Senior Citizens, 925 15th Street, Washington DC 20005 (tel: (202) 347 8800).

Sport
Aeroclubs There are plenty of aeroclubs in Spain, covering gliding, ultralights, sports planes, ballooning and parachuting: government permits are needed for aero sports. Information can be obtained from the Spanish Aerial Sports Federation (FENDA), Ferraz 16, 28008 Madrid (tel: (91) 247 5922 or 248 9701).

Fishing Spain can provide deep-sea fishing in the Atlantic or Mediterranean, or underwater fishing, in the Mediterranean, on the Costa Brava and in the area around Almería. There are also over 120,000km of rivers and streams. Information is available from the Spanish Fishing Federation, Navas de Tolosa 3, 28013 Madrid (tel: (91) 232 8353).

Golf There are over 90 courses throughout Spain, many of them along the Mediterranean coast. Most golf clubs are members of the Royal Spanish Golf Federation, Capitan Haya 9, 28020 Madrid (tel: (91) 455 2682 and 455 2757). Visitors can join the federation to gain access to the courses.

Riding The Spanish Riding Federation, Monte Esquinza 8, 28010 Madrid (tel: (91) 419 0233/419 0232) can give information about

On the road behind the Costa del Sol. There are good long-distance bus services between main towns throughout Spain

Taking a taxi in Barcelona. A green light means 'available for hire'

riding, and also issues a membership card for tourists. This gives access to race meetings without charge, and allows use of local riding club facilities.

Sailing Information on marinas, landing stages and official sailing competitions can be obtained from the Spanish Motor Boat Federation, Avenida de America 33-4 B, 28002 Madrid (tel: (91) 415 9327).
For further information on facilities and local clubs, contact the Spanish Sailing Federation, Juan Vigon 23, 28003 Madrid (tel: (91) 233 5305 or 233 5304).

Skiing The Pyrenees and Cantabrian ranges offer a wide choice of ski resorts in the north. In central Spain there are three resorts close to Madrid: Navacerrada, Valdesquí and Valcotos; and in the south, there is Solynieve in the Sierra Nevada. The season is usually November to May. For information on skiing resorts contact ATUDEM (Tourist Association of Skiing and Mountain Resorts) on Madrid (91) 458 1557; or the Spanish Winter Sports Federation, Claudio Coello 32, 28001 Madrid (tel: (91) 275 8943 or 275 0397).

Tennis The Royal Spanish Tennis Federation is based at Avinguda Diagonal 618, 08028 Barcelona (tel: (93) 201 0844 or 200 5355 or 201 5586), and can provide information on tournaments and local tennis clubs.
Many tennis clubs are for members only, but you may be able to get day membership. Large modern hotels often have courts for rent, and municipal sports centres also provide tennis courts, often cheaper than hotels.

Student and Youth Travel
Enjoying yourself can be expensive, but the Student Identification Card and – for people under 26 – the International Youth Card, will help you to cut costs. They entitle you to discounts on museum and gallery entrance, transport and accommodation. Other hints:
• Students can get information about the Student Identification Card from their school or college student body.
• Contact the Federation of International Youth Travel Organisations, 81 Island Brugge, DK2300, Copenhagen S, Denmark for further information about the International Youth Card.
• The Spanish Youth Hostel

Organisation – Red Española de Albergues Juveniles – gives priority at its hostels to travellers under the age of 26. The youth hostel organisation and the young people's travel information body, TIVE, can both be contacted at José Ortega y Gasset 71, 28006 Madrid (tel: (91) 347 7700).
The International Youth Hostel Federation publishes a *Guide to Budget Accommodation*, covering Europe and the Mediterranean, with a section on hostels in Spain.

Telephones
The international phone system is generally effective, but long-distance calls have a tendency to get blocked up and there can be delays.

Public phone boxes. Look for the Teléfono signs; they use 5, 25, 50 and 100 peseta coins (put the money in the slot before lifting the receiver). Cheap rate operates between 22.00 and 08.00hrs; it's usually cheaper to use a public call box rather than a hotel phone.

International phones These are signed 'Teléfono Internacional' Instructions on how to use the phone are usually given in several languages. To make an international call dial 07 then wait for a high pitched continuous tone; then dial the country and area codes (omit the initial '0' of the area code) and the number itself.
International codes from Spain are: Australia 61, Irish Republic 353, New Zealand 64, UK 44, US and Canada 1.

Help Major towns have telephone bureaux (Locutorios Telefónicos) where help is at hand if you need it – and you don't have to struggle with change; just pay after you've made the call.
In Spain, for information about making domestic calls dial 003; for international information dial 008 for calls to Europe, otherwise 005 .

Time
Daylight Saving Time, when the clocks move forward one hour, is from the morning of the last Sunday

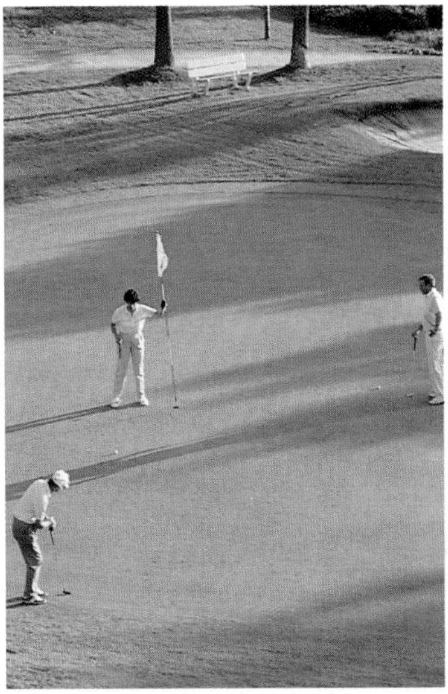

Golf is an ever-increasing activity along the coast

in March to the first Sunday in September. Spain is one hour ahead of Greenwich Mean Time; two hours ahead during Daylight Saving Time.

Clock times compared with Spain (Standard Time) are as follows:
Australia: 7–9 hours ahead
Canada: $4\frac{1}{2}$–9 hours behind
New Zealand: 11 hours ahead
UK and Irish Republic: 1 hour behind
US: 6–9 hours behind

Tipping
Most hotel and restaurant bills now include a service charge, but it is still customary to leave something – between 5 and 10 per cent – as a tip to show your appreciation.
Small tips are usually given in bars and to taxi-drivers from small change. Car park attendants, doormen, hairdressers, lavatory attendants, shoe shines and tour guides also generally receive small tips.

Toilets
Public toilets are pretty thin on the ground. The best places to look for toilets (*los servicios*) are in large department stores, some museums and places of interest. Bars and

On court at Los Monteros tennis centre in Málaga province

restaurants have facilities for their customers. If you go into a bar to use the toilet it is good form to buy something.

Tourist Offices

Spanish tourist offices abroad (addresses below) can provide you with information and advice on holidays in Spain, but they are not travel agencies and do not book or arrange individual holidays.

Australia and New Zealand: 203 Castlereagh Street, Suite 21a, PO Box A 675, Sydney South, NSW 2000 (tel: (02) 264 79 66).

Canada: 102 Bloor Street West, 14 Floor, Toronto, Ontario M5S 1M8 (tel: (416) 961 3131)

UK and Irish Republic: 57–8 St James Street, London, SW1A 1LD (tel: (071) 499 1169 or 499 0901)

US: *Chicago* – Water Tower Place, Suite 915 East, 845 N Michigan Avenue, Chicago Ill 60611 (tel: (312) 944 0215)

Los Angeles – 8383 Wilshire Boulevard, Suite 960, Beverly Hills, CA 90211 (tel: (213) 658 7192)

Miami – 1221 Brickell Avenue, Miami, Fla 33131 (tel: (305) 358 1992)

New York – 665 Fifth Avenue, New York 10022 (tel: (212) 759 8822)

The following are the tourist information centres in the principal regional towns throughout Spain:

Barcelona: Gran Via de les Corts Catalanes 658 (tel: ((93) 301 7443)

Logroño: Miguel Villanueva 10 (tel: (941) 29 1260)

Madrid: Princesa 1, Edifico Torre de Madrid (tel: (91) 241 2325)

Mérida: Pedro M Plano (tel: (924) 31 5353)

Murcia: Alejandro Séiquet 4 (tel: (968) 22 2800)

Oviedo: Plaza de Alfonso II El Casto 6 (tel: (98) 521 3385)

Pamplona: Duque de Ahumada 3 (tel: (948) 10 7741)

Santiago de Compostela: Rúa del Villar 43 (tel: (981) 58 4081)

Santander: Plaza de Porticada 1 (tel: (942) 31 0708)

Seville: Avda de la Constitución, 21 (tel: (95) 422 1404)

Toledo: Puerta de Bisagra (tel: (925) 22 0843)

Valencia: Calle de la Paz 48 (tel: (96) 35 2287)

Valladolid: Plaza de Zorrilla 3 (tel: (983) 35 1801)

Vitoria (Alava); Parque de la Florida (tel: (945) 13 13 21)

Zaragoza (Saragossa): Torreón de la Zuda, Glorieta Pio XII (tel: (976) 23 0027)

Valeting and Laundry
Most hotels handle laundry and dry cleaning but they tend to charge more than local laundries and dry cleaners.

Walking and Hiking
Popular walking areas are the Sierra Nevada range in the south and, in the north, the historic Pilgrims' Way of St James (see pages 168–9) running through the Cantabrian mountains. The Picos de Europa, also in the Cantabrian range, offer spectacular treks.
Many national parks, such as the Ordesa Park in the Aragonese Pyrenees (see page 111), have signposted walks and trails for the serious and not so serious walker. Serviceable walking maps can be bought locally, but to plan routes beforehand, obtain walking maps from the **Instituto Geográfico Nacional** (see **Maps**, page 265) and from the **Federación Española de Montañismo**.
When walking in Spain, follow the usual advice:
• Wear comfortable walking boots which are already broken in, and casual, comfortable clothing, remembering to take suitable clothes for cold and wet weather
• Be prepared for emergencies, with a torch, whistle and some energy-giving food such as chocolate
• Also check with your insurance company that you are covered in case of accident.

Hotels are government regulated

Many of the hotels in the listings below are paradors. Originally a parador was an inn for the gentry. Today the state-run paradors still have an up-market image. Many are in historic or beautiful old buildings; others are in particularly fine positions; all give a guarantee of good standards of service and accommodation.
All hotels in Spain are government regulated and classified according to facilities. In addition to full hotels, there are *hotel residencias* (usually without a restaurant), and the more basic but reliable *hostales* and *pensiones*. The latter provide full board.

MADRID

Accommodation

Expensive

Meliá Castilla, Cpt Haya 43 (tel: (91) 571 2211). Business style hotel well into the conference scene.
Palace, Plaza de las Cortes 7 (tel: (91)429 7551). Much of the atmosphere of this large sumptuous hotel has survived refurbishment. You are likely to glimpse politicians under the stained glass rotunda.
Ritz, Plaza de la Lealtad 5 (tel: (91) 521 2857). Though male guests must wear ties beyond reception, the Ritz – one of Europe's great old hotels – is not stuffy.
Villa Magna, Paseo de la Castellana 22 (tel: (91) 576 7500). Very exclusive hotel, modern but with Charles IV décor. Gardens.

Moderate

Carlos V, Maestro Vitoria 5 (tel: (91) 531 4100). City centre hotel (can be noisy). Well furnished public areas. Bed and breakfast only.
Gran Hotel Reina Victoria, Plaza del Angel 7 (tel: (91) 531 4500). Well placed for old Madrid, this has been recently refurbished. Bullfighters stay here on fight nights. Bed and breakfast only.
Santander, Echegaray 1 (tel: (91)429 9551). In a lively old city tapas area.

Budget

Ingles, Echegaray 8 (tel: (91) 429 6551). Spacious and characterful, up the road from the Santander.

Restaurants

Expensive

Horcher, Alfonso XII (tel: (91) 522 0731). Top business people lunch here. Specialises in game dishes.
Zalacaín, Alvarez de Baena 4 (tel: (91) 561 1079). With the reputation of being Madrid's top restaurant, the Zalacaín serves an international menu and Basque specialities. Closed Saturday midday, Sundays August and Holy Week.

Moderate

Botín, Cuchilleros 17 (tel: (91) 366 4217). An ancient Castilian suckling pig restaurant, providing a good evening out in pretty Castilian-style dining rooms. Touristy but good.
Casa Paco, Puerta Cerrada 11 (tel: (91) 366 3166). Steaks come on sizzling platters and go well with lashings of red wine. Reserve your table. Closed Sundays and throughout August.
La Gran Tasca, Santa Engracia 24 (tel: (91) 448 7779). Not in the most salubrious area, but good Castilian food as grandmother made it. Lunch only. Closed Sundays, holidays and throughout August.
Gure-Etxea, Plaza de la Paja 12 (tel: (91) 365 6149). Basque cuisine is served in an atmosphere of 18th-century Madrid. Closed Sundays and throughout August.
El Pescador, José Ortega y Gasset 75 (tel: (91) 402 1290). A fish restaurant as its name suggests, this provides reliable quality. Closed Sundays and mid-August to mid-September.
El Schotis, Cava Baja 11 (tel: (91) 365 3230). Steak house but also serving a wide-ranging Spanish menu. Closed Mondays and in August.

Budget

Madrid has a wealth of tapas bars, cafés and cheap restaurants. Explore the area where you are staying for places that appeal.

GALICIA

Accommodation

Expensive

Araguaney, Alfredo Branas 5, Santiago de Compostela, La Coruña (tel: (981) 59 5900). Modern hotel in the newer part of town.
Finisterre, Paseo del Parrote, La Coruña (tel: (981) 20 5400). Modern hotel with its own sports complex. Atlantic views.
Gran, Isla de la Toja, El Grove, Pontevedra (tel: (986) 73 0025). Turn-of the-century hotel in a pine wood.
Parador Nacional Condes de Villalba, Valeriano Valesuso, Villalba, Lugo (tel: (982) 51 0011). Only six rooms in this fortified octagonal tower, so book ahead.
Parador Nacional Los Reyes Catolicos, Plaza del Obradoiro, Santiago de Compostela, La Coruña (tel: (981) 58 2200). Founded as a pilgrims' hospital by Ferdinand and Isabella in

1499, this vies with the San Marcos in León as the grandest in the parador chain. Deeply memorable.

Moderate

Hotel Louxo, Isla de la Toja, Pontevedra (tel: (986) 73 0200). Resort hotel with good *ría* views from glass balconies and dining-room.
Hotel Pazo O'Rial, El Rial 1, Villagarcia de Arosa, Pontevedra (tel: (986) 50 7011). Converted manor house; good restaurant.
Parador de Ribadeo, Amador Fernandez, Ribadeo, Lugo (tel: (982) 11 0825). Excellent views of the Eo *ría* from this modern parador.
Parador Nacional Casa del Barón, Calle Maceda, Pontevedra (tel: (986) 85

HOTELS AND RESTAURANTS

5800). An 18th-century *pazo* (unfortified manor house), well placed for the town and for touring the *rías*.
Parador Nacional de Monterrey, Verín, Orense (tel: (988) 41 0075). Modern parador in fortified manor style, looking across at Galicia's finest castle.
Parador Nacional San Telmo, Tui, Pontevedra (tel: (986) 60 0309). Modern parador in *pazo* (manor house) style on the River Miño overlooking Portugal.
Peregrino, Avenida Rosalia de Castro, Santiago de Compostela, La Coruña (tel: (981) 52 1850). This modern inn is at the top end of the moderate range.

Budget

Barcelona, Avenida Pontevedra 13, Orense (tel: (988) 22 0800). Smallish hotel, some rooms with bath/shower.
La Estela, Rajoy 1, Santiago de Compostela, La Coruña (tel: (981) 58 2796). Basic, but good value for bed and breakfast.
Hostal Fidelmar, Playa Arena Grande, La Guardia, Pontevedra (tel: (986) 61 0208). Family hotel on a small bay.
Mapoula, Entremurallas 10, Santiago de Compostela, La Coruña (tel: (981) 58 0124). Well run *hostal-residencia* in private apartment block. Clean and comfortable.

Restaurants

Expensive

Anexo Vilas, Avenida Villagarcia 21, Santiago de Compostela, La Coruña (tel: (981) 59 8387). This very Galician seafood restaurant, within walking distance of the city centre, has been run by the same family for generations.
Chocolate, Villajuan, Pontevedra (tel: (986) 50 1199). 2km from Villagarcia de Arosa, this is one of Galicia's top restaurants. Particularly strong on seafood.
El Rapido, Estrella 7, La Coruña (tel: (981) 22 4221). Reservations often necessary at this seafood restaurant. Closed Sunday evening and last two weeks in December.
San Miguel, San Miguel 12-14, Orense (tel: (988) 22 1245). This restaurant has a high reputation in Galicia, using first-class ingredients. Closed Tuesdays.

Moderate

Casa Solla, Carretera El Grove, Pontevedra (tel: (986) 85 2678). Excellent seafood; reservations usually needed. Closed Thursdays and Sunday evenings.
Mesón de la Cazuela, Callejón de la Estacada 1, La Coruña (tel: (981) 22 2448). Good value home cooking.
Posada del Mar, Castelao 202, El Grove, Pontevedra (tel: (986) 73 0106). Seafood specialities include scallop pie (good for pilgrims). Busy at weekends. Closed Sunday evenings and mid-December to January.
San Clemente, San Clemente 6, Santiago de Compostela, La Coruña (tel: (981) 58 0882) Non-stop reasonably priced seafood from 08.00 to 02.00 hrs.

Budget

Mar y Cielo, Monte de Santa Tecla, La Guardia, Pontevedra (tel: (986) 61 1164). You get tapas on the first floor of this restaurant perched on a crag above the River Miño and the Atlantic; fish and meat restaurant on second floor.

THE NORTH COAST

Accommodation

Expensive

Gayoso, Paseo de Gómez 4, Luarca, Asturias (tel: (98) 564 0050). Family-run (for 120 years) comfortable small hotel.
Husa Carlton, Plaza F Moyua 2, Bilbao, Vizcaya (tel: (94) 416 2200). This grand old hotel was a haunt of Basque republicans in the Civil War.
Londres y de Inglaterra, Zubieta 2, San Sebastián, Guipúzcoa (tel: (943) 42 6989). Elegant turn-of-the-century hotel right on La Concha beach. This popular town rendezvous point has a casino and restaurant.
Pampinot, Calle Mayor 3, Funterrabía, Guipúzcoa (tel: (943) 64 0600). Small charming town hotel in converted mansion. Closed in February.
Parador Nacional El Molino Viejo, Parque Isabel la Católica, Gijón, Asturias (tel: (98) 537 0511). Attractively sited by the park, this modern parador's bar and restaurant are popular with locals. Pleasant garden.
Reconquista, Gil de Jaz 16, Oviedo, Asturias (tel: (98) 524 1100). Asturias' leading hotel, host to all the top people including royalty, is a converted 18th-century orphanage.
La Rectoral, 33775 Taramundi, Asturias (tel: (98) 564 6767). Outstanding hotel in a converted rectory. Specialises in 'green tourism' in this beautiful hill district.
Santemar, J-Costa 28, Santander, Cantabria (tel: (942) 27 2900). Well placed for the beach, though rather a business hotel atmosphere.

Moderate

Arocena, San Juan 12, Cestona, Guipúzcoa (tel: (943) 14 7040). Refurbished 'Belle Epoque' hotel.
Clarín, Calle Caveda 23, Oviedo, Asturias (tel: (98) 522 7272). Central, attractive hotel. Car parking in garage opposite can be a struggle. Disabled access. Restaurant.
Maroño, Correo 21, Bilbao, Vizcaya (tel: (94) 416 5851). Close to the cathedral. Meals are served.
Montemar, Avenida Genaro Riestra 8, Llanes, Asturias (tel: (98) 540 0100). Efficient smallish hotel in '60s-style block. Near sea and with good mountain views.

Palacete Peñalba, Figueras del Mar, Castropol, Asturias (tel: (98) 562 3150). Modernista-style 1912 building, fancifully decorated in and out. Not suitable for families.
Parador de Gil Blas, Plaza Ramón Pelayo 11, Santillana del Mar, Cantabria (tel: 942) 81 8000). Has old (15th- to 16th-century) and new parts, both pleasant. Good restaurant.
Parador de Hondarribia, Plaza de Armas del Castillo, Fuenterrabía, Guipúzcoa (tel: (943) 64 2140). Small parador once associated with Charles V. Splendid location and good décor but no restaurant.
Parador Nacional del Río Deva, Fuente Dé, Cantabria (tel: (942) 73 0001). Magnificently sited under a rock wall on the side of Picos de Europa near ascending cable-car. Architecturally unimpressive however.
Sardinero, Plaza Italia 1, Santander, Cantabria (tel: (942) 27 1100). In a pleasant building close to the beach.
Budget
Arana, Bidebarrieta 2, Bilbao, Vizcaya (tel: (94) 415 6411). Bed and breakfast in the old quarter.
Castillo de Valdés-Salas, Plaza General Aranda, Salas, Asturias (tel: (98) 583 1037). Simple hotel in a converted 16th-century castle. Plenty of character and friendly service.
Luzón, Avenida Miramar 1. San Vicente de la Barquera, Cantabria (942) 71 0050. Friendly family-run hotel.

Restaurants
Expensive
Arzak, Alto de Miracruz 2, San Sebastián, Guipúzcoa (tel: (943) 28 5593). Reputed for its Basque cuisine – top restaurant in a foody city.
Dos Hermanas, Madre Vedruna 10, Vitoria, Alava (tel: (945) 13 2934). Over 100 years old and popular with Basque parliamentarians. Classic Basque cooking. Good local wines.
Goizeko-Kabi, Particular de Estraunza 4 and 6, Bilbao, Vizcaya (tel: (94) 442 1129). One of Spain's top restaurants, serving Bilbao (and own) specialities.
Peñalba, Avenida de José Tenor, Figueras del Mar, Asturias (tel: (98) 562 3760). Delicious fish in this restaurant owned by hotel Palacete Peñalba.
Ramon Roteta, Villa Ainara, Irun s/n, Fuenterrabía, Guipúzcoa (tel: (943) 64 1693). Great food in an old villa.
Moderate
Casa Victor, Carmen 11, Gijón, Asturias (tel: 98) 535 0093). Seafood and traditional cuisine. Good wines. Closed November, Sunday evenings and Thursdays.
Patxiku Quintana, San Jeronimo 22, San Sebastián, Guipúzcoa (tel: (943) 42 6399). Traditional Basque fish dishes are served in this Old Town restaurant. Closed Tuesday evenings and Wednesdays, also 15 December to 8 January.
El Raitan, Plaza Trascorrales 6, Oviedo, Asturias (tel: 98) 521 4218). Fixed Asturian menu – excellent and hearty food. Lunch only except Fridays and Saturdays; closed Sundays.
Retolaza, Tendería 1, Bilbao, Vizcaya (tel: (94) 415 0643). Very authentic Old Town restaurant offering classic Vizcayan cuisine. Closed late July to mid-August, Easter and Sundays and Mondays.
Trascorrales, Plaza Trascorrales 19, Oviedo, Asturias (tel: (98) 522 2441). Often reckoned the top restaurant in Asturias, this serves Spanish nouvelle cuisine.
Budget
Bodega del Riojana, Rio de la Pila 5, Santander, Cantabria (tel: (942) 21 6750). This restaurant in a 16th-century wine cellar is popular and very crowded in summer. Closed Sundays.

ARAGON AND NAVARRE

Accommodation
Expensive
Albarracín, Calle Azgara, Albarracín, Teruel (tel: (978) 71 0011). Converted 16th-century palace on hillside.
Goya, Cinco de Marzo 5, Zaragoza (tel: (976) 22 9331). Largish hotel, well placed for exploring the town centre.
Maisonnave, Calle Nueva 20, Pamplona, Navarra (tel: (948) 22 2600). Big business-style town centre hotel with garage and restaurant.

Pedro I de Aragón, Avenida del Parque 34, Huesca (tel: (974) 22 0300). Huesca's best hotel is just outside the centre.
Reina Cristina, Paseo del Ovaló 1, Teruel (tel: (978) 60 6860). Conveniently placed for the town centre. Air conditioning; restaurant.
Moderate
Gran, Paseo de la Constitución 1, Jaca, Huesca (tel: (974) 36 0900). Somewhat soulless resort-type hotel, but comfortable and efficient.
Hospedería de Leyre, Monasterio de Leyre, Yesa, Navarra (tel: (948) 88 4100). The 30-room traditional *hospedería* is run by monks.
Monasterio de Piedra, 50210 Nuevalos, Zaragoza (tel: (976) 84 9011). The bedrooms are slightly run-down, though public areas are impressive in this 12th-century Cistercian monastery set in a lovely park. Atmospheric, if gloomy.
Parador Nacional, Teruel (tel: (978) 60 1800). Modern parador 2km out of town on

the Zaragoza road. Pleasant gardens and agreeable dining room serving local cuisine.
Parador Nacional de la Concordia, Castillo de los Calatravos, Alcañiz, Teruel (tel: (978) 83 0400). This small (12 rooms) parador occupies part of the castle dating from 1728. Good Aragonese food in restaurant.
Parador Nacional Fernando de Aragón, Sos del Rey Católico, Zaragoza (tel: (976) 88 8011). This parador, though modern, successfully evokes traditional Aragonese style. Good dining.
Parador Príncipe de Viana, Plaza de los Teobaldas 2, Olite, Navarra (tel: (948) 74 0000). Stay in the castle of the kings of Navarre, with suitably medieval décor. Centrally placed but with fine country views from the castle.
Sant Antón, Carretera a Francia, Benasque, Huesca (tel: (974), 55 1611). Comfortable modern hotel on the southern side of town, with popular Don Pedro restaurant. Closed November.

Tudela, Avenida de Zaragoza 56, Tudela, Navarra (tel: 948) 41 0802). Modest small hotel with restaurant.

Budget
Conde Aznar, General Franco 3, Jaca, Huesca (tel: (974) 36 1050). Agreeable small hotel, with antlers and beams providing a mountain atmosphere. Good Aragonese food.
Lleida, Glorieta Joaquín Costa, Graus, Huesca (tel: (974) 54 0925). Adequate overnight stopping-point for motorists. Friendly service and local-type restaurant.
La Perla, Plaza del Castillol, Pamplona, Navarra (948) 22 7706. Fair-sized hotel (67 rooms), conveniently placed.

Note: this area, Navarre in particular, has plenty of self-catering houses and apartments in country areas. Ask in tourist offices for *Guía de Casas Rurales.*

Restaurants
Expensive
Josetxo, Plaza Principe de Viana 1, Pamplona, Navarra (tel: (948) 22 2097). Pamplona's smartest restaurant, serving Navarrese cuisine.

Moderate
Casa Paco, La Salud 10, Jaca, Huesca (tel: (974) 36 1618). Fresh local produce is used for Aragonese nouvelle cuisine.
Meseguer, Avenida del Maestrazgo 9, Alcañiz, Teruel (tel: (974) 83 1002). Good-value restaurant, popular with locals. Closed Sundays, holiday evenings and late September.

Budget
Erburu, San Lorenzo 19-21, Pamplona, Navarra (tel: (948) 22 5169). This inexpensive restaurant in Pamplona's nightlife district is a favourite with locals.

BARCELONA
Accommodation
Expensive
Condes de Barcelona, Passeig de Gràcia 75 (tel: (93) 484 8600). Modern hotel behind a Modernista façade, elegant and comfortable.
Gran Derby, Loreto 28 (tel: (93) 322 3215). Well furnished and equipped apartments with many of the facilities of a hotel.
Meridien, La Rambla 111 (tel: (93) 318 6200). Stay here to combine exploring old Barcelona with a touch of luxury.
Princesa Sofía, Plaça Pius XII (tel: (93) 330 7111). Big business-style hotel with décor featuring marble and bronze. Three restaurants, one serving Catalan Empordà-style cuisine. Indoor and outdoor swimming pools.
Rey Juan Carlos I, Avinguda Diagonal 661–71 (tel: (93) 448 0808). Opened in 1992, this sumptuous five-star hotel is convenient for airport and motorway. **Hotel Ritz**, Gran Via de les Corts Catalanes 668 (tel: (93) 318 5200). Long Barcelona's grandest hotel; the public areas retain a real turn-of-the-century feeling.

Moderate
Continental, La Rambla 138 (tel: (93) 301 2570). Efficiently run small hotel. Front rooms are good for observing the Ramblas, though noisy.
Gaudí, Nou de la Rambla 12 (tel: (93) 317 9032). Well situated opposite Gaudí's Palacio Güell.
Gran Via, Gran Via de les Corts Catalanes 642 (tel: (93) 318 1900). Palatial surroundings at a reasonable price. Good sized bedrooms – ask for a back one if you want quiet.
Oriente, Rambla 45 (tel: (93) 302 2558). Wonderfully old-fashioned and slightly faded, dating from 1842, the Oriente has a Modernista-style restaurant.

Restaurants
Expensive
Florian, Bertrand i Serra 20 (tel: (93) 212 4627). Very small and intimate, this is one of Barcelona's best restaurants. Good wine list. Closed Sundays and in July.
Eldorado Petit Dolors Monserdà 51 (tel: (93) 204 5506). Situated in a villa above the city, this is one of Spain's top restaurants, serving Catalan nouvelle cuisine based on the dishes of the Empordà region. Reservations essential for lunch or dinner.

Moderate
Agut, Ginyas 16 (tel: (93) 315 1709). Classic Catalan cooking in the Barri Gòtic.
Can Costa, Passeig Nacional, 70 (tel: (93) 221 9511. Excellent seafood restaurant in the Barceloneta district, where fish restaurants abound.

Els Perols de l'Empordà, Villaroel 88 (tel: (93) 323 1033). Good food from the Empordà region in this very quiet restaurant. Slightly shabby, but pleasant domestic atmosphere. Closed Sunday evenings, Mondays, Holy Week and second half of August.
Els Quatre Gats, Montsiò 3 (tel: (93) 302 4140). There is a Modernista atmosphere in this café-restaurant, formerly a café haunted by artists, including Picasso, early this century. Light meals available – mainly Catalan dishes.
7 Portes, Passeig Isabel II 14 (tel: (93) 319 3033). In business since 1836, this rather formal restaurant has a huge menu.

Budget
Can Culleretes, Quintana 5 (tel: (93) 317 6485). Very old restaurant in the Barri Gòtic serving Catalan dishes. Closed Sunday evenings, Mondays and 1–21 July.
Egipte, Jerusalem 12 (tel: (93) 317 7480). Catalan food and good puddings served in this popular restaurant. Lively and stylish clientele. Closed Sundays.
Mordisco, Rosselló 265 (tel: (93) 218 3314). Busy eatery serving imaginative food. Open till the early hours of the morning.

CATALONIA

Accommodation

Expensive
Condes de Urgel, Avenida de Barcelona 17–27, Lleida, (tel: (973) 20 2300). Comfortable modern largish hotel away from the town centre.
Imperial Tarraco, Paseo Palmeras, Tarragona (tel: (977) 23 3040). Comfortable large hotel, centrally placed and overlooking the sea. Pool, tennis court.
Parador de Aiguablava, Aigua Blava, Girona (tel: 972) 62 2162). Beautifully situated among pines near one of the Costa Brava's most dramatic rockscapes, this is a modern parador. No prizes for the cuisine, however.
Sol Girona, Carrer de Barcelona 112, Girona (tel: (972) 40 0500). Big, business-style hotel on city outskirts (exit 7or 8 from A7 motorway). Useful as a stopover.
Moderate
Ampurdán, Carretera General Madrid-Francia, Figueres, Girona (tel: (972) 50 0562). Centrally placed main-road stopover-type hotel distinguished by its excellent restaurant.
Hotel Balneario Vichy Catalán, Avenida Furest, Caldas de Malavella, Girona (tel: 972) 47 0000). One of the region's most agreeable spa hotels in the home of the top mineral water.
Parador Nacional, Paraje el Bach de Sau, Vic, Barcelona (tel: (93)812 2323). Modern parador in traditional Catalan farmhouse style, about 15km northeast of Vic.
Parador Nacional, Santo Domingo, Seo de Urgel, Lleida (tel: (973) 35 2000). Modern parador near the cathedral. Restaurant serves Catalan dishes.
Parador Nacional Castillo de la Zuda, Tortosa, Tarragona (tel: (977) 44 4450).There are fine views of the town and River Ebro from this hilltop parador in an old Moorish fortress. Garden and pool.
Parador Nacional Duques de Cardona, Castillo, Cardona, Barcelona (tel: (93) 869 1275). Stay in one of Spain's most impressive hilltop castles. Medieval décor including four-poster beds. Well reputed restaurant serving local specialities.
Parador Turismo Don Gaspar de Portolá, Artiés, Lleida (tel: (973) 64 1103). Very comfortable, basically modern parador in local mountain style. Catalan cuisine.
Plaça, Plaça Mercat 22, Sant Feliu de Guíxols, Girona (tel: (972) 32 5155). New, very agreeable hotel on the market square of Sant Feliu open all year. Roof terrace; café but no restaurant.
Budget
Edelweiss, Artiés, Lleida (tel: (973) 64 0902). Straightforward and welcoming hotel. Closed first half of May and in November.
Gaudí, Arrabal Robuster 49, Reus, Tarragona (tel: (977) 30 5545). Central *hostal* in Gaudí's birthplace.
Llevant, Francisco de Blanes 5, Llafranc, Girona (tel: (972) 30 0366). Pleasant small hotel on the main promenade. Good restaurant serving French-influenced Catalan food.
Oasis, Roca Maura 28, L'Estartit, Girona (tel: (972) 7575 15). Simple and good-hearted resort hotel.
Port Lligat, Cadaqués, Girona (tel: (972) 25 8162).

Fairly simple hotel near Dalí's home. Good views.
Romantic, San Isidro 33, Sitges, Barcelona (tel: (93) 894 8375). Conversion of three 19th-century villas in town centre. Large garden. Bed and breakfast only.

Restaurants

Expensive
Albatros, Bruselas 60, Salou, Tarragona (tel: (977) 38 5070). Specialises in seafood. Closed Sunday evenings, Mondays and 20 December to 15 January.
Bahía, Passeig del Mar 17–18, Sant Feliu de

Guíxols, Girona (tel: (972) 32 0219). Behind the promenade; specialises in seafood.
Casa Irene, Calle Mayor 3 , Artiés, Lleida (tel: (973) 64 0900). Enjoy a gastronomic blow-out, French and Pyrenean style. Good value.

Mas Pau, Avinyonet de Puìgventos, Figueres, Girona (tel: (972) 54 6154). Specialises in game dishes.
Sol-Ric, Via Augusta 227, Tarragona (tel: (997) 23 2032). Varied menu specialising in Catalan dishes; accompanied by a good wine list. Closed Sunday evenings, Mondays and 15 December to 15 January.

Moderate

Casa Hidalgo, Sant Pau 12, Sitges, Barcelona (tel: (93) 894 3895). An intimate restaurant serving well-presented Catalan food.
El Pescador, Nemesio Llorens, Cadaqués, Girona (tel: (972) 25 8859). Seafront seafood restaurant on two floors. Closed November and January.
Garreta, Platja d'Aiguablava, Aigua Blava, Girona (tel: 972) 62 3033). Agreeable fish restaurant situated just behind the beach.
L'Hostalet del Call, Calle Battle, Prats 4, Girona (tel: (972) 21 2688). Rich and adventurous Catalan cuisine.
Capri, Paseo del Mar 17, Tossa de Mar, Girona (tel: (972) 34 2393). Pizzas and fast food situated behind the beach. Closed February.
La Puda, Muelle Pescadores 25, Tarragona (tel: (977) 21 1511). Good food next to the quay.

CASTILLA, LEON AND LA RIOJA

Accommodation

Expensive

Landa Palace, Carretera de Madrid-Irún, Burgos (tel: 947) 20 6343). Fanciful architecture distinguishes this modern hotel in the Relais and Châteaux chain. Good restaurant serving Castilian roasts, etc.
Palacio Valderrabanos, Plaza Catedral 9, Avila (tel: (920) 21 1023). Slightly gloomy hotel in a 15th-century bishop's palace, but it is well located within 50m of the cathedral.
Parador Nacional, Teso de la Feria 2, Salamanca (tel: (923) 26 8700). Though unrivalled as the ugliest building in the parador chain, this out-of-centre hotel has great city views.
Parador Nacional Condes de Alba y Aliste, Plaza Viriato 5, Zamora (tel: (988) 51 4497). This parador in a Renaissance palace is small enough to seem more welcoming than grand. There's a fine patio and staircase. Swimming pool in the garden.
Parador Nacional de Segovia, Carretera de Valladolid, Segovia (tel: (921) 44 3737). Elegant, brick-built modern parador. Great floodlit town views at night. Good restaurant.
San Marcos, Plaza San Marcos, León (tel: (987) 23 7300). One of the great hotels of Spain, this parador was once a monastery and is graced with magnificent façade, staircase and patio. Try to get one of the old rooms furnished with antiques (there is also a modern annexe).

Moderate

Hotel Gaudí, Plaza Eduardo de Castro 6, Astorga, León (tel: (987) 61 5654). Pleasant modern hotel.
Los Linajes, Dr Velasco 9, Segovia (tel: (921) 460475). In an old town house (with new annexe), this is a quiet place to stay in the heart of old Segovia.
Parador Rey Fernándo II de León, Parque de la Marina Española, Benavente, Zamora (tel: (988) 63 0300). Modern parador based on an old castle keep.
Parador Nacional Enrique II, Plaza del Castillo 1, Ciudad-Rodrigo, Salamanca (tel: (923) 46 0150). Though comfortable and well modernised, the castle building is still redolent of medieval Spain.
Parador Nacional de Gredos, Gredos, Avila (tel: (920) 34 8048). Built in 1928 on a site chosen personally by King Alfonso XIII, this was the first-ever parador. Views of Circo de Gredos.
Parador Nacional Marco Fabio Quintiliano, Avenida Generalismo, Calahorra, Rioja (tel: (941) 13 0358). Unexceptional modern brick building, but with a good kitchen. A recommended stopover.
Parador Nacional Raimundo de Borgona, Marqués de Canales de Chozas 16, Avila (tel: (920) 21 1340). Just out of the centre but within the city walls built by Count Raymond of Burgundy. Garden; good restaurant.
Parador Nacional de Tordesillas, Carretera N620, Tordesillas, Valladolid (tel: (983) 77 0051). Stately modern parador, very comfortable and convenient for visiting Tordesillas. Useful stopover.
Parador Nacional de Villafranca del Bierzo, Avenida de Calvo Sotelo, Villafranca del Bierzo, León (tel: (987) 54 0175). Modern but well located parador on the Camino de Santiago. Good atmosphere; local produce in restaurant.
Quindos, Avenida J-Antonio 24, León (tel: (987) 23 6200). This modern block hotel is far better than its two stars suggest. Well decorated by a proprietor with an eye for art.

Budget

España, Paseo de Espolón 32, Burgos (tel: 947) 20 6340). City-centre location; modern rooms.

Hotel Juan II, Paseo del Espolón, Toro, Zamora (tel: (988) 69 0300). In the centre of Toro (33km from Zamora), this has basic rooms and public areas and good views over the Duero river. A surprisingly good, if simple, stopover.

Restaurants

Expensive

Hostería Nacional Pintor Zuloaga, Matadero 1, Pedraza, Segovia (tel: (921) 50 9835). You face serious eating in this restaurant which is part of the parador chain (no rooms). Castilian cuisine.

Mesón Cervantes, Del Rastro 6, Valladolid (tel: (983) 308553). You get a warm welcome in this Castilian restaurant which also serves fish and seafood.

Moderate

Adonias, Santa Nonia 16, León (tel: (987) 20 6768). Lively ceramic decorations and good regional cuisine characterise this restaurant.

Fernán González, Calera 19, Burgos (tel: (947) 20 9441). Interesting menu in this hotel restaurant. Wines are from the proprietor's own vineyard.

Maroto, Paseo del Espolón, Soria (tel: (975) 22 4086). Named after its proprietor, this is the most popular of Soria's better restaurants.

Regional menu with some novelties.

Mesón de Cándido, Plaza del Azoguejo 5, Segovia (tel: (921) 42 5911). One of the best suckling pig eateries in Spain, which makes it almost too popular.

Mesón del Rastro, Plaza Rastro 1, Avila (tel: 920) 21 1218). Hearty Castilian cooking served in a medieval setting.

El Molino de la Losa, Bajada de la Losa 12, Avila (tel: (920) 21 1101). Local restaurant in a 15th-century mill. Good for families as there is a garden with play area.

La Posada, Aire y Azucena 1, Salamanca (tel: (923) 21 7251). Main dining room is unprepossessingly in the basement, but the food is worth seeking out. Mainly Castilian specialities.

EXTREMADURA

Accommodation

Expensive

Gran Zurbarán, Paseo Castelar, Badajoz (tel: (924) 22 3741). Modern luxury hotel offering many facilities (shops, tennis, swimming pool, etc).

Parador Nacional de Cáceres, Ancha 6, Cáceres (tel: (927) 21 1759). The hotel, in a 15th-century palace, is wonderfully atmospheric.

Parador Nacional Hernán Cortés, Plaza Corazon María, Zafra, Badajoz (tel: (924) 55 4540). This hotel in a 15th-century castle once used by Cortés is much admired, but the recently refurbished marbled Renaissance patio has rather a formal look.

Parador Nacional Via de la Plata, Plaza de la Constitución 3, Mérida, Badajoz (tel: (924) 31 3800). In the town centre but quiet, this parador is well run and friendly, and most attractive in its convent setting.

Moderate

Hospedería del Real Monasterio, Plaza Juan Carlos I, Guadalupe, Cáceres (tel: (927) 36 7000). Simple and peaceful in a still functioning monastery, gathered around one of Spain's most beautiful cloisters, this is superb. There is also a restaurant serving local food.

Parador Nacional Carlos V, Carretera Plasencia, Jarandilla, Cáceres (tel: (927) 56 0117). A castle once used by Charles V, this is a high-style stopover in the beautiful Tiétar valley.

Parador Nacional de Trujillo, Plaza Santa Clara, Trujillo, Cáceres (tel: (927) 32 1350). In a former convent of the Poor Clares. Garden and pool.

Parador Nacional de Zurbarán, Marqués de la Romana 10, Guadalupe, Cáceres (tel: (927) 36 7075). This 15th-century pilgrims' hostel is one of the most attractive of all paradors, with a delightful patio.

Budget

Mesón la Cadena, Plaza Mayor 8, Trujillo, Cáceres (tel: (927) 32 1463). Hotel in a small palace.

Restaurants

Expensive

La Toja, Avenida Alvas 21, Badajoz (tel: (924) 23 7477). Specialises in Galician and local food.

Moderate

El Figón de Eustaquio, Plaza San Juan 12, Cáceres (tel: (927) 24 8194). This is good fun with a real sense of gastronomic regionalism.

CASTILLA-LA MANCHA AND MADRID REGION

Accommodation

Expensive

Parador Conde de Orgaz, Paseo Emperador, Toledo (tel: (925) 22 1850). Modern comfortable parador with view of the city very much as painted by El Greco. Best rooms have balconies.

Parador Nacional Castillo de Sigüenza, Plaza del Castillo , Sigüenza, Guadalajara (tel: (911) 39 0100). Castle overlooking the town which has played host to royalty. Today it is a sumptuous hotel. Many rooms open on to central Patio de las Armas. Early booking essential (especially weekends).

Santa María del Paular, El Paular, Rascafría, Madrid (tel: (91) 869 1011). Luxury hotel in a former monastery and adjoining a still functioning monastery. Beautiful building and views, though the contrast with the austere lifestyle next door can be sobering.

Moderate

Carlos V, Trastamara, Toledo (tel: (925) 22 2100). Modest hotel in the centre of town within walking distance of monuments.

Leonor de Aquitánia, San Pedro 60, Cuenca (tel: (969) 23 1000). Opened in 1991, this is a comfortable, friendly hotel in the high town and central to main monuments. Recommended.

Parador Nacional, Ronda de San Francisco, Almagro, Ciudad Real (tel: (926) 86 0100). Charming parador in an old convent with patios and lovely tile work. An easy walk to the centre of this lovely town.

Parador del Marqués de Villena, Alarcón, Cuenca (tel: (969) 33 1350). In a spectacular castle setting on a rocky promontory above a gorge. Exceptionally handsome bar/lounge and popular restaurant.

Posada de San José, Julián Romero 4, Cuenca (tel: (969) 21 1300). Set in an ancient convent/inn of medieval aspect, this is a homely, delightful and restful place to stay. Good views over the gorge.

Budget

Hostal El Doncel, Paseo de la Alameda, Sigüenza, Guadalajara (tel: (949) 39 0001). Situated at the bottom of town, where the evening *paseo* takes place.

Almazara, Carretera de Cuerva, Apartado Postal 6, Toledo (tel: (925) 22 3866). Bed and breakfast only. Located on the edge of town, with great views.

Restaurants

Expensive

Asador Adolfo, Granada 6 and Hombre de Palo 7, Toledo (tel: (925) 22 7321). Central location in an old house. Local cuisine.

Figón de Pedro, Cervantes 13, Cuenca (tel: (969) 22 6821). Good local cuisine in one of Cuenca's best restaurants.

Mesón Casas Colgadas, Canónigas, Cuenca (tel: (969) 22 3509). Famous for its situation and excellent local food.

Medium

Hostal del Cardenal, Paseo de Recaredo 24, Toledo (tel: (925) 22 0862). The restaurant is attached to the inn of the same name. Local dishes served.

Los Claveles, 18 de Julio 32, Cuenca (tel: (969) 21 3824). Regional dishes are served in this new town restaurant. Closed Thursdays and in September.

Venta de Aires, Circo Romano 35, Toledo (tel: (925) 22 0545). Both partridges and marzipan feature on the menu here. Closed Sunday evenings.

Venta del Quixote, El Molino 4, Puerto Lápice, (tel: (926) 57 6110). Ancient inn built round a yard of the kind from which Don Quixote set off on his adventures. The bar has giant wine storage jars typical of the Valdepeñas region. Touristy but fun.

LEVANTE

Accommodation

Expensive

Huerto del Cura, Federico García-Sanchiz, Elche, Alicante (tel: (96) 545 8040). The accommodation is in bungalows in the extensive gardens. Lovely swimming pool under palms, tennis court. Good restaurant.

Meliá Alicante, Playa de Postiguet, Alicante (tel: (96) 520 5000). Very large block of a hotel, but selfishly

situated at the end of the town beach with fine views.

Parador Nacional Costa Blanca, Playa del Arenal 2, Jávea, Alicante (tel: (965) 79 0200). This comfortable purpose-built parador looks over a hoop of excellent town beach.

Reina Victoria, Calle de las Barcas 4, Valencia (tel: (96) 352 0487). Central, traditional city hotel, recently renovated, but unfortunately, noisy.

Rincón de Pepe, Apóstoles 34, Murcia (tel: (968) 21 2239). Centrally situated hotel with the best restaurant in the region.

Moderate

Don Pancho, Avenida Mediterraneo 39, Benidorm, Alicante (tel: (96) 585 2950). A bit of character amid Benidorm's hotel jungle.

Hosteria del Mar, Carretera Benicarlo-Peñiscola, Peñiscola, Castellón (tel: (964) 48 0600). Modern, but with traditional décor. Near beach with views of old town.

Hotel Inglés, Marqués de Dos Aguas 6, Valencia (tel: (96) 351 6426). Opposite the Ceramics Museum, this is an intriguing mixture of Spanish and English décor. Bar serves good tapas.

Palas, Cervantes 5, Alicante (tel: (96) 520 9310). Slightly tatty but charming Belle Epoque hotel near the beach and harbour. Closed in November.

Parador Nacional de Puerto Lumbreras, Puerto Lumbreras, Murcia (tel: (968) 40 2025). South of Lorca, this makes a great stopover on the way to Granada. Cool flagged floors, ceramics, garden and swimming pool give the feeling of an oasis.

Budget

Hostal Elías, Calle Colomer 7, Morella, Castellón (tel: (964) 16 0092). In the centre of town. No meals provided.

Restaurants

Expensive

Civera, Lérida 11, Valencia (tel: (96) 347 5917). Family-run seafood restaurant; house speciality is *caldereta de langosta mediterranea* (lobster casserole). Good selection of wines from Rioja and Valencia. Closed Mondays and August.

El Delfín, Esplanada de España 12, Alicante (tel: (96) 521 4911). Excellent first-floor restaurant facing the Esplanada and serving top-class local cuisine.
Rincón de Pepe see Accommodation – Expensive

Moderate
Casa Roque, Segura Barreda 8, Morella, Castellón (tel: (964) 16 0336). Truffles are a speciality.
Easo Berri, Santo Domingo 14, Benidorm, Alicante (tel: (96) 586 4350). Basque cuisine served here.

Estimat, Paseo Neptuno 16, Valencia (tel: (96) 371 1018). Popular rice and seafood restaurant.
Gargantua, Navarro Reventer 18, Valencia (tel: (96) 334 6849). Serves authentic Valencian cuisine. Closed Sunday evenings and Mondays.
Los Habaneros, San Diego 60, Cartagena, Murcia (tel: (968) 50 5250). Recommended by locals, this is the best fish and seafood restaurant in town and worth the quite high prices. Closed Sunday evenings.
Mesón el Granaino, José Maria Buch 40, Elche, Alicante (tel: (965) 46 0147). Good regional food on the menu. Closed Sunday evenings.

Budget
Cándido, Santo Domingo 13, Lorca, Murcia (tel: (968) 46 6907). Cooking inspired by regional dishes from the surrounding area. Closed Sundays in summer.
Quo Vadis, Plaza Santisssima Faz 3, Alicante (tel: (96) 521 6660). Tapas are good in this lively restaurant, also grilled fish. You can eat on the terrace.

ANDALUCIA

Accommodation

Expensive

Alfonso XIII, San Fernando 2, Sevilla (tel: (95) 422 2850). This is the top hotel in town with livery-clad staff, Edwardian/Moorish splendour and huge bedrooms.
Almería, Gran Avenida Reina Regente 8, Almería (tel: (950) 23 8011). Functional rather than luxurious, the hotel has views of the bay and harbour.
La Bobadilla, Finca La Bobadilla, Loja, Granada (tel: (958) 32 1861). Probably Spain's most spectacular country hotel. Purpose built to resemble an Andalucian village, it is true *grande luxe* with every facility, including riding on the estate through sweeping countryside.
Casas de la Judería, Callejón de Dos Hermanos 7, Sevilla (tel: (95) 441 5150). A small group of ancient houses has been converted into serviced apartments, well furnished with antique décor.
Colón, Canalejas 1, Sevilla (tel: (95) 422 2900). Bullfighters dress for the ring in the luxurious surroundings here, then hold court after the fight. Rooms slightly small for the five-star prices, but satisfyingly Spanish atmosphere.
Meliá Don Pepe, Finca las Merinas, Marbella, Málaga (tel: (952) 770 300). Prestigious town hotel with good access to golf, tennis and horseriding.
Hotel Doña Maria, Don Remondo 19, Sevilla (tel: (95) 422 4990). You can't get closer to Seville's old quarter than here. The rooftop swimming pool looks on to the cathedral.
Parador Nacional Alcázar Rey Don Pedro, Carmona, Sevilla (tel: (95) 414 1010). A modern structure within fortress walls that once belonged to Pedro I of Castile (the Cruel). Moorish-style patio; old-fashioned rooms with fine views.
Parador Nacional de la Arruzafa, Avenida de la Arruzafa, Córdoba (tel: (957) 27 5900). The site of the 8th-century palace of Abd al-Rahman I is now in a definitely suburban setting. Good views, however.
Parador Nacional Casa del Corregidor, Plaza d'España, Arcos de la Frontera, Cádiz (tel: (956) 70 0500). In the main square of this 'White Town', spectacularly perched on top of a cliff, the parador has superb views over the Guadalete valley.
Parador Castillo de Santa Catalina, Jaén (tel: (953) 26 4411). A visit to this historic crag, if only for a coffee, is essential to the Jaén experience. Its capture in 1246 was the key to the Christian conquest of western Andalucía.
Parador Nacional Condestable-Dávalos, Plaza de Vázquez de Molina, Ubeda, Jáen (tel: (953) 75 0345). Small in scale (only 31 rooms), this is nevertheless one of the great places to stay. It is housed in a 16th-century palace on the town square.
Parador Nacional Cristóbal Colón, Carretera Mazagón-Moguer, Mazagón, Huelva (tel: (959) 53 6300). Well placed for visiting Columbus sites, the parador is situated on a clifftop above the sea.
Parador de Málaga-Gibralfaro, Gibralfaro, Málaga (tel: (952) 22 1903). This quiet, small parador stands in a lovely wooded position above Málaga, near the castle.
Parador de Nerja, Almuñecar 8 , Nerja, Málaga (tel: (952) 52 0050). Despite good décor, this is one of the more functional-style paradors. Wonderful position and views. Lift down to the beach.
Parador Nacional de San Francisco, Real de la Alhambra, Granada (tel: (958) 22 1440). A former convent built right inside the Alhambra. You need to book one of the 39 rooms months in advance.
Reina Cristina, Paseo de las Conferencias, Algeciras,

Cádiz (tel: (956) 60 2622). Despite the growth of industrial Algeciras, this remains a charming hotel.
Reina Victoria, Calle Jerez 25, Ronda, Málaga (tel: (95) 87 1240). Showing signs of age, but comfortable and with fine views over the town and mountain landscape.

Moderate
América, Real Alhambra 53, Granada (tel: (958) 22 7471). Some of the rooms in this hotel, right inside the Alhambra precincts, are very tiny. Knowledgeable and loyal clientele.
Cervantes, Cervantes 10, Sevilla (tel: (95) 490 0280). New hotel in a quiet street. Patioed, small and intimate, it has a dashing décor.
Costasol, Paseo de Almería 58, Almería (tel: (950) 23 4011). Central, this is an adequate small and modern hotel.
Marisa, Cardenal Herrero 6, Córdoba (tel: (957) 47 3142). Simple white hotel near the Mezquita.
Parador de Bailén, Bailén, Jaén (tel: (953) 67 0100). A good stopover point. The restaurant serves Andaluz and Jaén specialities and game in season.
Plaza Sevilla, Canalejas 2, Sevilla (tel: (954) 21 7149). This *hostal*, just across from the luxury Colón hotel, though spartan, is clean, efficient and pleasing.
Simon, García de Vinuesa 19, Sevilla (tel: (95) 422 6660). If you sacrifice some comfort here, you make up for it aesthetically with beautifully tiled rooms around the patio.
Budget
Lis, Calle Córdoba 7, Málaga (tel: (95) 222 7300). Comfortable simple hotel with some apartments. No dining room.
Madrid, San Pedro Martír 22, Sevilla (tel: (95) 421 4307). Small (21 rooms), basic but clean hotel.

Restaurants
Expensive
Antonio Martín, Paseo Maritimo, Málaga (tel: (952) 22 2113). Seafood is the speciality in Málaga's top restaurant. Seafront position, with a terrace.
El Churrasco, Romero 16, Córdoba (tel: (957) 29 0819). Restaurant in the Judería specialising in Andalucian cuisine and meat dishes.
Egana-Oriza, San Fernando 41, Sevilla (tel: (95) 422 7211). Basque and international cooking. Light meals available and nice bar with seats outside.
La Hacienda, Urbanización Hacienda Las Chapas, N340, Marbella, Málaga (tel: (95) 83 1116). The chef's personal version of French/Spanish cuisine is served in a villa-like ambience. Five-course gastronomic menu available. Closed Mondays and Tuesdays.
Ruta del Veleta, Carretera de la Sierra, Granada (tel: (958) 48 6134). This mountain restaurant, 5km out of Granada, provides the best cooking in and around the city. Cuisine of Andalucía and the regions. Many loyal regulars.
Moderate
El Figón de Bonilla, Cervantes, Edificio Horizonte, Málaga (tel: (95) 222 3123). Fish and local dishes; also good tapas. Closed Sundays.
Florida, Casablanca 15, Torremolinos, Málaga (tel: (95) 238 5095). Open buffet style restaurant.
Gran Marisquería Santiago, Duque de Ahumada 50, Marbella, Málaga (tel: (952) 77 4339). This is one of Marbella's best seafood restaurants. Popular with the locals.
La Langosta, Francisco Cano s/n, Fuengirola, Málaga (tel: (952) 47 5049). Well established town restaurant; international menu with the emphasis on seafood.
Mesón Don Raimundo, Argote de Molina 26, Sevilla (tel: (95) 422 3355). In an attractive alley near the Giralda, serves traditional dishes with original touches. Interesting décor.
Mirador de Morayma, Callejón de las Vacas 2, Albaicín, Granada (tel: (958) 22 8290). Andalucian food is served in a charming *carmen* – ancient house of the Albaicín.
Pedro Romero, Virgen de la Paz 18, Ronda, Málaga (tel: (95) 287 1110). Situated opposite Ronda's famous bullring, the restaurant is predictably rich in bullfighting paraphernalia. Local and international dishes served. Touristy, but acceptably so.
Rio Grande, Betis 70, Sevilla (tel: (95) 427 3956). Wonderfully positioned, with a terrace on the river looking across at the Torre del Oro and the Giralda tower. Cuisine (not great) is international and Spanish.
Budget
Casa Pedro, Quitapeñas 121, El Palo, Málaga (tel: (952) 29 0013). Large popular restaurant. Sardines and paella are tourist favourites. Closed Monday evenings.

Confederación de Peñas, Calle Luque s/n, Córdoba (tel: (957) 47 5427). Simple food served here, inside or on the patio.
La Posada, San Juan de Dios 4, Marbella, Málaga. Basic local food in a characterful setting.

Index

A

Agreda 152
Aguadulce 236
Aguilar de Campóo 152
Aguilas 215
Aiguablava 134
Aigües Tortes (Aigüestortes) 130
airports and air services 256, 268
Alarcón 192
Alba de Tormes 152
Albacete 192
Albarracín 100
La Alberca 152
La Albufera 211
Alcalá de Henares 192
Alcalá del Júcar 192
Alcañiz 100
Alcántara 182
Alcaraz 193
Alcocéber 213
L'Alcora 221
Alcoy 19, 210
Alfaro 152
Algeciras 226
Alhama de Granada 226
Alhambra 242, 243–4
Alicante 214
Allariz 74
Almagro 193
Almansa 193
Almazán 152
Almería 226
Almerimar 236
Almuñécar 238
Las Alpujarras 226, 252
Alquézar 101
Alsasua (Altsasu) 101
Altamira 88–9
Altea 214
L'Ampolla 136
Ancares, Reserva Nacional Dos 81
Andalucía 21,224–54, 283–4
Andújar 226
Antequera 227
Aracena 227
Aragon and Navarre 98–113, 277–8
Arán, Vall de 139, 148, 149
Aranda de Duero 153
Aranjuez 193
Arcos de la Frontera 227
Arévalo 153
Argentona 131
Arnedo 153
Astorga 153
Astudillo 156
attitudes and etiquette 261–2
Avila 154–5
Avilés 86

B

Badajoz 182
Baeza 228
Bagur (Begur) 134
Bakio 85
banks 266
Bañolas (Banyoles) 131
Barbastro 101, 109
Barcelona 114–27, 278–9
Bareyo 84
Basque Country 22, 23, 83
Bayona (Baiona) 74
Baztàn 101
beaches 257
Béjar 156
Belmonte 194, 199
Benalmádena 238
Benasque 101
Benavente 156
Benicarló 213
Benicasim 213
Benidorm 214
Berlanga de Duero 156
Bermeo 85
Besalú 131
Betanzos 74
Bilbao (Bilbo) 83
Blanes 134
Boí, Vall de 139, 148, 149
Brihuega 194
Briviesca 156
bullfighting 18, 240–1
Burgos 156–8
bus services 268

C

Cabo de Gata 236
Cabo de San Antonio 215
Cabo Vidio 86
Cáceres 183
Cadaqués 131
Cádiz 230
Caidos, Valle de 194
Calatayúd 101
Calatrava 194, 218–19
Caldes de Malavella 131
Calpe 214
Camariñas 74
Cambrils 136
camping 257
Canelobre caves 215
Cangas de Onis 92
car rental 260–1
Caravaca de la Cruz 210
Cardona 131
Carmona 231
Carrión de los Condes 159
Cartagena 19, 210
Casares 231
Cascada de Cola de Caballo 111
Castellón de la Plana 210
Castilla-La Mancha and the Madrid region 21, 190–207, 281–2
see also Madrid
Castilla, León and La Rioja 150–79, 280–1
Castro-Urdiales 84
Castropol 86
Catalonia 21, 128–49, 279–80
see also Barcelona
cave paintings 88–9
Cazorla 231
Cebreiro 74
Celanova 74
Cervatos 83
Cervera 131
Cervera de Pisuerga 159
children in Spain 257
Chinchilla de Monte Aragón 196
Chinchón 196
Ciudad Encantada 195
Ciudad Real 196
Ciudad Rodrigo 159
climate 257–8
Coca Castle 160
Collado de Llesba 93
Comillas 84
Consuegra 198
Córdoba 232–5
Coria 182
La Coruña (A Coruña) 74–5
Costa de Almería 236
Costa del Azahar 213
Costa Blanca 214–15
Costa Brava 132, 134–5, 137, 143
Costa Calida 215
Costa de Cantabria 84
Costa Dorada 136
Costa de la Luz 237
Costa de la Muerte (Costa da Morte) 76
Costa del Sol 238–9
Costa Vasca 85
Costa Verde 86
Coto Doñana 229
Covadonga 92
Covarrubias 160

crime 13, 258
Cudillero 86
Cuenca 197, 203
Cullera 213
customs regulations 258

D

Daroca 101
Delta del Ebro 136
Denia 215
disabled travellers 258–9
driving 259–61
Durango 90

E

Ebro delta 136
Elantxobe 85
Elche 216
Elorrio 90
embassies and consulates 261
emergency telephone numbers 261
Empúries (Ampurias) 133
entry formalities 256
environmental 24–5
El Escorial 38, 200
L'Estartit 134
Estella (Lizarra) 102
Estepona 238
Estudio y Museo de Sorolla 58
Expo 92 13, 254
Extremadura 180–9, 281

F

El Ferrol (Ferrol) 76
ferry services 256
Figueras (Figueres) 137
Fitero 102
flamenco 19, 68, 243
food and drink
  eating out *see* regional information
  Spanish cuisine 20–1
Frías 160
Frómista 160
Fuendetodos 102
Fuengirola 238
Fuente Dé 93
Fuenterrabía (Hondarribia) 90

G

Galicia 20-1, 72-82, 274, 276
Gandia 215
Garrucha 236
Gerona (Girona) 137
Getaria 85
Gijón (Xixon) 90
Granada 242-5
Gredos, Sierra de 161
Grutas de San Josep 213
Guadalajara 201
Guadalest 217
Guadalupe 184
Guadarrama 201
Guernica (Gernika) 90

H

Haro 165
health matters 262–3
history of Spain 26–49
hitch-hiking 263
Huesca 103, 106

I

Illes Medés 134
Irache (Iranzu) 102
Isla Cristina 237

J

Jaca 106
Jarandilla 182
Játiva 217
Jerez de los Caballeros 185
Jijona 214
Jimena 253

L

Laguna Negra 177
language 22, 263–5
Lanjarón 252
Laredo 84
Lastres 86
Lebeña 93
Lekeitio 85
León 162–4
Lérida (Lleida) 137
Lerma 165
Levante 208–23, 282–3
Leyre 106
Llanes 86
Lloret de Mar 134–5
Loarre, Castillo de 103
local time 271
Logroño 165
Lorca 217
lost property 265
Loyola 91
Luanco 86
Lugo 76

M

Madrid 50–71, 274
Maestrazgo 218–19
Málaga 238
Maluenda 101
Manzanares El Real 201
maps
  Alhambra 243
  Andalucía 224–5
  Aragon and Navarre 98
  Avila 154
  Barcelona 114
  Barri Gòtic (Barcelona) 116
  Cantabrian coast 84–5
  Castilla-La Mancha 190–1
  Castilla, León and La Rioja 150–1
  Catalonia 128
  Córdoba 232
  El Escorial 200
  Extremadura 180
  Galicia 72
  Granada 242
  Guadalupe monastery 184
  León 162
  Levante 208
  Madrid 50–1
  Santiago de Compostela 79
  Segovia 175
  Seville 248
  sources of 265
  Spain 10–11, 26
  Tarragona 146
  Toledo 204
  Valencia 222
Mar de Castilla 201
Mar Menor 215
Marbella 239
Matalascañas 237
measurements and sizes 265
Medellín 185
media 266
medical treatment 262–3
Medina Azahara 235
Medina del Campo 165
Medina de Rioseco 166
Medinaceli 165
Mérida 185
Mezquita 233–4
Mijas 239
Mojácar 236
Molina de Aragón 201
Mondoñedo 77
money 266
Monfragüe, Parque Nacional de 105
Montblanc 138

Montes de Toledo 201
Montesinos 199
Montseny 138
Montserrat 138
Moraira 215
Morella 217
Murcia 220
Muros 82
music and dance 19
Muxia 74

N

Nájera 166
Naranjo de Bulnes 92
national holidays 266
national parks 104
Navia, Valle de 91
Nerja 239
Noja 84
North Coast 83–97, 276–7
Nuevalos 107
Numantia 178
Nuestra Señora del Rocio 141

O

Olèrdola 149
Olite 107
La Oliva 107
Olivenza 185
Olmedo 166
Olot 132, 138
Oña 166
Oñate (Oñati) 91
Onda 220
Ondarroa 85
opening times 266–7
Ordesa y Monte Perdido, Parque Nacional 108, 111
Orense (Ourense) 77
Orihuela 220
Oronoz 111
Oropesa del Mar 213
Osera (Oseira) Monastery 77
Oviedo (Uviéu) 91

P

package tours 267
Padrón 77, 82
Pajares, Puerto de 166
Palacio Real 56
Palamós 135
Palencia 166
El Palmar 211
Pals 135
Pamplona 107
Pancorvo, Desfiladero de 167
Panes 93
paradors 25, 274
Pasajes (Pasaia) 91
Pastrana 202
El Paular 201
Pedraza de la Sierra 167
Peñafiel 167
Peñaranda de Duero 167
Peñiscola 220
Peralada 138
Peratallada 138
pharmacies 267
Picos de Europa 92–3
Piedra, Monasterio de 107
Pilgrims' Way 168–9
Pindal 89
Piornedo 81
places of worship 267
Plasencia 187
Poblet 142
police 17, 267–8
Ponferrada 167
Pontedeume 77
Pontevedra 77
Portlligat 131
Posada de Valdeón 93
post offices 268
Potes 93
Pre-Pyrenees 139
Priego 202
public transport 268
Puebla de Sanabria 167
Pueblos Blancos (White Towns) 253
Puente la Reina 107
Puente Viesgo 89
Puerto Banús 239
Puerto Lápice 198
Puerto de Mazarrón 220
Puerto de Santa María 237
Puig 220
Puigcerdà 142
Pyrenees (Aragon/Navarre) 104,108–9
Pyrenees (Catalan) 139

Q

Quindos 81
Quintanilla de las Viñas 167
Quixote route 198–9

R

rail services 256–7, 268
religious festivals 19, 140–1, 249
Requena 221
Reus 142
rías (sea inlets) 76
Riaza 177
Ribadeo 80
Ribadesella 86
Ripoll 132, 142
Roncal valley 109
Roncesvalles 110
Ronda 247
Roquetas 236
Rosas (Roses) 135
Rota 237
Ruidera 202
Ruta de Plata 171

S

S'Agaró 135
Sabiñánigo 109
Sagrada Família 123
Sagunto 221
Salamanca 170–3
El Saler 211
Sallent de Gállego 109
Salou 136
San Esteban Dam 80
San Juan des Gastelguche 85
San Juan de la Peña 110
San Martín de Valdeiglesias 202
San Millán de la Cogolla 174
San Sebastián (Donostia) 20, 94–5
San Vicente de la Barquera 84
Sangüesa (Zangoza) 110
Sanlúcar de Barrameda 237
Sant Cugat del Vallès (San Cugat del Vallés) 143
Sant Feliu de Guíxols 135
San Juan de las Abadesas (Sant Joan de les Abadesses) 142
Sant Pere de Rodes 135
Santa Clara, island 94, 95
Santa María de la Huerta 174
Santander 96
Santes Creus 143
Santiago de Compostela 78–9, 168
Santillana del Mar 96
Santo Domingo de la Calzada 174
Santo Domingo de Silos 174
Santoña 84
Sargadelos 80
Segorbe 221
Segovia 175–6
senior citizens 268–9

Seo de Urgel (La Seu d'Urgell) 143
Sepúlveda 177
Sete Caballos 81
Sevilla (Seville) 248–51
shop hours 266
Sierra Nevada 105, 245, 252
Sigüenza 203, 207
Sitges 143
Sobrón, Embalse de 177
Solsona 143
Somiedo, Reserva Nacional de 94
Somport Pass 109
Sorbas 254
Soria 177
Spanish Civil War 46–7
sport and leisure 18, 269–70
student/youth travel 270–1

T

Tabernas 254
Tablas de Daimiel, Parque Nacional de las 195
Talavera de la Reina 207
Taramundi 87
Tarazona 110
Tarifa 237
Tarragona 146–7
Tarrassa (Terrassa) 148
taxis 268
telephones 271
Teruel 112
Texois 87
Tiétar Valley 186
tipping 271
Tito Bustillo cave 89
El Toboso 199
toilets 271–2
Toledo 204–6
El Torcal de Antequera 231
Tordesillas 177
Torla 111
Toro 178
Torremolinos 239
Torrevieja 215
Tortosa 148
Tossa de Mar 135
tourism 25
tourist offices 272
travelling to Spain 256–7
Trevélez 252
Trujillo 187
Tudela 112
Turégano 178
Túy (Tui) 80

U

Úbeda 254
Uclés 207
Ujué 112
Urkiola 90

V

Valdediós 97
Valdepeñas 207
Valderrobres 112
Valencia 21, 212, 222–3
Valladolid 179
Valls 148
Valverde de la Vera 186
Veigas 87
Vejér de la Frontera 254
El Vendrell (El Vendril) 136
Verín 80
Veruela 112
Viana 112
Vich (Vic) 148–9
Vigo 80, 81
Vilafamés 221
Vilanova i la Geltrú 136
Villafranca (Vilafranca del Penedès) 149
Villajoyosa 215
Villanueva de los Infantes 207
Villaviciosa 97
Villena 221
Vinaroz 213
Vitoria (Gasteiz) 97
voltage 261

W

walking and hiking 273
wildlife 104–5
words and phrases 263–5

Y

youth hostels 271
Yuste 182

Z

Zafra 187
Zahara de los Atunes 237
Zamora 178
Zaragoza 113
Zarauz 85
Zumaya (Zumaia) 97

Acknowledgements

The Automobile Association would like to thank the following photographers, libraries and associations for their assistance in the preparation of this book.

J ALLAN CASH PHOTOLIBRARY 211 La Albufera

ANCIENT ART & ARCHITECTURE COLLECTION 88 Hunters, Altamira cave painting, 89 Hand of palaeolithic man.

BILBAO TOURIST BOARD 83 Bilbao

ADAM HOPKINS 15 Picos de Europa, 16 Oviedo, 18 San Sebastián, 23 Mountain folk, 73 Galicia, 87 Veigas, 92 Picos de Europa, 97 Bridge, Alto Campoo, 110 Ordesa, 114 & 115 Barcelona, Las Ramblas, 160 Coca Castle, 162 León, San Isidoro, 164 León, San Isidoro, 197 Cuenca, 199 Statue, 200 Sigüenza fiesta.

NATURE PHOTOGRAPHERS LTD 104 White stork (A D Schilling), 105 Tongue orchid (P R Sterry).

MARY EVANS PICTURE LIBRARY 32 Alfonso VI, 34 Isabella I, 35 Ferdinand II, 37 Philip II, 38 Diego Velázquez de Silva, 40 Siege of Barcelona, 41 Naval Victory at Viego, 42 Isabella II, 44 Primo de Rivera, 45 Civil War, 46 Franco, 48 'La Falange', 168 & 169 Pilgrims, 218 Knights Templar.

REX FEATURES LTD 49 King Juan Carlos.

SPECTRUM COLOUR LIBRARY 24/5 San Sebastián, 30/1 San Juan de los Reyes, 94 & 95 San Sebastián, 140 Riders, 141 God's Day Festival, 205 New Bisagra Gate, 207 Wine tasting, 212/3 Valencia, 216 Elche.

THE MANSELL COLLECTION 36 Charles V, 188/9 Spanish ships.

All remaining pictures are held in the Association's own library (AA PHOTO LIBRARY) with contributions from: J EDMUNSON, P ENTICKNAP, A MOLYNEUX, T OLIVER, J POULSEN, D ROBERTSON, P WILSON.